PUZZLE AND PARADOX

Madagascar's long-term trajectory is unique: not only has GDP per capita been trending downward since 1960 (the puzzle), but every time the country has set out on path of growth, it has been stopped in its tracks by a socio-political crisis that has shattered the hopes it raised (the paradox). No satisfactory explanation of this failure has been provided so far. This book elaborates a model of intelligibility of Madagascar's downfall, based on an integrated political economy approach as well as mobilizing the most recent development theories. Combining a review of historical literature with original and sometimes unique statistical surveys, it proposes a general interpretative framework for the workings of Malagasy society. Richly documented and accessible, Puzzle and Paradox allows readers to understand Madagascar's sociopolitical history while more broadly offering an opportunity to grasp the different dimensions of development in the Global South.

Mireille Razafindrakoto is Senior Researcher at the French Institute of Research for Sustainable Development (IRD). She is the co-editor of many books, including *Madagascar d'une crise l'autre: ruptures et continuité* (2018), *The Informal Economy in Developing Countries* (2014) and *The New International Poverty Reduction Strategies* (2003).

François Roubaud is Senior Research Fellow at the French Institute of Research for Sustainable Development (IRD). He is the co-editor of many books, including *Randomized Control Trials in the Field of Development: Critical Perspectives* (2020), *Madagascar d'une crise l'autre: ruptures et continuité* (2018), and *The New International Poverty Reduction Strategies* (2003).

Jean-Michel Wachsberger is a Lecturer of Sociology at the University of Lille. He is the co-editor of many books, including *Madagascar d'une crise l'autre: ruptures et continuité* (2018) and *L'intégration sociale hiérarchisée: L'exemple d'une métropole en développement* (2014).

Puzzle and Paradox

A Political Economy of Madagascar

MIREILLE RAZAFINDRAKOTO
French Research Institute for Sustainable Development

FRANÇOIS ROUBAUD
French Research Institute for Sustainable Development

JEAN-MICHEL WACHSBERGER
University of Lille

CAMBRIDGE
UNIVERSITY PRESS

CAMBRIDGE
UNIVERSITY PRESS

University Printing House, Cambridge CB2 8BS, United Kingdom

One Liberty Plaza, 20th Floor, New York, NY 10006, USA

477 Williamstown Road, Port Melbourne, VIC 3207, Australia

314–321, 3rd Floor, Plot 3, Splendor Forum, Jasola District Centre, New Delhi – 110025, India

79 Anson Road, #06–04/06, Singapore 079906

Cambridge University Press is part of the University of Cambridge.

It furthers the University's mission by disseminating knowledge in the pursuit of education, learning, and research at the highest international levels of excellence.

www.cambridge.org
Information on this title: www.cambridge.org/9781108488334
DOI: 10.1017/9781108770231

This edition first published 2020

Printed in the United Kingdom by TJ International Ltd, Padstow Cornwall

A catalogue record for this publication is available from the British Library.

ISBN 978-1-108-48833-4 Hardback

Contents

Figures and Maps

Figures

Maps

Tables

Boxes

Foreword

JOHN JOSEPH WALLIS

The title of *Puzzle and Paradox* captures two essential features of late twentieth and early twenty-first century Madagascar. Madagascar is one of the poorest and poorest performing countries in the world. Since independence in 1960, the time path of gross domestic product (GDP) per capita follows a downward path, but it is not inexorable. The downward trend results from five consecutive "scallops." Figure 1.2 dramatically illustrates the history. In the first scallop income rises a few years after independence. A political crisis in 1972 results in sharply declining income for a time, followed by rising income (the scallop), then followed by another political crisis in 1991 and another scallop. The scallop pattern continues to the present day. What explains this pattern and the long decline in income? That is the puzzle.

Yet, unlike most of the other extremely poor nations, Madagascar has not been beset by a series of civil wars; the society is not particularly violent and has a strong cultural inheritance that limits violence and values order; it has resources, both productive land and mineral wealth, but has not been ravaged by a resource curse; and its population exhibits strong support for open democratic values. Nonetheless, each economic recovery ends in a political crisis that chokes off economic growth. That is the paradox.

Mireille Razafindrakoto, Francois Roubaud, and Jean-Michel Wachsberger weave together the puzzle and paradox to make a convincing case that there are no easy answers to why Madagascar finds itself in its current predicament. The standard diagnoses for why economies fail do not apply neatly to Madagascar, and the authors make their analysis particularly convincing by a close and careful comparison of Madagascar with the rest of Africa. While Madagascar's economy is one of the worst performing in

Africa, Madagascar ranks somewhere in the middle of African countries with respect to literacy, life expectancy, roads, the quality of governance, and the distortion of agricultural prices, although it does have low fixed capital per capita. The lack of capital is almost certainly a result, rather than a cause, of poor economic performance. Africa is the most ethnically diverse region in the world, and Madagascar is among the most ethnically fragmented societies in Africa. Yet, Madagascar is also the most linguistically homogeneous society in Africa and ethnic divisions and conflict appear to play a smaller role in Madagascar than other African societies. The paradox is a paradox indeed.

The second chapter illuminates the paradox by laying out the history of Madagascar's "scallops." Periods of economic recovery usually end in a political crisis in which a new government is elected and policies change. Political crises are accompanied by low levels of violence but significant amounts of political protest. New regimes change the rules and policies, and the economy suffers for a time. The economy begins to grow again, another political crisis emerges, and a new regime suffers through an initial period of economic shrinking. The cycles are not only persistent, but they appear to be occurring more frequently. Again, a paradox. Why is Madagascar unable to solve the problem of repeated political uncertainty and regime change, and along with it significant disruption to institutions and policies that, nonetheless, fail to produce positive results?

Chapter 3 briefly steps back from the granular history to consider very general frameworks for thinking about the problem of development. The three considered are North, Wallis, and Weingast (2009); Acemoglu and Robinson (2005 and 2012); and Kahn (2010). For the most part, the book uses the North, Wallis, and Weingast (NWW) as a scaffolding for the analysis of Madagascar. NWW theorize about how societies create and sustain social order within the threat of disorder and violence. They focus on elites and intra-elite bargains that create rents for elites that enable intra-elite bargains to be credible and sustainable. Stable elite bargains limit violence among the elites. The framework operates at a high level of generality, very different from the granular detailed history that Razafindrakoto, Roubaud, and Waschsberger provide. The difference provides a useful tension in the argument and a clear organizational structure for the book. On key points Razafindrakoto, Roubaud, and Waschsberger disagree with NWW. They do not show that NWW explain the details of Madagascar's history, but use the framework as it was intended, as a framework for asking questions about the nature of societies. Another benefit of the framing is to quite effortlessly place the Madagascar experience, and the lessons we might draw from it, in the larger development context. This is done nicely in the book without straining at parallels or analogies. This is accomplished by carefully placing Madagascar both in the African context and in the larger development literature, which the authors know very well.

Having done a careful job of eliminating the usual candidates for poor economic performance in Chapter 1, highlighting the role of political instability at key inflection points in Madagascar's recent history in Chapter 2, the conceptual framework, building on NWW, draws attention to the central role played by elites in Malagasy society and, potentially, in the periodic political crises that stymie economic growth. Chapter 4 finds that non-elites in Madagascar are relatively unorganized. Non-elites are atomistic in the sense that their organizational structures are limited, and not very trusting (again, in comparison to other African societies). In other words, civil society is weak in Madagascar. The organizational structures that people belong to and can tap into to help coordinate their lives are weak.

Chapter 5 is where the real pay-off comes. Using a unique and innovative way of gathering and measuring elite experiences, building on a network of elite contacts that the authors created and nurtured, the authors investigate how networks of elite relationships operate. Madagascar has a long history of hierarchical, status-dominated social relationships. The class structure is not impermeable, but it is real. Beginning by interviewing thirty members of the elite who the team members were connected with (the team members recognizing that they themselves were elites), the initial interviewees conducted additional rounds of interview with elites the original thirty "super-interviewers" identified (the methods are described in Box 5.2 of Chapter 5). Each interview ended with a request to list eight other elites who might be interviewed, and then built out a network of elite by following up the suggested contacts. In all, 1,000 elites were interviewed. Critically, all the elites were interviewed by other elites. The survey of elites in Madagascar is called ELIMAD, and is, among the many valuable contributions of the book, a true innovation.

The ELIMAD survey shows that elites are not only better organized – 80% of elites are members of some association compared to 20% of non-elites – but they are also better connected with each other. Nine spheres of elite spheres of power are identified. More powerful elites "straddle" multiple spheres. Connection across groups of elites is positively associated with the power and status of individual elites. These are fascinating results, for they show how the elites reconstitute themselves through time and the stark difference in the organizational capacity of elites and non-elites.

How does this help us understand the puzzle and paradox of Madagascar? The authors' research and insights into the organization of elites, non-elites, and the dynamics of Malagasy society offers several possible explanations. What follows are the lessons that I have learned from their research, perhaps more pointed than the authors can draw given their requirement to consider the feasible alternative explanations.

Over time, certainly in the nineteenth and early twentieth century, domination of Malagasy society was secured by a set of privileged elite arrangements dominated by an ethnic highland group, the *Merina*, who established norms and formal rules recognizing and implementing a set of privileges possessed by identifiable status groups, the *Andriana* and *Hova*. These groups were stable, but not closed. They were very successful at limiting violence and instilling a social norm against the use of violence. But instilling a social norm against violence was an outcome; it was not the source of peace. The source of peace, of social order, was the interlocking privileges created and sustained within the elites and their organizations. Those groups remain at the top of the elite social structure today.

With the arrival of the British and the French, the Malagasy elite was not removed, but it was challenged to accommodate new and powerful individuals who could call on external resources. This meant, gradually or not, that the most powerful elites, or perhaps more accurately the highest status Malagasy elite(s), were no longer identified as the elites who ran the government. Elites retained their privileges and their organizations, but within elite status did not determine who controlled the government.

Perhaps this was a necessity under colonialism, when foreign colonial officers necessarily occupied positions of government authority. The arrangement became institutionalized after independence. Political leaders continued to come from the *Andriana* and *Hova*, but their status within the elite hierarchies had little to do with whether they became political leaders. Society as a whole remained markedly disorganized when compared to elites, but the general population was allowed to select leaders through elections that were usually open and fair, but initially returned winning candidates with 80% or more of the vote. That is a result that does not occur at random. It requires organization, but perhaps organization that is not overtly political.

For reasons that are not clear, the Malagasy elites were unwilling or unable to reach an intra-elite agreement in which political leadership came out of an intra-elite agreement. Nonetheless, the elite agreement maintains social order and ensured existing elite privileges (with some mobility but very limited entry) in the face of changing conditions. The elite agreement has yet to break down: specifically, civil war between the elites had been avoided. The military elites have substantially honored their agreement to remain both outside and above politics. But the costs of maintaining that agreement have been enormous for the rest of society.

Periodically and with growing frequency, political leadership collapses. New leaders are chosen democratically and legitimately (most of the time), and no regime has significantly altered the privileges and agreements within the elites, as evidenced by the continued existence, education, wealth, status, and power of the elites identified in Chapter 5.

But new regimes have shown no reluctance to completely alter other institutional rules governing the economy, as detailed in Chapter 2. The result has been chaos. Every time a new regime enters, the rules change. Things fall apart. As the economy begins to recover, the depredations of the existing regime create circumstances that mobilize a new political competitor. The existing regime falls, the rules change, the economy suffers, people become poorer and the elites remain the elites.

This foreword only scratches the surface of the deep learning and research *Puzzle and Paradox* represents. I learned a tremendous amount from this research and it has influenced my thinking about the problems of both development and the relationships between elites and larger societies. My connection to the book has been through the research project of the Agence Française de Developpement under the organization and direction of Nicolas Meisel. With time, the project may produce more book length case studies, and we can only hope that they are of such high quality as this one.

Acknowledgements

We are grateful to all those who contributed to this book. We cannot mention everyone by name, as the book draws on nearly a quarter of a century of research in Madagascar. The following are just some of those we have the space to acknowledge here (if those omitted reprehend, if you pardon, we will mend):

- The French Research Institute for Sustainable Development (IRD) departments and teams in France and Madagascar for their help and support with the research conducted with the Malagasy institutions and Editions de l'IRD for their care and speed in the home straight that enabled us to be ready to present the original work published in French (*L'énigme et le paradoxe: économie politique de Madagascar*, 2017) to the diaspora (Zama, July 2017).
- Diane Bertrand, our English translator, whose sharp eye picked up so many typos in the French manuscript and especially whose close working relationship built up with us over so many years has given her such a good grasp of our sometimes convoluted prose, which she so faithfully and melodiously translated into her beautiful language.
- Our sponsors – French Agency for Development (AFD), the EU Nopoor programme, etc. – which funded our research in part so that we could, to use a sporting metaphor, take on each match with a degree of composure. We are particularly grateful to the AFD team for their financial contribution to the translation of the original French publication, which formed the basis for this book.
- Our many (more or less) anonymous editors for their inspiring comments and remarks.
- Rijasolo, for the quality of his photographs and the on-the-ground realities he gives us to see. We are grateful for the pictures he provides that

marvelously illustrate the original work published in French and this book.

- Madagascar National Statistics Office (INSTAT) for our close partnership spanning decades since the start of the *MAdagascar-Dial-Instat-Orstom* (MADIO) project in 1994: we are particularly grateful to the successive directors-general (ten in all over twenty years: Armand, Daniel, Christian, Charles, Philippe, Mpianina, Jean, Gérard, Ida and Zefania) for placing their trust in us, and to Faly Rakotomanana for the major role he played in our work together, all too modestly and unfailingly to the point of exhaustion.
- The *Conseil-Expertise-Formation* (COEF) Ressources team, with their conductor Désiré Razafindrazaka, assisted by Laetitia Razafimamonjy, for their valuable, dependable, warm partnership despite the trials and tribulations of managing time and space.
- All our colleagues and friends, Malagasy by birth or by heart, for helping us each in their own way to move forward with our thinking: Alain, Alban, Brice, David, Denis-Alexandre, Erick, Geneviève, Gil, Jean, Linda, Michel, Nicolas, Nirintsoa, Patrick, Samuel, Thomas, etc., not forgetting our co-authors of the new book we co-edited entitled *Madagascar d'une crise l'autre: ruptures et continuité*, published in French May 2018; the list is too long to mention you all, but we spare a special thought here for Christian, Lala and Dieudonné, and ultimately Philippe and Raymond, who sadly passed away and handed on the baton.
- Our friends and families for encouraging us and tolerating the hours and days we spent in the maze of the Malagasy 'mystery'.
- All those who agreed to take time out to participate in the dozens of statistical surveys and hundreds of qualitative interviews. May the time they have given to answer relatively tedious and intrusive questions find a form of gratification in the analyses, thinking and debates prompted by this book.

Abbreviations and Acronyms

ACMIL	*Académie Militaire d'Antsirabé* (Antsirabe Military Academy)
AFD	*Agence Française de Développement* (French Agency for Development)
AfDB	African Development Bank
AGOA	African Growth and Opportunity Act
AKFM	*Antokon'ny Kongresin'ny Fahaleovantenan'i Madagasikara* (Congress Party for the Independence of Madagascar)
AREMA	*Avant-garde de la Révolution Malgache* (Vanguard of the Malagasy Revolution)
AVI	*Asa Vita no Ifampitsarana* (Judged By Your Work Party)
BIANCO	*Bureau Indépendant Anti-Corruption* (Independent Anti-Corruption Bureau)
CAPSAT	*Corps d'Administration des Personnels et Services de l'Armée de Terre* (Army Corps of Personnel and Administrative and Technical Services)
CAR	*Communes Autochtones Rurales* (Rural Indigenous Authority)
CASEP	*Crédit à l'Ajustement Structurel des Entreprises Publiques* (Public Enterprise Structural Adjustment Credit)
CASPIC	*Crédit d'Ajustement Structurel de la Politique Industrielle et Commerciale* (Industrial and Trade Policy Structural Adjustment Credit)
CEAMP	*Centrale d'Equipement Agricole et de Modernisation du Paysannat* (Central Agricultural Equipment and Farming Modernisation Stores)
CNDP	*Conseil National Populaire pour le Développement* (National Popular Council for Development)

CNOSC	*Coordination Nationale des Organisations de la Société Civile* (Consortium of Solidarity with Madagascar)
CONECS	*Conseil National Economique et Social* (National Economic and Social Council)
CPIA	Country Policy and Institutional Assessment
CRES	*Comité pour le Redressement Economique et Social* (Committee for Economic and Social Recovery)
CSR	*Conseil Suprême de la Révolution* (Supreme Revolutionary Council)
CSLCC	*Conseil Supérieur de la Lutte Contre la Corruption* (Anti-Corruption High Council)
CST	*Conseil Supérieur de la Transition* (High Transitional Council)
CT	*Congrès de la Transition* (Transitional Congress)
DCAN	*Direction de la Construction et de l'Armement Naval* (Shipbuilding and Navy Armaments Division)
DIAL	*Développement, Institutions & Mondialisation* (Joint Research Unit IRD – Université Paris-Dauphine)
EBA	Everything But Arms
EDBM	Economic Development Board of Madagascar
DHS	Demographic and Health Survey
EKAR	*Eglizy Katolika Apostolika Romana* (Roman Catholic Church)
ENEMPSI	*Enquête Nationale sur l'Emploi et le Secteur Informel* (National Survey on Employment and the Informal Sector)
FCF	Fixed Capital Formation
FFKM	*Fikambanan'ny Fiangonana Kristianina eto Madagasikara* (Malagasy Council of Christian Churches)
FIDES	*Fonds d'Investissement pour le Développement Economique et Social* (Investment Fund for Economic and Social Development)
FJKM	*Fiangonan'i Jesoa Kristy eto Madagasikara* (Church of Jesus Christ in Madagascar)
FNDR	*Front National de Défense de la Révolution* (National Front for the Defence of the Revolution)
FRS	*Force de Sécurité Républicaine* (Republican Security Forces)
GDP	gross domestic product
GEFP	*Groupement des Entreprises Franches et Partenaires* (Madagascar Export Processing Zone Association)
GEM	*Groupement des Entreprises de Madagascar* (Confederation of Trade Organisations of Madagascar)
GPM	*Groupement de Police Mobile* (Mobile Police Group)

HAE	*Haute Autorité de l'Etat* (High State Authority)
HAT	*Haute Autorité de la Transition* (High Transitional Authority)
HCC	*Haute Cour Constitutionnelle* (High Constitutional Court)
HIPC	Heavily Indebted Poor Countries Initiative
HVM	*Hery Vaovao ho an'i Madagasikara* (New Forces for Madagascar)
IFI	International Financial Institution
IMF	International Monetary Fund
INSTAT	*Institut National de la Statistique* (Madagascar National Statistics Office)
IPD	Institutional Profiles Database
IRD	*Institut de Recherche pour le Développement* (French Research Institute for Sustainable Development)
JINA	*Jeunesse Nationaliste* (Nationalist Youth; secret society)
JPM	*Jery sy Paikady ho an`i Madagsikara* (Young Business Heads of Madagascar)
KIM	*Komity Iombonan'ny Mpitolona* (Committee for the Coordination of the Struggle)
KMF/CNOE	*Komity Mpanaramaso ny Fifidianana/Comité National pour l'Observation des Elections* (National Election Observation Committee, founded in 1989)
LAO	limited access order
LMS	London Missionary Society
MAP	Madagascar Action Plan
MDG	Millennium Development Goals
MDRM	*Mouvement Démocratique de la Rénovation Malgache* (Democratic Movement for Malagasy Renewal)
MFA	Multi Fiber Agreement
MFM	*Mpitolona ho amin'ny Fandrosoan'i Madagasikara* (Party for Proletarian Power)
MGF	Malagasy franc
MONIMA	*Mouvement national pour l'indépendance de Madagascar* (Madagascar for the Malagasy; people's peasant, anti-imperialist party)
NIC	National Investment Company
NPA	National People's Assembly (*Assemblée Nationale Populaire*)
OAO	open access order
ODA	Official Development Assistance
OECD	Organisation for Economic Co-operation and Development

OMNIS	*Office des Mines Nationales et des Industries Stratégiques* (National Military Agency for Strategic Industries)
PADESM	*Parti des Déshérités de Madagascar* (Party of the Disinherited of Madagascar)
PAPMAD	*Papèterie de Madagascar* (Paper Mill of Madagascar)
PDS	*Président de la la Délégation Spéciale* (Chairman of the Special Delegation)
PRSP	Poverty Reduction Strategy Paper
PSD	*Parti Social-Démocrate* (Social Democratic Party)
PSM	*Parti Socialiste Malgache* (Malagasy Socialist Party)
R&D	research and development
SADC	Southern African Development Community
SAP	Structural Adjustment Programme
SeFaFi	*Sehatra Fanaraha-maso ny Fiainam-pirenena* (Public Life Observatory)
SEM	*Société d'Electricité de Madagasar* (Madagascar Electricity Board)
SIM	*Syndicat des Industries de Madagascar* (Federation of Malagasy Industries)
SINPA	*Société d'Intérêt National des Produits Agricoles* (National Farm Produce Marketing Board)
SMOTIG	*Service de la Main-d'Œuvre des Travaux Publics d'Intérêt Général* (Manpower Service for Public Works)
SMR	*Société Malgache de Raffinage* (Malagasy Refinery)
SMTM	*Société Malgache de Transport Maritime* (Malagasy Society of Maritime Transport)
SONACO	*Société National du Commerce Extérieur* (National Foreign Trade Company)
SOTEMA	*Société textile de Mahajanga* (Mahajanga Textile Company)
TFP	total factor productivity
TGV	*Tanora malaGasy Vonona* (Determined Malagasy Youth)
TIM	*Tiako i Madagasikara* ('I Love Madagascar', the president Marc Ravalomanana party)
TTS	*Tanora Tonga Saina* ('Aware Youth')
UDECMA	*Union des Démocrates Chrétiens de Madagascar* (Union of Christian Democrats; membre du FNDR sous la IIe République)
UDSM	*Union Démocratique et Socialiste de Fianarantsoa et Tuléar* (Union of Social Democrats of Fianarantsoa and Toliara)
UNDP	United Nations Development Programme

UNISDR	United Nations Office for Disaster Risk Reduction
UPM	*Union des Populations Malgaches* (Union of Malagasy Peoples)
VITM	*Vonjy Iray Tsy Mivaky* (Popular Movement for the Unity of Madagascar)
VVS	*Vy, Vato Sakelika* (Iron, Stone, Branching; secret political society)
WDIs	World Development Indicators
ZOAM	*Zatovo Orin'asa* (Unemployed Youth)
ZWAM	*Zatovo Western Andevo Malagasy* (Malagasy Western Slave Youth)

General Introduction

Madagascar is one of the poorest countries in the world today, with gross domestic product (GDP) per capita of less than 400 dollars in 2016 and a colossal rate of monetary poverty (over 90% on the international poverty line). Yet nothing appears to have ever marked the country out for such a terrible fate. Far from it, in fact. Although the latest political crisis that started in early 2009 and found an electoral conclusion in late 2013 has played a role, it is a mere blip on the historical radar. Madagascar's long-term economic trajectory is a real mystery, which raises farther-reaching questions as to what is behind the divergent development processes observed in the world today. Not only has per capita GDP been trending downward since 1960, but also every time the country has set out on a growth path, it has been stopped in its tracks by a socio-political crisis that has shattered the hopes it raised.

This study sets out to find some answers to a mystery that seems to defy imitation elsewhere in the world. It proposes an interpretive framework for Madagascar's very long-term trajectory (spanning nearly three centuries) by tracing the defining elements that have structured the country's political economy. This involves an analysis of the economic phenomena taking into account the diversity of social players and their organisations, the nature of the accumulation regime(s)[1] and any internal contradictions they may have and the economic and social modes of regulation put in place in each period. The book throughout explores specific areas, testing the proposed framework to either confirm its relevance or identify its limitations and flaws.

[1] The expression is used here in the ordinary sense of the term. Although it might be construed as referring to the regulation school, this study does not take up its concepts (mode of regulation, accumulation regime or institutional forms).

The book builds on and aspires to improve on previous studies that have considered Madagascar's recurrent crises (including the authors' own). Among them is a series of special issues of scientific journals on these questions. In 1993, for example, *Politique Africaine* published an issue on the political transition and the accession of Forces Vives (Raison-Jourde, 1993). The journal gave a repeat performance in 2002 as the dust was barely settling on the new crisis (*Madagascar: The Ballot Box and the Street*; Raison-Jourde & Raison, 2002). *Afrique Contemporaine* in turn brought out its own double issue in 2002 entitled *Madagascar after the Storm: Ten Years of Political and Economic Transition* (Roubaud, 2002). This issue differed from the first two, focusing essentially on the political turn of events, with more in-depth analyses of the economic aspects of Madagascar's trajectory. Yet Madagascar subsequently dropped out of the picture, aside from a few sporadic articles. It was not until 2012 that a first co-authored book on the new crisis was published (*Madagascar, the 2009 Coup d'état*; Randrianja, 2012c). As its name suggests, the collection addresses essentially the events of the day, even though some of the authors ventured into a longer timeframe. More recently, *Afrique Contemporaine* published a new special issue in 2014, coordinated by this book's authors and entitled *Madagascar: Anatomy of a Crisis State* (Razafindrakoto *et al.*, 2014c). The issue updates the previous publications based on all the information available through to the end of 2014, thereby taking nearly a year's distance from the 'crisis exit' electoral process.

The main originality of this particular book, and the aforementioned special issue of *Afrique Contemporaine* – two closely linked, complementary editorial perspectives viewed through a common lens – is to shed light on how and why crises keep recurring in Madagascar. Whereas the authors of the special issue presented an on-the-spot focus on one crisis in particular (the most recent at the time of writing), this book covers all the crises in order to explore what makes them systemic.[2]

What appears self-evident today in the way of setting out the Malagasy equation is the result of a long gestation period covering more than two decades of work by the authors. Analysis of the two democratic changes of power and resumed growth in the second half of the 1990s initially led us to draw a relatively optimistic conclusion and consider the possibility of a Malagasy exception (Roubaud, 2000). The 2002 crisis caused us to revise

[2] *Afrique Contemporaine* published an article in 2010 that put the question in similar terms (Véron, 2010). Yet although it offered some interpretations of the Malagasy crises, it pointed to the need for further research, which is precisely what we have taken up here.

our judgement, which we worded in these terms in the introduction to the 2002 *Afrique Contemporaine* article: 'Economic growth and political crisis: does Madagascar refuse to develop?' (Roubaud, 2002). Yet aside from differing in their analyses of the course of events, these studies revolved around two pillars: an interconnection between political and economic cycles and the major role of governance in every sense of the word. The elements of the Malagasy equation were already in place: Madagascar's divergent economic growth pattern with its few rare spurts of growth wiped out by popular protest in a phenomenon that we were, to our knowledge, the first to identify and which we called a 'real iron law' (Razafindrakoto & Roubaud, 2002a).

It was eventually the 2009 crisis, albeit disastrous for Madagascar, that brought the decisive element of support for our earlier conjecture. And it was a particularly conclusive demonstration in that the crisis caught many observers unawares, the vast majority of whom had been impressed by the momentum built by Marc Ravalomanana. This bolt from the blue had us reading back methodically over all the past crises to stabilise our definition of their characteristics. This definition is based on three elements: (1) Madagascar's long-term downward spiral (the puzzle); (2) the increasingly short cyclicality of the crises; and (3) the association between economic growth and political crisis (the paradox). This is the complex (the mystery) that we proposed to study in 2010 in a French Agency for Development (AFD – *Agence Française de Développement*) research study entitled *Governance, Institutions and Long-Term Growth* covering a dozen developing countries and engaging as many teams of researchers.

This potted history of ideas is particularly interesting in that there is now more or less unanimous agreement that these are the terms of the Malagasy equation. It has even become institutionalised. Our Puzzle and our Paradox, illustrated by the divergence in per capita GDP between Madagascar and Africa and the correlation of economic cycles and political crises (Figures 1.1 and 1.2 of Chapter 1), open two recent official documents from the World Bank (2015: *Systematic Country Diagnostic*) and the International Monetary Fund (2015: *Article IV Consultation*), both designed to guide the two Bretton Woods institutions' assistance policies in Madagascar. Yet this has not always been the case. The spread of this way of putting the equation is even very recent. It started appearing in World Bank documents at the beginning of the decade, even though the institution considered the reasons for economic decline ('the puzzle') mainly from a governance angle (Morisset, 2010). The idea was then taken up in a number of World Bank studies in Madagascar (2014 and 2015) and, more interestingly, by various Malagasy initiatives funded by the World Bank (VANF, 2012; IEP and World Bank, 2014). This less economic lens is also more general, as shown by the new World Development Report 2017 on governance (World Bank, 2017). However, despite this broader reach, the two institutions continue to prefer more strictly economic approaches.[3]

This book has had to come to terms with some severe constraints. For example, as with most poor countries, available written sources are terribly patchy. Although there is a certain historical tradition of writing in (and on) Madagascar, it is more political and religious and merely skims economic issues. Moreover, none of the quantitative macroeconomic data (virtually non-existent before 1960 and incomplete thereafter) are entirely reliable, including the most recent data (Devarajan, 2013; Jerven, 2013). We have therefore had to bear these limitations in mind and take a modest approach to the ambitious task in hand (another paradox). In particular, some of our conclusions remain fragile and some may remain impossible to firmly corroborate owing to a lack of adequate retrospective data.

Not to end on a pessimistic note, this book takes two main innovative directions. First, it conducts a critical review of existing research, examined in the light of recent political economy theories, endeavouring to more consistently link up two fields of history – economic history and political and social history – which are often studied separately, in this country as in others. It then seeks to optimise the use of existing empirical resources on the social players, more specifically the people and the elites. There are two advantages to this original use of statistical surveys developed largely by the authors. Unlike aggregate data, these surveys are representative and reliable. Their data can be disaggregated for more in-depth analyses to get right down to the 'flesh and blood' players, who are ultimately the real agents acting unseen behind the concepts of institutions, organisations and

[3] Although the World Bank (2014) report considers 'breaking the cycle of recurrent crises' to be one of the main challenges in Madagascar, the issue is addressed only by part of the report on macroeconomic policy and the proposed solutions are virtually all economic. Similarly, the IMF report (2015b) acknowledges that 'Over the last fifty years, all heads of state (excluding the current president) have either gained or lost power in the context of an unconstitutional event. Uncertainties linked to political instability, weak institutions, and weak governance have eroded the foundation for solid economic growth, with short-term rent-seeking having taken precedence over longer-term nation building.' Yet it does not go on to analyse how rents are extracted and the sets of players in the field. More broadly speaking, although a highly technical analysis of national taxation systems shows that their shortcomings in poor countries are partly due to low rates of taxation and massive tax breaks (Fenochiettto & Pessino, 2013), at no moment in time is the question put as to why. In both cases, the analysis stops short at the doorway to political economy, despite the rich potential of this lens, as we propose to demonstrate in this book.

so on. In this, the surveys transcend the usual framework of inevitably approximate (and sometimes erroneous) stylised facts found in many political economy studies. They also bring the people back to the stage as full-fledged players when they are astonishingly absent from the analytic framework discussed here, which is centred exclusively on the role of the elites and fractions of the elites as the driving force of history. More generally speaking, we hope that the wealth of the empirical material in support of the theses developed in this book will demonstrate the validity of a long-run scientific approach. This book is the result of nearly a quarter of a century of investment in and on Madagascar, as much in terms of building institutional partnerships (primarily with the national statistics office, but also with other public administration bodies and the university and research centres) as in terms of deepening research focuses, including developing innovative statistical surveys; a good illustration of IRD's research modus operandi.

This book contains five chapters. The first presents the data on the Malagasy mystery and looks into its causes based on traditional and modern economic theories of long-term growth. This first sweep fails to provide satisfactory answers to our questions and even adds to the veil of mystery surrounding Madagascar's trajectory, in that most of the conditions found appear to be positive. This leads us to make a foray into political economy as a potential solution to the problem. The second chapter therefore dons political economy glasses to review Madagascar's economic and political history from precolonial times to the present day, using the analytic categories proposed by the discipline's most recent studies. More particularly, it draws on the theories developed by North and his co-authors (NWW, 2009, 2012b), Acemoglu and Robinson (2005, 2012) and Khan (2010) and applies the concepts they have fashioned (institutions, social orders, control of violence and rents, elite coalitions, etc.) to the Malagasy case. The following two chapters set out to piece together the previous chapter's information in order to build an explanatory framework as to how Madagascar works and its underlying institutional arrangements. The third chapter first of all discusses the country's key structural assets. The fourth chapter then identifies the main obstacles. The fifth and final chapter focuses on an overlooked, yet crucial player in the Malagasy tragedy in the form of the elites. The chapter draws on a survey of a representative sample conducted by this research programme – a first in this field – to present a detailed sociography of the elites, their reproduction strategies and their values.

This book is part of a broader editorial project. To use an analogy with *The Alexandria Quartet* – Lawrence Durrell's tetralogy penned from 1957 to 1960 on different angles of love regarding the same set of events and people in Alexandria – we could call our project *The Red Island Quartet*, where the crises replace the love and Madagascar takes the place of Alexandria. In addition to the issue of *Afrique Contemporaine* published in 2014 (*Madagascar: Anatomy of a Crisis State*) and the original publication in French ((*L'énigme et le paradoxe: économie politique de Madagascar*; Razafindrakoto *et al.*, 2017) which was a basis for this book, the project includes a co-authored book of comparative perspectives on the same theme published in 2018 (*Madagascar Crisis to Crisis: Breaks and Continuity*) and a final opus on the elites and the relationship between power and the people, a subject on which the last chapter of this book offers an introductory prelude.

1

The Malagasy Mystery through the Lens of Economic Growth and Development Theories

1.1 Introduction

As with all countries that work in mysterious ways that need explaining, an understanding of which is the exact purpose of this book, Madagascar in all its historical depth and subtle player interactions is far too complex to reveal itself outright. A key needs to be found if there is to be any hope of progressing towards this ambitious and ostensibly unattainable goal, for us in any case. In research, the greatest scientific discoveries have often sprung from a simple question whose ramifications are not always immediately apparent. We obviously do not pretend to aspire to these heights, but our approach has evolved from the same starting point. It is no secret that Madagascar is 'in a bad way', with so many areas in which its performance is sorry, if not dire. Yet once this patent diagnosis has been made, where does one start? In our case, the simple question we asked as a way in to the Malagasy equation concerned economic growth, not because it is the only or most important question, but because it has certain advantages for our case in hand. First, a straightforward curve gives a clear idea of the situation, at least over the years since the early 1970s. Second, the growth question is probably the issue that has most engaged economists, and many others besides, for centuries. We could therefore hope to draw on their theories to explain Madagascar's economic trajectory. Of course, things are never as easy as they seem. Yet it was precisely this initial, very narrow road that opened up into others, the single thread that finally wove into a much larger tapestry – that, and a stroke of luck.

The first part of this chapter sets out the elements of the Malagasy equation as concisely and accurately as possible to describe the issue addressed by this book (a mystery made up of a puzzle and a paradox) and makes sure that this is really the right way of asking the question. The huge amount of uncertainty surrounding our knowledge of the economic and social phenomena in Madagascar, especially when captured by statistics, is such that existing sources have to be compared and triangulated to ensure their robustness and even the veracity of the facts stated. The second part of the chapter considers 'orthodox' economic theories of growth and development from the oldest to the most recent, from the simplest to the most sophisticated, to find elements to interpret the Malagasy mystery. Yet the fact is that none of these theories provides any conclusive answers – quite the opposite. The third part of the chapter therefore makes a preliminary foray into political economy, which proves just as inconclusive. If, at the end of this chapter, there is still no key to be found to unlock an even denser Malagasy mystery, readers are at least less in the dark. They can now rule out the interpretations that do not work. They know the answer lies elsewhere.

1.2 The Facts of the Problem: The Malagasy Equation to Be Solved

The mystery of the Malagasy economy is first of all a *puzzle*. The country has been on a stubborn downward trend since independence more than a half a century ago, and nothing seems able to shift it. Few countries, including in sub-Saharan Africa, demonstrate such poor growth performance. If the Malagasy economy displays any clear constancy, it is mainly in its inexorable tendency to go downhill. Data compiled by the World Bank (2017) estimated per capita gross domestic product (GDP) at US$132 in 1960 and US$402 in 2015 (Figure 1.1). At the same time, per capita GDP in sub-Saharan Africa as a whole rose from its slightly lower starting level of US$117 to fourteen times that sum (US$1,588) in 2015, four times the level in Madagascar. Yet Africa's performance record is far from outstanding. Southeast Asia and the Pacific, poorer by a third with just US$90 at the beginning of the period, were sixteen times better off than Madagascar in 2015, with an average per capita GDP of US$6,552. This comparison in current dollars clouds part of the story, which is revealed by the long time series put together by Maddison (2011) and his team. In constant dollars, not only does Madagascar fail to keep up with the continent, itself lagging largely behind other world regions, but the Red Island's inhabitants also saw their purchasing power slashed by one-third in value from 1950 to 2015, when it virtually tripled (2.8) in sub-Saharan Africa.

Behind these expressionless averages, a more palpable gauge of Madagascar's downfall can be gleaned from a comparison with other

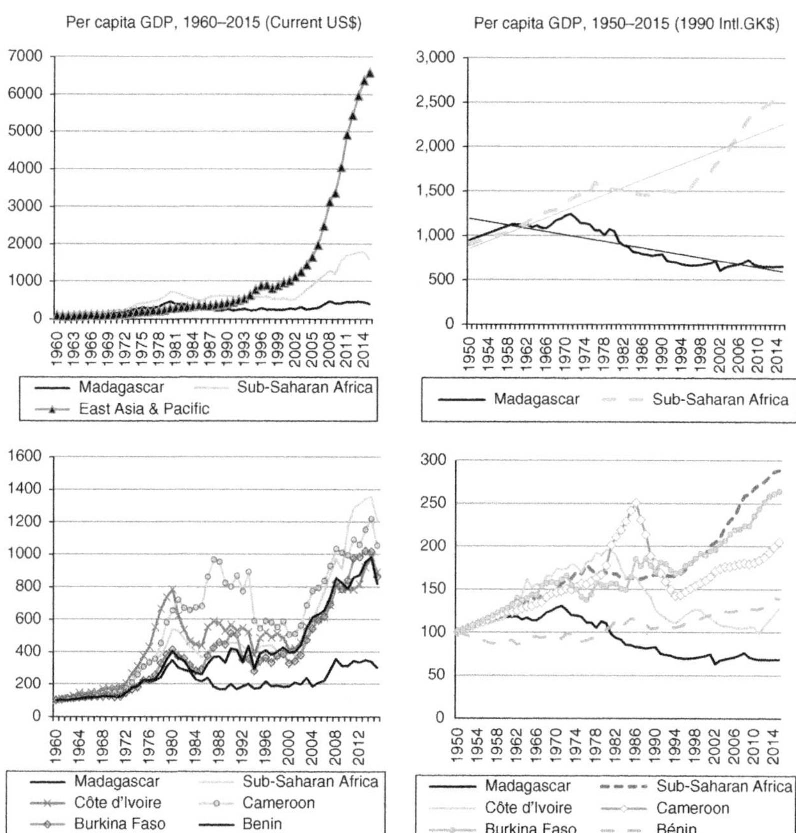

Figure 1.1 The Malagasy puzzle: Inexorable economic decline.
Source: Maddison (2011); World Development Indicators (2017, https://databank.worldbank.org/source/world-development-indicators); authors' calculations.
Note: The left-hand charts cover developing countries in sub-Saharan Africa and East Asia only. The right-hand charts are estimated in 1990 international Geary–Khamis dollars through to 2009 when the Maddison series ends. The growth rates for the 2009–15 period are taken from the 2017 WDIs (measured in 2011 constant international dollars, in purchasing power parity).

African countries. The comparison countries chosen here by way of illustration are

- Cameroon and Côte d'Ivoire, two countries of similar population size, which are also former French colonies and were each the hub of development in their respective regions of Central Africa and West Africa

- Benin, with which Madagascar shares many similarities in terms of political history
- Burkina Faso, the other French-speaking African country in which the same political economy approach has been taken by a joint research programme (Koussoubé *et al.*, 2015)

Madagascar is outdistanced by all these countries and alone carves out a resolutely downward path. Cameroon and Côte d'Ivoire may well post sharper variations because of world commodity prices and civil war (for the latter), but both countries have managed to set in motion the sustainable (albeit reversible) growth processes of which Madagascar has proved incapable. Madagascar not only loses ground to these two countries, but it also does not bear comparison with Benin and Burkina Faso, both infinitely less well endowed on all counts. In current dollars, Madagascar's per capita GDP in 1960 was twice that of Burkina Faso. Fifty years on, it was 33% lower. Benin's lag of 30% at independence had turned into a lead of nearly double the GDP of Madagascar by the end of the period. These two countries, both very poor performers on a global scale, have grown around three times faster on average than Madagascar.

While Madagascar's economic trajectory is a puzzle, it is also a *paradox*. Herein lies the second element of the Malagasy mystery we seek to solve. On closer examination, Madagascar's history has not actually been one long, steady downhill slide. The country seems to have embarked on a growth cycle on numerous occasions. Yet each time Madagascar showed signs of an economic take-off, the upturn ended a few years later in a major political crisis (for growth), dragging down the positive momentum with it (Figure 1.2). This happened in the early 1970s, 1990s and in the early 2000s and at the turn of the 2010s in the late 2000s. In a parody of Marx's words, Madagascar's tragic history repeats itself as farce, ad nauseum.

Madagascar showed the first signs of economic take-off in the second half of the 1960s following a sluggish first half-decade. From 1964 to 1971, GDP grew nearly 5% per year. Yet the 1972 student and urban movements, preceded by farmer revolts in the south of the country the previous year, broke the momentum and led to the fall of the First Republic. It was not until the end of the 1980s that the country resumed a growth path and started to pick up speed. From 1986 to 1990, per capita GDP rose 3% per year. The structural adjustment policies in place since the beginning of the decade finally appeared to be paying off. Alas, the popular movement for democracy launched in 1991 brought down President Ratsiraka and the Second Republic and ruptured the economic

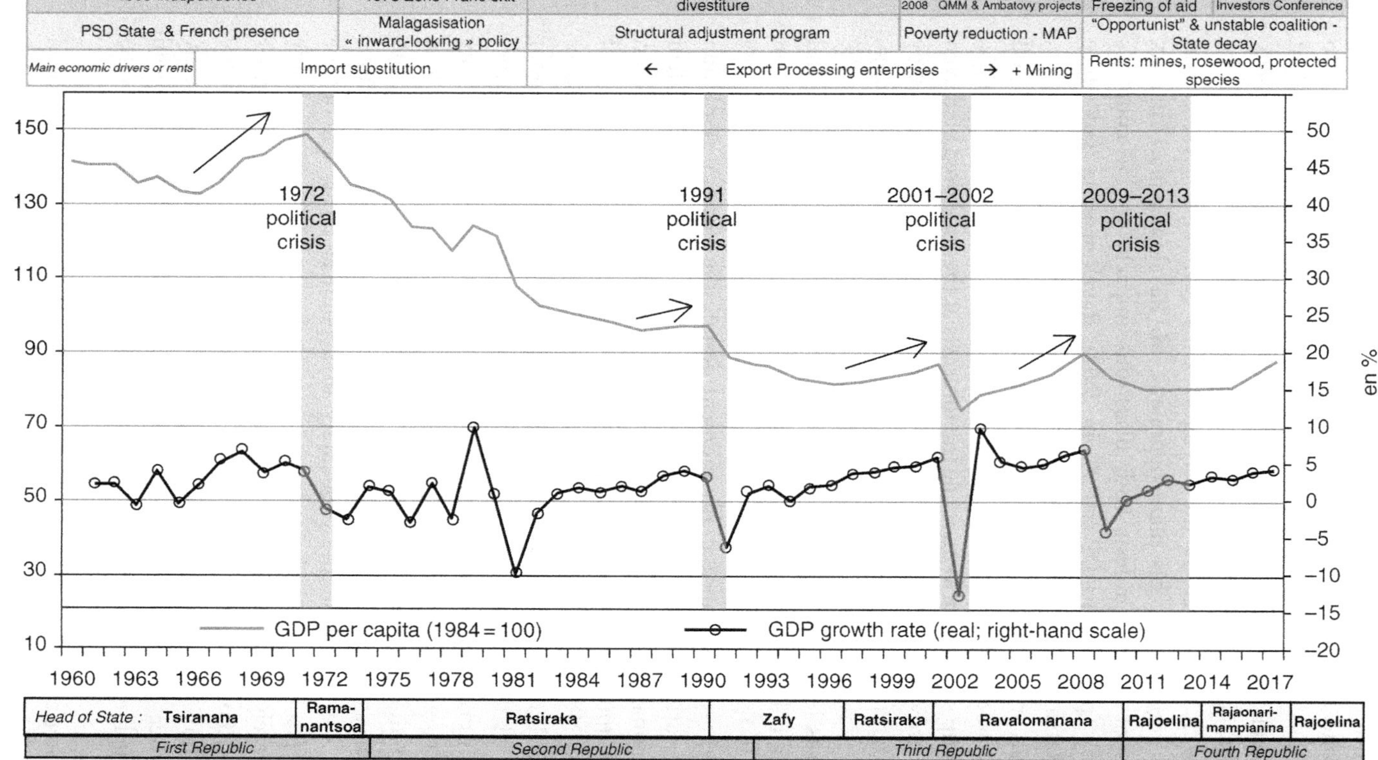

Figure 1.2 The Malagasy paradox: Growth and socio-political crises, 1960–2017.
Source: INSTAT (2018, www.instat.mg/); World Development Indicators (2018, https://databank.worldbank.org/source/world-development-indicators); authors' calculations.
Note: Per capita GDP in 1984 constant Malagasy francs.

momentum underway (Raison-Jourde, 1993). The country was into the second half of the 1990s before the growth engine sputtered back to life and started moving again under the leadership of President D. Ratsiraka back in office, but this time democratically elected in 1996. However, the outcome of the 2001 presidential election for which he stood with confidence on the strength of his economic successes was bitterly contested by his main opponent, M. Ravalomanana. After six months of violent protests with disastrous impacts on the country's economy (per capita GDP fell 9% in 2002), Ravalomanana took office while Ratsiraka went into exile in France (Roubaud, 2002). Once again, Madagascar recovered from this troubled episode and growth took off again at a brisk pace. From 2004 to 2008, GDP rose nearly 6% on average, picking up speed as it went, while the forecasts at the time predicted even higher growth for the coming years. Yet Ravalomanana's increasingly authoritarian rule was to trigger a coup d'état in early 2009 (Randrianja, 2012a). Ravalomanana in turn went into exile in South Africa as the putschists led by A. Rajoelina held the country at ransom in a legal and institutional imbroglio. The economy stagnated in an appalling state, in which it is still mired today, raising fears that the regime (and the country) would collapse at any moment despite the electoral resolution of the crisis in late 2013 and voting into office of President H. Rajaonarimampianina (see Chapter 2). Madagascar did, however, post an upturn in growth during his term of office, with an increase of 3% in GDP in 2014 and 2015, 1 percentage point in 2016 and just over 4% in 2017. Yet these figures are highly questionable in view of the poor quality of their associated macroeconomic data. The country's performance during this period even turns out to be quite disappointing considering the demographic growth rate of 2.8%, especially in view of the fact that the international donors resumed their programmes and financial assistance. Election years are generally periods of political unrest, with peaks in the probability of a political crisis. Yet despite many episodes of disorder (protests, a move by the National Assembly to impeach the president, etc.), Madagascar managed to avoid further collapse. Following relatively transparent elections, Rajoelina won at the ballot box and took office in early 2019. However, there is barely a glimmer of any hope of a real game change. In Madagascar, it will take much more than the election of a new head of state to really turn the tide.

Barring each period's particularities, analysed in detail in the second part of this chapter, Madagascar therefore appears doomed to a baffling iron law: any growth spurt is met with a political upheaval that immediately erases all trace of it. The only exception to this rule in the country's last half-century of history is the 'all-out investment' period in the late 1970s. Yet the shine dulls even on this in that the growth episode due entirely to a massive injection of public investment, unsustainable on all counts, lasted just one year (+10% in 1979) and ended abruptly (+1% in 1980), with the country plunging into deep recession for a year (−10% in 1981).

Before embarking on attempts to explain the Malagasy mystery, we need to make sure that it is indeed a mystery. Our diagnosis is based on GDP data calculated by the Madagascar National Statistics Office (INSTAT) and compiled by leading international databases such as the World Bank World Development Indicators, the Penn Tables and the series put together by Maddison and his team at the University of Groningen. These are the world's three leading reference sources.

In the case of Africa, these data have been severely criticised for their lack of reliability and transparency (Jerven, 2010a, 2011). The most illustrative example of this is the 60% increase in Ghana's GDP when it was re-evaluated in 2010 (upgrading the country to middle-income status). The uncertainty that mars growth figures in Africa led a leading expert on the subject to call one of his articles 'Random Growth in Africa?', based on a close examination of the data on Botswana, Kenya, Tanzania and Zambia (Jerven, 2010b). This problem, which we raised back in the early 2000s (Razafindrakoto & Roubaud, 2003c), is starting to be taken increasingly seriously at the international level (Devarajan, 2013; Jerven, 2013, 2015). Madagascar is no exception to this rule. Our own explorations in the late 1990s showed just how unreliable the figures on the country's GDP, growth and all the national accounts could be (Roubaud, 1999). More recently, the different measurements of GDP growth in 2009 (officially estimated at +0.6% by INSTAT, but at −5% by the International Monetary Fund; Rakotomanana *et al.*, 2010) show that the problem has not gone away. How far can the Malagasy national accounts be trusted when entire swaths of the economy (such as household consumption, the informal sector and private investment) are not directly measured by statistics and when even the most visible, formal parts of the economy (public and private) are only partially measured? Even foreign trade is captured better by 'mirror statistics', reported by supplier country (for imports) and destination country (for exports), than by national statistics.

We therefore need to look to other sources of information on which to base our diagnosis. The best candidate for this is household consumption surveys, which present two advantages: first, information sources can be

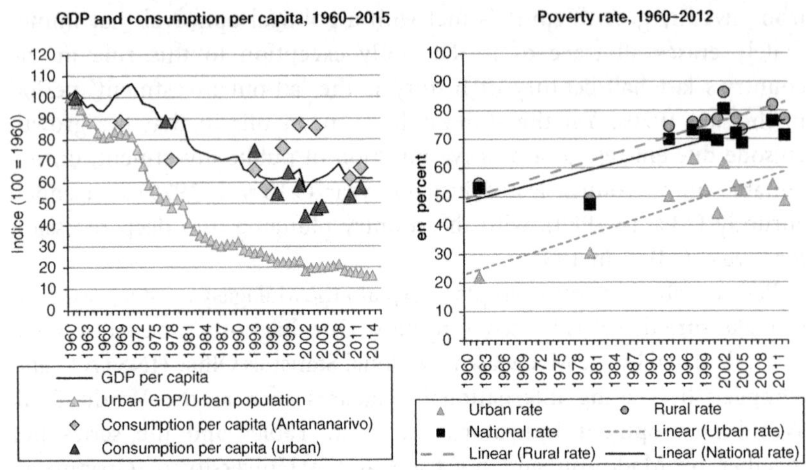

Figure 1.3 The paradox confirmed.
Source: INSTAT, MADIO, DIAL, system of national accounts and different household surveys; authors' calculations.

compared and triangulated for a robust diagnosis because the surveys are totally separate from the system of national accounts (which has never made use of them); and second, the surveys by nature reflect the population's standard of living better than per capita GDP, which includes a certain number of components (private and public investment, etc.) from which the households do not benefit. This type of exercise has long been in operation (Ravelosoa & Roubaud, 1998) and has recently been updated (Razafindrakoto & Roubaud, 2002a, 2010a). We dispense here with details on the methods and their limitations and all the possible results of these approaches (see the aforementioned articles for fuller analyses) to concentrate on the crux of the matter in hand.

Figure 1.3 presents long-run GDP growth and per capita consumption alongside the poverty rate, as reported by all the representative surveys conducted since independence. Two stylised facts emerge from the analysis. First, the Malagasy standard of living has indeed dropped since independence. For example, urban consumption per capita in 2010 stood at half its level in 1962, when the first survey was taken. The urban monetary poverty rate in turn escalated from an estimated 22% at the beginning of the period to more than double that in 2010 (54%).[1] The same downward

[1] The five-point drop in the poverty rate from 2010 to 2012, the latest survey date available, is subject to caution. The authors themselves believe that this drop could be due to the fact that the 2012–13 survey was conducted at the end of the year over the festive period

trend can be found in the countryside, albeit not as sharp. Second, the upturns do indeed appear to have been real and are not simply statistical artefacts. The only upswing that the surveys can really diagnose accurately is that which preceded the 2001–2002 crisis. Urban household consumption picked up in response to the growth cycle that started in the late 1990s, with a particularly spectacular leap in the capital Antananarivo (Razafindrakoto & Roubaud, 2002a, 2010a). Last but not least, aside from differences observed in the intensity of the phenomenon, both data sources (national accounts and surveys) confirm the very real existence of the Malagasy puzzle and paradox that this chapter seeks to understand.

1.3 First Steps in Interpretation: The Usual Theories Do Not Work

Once the problem has been clearly stated, the challenge is then to put forward factors to explain the Malagasy mystery. We look for them first in the economists' toolbox, i.e. growth theory and its offshoots. When these prove unable to explain Madagascar's economic trajectory, we then make a preliminary foray into political economy, which we believe is best able to shed light on our puzzle. Two comments on method are called for here. First, bear in mind that, as the Malagasy mystery is unique, so too do its sought 'causes' need to be unique. Assume, for example, that corruption inhibits growth. It is not enough to observe that corruption is rife in Madagascar (and consequently that Malagasy growth is curbed by corruption). Proof is needed that corruption is more acute here than elsewhere. This same condition holds for any factor identified. Second, the purpose here is not to perform a sophisticated growth analysis, but to sound out a broad spectrum of possible determinants to decide whether any of them display dynamics tentatively specific and deficient enough to be potential suspects to explain Madagascar's misfortune.

We start by looking at the classic economic factors, drawing mainly on the most comprehensive and widely used international database, i.e. the World Development Indicators (WDIs) compiled by the World Bank, which form the basis for a large part of the empirical literature on economic growth worldwide. As we move away from standard economic factors, so the

(INSTAT, 2015). The figures revised by the World Bank (2015) moreover show a six-point increase in urban poverty and a two-point decrease in rural poverty. However, the reconstructed series is not compatible with the pre-2001 data.

databases used become more micro, although representative (household surveys) and paradoxically generally of better quality than the aggregate macroeconomic indicators. A last introductory remark before embarking on our exploration is that, as our approach takes a structural angle to paint a global picture of stylised features, we do not get caught up in methodological refinements at this point, which would serve no purpose in any case given the quality of the data. In particular, wherever possible, we take the long time series (one of the major advantages of the WDIs) to calculate averages over a number of decades, generally half a century (1960–2015). This choice in effect smooths over the details, especially the profiles and dynamics of the phenomena. Yet we contend that our general conclusions are robust enough to dispense with the need to be tested by more detailed approaches on one or other point, notwithstanding the merits of conducting such approaches wherever conditions, especially access to data, allow.

It's the Economy, 'Stupid'?

Is the economy enough as an explanation? [2] In good classical economic theory, the usual suspects taken to explain a structural economic growth deficit are the factors of production: labour and physical capital, to which land could be added in an economy where more than two-thirds of the population work in agriculture. There is obviously no intention here of revisiting growth theory, a central focus that has engaged generations of economists from its beginnings and founding fathers through to the most sophisticated endogenous growth developments (Barro & Sala-i-Martin, 2004). Data on Madagascar are so scant that such an undertaking would make no sense. However, growth theory does provide a convenient analytic framework within which to consider our question and lay the groundwork for our thinking. The annual wealth produced in Madagascar (approximated by its GDP) could be perceived as the outcome of a production function making use of the country's available labour and capital. The combination of factors more or less efficiently incorporates 'technical progress', a term taken by economists to mean everything that increases the efficiency of the production process, i.e. raises output for a given volume of inputs.[3] In this heuristic framework, a growth deficit may

[2] The title of this subsection is in reference to Bill Clinton's 1992 election campaign slogan about the decisive importance of the economy when his opponent – George Bush – was plugging his foreign policy achievements.

[3] Otherwise known as total factor productivity (TFP) or multifactor productivity.

come from two, potentially linked causes: a deficient factor accumulation process or the suboptimal use of these factors or both.

Looking first at labour, the traditional decompositions make labour a key factor of growth. Most of the indicators concur that Madagascar is fairly well endowed on this front, in both quantity and quality. First, demographic growth (given the little we know, as the last population census dates back to 1993![4]) is approximately the same in Madagascar as in sub-Saharan Africa (Table 1.1). Manpower[5] even posts slightly sharper growth in Madagascar (3.6% per year on average compared with 3% on the continent as a whole from 2005 to 2014). Second, population age structure and labour market functioning are quite positive in Madagascar, transforming the demographic dividend into an economic dividend. The employment rate, i.e. the percentage of the population (aged 15 and over) working averages 84%, which is 20 points higher than in sub-Saharan Africa and higher than in our four comparison countries. Lastly, this growth potential is even greater considering that the Malagasy labour force is more skilled on average and therefore (again potentially) more productive (quality effect). For example, the adult (aged 15 and over) literacy rate stood at an estimated 71% in Madagascar in 2000 as opposed to 57% in Africa as a whole in the same year (and 61% in 2010). Once again, even though its initial advantage is slipping, Madagascar's long-run average is higher than in our four comparison countries (Cameroon comes closest) and sub-Saharan Africa in general (Table 1.1). The WDIs estimate that nearly one-quarter of the manpower has secondary education at least (the database unfortunately provides no information on either our comparison countries or Africa in general). Malagasy manpower is not only more educated but also healthier, as shown by life expectancy at birth (three years more on average than in sub-Saharan Africa, all countries combined). It is this combination of health and education that explains why Madagascar systematically ranks much higher in the Human Development Index country ranking than when classed by per capita GDP. The new Human Capital Index (HCI) developed by the World Bank (2018) provides a more comprehensive measurement than previous indicators, as it considers health and education in terms of quantity and quality. Madagascar performs poorly at the global level but comes out at around the average for sub-Saharan Africa. An HCI of 0.37 means that

[4] The next, much-postponed census took place in May 2018. But the results will not be available until mid-2019.

[5] Working-age population (conventionally aged 15 years and over).

Table 1.1 *Accumulation of production factors, (1960–2015)*

	Madagascar	Sub-Saharan Africa	Benin	Burkina Faso	Côte d'Ivoire	Cameroon
Labour						
Population (% growth rate)	2.8	2.6	2.7	2.4	3.4	2.7
Employment rate (15 years and over)	84.1	63.6	71.9	81.0	64.0	65.3
Adult literacy rate	66.6	58.9	29.1	22.7	40.7	65.3
Life expectancy at birth	52.0	48.9	50.0	47.0	47.7	50.4
Physical capital						
Fixed capital formation/ capita ($2010)	61	228	141	81	168	214
Road density (km/1,000 ha)	3.0	2.4	1.7	5.5	3.7	2.5
Land						
Arable land per capita (ha)	0.45	0.89	0.67	1.01	1.24	0.93
Irrigation potential (% arable land)	19.0	6.0	4.6	1.8	2.3	1.9

Source: WDI, 2017, FAO, 2005; authors' calculations.
Note: FCF reports the averages for the entire period. The series starts in 1965 for Burkina Faso, 1981 for sub-Saharan Africa and 2008 for Côte d'Ivoire.

children born in Madagascar today will be 37% as productive in adulthood as they might have been with full education and health. The country's HCI ranking slid back from 2012 to 2017. Yet the HCI for Madagascar is still higher than expected given its income level. This means that the stock of human capital, despite an accumulation rate well below par, cannot be held responsible for Madagascar's stalled economic growth.

Physical capital is more problematic for a number of reasons. First, although statistical data present a major challenge in Africa (Jerven, 2013, 2015), the problem is even more acute, if not insurmountable, when it comes to measuring physical capital. There are quite simply no capital stock series, while flows (investment) are particularly poorly measured. We therefore have to make do with rough approximations, as with everything found in the literature even though all too often no mention is made of these shortcomings. Our partial indicators point to a capital underaccumulation phenomenon. The most reasonable capital stock approximation that we can make from the WDIs, with all the usual reservations, is the sum of year-on-year per capita fixed capital formation (FCF), public and private, in constant currency. On average, between 1981 and 2015, FCF in Madagascar stood at US$58 (2010 constant) per capita (US$61 from 1960 to 2015). By contrast, this ratio was US$228 for sub-Saharan Africa as a whole, which is four times higher than in Madagascar. Taking our comparison countries again, Madagascar has categorically the lowest level of accumulation. The comparative sums are US$141 for Benin and US$214 for Cameroon for the entire period, and US$81 for Burkina Faso (since 1965). The case of Côte d'Ivoire is not very significant, as no data are available for the years before 2008. Considering that the level of capital was probably higher in Madagascar than in other former French colonies, including our comparison countries, owing to the greater importance placed on Madagascar by mainland France compared with most of the other sub-Saharan African zones, the question then boils down to why the country has an investment deficit, in both amount and percentage of GDP. At approximately 16% of GDP (on average since 1980), Madagascar's fixed capital formation is lower than in sub-Saharan Africa as a whole (18%).

We sought to support our diagnosis with an example, with a capital indicator that would be illustrative, more compelling and, most importantly, less subject to measurement errors. We found road density to be a good candidate. Obviously, it is itself highly imperfect: it is biased (counting only one type of infrastructure, mainly public, not machines, buildings, etc.) and disputable (what is actually being counted?). The outcome of our test is inconclusive. With 3 kilometres of road per 1,000 hectares (in 2011), Madagascar is better equipped than Africa as a whole on average (2.4 kilometres). It is on the positive side of the continental ranking (31st of 50 countries ranked). This average position is found again when looking at our comparison countries: Madagascar appears to be better connected than Cameroon and especially Benin, but less well off than Côte d'Ivoire and Burkina Faso. This finding is particularly surprising considering that road density is generated primarily by public investment, whose (relative) inadequacy was mentioned earlier. To conclude, not to take the existing indicators at face value, our qualitative diagnosis of capital underaccumulation, public especially, appears to be reasonable and all the more credible in that it has also been advanced by two recent studies on the subject (D'Hoore, 2018; Naudet & Rua, 2018).

Land is obviously a crucial issue in a country like Madagascar. Here again, as always, the question of data and data quality is key. We stick to the best practices in this field, i.e. the FAO data, combined with the more classic WDI data, as in the previous paragraphs. Madagascar is a large, underpopulated country, but that does not necessarily make it a country rich in land. The FAO estimates that Madagascar had 0.45 hectare of 'arable' land per person in 2005, half the surface area for sub-Saharan Africa in general (0.89) and less than each of all four comparison countries. Yet this finding needs qualifying. First, there is nothing unusual about Madagascar from this point of view: it is in 20th place (in a 53-country ranking) of the least well-endowed countries, between South Africa (0.41) and Ghana (0.47), but ahead of countries such as Ethiopia (0.18), Kenya (0.31) and Senegal (0.37). Second, Madagascar's picture brightens up when it comes to the irrigation potential of this arable land with a share, at nearly 20%, three times higher than in Africa as a whole (6%). In 2005, Madagascar came out on top overall for its irrigation potential. At 0.09 hectare per person, the Red Island ranks 42nd of the countries on the continent in ascending order of surface area, with the African average being 0.05 hectare per person; each of all our four comparison countries are below this line. Here again, although our admittedly crude analyses show that Madagascar cannot claim outstanding land factor endowment, it is hardly particularly deficient either. This is evidenced by the scale of the land grab phenomenon, including the famous 'Daewoo affair' (we will come back to this in later chapters). In any case, there is nothing in this area to explain Madagascar's disastrous growth performance.

Measuring technical progress is even more problematic than measuring factors of production. As mentioned earlier, technical progress is identified as the unexplained growth residual (where growth in production is higher than growth in the quantity of labour and capital factor inputs). It is therefore reflected by both the quality of the production factors and the efficiency of their use. Patents filed and the number of researchers in a country are indirect indicators of the technical progress associated with research and development (R&D). These data are available in the WDIs. From 1994 to 2014, 37 patents a year were filed by non-residents and barely eight a year by residents in Madagascar. The human resources figures are equally meagre: Madagascar counted 65 executives working in R&D per million inhabitants over the period (41 researchers and 24 technicians). Unfortunately, none of these indicators is available for our four comparison countries, any more than for sub-Saharan Africa (which points to the underlying weakness of these elements).

The strategy employed by economists to overcome this problem of indirect, imperfect indicators is to calculate the famous total factor productivity (TFP), i.e. the residual that 'explains' growth after deducting the contribution of production factors. In developing countries, this calculation often calls for heroic assumptions as to the form and parameters of the production function. The Penn Tables, the benchmark database in this area, systematically propose an estimate of TFP for most of the world's countries. Yet the data on Madagascar were judged inadequate to be able to provide a credible estimate, as was the case with a certain number of other African countries. We agree with this point of view, with the result that it is impossible to conduct a standard decomposition of growth. In these circumstances and considering our simplified production function, the only conclusion we can draw at this stage from our preceding analyses is that Madagascar's growth deficit is due either to poor physical capital accumulation or to weak TFP gains or both.

To conclude, Madagascar does not appear to be less endowed with production factors, with the plausible exception of physical capital. Nevertheless, and even if this 'anomaly' were firmly established, the question arises as to why. Capital accumulation is indeed largely endogenous: on the one hand, poor growth, and therefore sluggish demand, reduces investment (a mechanism known as the accelerator effect); on the other hand, the same factors may hinder both growth and capital. Our exploration has therefore only managed to take one step on the road to the causes: if Madagascar accumulates less capital, why? Furthermore, for a given volume of factors, other elements may explain why their combination produces poorer results in Madagascar than elsewhere, i.e. the famous embodied 'technical progress', in the broad sense of the term, whose many dimensions can be explored using an augmented production function. This is what we undertake next in this chapter.

Historical and Geographical Circumstances?

Madagascar's poor economic performance is even more intriguing considering the country's remarkably favourable historical and geographical 'circumstances'. First of all, Madagascar has a wealth of natural resources and human capital, and a fair share of arable land. It has the advantages of natural borders and cultural and linguistic unity (notwithstanding a few local variations), which owe nothing to the colonial carve-up.

Madagascar's biodiversity is beyond compare, with outstanding flora and fauna endemic to the island. As with many intertropical regions, the country's ecosystem is fragile and in a state of degradation. However, this remains contained (relatively to other countries) as anthropogenic pressure is low. The country's natural resources (mineral and agricultural) are fairly evenly balanced, hitherto sparing the island from the 'resource curse' that has befallen so many other countries. This is also probably one of the reasons why Madagascar has never been paralysed by domestic armed conflict for long, any more than it has been by external conflicts as it has no potential enemies on its borders. All of these elements form structural advantages (agro-climatic, human and political) that are undoubtedly the envy of many a poor country (especially in the Sudano-Sahelian region).

It is important to say a word about natural disasters given the severity of the problem globally, and in Madagascar in particular. Madagascar is prone to a whole host of recurrent events on the increase in recent years as a result of climate change: cyclones, floods, drought, locust infestations, etc. Madagascar is also classified as one of the most vulnerable countries to hydrometeorological risks. The international EM-DAT benchmark database on natural disasters worldwide[6] counts no fewer than 76 events since 1968 (date of the first entry in the base). The events are mainly cyclones (80%), but all occur with increasing frequency over time (48 of the 76 since 2000). These natural disasters have caused nearly 5,000 deaths and affected more than 16 million people to date. So Madagascar is clearly subject to natural disasters. Yet the question of interest here is whether it is more vulnerable than others. The answer to this question is no – or it depends on the type of impact considered. The number of disasters, as a ratio of the (current) population for indicator comparability (surface area could also have been used), comes to 3 episodes on average (per million inhabitants) as opposed to 2.4 on average in Africa, which makes for slightly higher prevalence. From this point of view, then, the occurrence of extreme weather does not appear to be extremely high. Madagascar ranks between Cameroon and Côte d'Ivoire (both less affected) and Benin and Burkina Faso (more affected). Obviously, extreme weather events vary in intensity and the damage they cause. Yet Madagascar does not appear to be particularly hard hit in terms of this impact either, as extreme weather claims fewer lives on the island than in many other countries. Each episode

[6] The base includes only the largest disasters that conform to at least one of the three following criteria: 10 or more people dead; 100 or more people affected; a call made for international assistance or a state of emergency declared.

averages a death toll of around 60 in Madagascar as opposed to nearly 550 in Africa. All in all, as a ratio of the population, natural disasters claim nearly five times fewer lives than in Africa. However, the number of people affected by these disasters is slightly higher in Madagascar: 223,000 compared with 210,000 in Africa on average for each event. In cumulative terms, the Malagasy have a marginally higher probability of being affected than Africans as a whole. And although no reliable indicators are available on economic loss and damage caused by natural disasters, Madagascar has clearly never been hit by a severe disaster in this way. Ultimately, it would seem that although Madagascar suffers from extreme weather, its situation is not (yet) extraordinary. So extreme weather cannot be put forward to explain the country's divergent growth. Damage (human and material) from natural disasters is caused by the interaction between the physical intensity of the extreme weather event and household socioeconomic vulnerability (Wisner *et al.*, 2014). Causality therefore runs in the opposite direction to that expected here: the level of damage is high because a country is poor, rather than vice versa. This conclusion is shared by D'Hoore (2018) in his exploration of the Malagasy puzzle. Yet this does not mean that disasters are not set to play an increasingly important role in the future (see the book's conclusion on this point).

Turning to the historical angle, Madagascar at independence displayed all the advantages it needed for a successful economic take-off. The country had been on a path of homegrown political unification prior to colonisation. The budding *Merina*[7] state had much in common with Asian nations (state centralisation, bureaucracy, irrigation works, taxation, etc.), to the extent that its economic organisation could be termed an Asiatic mode of production (to borrow Marxist terminology). This singularity is largely held to be an asset today in view of contemporary development experiences. Madagascar also exhibited the ability to relatively painlessly absorb the elements of societal change introduced by the early Western incursions (especially on the economic, education and religious fronts). School, for example, became compulsory in 1876, five years ahead of France. Although there is no denying the traumatic impact of an unjust, repressive system of colonisation and the disruption it caused, the rupture was much smaller than elsewhere. It was during this period that Madagascar, held up as a jewel of the French colonial empire, started to transform economically. The country's appeal can be gauged from the significant number of settlers established on the Red Island, albeit never an actual settlement colony. The

[7] *Merina*: one of the ethnic groups from the Central Highlands of Madagascar.

Empire accounts compiled by the Afristory project (Cogneau *et al.*, 2017) show that Madagascar counted some 30,000 settlers (mainly French) in the 1930s, as much as French West Africa and French Equatorial Africa combined. This point is worth stressing, as some studies have made the rate of settlement the main explanatory factor for the nature of the (extraction-based) institutions put in place at the time, with their decisive repercussions on both today's institutions and the country's long-run development potential (Acemoglu *et al.*, 2001). Following independence, the country's productive structures and socio-political fabric were in better condition than most of the other colonies that gained independence at the same time.

Economic Policy?

Considering these patent comparative advantages, the country's disastrous post-independence economic performance can hardly be explained by economic policy choices alone. Madagascar has basically explored in turn most of the options available on the development 'market' at any particular time (import substitution, structural adjustment and poverty reduction) without any lasting success. Some have seen the socialist experiment of the 1970s as the decisive break that set Madagascar into a fatal tailspin. We view this interpretation as stereotyped and misguided. The 'Malagasy-style socialism' promoted by D. Ratsiraka in the 1970s was nothing like the European, Asian or even African models of socialism. It was neither brutal nor radical in its economic and political outlook, which only marginally departed from the policies run by countries remaining in the Western fold (such as Côte d'Ivoire): central role of the state, managed economy, Ivoirianisation, nationalisation, domination of the presidential party, etc. Furthermore, it lasted a mere fleeting interlude of a few years before a sharp shift to structural adjustment in the early 1980s. Lastly, other countries that went further and longer down the socialism road steered their conversion much better (see the typical example of Ghana, or else Benin). Dispensing then with the idea of the "socialist" episode as the God in the machine of later failings, when it was itself a mere epiphenomenon, Madagascar has by and large taken the line of admittedly contradictory policies, but donor-recommended policies all the same (relatively well-timed adoption of 'good policies', to use a current buzzword), without making any major departure from the other developing countries (African in particular).

Agricultural price management policies offer a good – partial, but illustrative – way of providing objective, quantitative evidence in support of this reading of Madagascar's economic history. Cash crop sector administration was (and still is) a major public policy lever in developing countries. As a leading source of public and export revenues, these sectors formed a major test bed for economic policy in two ways: command economy versus market economy, and import substitution strategy versus extraversion strategy (trade-off between tradeable and non-tradeable goods; World Bank, 2008). The most representative examples of this are the creation and then dismantling of the famous commodities marketing boards and exchange rate manipulation.

This is probably what prompted the World Bank to launch a vast research project called *Distortions to Agricultural Incentives* in the 2000s. The project produced an international database to measure the level of intervention on the agricultural markets. It basically calculates the differential between the market price and the often-administered prices actually paid producers and estimates the loss (or gain) in terms of foreign trade or welfare (GDP). This programme also gave rise to a large number of publications, including country monographs, although unfortunately not including Madagascar (Anderson, 2009). The original database covered the main lines of production in 75 countries with annual information spanning a 50-year period (1955–2005) (Anderson & Valenzuela, 2008). The latest version of the database extends over 82 countries and runs through to 2010 (Anderson & Nelgen, 2013).

D'Hoore (2018) was the first to use these data in his seminal article to explore the 'Malagasy mystery'. The information covers the 10 main products in Madagascar (rice, sugar, vanilla, coffee, cocoa, pepper, cloves, cassava, maize and sweet potato). His main conclusion is that price distortions did indeed have an extremely adverse effect on producers (among the poorest) and the country's growth in general over a long 20-year period (1970–90), even though the drain was slowly (too slowly) plugged. Building on this first exploration, we have recalculated the distortion indicator, i.e. the volume of potential income denied producers as a percentage of GDP, for Madagascar and a certain number of comparison countries. Note that aside from some imprecision due to the data themselves (the database authors had to make a certain number of assumptions), the very design is 'ideologically' loaded and merits further discussion. The underlying idea is that the price differential, the drain when it is negative, is a distortion and cannot have been used productively, for example to invest in public infrastructure likely to have a positive impact on production. This is the problem with a strict accounting approach, in partial equilibrium, which does not take into consideration indirect and contraction effects, termed externalities or general equilibrium effects by economists.

We find the same results for Madagascar as D'Hoore (2018). If the aforementioned hypotheses are accepted, Madagascar displays a considerable urban bias. The drain on farmers, accounting for less than 5% of GDP throughout the entire First Republic, suddenly started shooting up in 1972 to reach nearly 13% of GDP in 1976. The differential began to recede in 1977, stagnating at 10% through to the early 1980s before being gradually absorbed with the implementation of structural adjustment. Yet the level did not fall to zero until the mid-1990s, when producers were assumed to be recovering the entire world price (minus delivery costs). The distortion curve coincides directly with the political cycle. However, the most interesting point, as predicted, is that Madagascar is not really a unique case at all (Figure 1.4). Our calculations show that many African countries exhibit similar trends. The distortion curves for five African countries chosen purposively (Cameroon, Côte d'Ivoire, Ghana, Kenya and Senegal) are similar to that observed for Madagascar. All curves are U-shaped with a peak in the 1970s. Although the level of the 'drain' shows up as higher for Madagascar at the lowest point (first half of the 1970s), possibly the greatest particularity displayed by the Red Island is the slow pace of absorption in the 1980s. Nevertheless, two major factors are of note. First, the drain turns into a surplus in the first half of the 2000s. Madagascar is the only country to experience this positive transfer. Second, and most importantly, the volume of the distortions is much lower than observed in Côte d'Ivoire, long considered a model success story in this area (see the emblematic example of the cocoa sector). From this point of view, President Houphouët-Boigny, despite being a professed proponent of free market economics, fared no better than President Ratsiraka, momentarily tempted by the sirens of socialism and branded among the West's enemies. The same type of conclusion could be drawn from a comparison of Ghana, also an erstwhile convert to socialism, and Côte d'Ivoire – two countries offering many points of comparison including a shared border, history and indigenous peoples – but also Senegal and Cameroon, less extreme than Côte d'Ivoire in terms of administered prices and ever-faithful to the capitalist fold.

Lastly, our comparative analyses show once again that Madagascar's cycle of economic policies is not entirely disconnected from that of our other comparison countries on the continent. So the reasons for the Malagasy mystery surely lie elsewhere. Our explorations add a further feature to the description of Madagascar's economy. Although there are rents, they are generally small sources compared with other countries. This

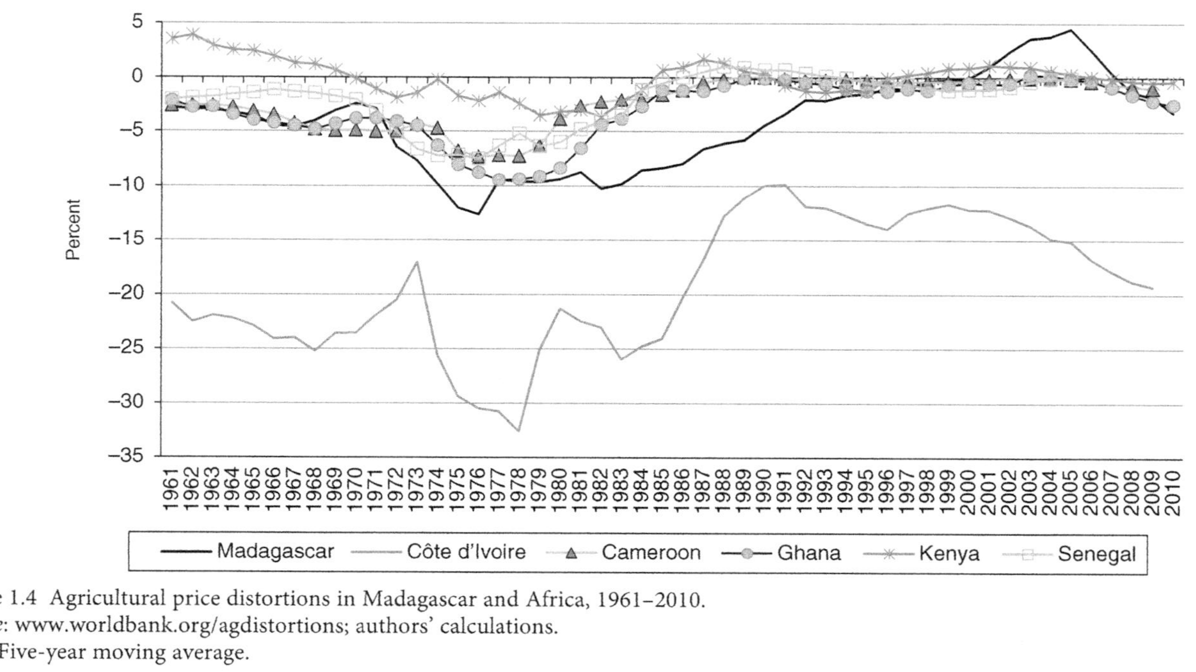

Figure 1.4 Agricultural price distortions in Madagascar and Africa, 1961–2010.
Source: www.worldbank.org/agdistortions; authors' calculations.
Note: Five-year moving average.

can be observed here for the agricultural sector. Yet it is also true of public resources, including taxation and international aid (see Chapter 4), and this is a constant throughout Madagascar's history (see Chapter 2). Rent capture strategies will therefore naturally be based on small bases.

Governance?

The explanation for Madagascar's economic failure is not to be found in the poor quality of its institutions and governance either, at least as measured by current official indicators. As we have seen, the country's institutions were in relatively better condition at independence than in other comparable developing countries. Neither are the governance indicators for Madagascar reported by the leading international databases significantly lower than the admittedly less than satisfactory indicators observed on the continent. The Worldwide Governance Indicators, developed by the World Bank and probably the most comprehensive source to date on governance (Kaufmann & Kraay, 2008), illustrate this statement for the 1996–2015 period.[8] Although this period includes two major crises (2002 and 2009), Madagascar's relative ranking in the community of nations is higher on average than sub-Saharan Africa, which in turn ranks higher than South-East Asia.

Figure 1.5 presents how Madagascar's mean relative positions have changed for the six dimensions of governance (*Voice & Accountability, Political Stability & Absence of Violence, Government Effectiveness, Regulatory Quality, Rule of Law* and *Control of Corruption*) among the 200 countries in the database. While sub-Saharan Africa sits along the 30th percentile for two decades, Madagascar progresses from the 40th to the 50th percentile before starting to fall off in 2007 and dipping slightly under the continental level with the onset of the 2009 political crisis (although the difference is not significant). Note that the improvement observed in the post-crisis period (2014–16) is barely perceptible. We take the same set of African countries considered in the foregoing growth comparison to further compare governance performance. Madagascar always ranks much higher than Cameroon and Côte d'Ivoire, except in the most recent period when Côte d'Ivoire made a spectacular recovery following the end of the civil war. Madagascar, previously neck and neck with Benin and Burkina Faso (even gaining a slight edge in the early 2000s), has fallen

[8] The first governance indicators emerged in the mid-1990s, which unfortunately rules out any earlier observations.

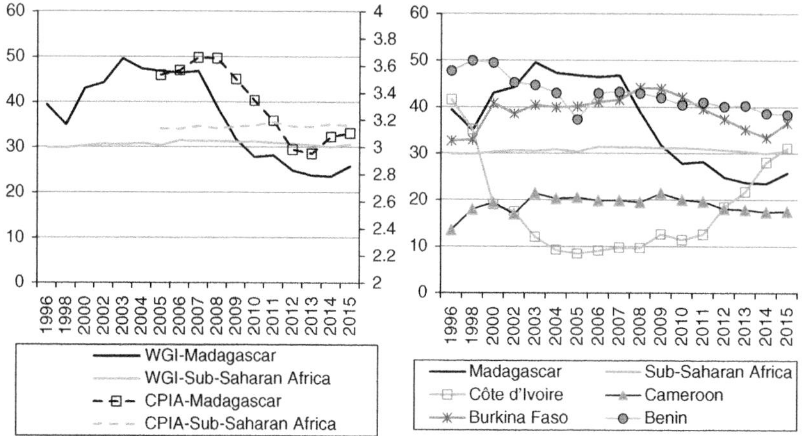

Figure 1.5 Comparative development of governance in Madagascar, 1996–2016.
Source: WGI, 2017; authors' calculations.
Note: The indicator corresponds to the arithmetic mean of the percentile for the six dimensions of governance covered by the WGIs. See note 9 for the definition of CPIA.

behind since the crisis in the late 2000s. Yet these countries all have economic records in a class of their own compared to the Red Island.

The elements taken to calculate the average levels of governance presented in Figure 1.5 are too heterogeneous to be able to do anything but skim the surface. Figure 1.6 (charts 1 to 3) therefore improves on the calculation by disaggregating each of the six individual dimensions over the entire 1996–2015 period. This exercise bears out the previous conclusions. Madagascar 'dominates' sub-Saharan Africa, Cameroon and Côte d'Ivoire on all fronts.

Burkina Faso has an astonishingly similar average governance profile to Madagascar. Benin unsurprisingly comes out on the whole ahead of Madagascar in the governance stakes, in two areas in particular: *Voice & Accountability* and *Political Stability & Absence of Violence*. However, the country performs less well in the *Control of Corruption*. Yet Benin's relatively good performance needs putting into perspective as it is largely due to the deterioration in Madagascar's situation with the advent of the 2009 coup d'état. In 2004, for example, Madagascar was level pegging with Benin in its two highest-scoring dimensions and, in 2007, when Madagascar's governance curve was still high, the Red Island ranked way ahead of Benin in four of the six indicators monitored.

The governance indicators, like the economic data, are far from entirely reliable (Arndt & Oman, 2006; Razafindrakoto & Roubaud, 2010b). Chart 4 of Figure 1.6 therefore presents the incidence of petty bureaucratic corruption in

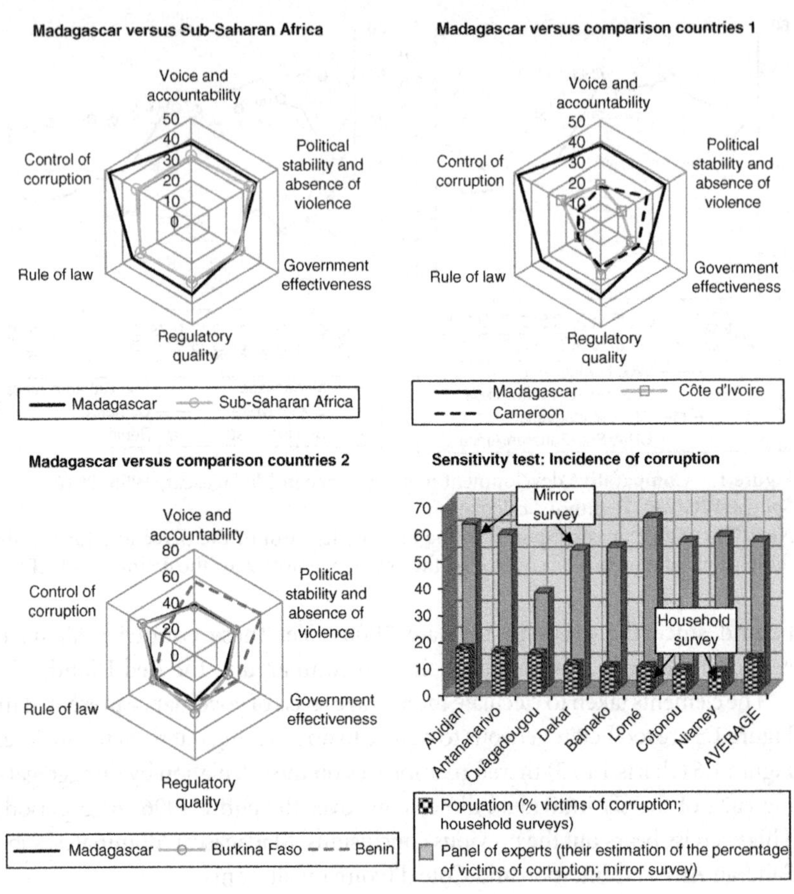

Figure 1.6 Individual dimensions of governance in Madagascar.
Source: WGI, 2017 (charts 1–3) Razafindrakoto & Roubaud, 2010b (chart 4); authors' calculations.
Note: The indicators in charts 1 to 3 correspond to the arithmetic mean of the percentile for each of the six dimensions of governance covered by the WGIs for the years 1996 to 2011.

eight African countries, including Madagascar, to ensure that Madagascar's relatively positive ranking is not due to international experts giving the country a boost in perception (as was found to be the case under M. Ravalomanana, one of the donor darlings in favour with the development community). Granted, this is only a partial robustness test as it covers just one of the dimensions of governance (and even then only one of its components as grand corruption is not measured – no more than it is measurable). Yet it does have the advantage of providing an objective measure (households' actual experience of corruption) rather than a perception, which is naturally more subjective.

The main conclusion that can be drawn from this comparison is that Madagascar ranks among the average of the eight test countries. The everyday corruption measures collected by the Afrobarometer surveys, this time at national level for a larger number of countries, come to a similar conclusion: Madagascar is in a median position in Africa, if not probably a better situation given that the surveys were conducted only in countries engaged in a democratic process, which might be considered to be less corrupt than others (Lavallée *et al.*, 2010). In any case, these findings confirm that the growth rate gap is not due, in principle, to a structural governance deficit.

All the other international databases concur: Madagascar is not a governance outlier. In the CPIA,[9] for example, Madagascar is rated on a par with sub-Saharan Africa in 2011 (in the midst of the crisis) and is still not considered a fragile state (World Bank, 2012), any more than it is in the CIFP Fragility Index (Naudé *et al.*, 2011) from 1999 to 2005. Assuming that a country's economic development is indeed closely associated with (if not due to) the quality of the institutions it has built, a first key to the Malagasy mystery is then that the proposed measures of these institutions are incapable of capturing Madagascar's Achilles' heel. Yet the new authorities elected to office in late 2013 and 2018 do not appear to have managed to turn the governance situation around, as they have in other areas, which raises the question as to whether there is not a chink in the armour of Madagascar's economy.

Ethnic Diversity: The Key to Madagascar's Woes?

In their endeavours to explain Africa's underperformance (the famous *Africa Dummy*), economists have turned en masse to an essentialist interpretation: the continent's ethnic diversity. A seminal article by Easterly and Levine (1997), entitled *Africa's Growth Tragedy*, marked the launch of a long line of studies focusing on ethnic diversity as the crux of the African problem. This interpretation still has wide currency in both academic and popular writing on sub-Saharan Africa, as it has the huge advantage of meeting with popular belief. Leaving aside discussion of the severe criticism made of this theory, let's take a look at Madagascar's own ethnic characteristics (see Map 1.1).

[9] The CPIA (Country Policy and Institutional Assessment) put together by World Bank experts is designed to rate the quality of improvements to public policies and institutions against a set of 16 indicators grouped in 4 clusters: economic management, structural policies, policies for social inclusion and equity and public sector management and institutions.

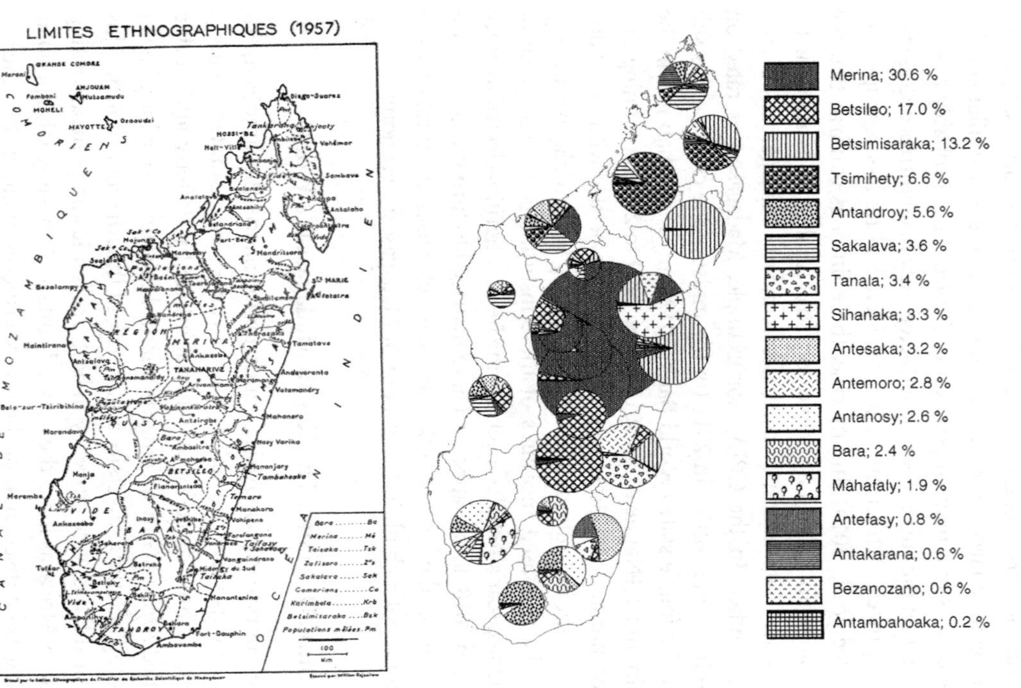

Map 1.1 Population distribution by region and ethnic group in 1957 and 2005.

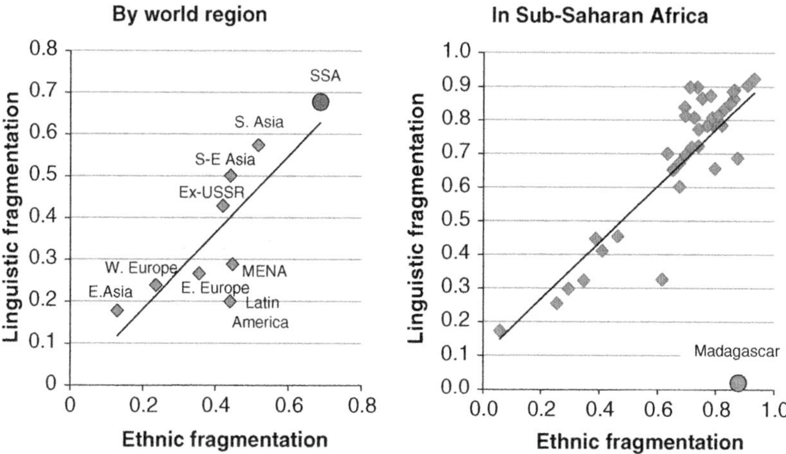

Figure 1.7 Madagascar's comparative ethnic and linguistic fragmentation.
Source: Based on Fearon (2003); authors' calculations.

At first glance, Madagascar is far from an exception to the rule, with ethnic fractionalisation in the country at its height and at one of the highest levels in sub-Saharan Africa (0.88). This observation supports many analyses that make the *Merina-côtier* divide pivotal to interpreting Madagascar's history right down the line from precolonial times (when the *Merina* kingdoms gradually subjugated the *côtier* political entities), through colonisation (the French authorities incessantly undermined the *Merina* elites' power to the advantage of the *côtier* elites in order to ensure their own domination), to the post-independence period (prior to the 2000s, *Merinas* were tacitly disqualified from standing for the presidency).

Figure 1.7, however, reveals a first anomaly in Madagascar's ethnolinguistic composition. Madagascar is an exception to the usual close correlation between ethnic and linguistic fragmentation. The level of linguistic fragmentation is by far the lowest in Africa (and one of the lowest in the world) at nearly zero (0.02). This reflects the country's above-mentioned linguistic unity and very strong cultural homogeneity in general.

Although ethnic fragmentation is high in Madagascar, ethnicity cannot necessarily be regarded as the be-all and end-all of the country's political, social and economic dynamics. The Afrobarometer surveys put this all-too common assumption to the test . . . and disprove it. As shown in Figure 1.8, Madagascar's politics and economy exhibit among the least (if not the least) pronounced ethnic dimension of all African countries (at least the 20

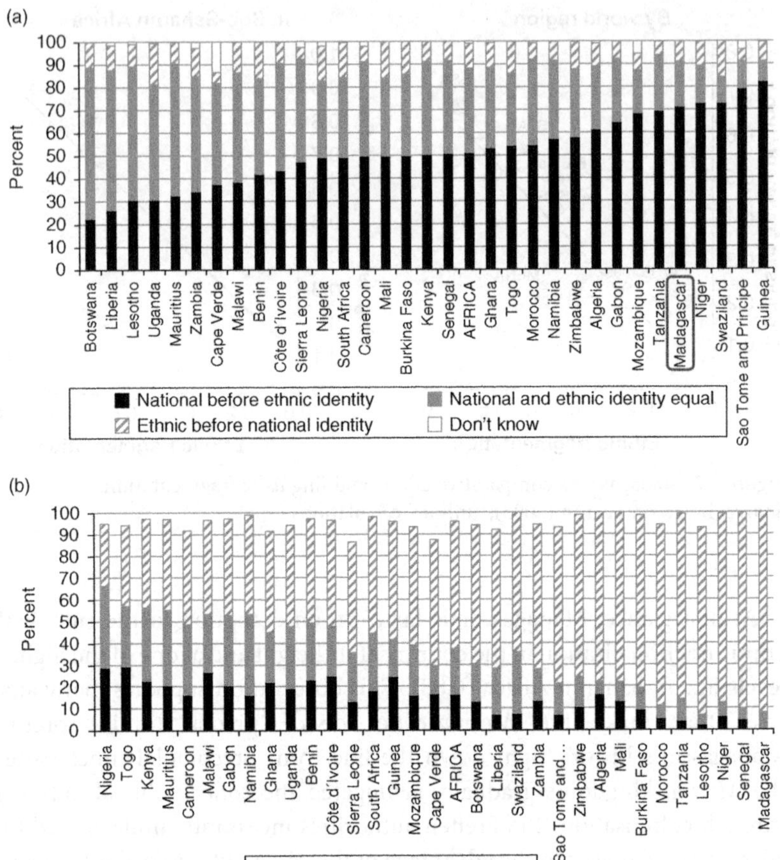

Figure 1.8 Low prevalence of ethnic issues in Madagascar. (a) National identity versus ethnic identity (b) Discrimination against ethnic groups.

Source: Afrobarometer surveys, round 6, 2014–15; authors' calculations.

Note: The questions are worded as follows: Assume you had to choose between being [Malagasy] and being [respondent's ethnic group], which of the following statements would best express your feelings? Are the [respondent's ethnic group] treated unfairly by the government?

countries where the surveys were conducted). An overwhelming majority of Malagasy place their national identity ahead of their ethnic identity (only a few countries are more attached to their national identity). They are by far the least likely to consider that certain ethnic groups are discriminated against (just over 10%, with only 3% believing this is often the case). The vast majority of Malagasy also hold the view that their ethnic group has neither more nor less political influence than other groups. Previous

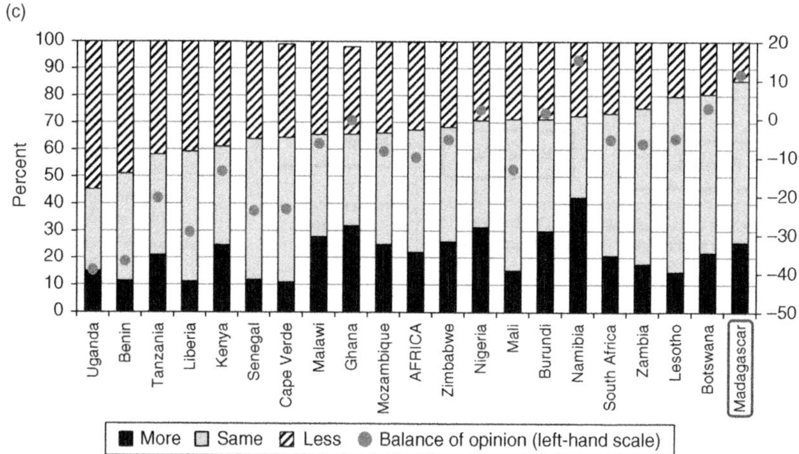

Figure 1.8(c) Comparative political influence of the different ethnic groups.
Source: Afrobarometer surveys, round 4, 2008; authors' calculations.
Note: The question is worded as follows: Do the members of your ethnic group have less, as much or more influence in politics than the other groups in the country?

studies (Roubaud, 2000; Ramamonjisoa, 2002) had already identified the low prevalence of ethnic issues in Madagascar, but never quite so conclusively. It is also telling that politicians' repeated attempts to play the ethnic card, such as in the 2002 crisis, have systematically failed.

1.4 A Preliminary Foray into Political Economy

At the end of this first sweep through the possible explanations for Madagascar's poor economic performance since independence, the plot has merely thickened. Most of the explanatory factors found in the literature come across as miscast since they tend to fare better on the whole than those observed in sub-Saharan Africa, whereas the country's long-run growth is significantly lower. Our study henceforth seeks to find the reasons for this unexplained residual, to use growth econometrics terminology. Where growth econometrics has set out to reduce the African dummy, we find ourselves in the paradoxical situation of having to explain the Malagasy dummy (in the African context).

This observation is nothing new to us. Ten years ago when considering the events of 2002, the systematic recurrence of political crises following (all-too) rare phases of economic growth already had us wondering whether Madagascar refused to develop, although we were unable to propose an entirely

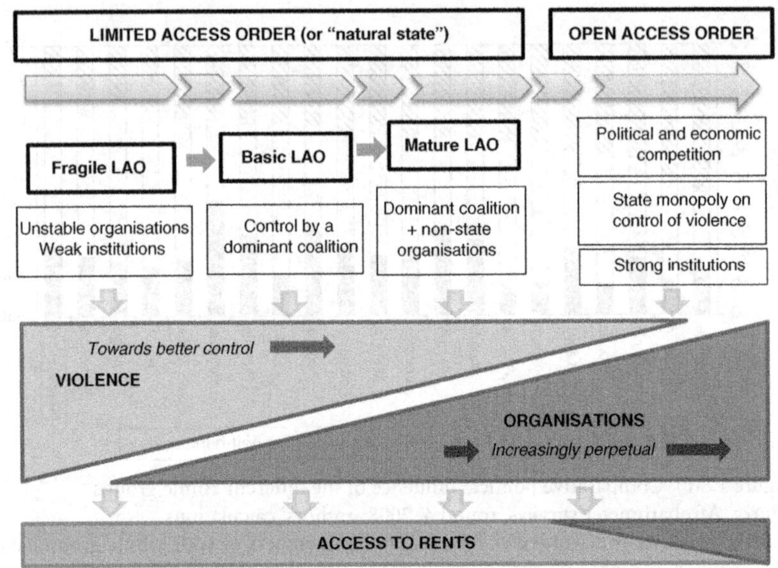

Figure 1.9 The conceptual framework developed by North et al. (2009, 2012a).
Source: authors.

satisfactory interpretive framework at the time. The main conclusion we drew from this phenomenon was that the economistic approach dominating the field of development policies in the sunset days of this adjustment period was incapable of understanding the country's overall trajectory. At the very least, a joint analysis of the interactions between political and economic transition, characteristic of the late-1990s, needed to be conducted in concert.[10] The new crisis has underscored this interconnection between economic and political cycles as it has the related paradox, now a truism in the eyes of most Madagascar analysts. Yet an analysis of this sort cannot just juxtapose economic and political histories or even study their interactions using the classic economic and political science approaches. The analysis has to be taken further to make sense of Madagascar's puzzle and paradox. This is precisely what the new political economy studies can do.

On this score, a promising conceptual framework (Figure 1.9) has been proposed by North, Wallis and Weingast (2009, 2012a; hereafter referred to

[10] Such was the initial purpose of the MADIO project that we launched in 1995 to analyse the dual economic and political transition process in Madagascar, with a first publication on the subject the following year (Razafindrakoto & Roubaud, 1996).

BOX 1.1 Brief Presentation of the Different Social Orders in NWW's Framework

LAO (Limited Access Order) or natural state: dominant coalition limiting access to political and economic power; enrichment associated with access to rents; social relations based on personal relationships (connections, loyalty, status and hierarchy). Environment not very conducive to development.

- Fragile LAO: Instability of organisations, absence of control of violence and weak institutions; state does not ensure the supply of public goods.
- Basic LAO: Government well established and durable; stable organisations (under the control of a dominant coalition); but violence controlled by a few scattered organisations.
- Mature LAO: Enforcement of the rule of law among the elites; better control of violence; strengthening of non-state organisations (private sector organisations, opposition and civil society).

OAO (Open Access Order): Open access allowing for competition in the political and economic arenas (which makes for innovation and the creation of values); state monopoly on the control of violence; social relations governed by impersonal exchange; strong institutions. Environment conducive to development.

as NWW) on the nature of natural states and open access orders (see Box 1.1 for a brief presentation of the different types of orders proposed by the authors). The conjunction of economic growth periods and political crises does indeed suggest that one of the main reasons for the country's problems might well be its poor ability to establish a stable political consensus on the wealth accumulation and distribution processes. Under this hypothesis, any attempt to understand the Malagasy puzzle and paradox calls for both an analysis of the economic mechanisms at work and consideration of the elements of the socio-political environment in which these mechanisms operate. Power games, elites and the institutions they fashion to their advantage are obviously central to the equation. It is also altogether symptomatic that the number of studies adopting this analytic framework shot up far beyond anything observed for other developing countries in response to the consternation at the 'discovery' of the Malagasy paradox, which caused a particularly large stir since pre-crisis Madagascar had (re)gained an image as one of Africa's rare development poster boys in the eyes of an international community in search of models. Several studies based on these premises – fast becoming the new *doxa* – have been published in this vein since the outbreak of the 2009 crisis, either explicitly (World Bank, 2010; Urfer, 2012a) or implicitly (Morisset, 2009; Jütersonke & Kartas, 2010).

On the face of it, the analytic framework proposed by NWW is very appealing, both generally and in terms of the use to which it can be put in the case of Madagascar. It reveals other key elements in addition to the discussed intrinsic link between economic and political trajectories. Political economy thinks outside of the box of methodological individualism and puts the social players (organisations, structured groups, etc.) back centre-stage of the economic dynamics at work. Among these players, the role they ascribe to the elites (*powerful groups*) and to the coalitions formed among these elites to share economic rents and control violence does indeed appear to be central to understanding the politico-economic dynamics in Madagascar. The extreme personalisation of the institutions and their hijacking by the elite groups for their own benefit means that even the formal organisations imported from the North operate nothing like their northern counterparts and fail to produce the same results as they do in open access orders.

We will have the opportunity to consider the application of these concepts to the Malagasy case in more detail and assess their relevance in the following chapters. Nevertheless, we feel it important at this juncture to show that these theories fall far short of providing the magic key to unlock Madagascar's mystery, at least from the point of view of attempts at their quantitative operationalisation. The first exploration is based on a recent article, which endeavours to conduct just such an operationalisation of NWW's theoretical framework and econometrically test its validity (Gollwitzer, Franke & Quintyn, 2014). This is obviously a hugely challenging ambition,[11] and the authors have to restrict their focus to one of the many hypotheses put forward by NWW, i.e. the conditions (*doorstep conditions*) for transition from a natural state (or limited access order) to an open access order. North *et al.* (2012) identify three such doorstep conditions: (1) rule of law for elites, (2) support for perpetually lived elite

[11] In this respect, Bluhm and Szirmai (2012) look into what kind of theory NWW's theses might be and whether they can be 'operationalised.' ('It is not quite clear to the reader whether the North *et al.* framework is really a theory of economic development, or rather a theory of overall modernization of society, or perhaps only an insightful typology.')

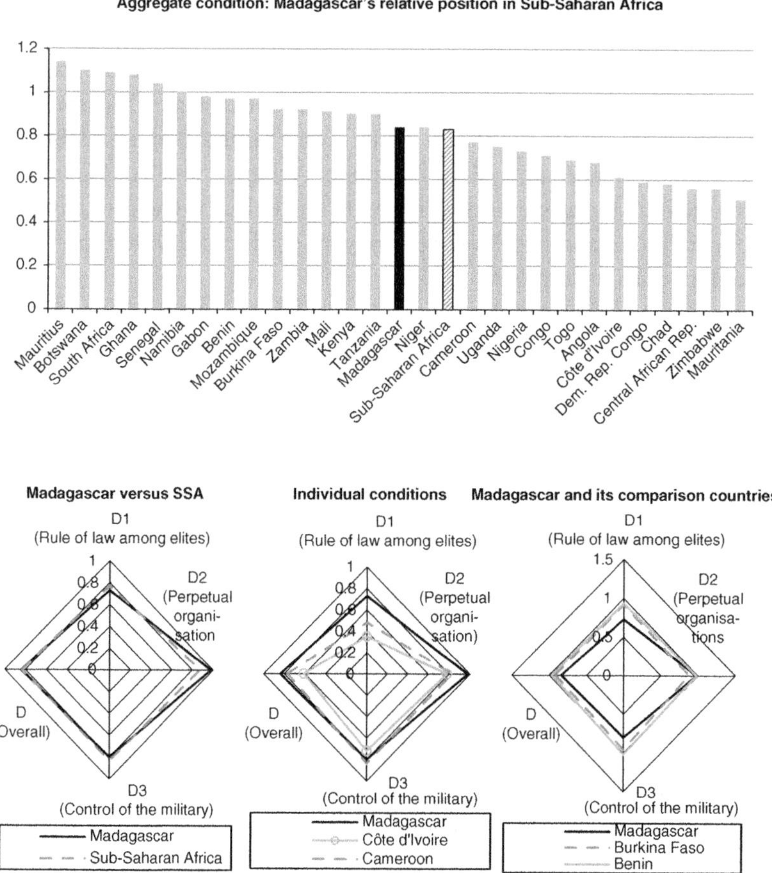

Figure 1.10 Madagascar and the conditions for transition to an open access order.
Source: Based on Gollwitzer, Franke and Quintyn (2014); authors' calculations.

organisations, and (3) political control of the organisations with violence capacity (Figure 1.10).

Taking different international databases, particularly the AFD's Institutional Profiles Database (IPD) (de Combrugghe *et al.*, 2010), arguably the most suitable to capture NWW's concepts, the authors construct composite measures of the three above-mentioned conditions of access (as well as an aggregate indicator). They then attempt to estimate the causal impact of the state of progress with these measures on different economic and political performance variables. Our purpose here is not to discuss the study's approach and conclusions, but to assess Madagascar's relative position. The results are not very convincing. The first chart in Figure 1.10 places Madagascar in an intermediate position in sub-Saharan Africa, more or less at the same level as the continental average for the aggregate indicator of access conditions.[12] The Red Island rates better than Cameroon and especially Côte d'Ivoire, but lags quite a way behind Benin and Burkina Faso. A more detailed analysis by component (charts 2 and 3 of Figure 1.10) bears out that Madagascar is no different to the African average for any of the three conditions, and even looks relatively more advanced with respect to the durability of its institutions.

1.5 Conclusion

This first chapter takes stock of Madagascar's long-run growth situation. It highlights what we call the Malagasy mystery of a steady downward trend (the puzzle) and the systematic recurrence of political crises during the rare spurts of growth (the paradox). It then takes a sweep of a broad spectrum of economic growth and development theories, including the most recent, with the potential to explain these two phenomena. The main conclusion that can be drawn from these initial analyses is that these theories prove incapable of explaining the Malagasy mystery, which not only remains unsolved, but even more impenetrable than it at first appeared. The next four chapters tackle the challenge of solving this mystery by extending the historical depth of our analyses (Chapter 2), using political economy tools to recompose all the existing, but scattered empirical elements to understand how Madagascar works (Chapters 3 and 4), and training the spotlight on the world of the elites, a universe as opaque as it is fantastic (Chapter 5).

[12] Note on the chart the position of Mali, engaged in open warfare from January 2012 to June 2015 and still destabilised by jihadists in the North today. This shows just how hard it is to capture institutional solidity and points up the indicator's poor predictive capacity.

2

Milestones for a Political Economy of Madagascar's Trajectory

2.1 Introduction

This chapter provides an interpretive framework for Madagascar's long-term trajectory by tracing the defining elements that have structured the country's political economy. The conjunction of economic growth periods and political crises suggests that one of the main causes of the country's problems is its poor ability to establish a stable political consensus on the wealth accumulation and distribution processes. This hypothesis calls for a review of the country's long history using a political economy analytic framework: who are the players in each period and how do they interact, what are the main sources of power and wealth, which institutions drive social regulation, and what are the system's contradictions?

Although many books have been published on Malagasy history and society, very few have taken this angle. The country's cultural history, economic history – as singularly deficient as it is – and political history are approached separately. And rare are the studies that take a very long-term view. This chapter sets out to address these limitations. It takes the main categories of political economy to review these studies and isolate what we believe to be the defining elements of Madagascar's trajectory. This places it fully in line with a series of recent research by economists in the same vein (North *et al.*, 2009, 2012b; Khan, 2010; Acemoglu & Robinson, 2012). This review of Madagascar's history identifies six main periods. Each period marks a clear break with the previous one, albeit retaining certain characteristics from the earlier periods without necessarily managing to solve their main contradictions. Each period features a relative change of ruling coalition, wealth production and extraction methods and social regulation elements. Each one is also marked by a major political crisis, which exposes the period's contradictions and precipitates its end. Not counting the last period still in progress, these periods are getting shorter in what is an indication of the successive regimes' loss of ability to ensure their stability.

The first period concerns the formation of the *Merina* State. We cover here only those elements of the historical analysis that we believe to be defining and to have left their mark on the country's long history: *Merina* supremacy, the Asiatic mode of production, social stratification in status groups and the symbolism of the ruling power as guardian of the political theology. The second period opens with French colonisation in 1895 and closes with the 1972 crisis. It inherits some of the traits from the first, but is also profoundly marked by colonial rule and the initial period of independence as seen from the domination of French interests, the rise of the "coastal" elites (*côtiers*) and a flourishing trading economy. The third period, from 1972 to 1991, is one of the economy's Malagasisation, promotion of meritocratic elites and development of state rent. The fourth period, which begins after the 1991 crisis and ends with the 2002 crisis, marks a time of relative economic and political openness as a factor for development and voice for new players, but also as a source of instability. The fifth period, ending with the 2009 coup d'état, features the attempt by the president and his affiliates to corner all the powers (economic, political and symbolic). The sixth period is still ongoing. It has been marked to date by the inability of the elites in power to form a stable coalition, control the violence and counter the spread of mafia practices.

2.2 From the Eighteenth Century to 1895: Development of the State

Madagascar's history as a political and cultural entity clearly precedes the colonial period, unlike many Black African countries that were formed not only late on, but often artificially by a set of arrangements among colonising countries. Cultural unification was accomplished in part well before political unification, as shown by the presence of a language common to the 18 officially recognised ethnic groups (albeit with significant regional differences) and the similarities between certain socio-political practices and values (holistic, hierarchical concept of society, references to identity-giving 'progenitor' ancestors, attachment to ancestral land, spatial hierarchy reproducing the social hierarchy, etc. – see Beaujard, 1991; Ottino, 1998; Andrianjafy-Andriamanindrisoa, 2004; Galibert, 2004). Political unification subsequently began with the expansion of the Merina kingdom by Andrianampoinimerina (1787–1810) in the late eighteenth century. It continued and spread into the nineteenth century under the influence of his successors, while the state tightened its hold over its subjects.

When the slave trade really began to take off in the mid-seventeenth century, Madagascar still comprised many competing royal fiefdoms, each controlling a swath of territory. The slave trade, however, brought relative expansion to some of them. This was firstly the case with the Sakalava kingdoms, originally established in the south-west of the island before spreading toward the centre and the north-west, depending on where their infighting took them (Lombard, 1988; Chazan-Gillig, 1991). The monarchs, whose names remain etched in history (such as Lahifotsy, Tsimenata and Toakafo), derived a good part of their power from their military and trade supremacy. With arms bought from Arab, Indian and then European traders, they were able to raise armies that would mount forays into the central regions to 'gather' slaves sold to traders on their return. Their wealth was therefore essentially a product of trade. This wealth, in the form of firearms, livestock and various items purchased from overseas merchants, remained undivided in their own and their minions' hands, sustaining and cultivating both the material and symbolic elements of their kingdom. Yet the political order that ensured their stability was not based solely on their coercive power. It was also underpinned by a symbolic system which held that the monarchs, as descendants of a superior ancestor, possessed royal *hasina* (Bloch, 1983), i.e. the invisible essence of power and fertility, and could bestow it on their descendants and subjects while receiving their *hasina* in return. It is from this capacity that the monarchs, seen by their subjects as demigods, drew their political legitimacy, regularly renewed by collective rites such as the circumcision ritual, the coronation ceremony, the royal bath ceremony and royal funerals. This type of political organisation was not specific to the Sakalava kingdoms. Similar versions of it were found in other regions, marking the spread of these political and organisational ideas from royalty down the roads taken by men in search of new settlements and seasonal trade (Randrianja & Ellis, 2009).[1] In the early seventeenth century, the *Merina* kingdoms, about which the most historical sources and studies can be found, were populated by immigrants of Austronesian origin organised

[1] Towards the end of the seventeenth century, however, the Sakalava kingdoms were in relative decline owing to the comparative shift from the slave trade to the East to meet the needs of colonial plantation development on the Mascarene Islands. This switch to the East fostered the rise of other kingdoms, more particularly Betsimisaraka in the north-east and *Merina* in the Imerina highlands.

along similar lines. Their sovereigns (*Mpanjaka*), who held the political power (*fanjakana*), lived on the highest central hilltop of the kingdom, exercising their symbolic and military power over the populations below who were socially stratified in descending order of altitude. The social hierarchy defined a number of status groups sometimes called castes.[2] At the top of this hierarchy were the *Andriana* castes (nobility), relatives of the king, followed by the *Hova* (white commoners), then the *Mainty* (black commoners)[3] and, at the bottom of the social ladder, the slaves (*Andevo*).

A combination of factors (higher population density, climate and land type, Austronesian origin of the people and no direct access to the sea) also drove the development of extensive rice-growing on the region's marshy plains. This gave the kings not only ritual domination, but also material domination over the people, with their offer of military protection in return for their allegiance and payments in rice and other goods.

These different kingdoms ended up united under the domination of a single sovereign in a movement similar to that described in Europe by N. Elias (Elias, 1975) as being consistent with 'the law of monopoly'. This movement was more particularly the work of one man, Andrianampoinimerina (ca. 1740–1810), in the late eighteenth century. His reforms marked a clear break with the way previous kingdoms had been organised, paving the way for real political institutionalisation. Once he had conquered the other highland kingdoms by either force or diplomacy, he stabilised his empire[4] by forming alliances with the most powerful neighbouring kingdoms: military and diplomatic agreements with the Sakalava kingdom of Boina and trade agreements with the Betsimisaraka kingdoms of the east coast (sale of slaves acquired from forays outside the kingdom). He also ensured the loyalty of the people under his control, first by introducing a veritable state religion based on the creation of a 'national pantheon' (Raison-Jourde, 1991) of

[2] Use of the term 'caste' in reference to Malagasy society has often been debated. Condominas (1991) prefers, for example, the term 'pseudo-castes' and Raison-Jourde (1991) prefers to say 'status groups', the term we also choose to use in this book.

[3] The social distinction between whites (*Fotsy*) and blacks (*Mainty*) is found throughout Madagascar. It is described in the mid-seventeenth century, for example, by Flacourt, representative of the Compagnie Française de l'Orient to Fort-Dauphin (south-eastern Madagascar), as structuring social relations in the societies he observed (Randrianja & Ellis, 2009). The terms *Fotsy* and *Mainty* are not purely symbolic designations, but also refer to differences in skin colour and origin (Austronesian vs. African). See Ramamonjisoa (1984); Razafindralambo (2005a, 2005b).

[4] See Randrianja and Ellis (2009) for a discussion of the term 'empire' applied to the *Merina* kingdom.

talismans (*sampy*) and the symbolic reinforcement of the image of sovereign as father and mother (*raiamandreny*) of the people. Second, he guaranteed the people his protection from the slave trade, in return for which the peasants had to pay taxes and provide their sovereign with all manner of services (*fanompoana*), including work on collective agricultural projects such as dykes and water supply systems. This gave rise to the expansion of rice-growing on the marshy plains (Raison J.-P., 1972), which in return settled the populations on their lands.

What resembled the Asiatic mode of production, as described by K. Marx and F. Engels in their time,[5] continued after Andrianampoinimerina's death, first under the reign of his son Radama I and then under the successive reigns of queens Rasoherina and Ranavalona I, II and III. Radama I's military conquests expanded his rule over Betsileo, the east coast, southern Menabe and then the Sakalava kingdom, while his alliance with Great Britain gave him key material support. The 1817 treaty recognised him as king of Madagascar and gave him international legitimacy in return for his prohibition of the slave trade, decreed by British Parliament since 1807. Andrianampoinimerina's successors also continued to institutionalise the *Merina* State with the establishment of a professional army,[6] the appointment of civil and military governors in the regions under their rule and the development of a bureaucratic administration trained in the schools set up by the London Missionary Society (LMS) missionaries following the 1817 treaty. These early, unpaid civil servants were recruited mainly from among the sons of the nobility and palace officers. Under the reign of Ranavalona I, it was explicitly 'prohibited to teach slaves or anyone not employed by the government to read' (Goguel, 2006). Following conversion to Protestantism by Queen Ranavalona II and her prime minister and husband Rainilaiarivony in 1869, the political government of the people was further expanded with the widespread introduction of primary school and military service (Raison-Jourde & Randrianja, 2002),[7] the establishment of a code of laws (101 in 1868 and 305 in 1881), and the formation of an eight-minister government based on the Western model (Randrianja & Ellis, 2009).

[5] A society based on two pillars: (1) the village communities inherited from the last stage of the primitive communistic mode of production, accounting for the majority of the population; and (2) forms of state organisation that centralise these villages and impose tribute on them. See Marx and Engels (1973, 2010).

[6] 'Recruited from among the population's wealthy echelons as they alone were able to procure rifles and uniforms' (Ramasy, 2010).

[7] However, the 1876 schooling obligation remained purely theoretical because most schooling was provided by Christian missions, with only vague state control (Ralaimihoatra, 1965, Vol. 1).

This state construction, led by the *Andriana*[8] aristocracy, paved the way for the appearance of a new administrative and commercial oligarchy, partially recruited from among the *Hova*. State positions, especially as high-ranking officers, gave them a considerable source of power and wealth from brigandage, forced labour and their control of the overseas export trade (first slaves and then livestock and rice. See Campbell, 2005). So it was that the members of this oligarchy gradually started competing with the *Merina* aristocracy[9] and ended up in a dominant position, particularly under the reign of Ranavalona II and her *Hova* prime minister Rainilaiarivony.[10] This, as well as the Queen's conversion to Protestantism in 1869 and destruction of the *sampy* amulets, clearly marked the weakening of the *Andriana* royalty by depriving it of an essential foundation of legitimacy. Yet rather than a shift from the rule of the aristocracy to an oligarchy of 'bourgeois families', what actually formed was an association 'with no clear distinctions, of powerful families with the same interests' (Archer, 1976). Rainilaiarivony was married successively to three queens (Rasoherina, Ranavalona II and Ranavalona III) and the same families stayed in power until the colonial period.

The vast majority of the population in the controlled regions remained not only excluded from sharing in the wealth, but also, for the freemen among them,[11] subject to the pressure of military conscription and forced labour (Condominas, 1961). Under Radama I, for example, labour duty or military service was required four days a week (Bloch, 1983). This explains the large number of gangs of bandits and 'brown' communities (*marofotsy*) of deserters from the army or forced labour as well as escaped slaves (Randrianja & Ellis, 2009). These groups were a source of recruitment for the leading *Menalamba*[12] rebels who were to destabilise the French colonial state's establishment

[8] Randrianja and Ellis (2009) report that there were initially so many small kingdoms that at least a quarter of the free population was considered to be Andriana in the nineteenth century.

[9] The 1863 assassination of Radama II, who succeeded his mother Ranavalona I in 1861, may have been caused by a conflict between the two ruling groups. The young king had endeavoured to counter the great *Hova* families by securing the political support of the French authorities in return for signing a charter awarding exclusive exploitation rights over the entire northern part of the island to a French business syndicate represented by Joseph Lambert.

[10] Himself from a prominent family long engaged in military service.

[11] An estimated 40% to 50% of Imerina's population were slaves in the nineteenth century (Randrianja & Ellis, 2009).

[12] From *mena*: red & *lamba*: shawl. The insurgents daubed their clothes red.

in Imerina from 1895 to 1898. This rebellion, often presented as an anti-French movement, was in reality chiefly the mark of a politico-social implosion in a situation of *Merina* State decay. In this light, the *Menalamba* revolt may express a form of reaction to the domination of the *Hova* oligarchy and the Christian principles on which it was based (Ellis, 1998; Campbell, 1991).

***

So on the eve of colonisation, the Malagasy State was a developing state. Part of the territory still escaped its control and the political formula on which it was built was still relatively fragile. A number of sources of power coexisted in the country. The *Merina Andriana* aristocracy drew their political power from the legitimacy conferred on them by their status as royal descendants. In a society historically compartmentalised into hierarchically stratified status groups, this royal pedigree, regularly renewed by religious rites, formed a key symbolic aspect of their superiority. M. Bloch has clearly shown how this 'cultural mystification' dissimulated 'the unscrupulous exploitation of a huge mass of subjects by a minority of sovereigns' behind the façade of a 'harmonious, ordered system ranked by a seemingly seamless social hierarchy' (Bloch, 1983). However, although the *Merina* kingdom's expansion extended its power beyond Imerina, it did not break up the power of its counterparts in other ancient kingdoms (especially Sakalava) with which alliances sometimes had to be formed. The development of trade and the institutionalisation of the state brought with them a new administrative, military and trade oligarchy born of the *Hova* 'high families'[13] in charge of the kingdom's conquests and administration. This oligarchy rose to a dominant position in the evolving Malagasy society at the very pinnacle of the state, even though it did not have the traditional legitimacy of the *Andriana* with whom it had to continue to compromise. Wealth came from levies on agricultural and livestock products and on trade in these products with foreign merchants. These levies forced the state to develop administratively, especially because its traditional legitimacy had been undercut by royalty's conversion to Christianity and the rise of the *Hova* oligarchy.

[13] The expression 'high families' is commonly used in Madagascar to refer to families of high-status origin whose influence (political and economic) dates back to the early days of the Malagasy state. This gives them a form of social legitimacy.

2.3 From 1895 to 1972: Colonial Upheaval and the First Republic

The Colonial Period: Racial Policy and Trading Economy

The colonial period radically changed this political and social order. Budding interest in colonial expansion in France under Ferry's government and Franco-British rivalries over missionary action sparked a first Franco-Malagasy war in 1884–5, making Madagascar a French protectorate. Following the 1890 Anglo-French agreements on sharing out the two countries' interests in Eastern Africa,[14] a second war with France in 1894–5 culminated in France's total annexation of the island. The monarchy was abolished and the queen and her leading courtiers exiled. Slavery was also prohibited and half a million slaves were freed. General Gallieni, appointed military governor, was placed in charge of implementing French colonial policy.

Political Organisation

As Madagascar, like all colonies, was required by the Act of 1900 to finance its needs from its own resources, General Gallieni introduced a direct tax alongside the indirect taxes (such as the consumer taxes levied by the *fokonolona*[15] or village councils). It was called the 'moralising tax' because, as an incentive to work, it was intended to generate a change of behaviour.[16] He also introduced the service system,[17] which evolved into the SMOTIG (*Service de la Main-d'Œuvre pour les Travaux d'Intérêt Général*; Manpower Service for Public Works) in 1926.[18] In so doing, he was merely extending an alternative version of the levy system on peasant manpower set up previously by the *Merina* State. This personal tax was moreover due solely by the Malagasy, which made it a sign of subjugation (Rajaonah, 1996).[19]

[14] France relinquished its interest in Zanzibar in exchange for a free hand in Madagascar.

[15] Traditional village communities.

[16] As shown by F. Braudel (1967) in his analysis of the development of capitalism in Europe, the introduction of a tax forces open the subsistence farming economy. In Madagascar, the sheer weight of the tax 'incomparable with the tax in Western Africa forced the indigenous people to seek waged work with the settlers' (Raison-Jourde & Roy, 2010).

[17] Fifty days of work per year were required of every male aged 16 to 60 (Ralaimihoatra, 1966).

[18] As an 'arm tax' replacing the 'blood tax', as the administration saw it, the SMOTIG assigned the fraction of indigenous conscripts not retained for compulsory military service to three years of compulsory labour (Ralaimihoatra, 1966).

[19] The capitation tax receipt also served as an ID card and was commonly referred to as 'paying your card' (Rajaonah, 1996).

In a move to bring the entire island under his command, many parts of which had actually escaped *Merina* State rule, he introduced his 'racial policy': 'Once the *Hova*[20] hegemony, the "conquering race", had been destroyed and all the purveyors of English influence, supposedly embedded in Madagascar via the London Missionary Society, had been eliminated, each "race" [was to be] governed by high-ranking natives chosen from its midst and placed under the command of the French administration' (Boetsch & Savarese, 2000). This indirect administration policy effectively gave power back to the traditional *côtier*[21] political elites. Nevertheless, the *Merina* high families' superior literacy and past administrative experience meant that they continued to hold the main colonial administrative positions. Lastly, Gallieni launched an education policy to smooth the populations' relations with the new *fanjakana* and meet the colonial power's needs. He set up rural schools and regional industrial and agricultural schools taught entirely in French by lay teachers specially trained in regional teacher training colleges. Education hence improved significantly during the colonial period, even though the improvement was highly uneven across the island with a very clear advantage to Tananarive Province compared with the others, especially the southern provinces. At the same time, the colonial administration established Le Myre de Vilers School in Tananarive (now Antananarivo) in 1896 to train civil servants (administration, railways, post office and telecommunications, topography, civil engineering and the medical sector), followed by primary school teachers as of 1905 (Hugon, 1976; Ratrimoarivony-Rakotoanosy, 1986; Goguel, 2006). It also simultaneously opened the Medical School to train 'colonial doctors' (Merlin, 2002). In keeping with the meritocratic principles of the Third French Republic, admission to these schools was by competitive examination, albeit with a regional quota system in accordance with the 'racial policy'. This system of education spawned the emergence of a new meritocratic elite from which were recruited the key nationalist leaders of the *Mouvement Démocratique de la Rénovation Malgache* (MDRM – Democratic Movement for Malagasy Renewal) and the future leaders of the Social Democratic Party (PSD, *Parti Social Démocrate*),[22] including Tsiranana himself.

[20] The French used the term *Hova* as a synonym of *Merina*.

[21] The term '*côtier*' (coastal dweller) was used from the start of colonial times to describe members of ethnic groups not from the central highlands (unlike the *Merina* and *Betsileo*) even when their land, as in the case of the Bara, was not open to the sea.

[22] See later for more on these political parties.

Economic Developments

At the beginning of the twentieth century, Madagascar was still a new country with vast expanses of uncultivated land and virtually untouched underground resources. This led the colonial administration to put into effect the French doctrine to 'develop' (Sarraut, 1923) the island by encouraging colonists to settle there[23] and opening it up to foreign trade with France. It revived rice-growing in the Central Highlands and introduced new export crops (coffee on the east coast, vanilla and cloves on the north-east coast, tea, rubber, etc.) while regulating the agricultural techniques used. It adopted tariff measures to encourage imports of French products and set about developing domestic travel by building roads and launching the construction of the Tananarive-Tamatave (now Antananarivo–Toamasina) railway. Nevertheless, this economic and social organisation generated but a small increase in the wealth produced. The 'moralising tax', far from stimulating production, weighed on the rural populations' resources and by the same token reduced market opportunities for imported products, while the use of forced labour limited the manpower available for the farms. The most prosperous economic activities remained in trade, dominated by a small number of large French companies (Compagnie Lyonnaise, Compagnie Marseillaise de Madagascar and Société Industrielle et Commerciale de l'Emyrne) with a torrent of often-foreign middlemen in their wake (Réunionese, Chinese and especially Karana[24]). These large companies theoretically ran a whole host of lines of business (mining, processing industries, livestock farming, harvesting natural products, plantations and river and land transport) with trading posts in every region. Yet they actually invested much less in production than in tertiary activities (shipping, road haulage, banks, etc.), establishing what is termed a 'trading economy'[25] (Jacob & Koerner, 1972). Madagascar started to display the fundamental elements of what have been analysed elsewhere as 'the impasses of colonial development' (Hémery & Brocheux, 2011). 'Development' had not changed a largely self-sufficient agrarian society but had actually widened the gulf

[23] For various reasons, however, Madagascar was never a settlement colony with only ever a small number of settlers.

[24] The name, derived from the Koran, was given to Indo-Pakistanis who arrived in Madagascar in the late seventeenth century.

[25] A 'trading economy' is an economic system steered by large foreign companies whereby the 'traders' buy, essentially for export, the products harvested by the farmers while keeping them in a situation of dependency by selling them imported products (provisions, seeds, household utensils, plastic items and industrial consumer goods) and giving them credit (see Badouin, 1967).

between a small oligarchy and the rest of the population. J. Fremigacci (2007a) produces a detailed analysis of this model's economic limitations in Madagascar: low wages cramped the use of technical progress and prevented the spread of waged work, which, 'seen as *fanompoana* (labour duty)', remained extremely undervalued. The Malagasy peasants 'switched to plantation crops to avoid the constraint of waged work while still paying the tax,' but spent most of their time and effort on food crops due to the low price guaranteed producers.

It was not until after World War II and new French concerns over the colonies' economic development (as shown by the 1946 establishment of the FIDES – Investment Fund for Economic and Social Development; *Fonds d'Investissement pour le Développement Economique et Social*) that the island's economy began to take off. The colonial administration opted for administrative restructuring with the 1950 creation of the rural indigenous authorities (CARs – *Collectivités Autochtones Rurales*) to stimulate the development of the rural sector, which had failed to develop other than highly superficially after half a century of colonial rule. These authorities headed by an elected representative, but reporting to the administration, were endowed with a budget and extended responsibilities. They could procure equipment at a reduced rate through the CEAMP (Central Agricultural Equipment and Farming Modernisation Stores; *Centrale d'Equipement Agricole et de Modernisation du Paysannat*) and could borrow at preferential rates from Crédit de Madagascar.[26] This massive economic intervention by the colonial government powered substantial progress in the agricultural sector[27] and the appearance of a class of small Malagasy planters (Randrianja & Ellis, 2009). However, the main economic principle remained the growing trading economy, driven by investment in road infrastructure. Foreign trade consequently posted a two-and-a-half-fold increase from 1948 to independence at the cost, however, of a sharp increase in foreign dependency on manufactured products: import-export coverage fell from 138% in 1938 to 76% in 1958. Conversely, the industrial sector remained very small. On the eve of independence, the country's industries (essentially processing agricultural

[26] The government also created SIM (Madagascar Property Investment Company) in 1951 and SEM (Madagascar Electricity Board) in 1952.

[27] Cropping of tens of thousands of hectares, increase in small-scale water engineering in agriculture, spread of ploughs and harrows, massive use of fertilisers, expansion of cotton-growing and rice-growing, development of fish farming, improvement in cattle and boom in export crops (vanilla, cloves and coffee). See Ralaimihoatra (1966) and Randrianja and Ellis (2009).

produce and livestock) could be listed on 'a table a few lines long' (Gendarme, 1960).

Political and Social Tensions

The colonial system's organisational principles contained the seeds of elements conducive to the emergence of nationalist movements: the 'racial policy' (reducing the power of the *Merina* 'high families') and the French corporate stranglehold on trade (restricting the people's possibilities for enrichment) drove the people to organise themselves politically; the spread of education fired new aspirations among those who attended the schools; and there was bitterness in both urban and rural worlds over the difference in treatment of citizens and French subjects, as laid down in the French Code of Indigenous Status (*Code de l'Indigénat*).

Freedom of the press and freedom of association did not exist at the start of the twentieth century. In particular, Malagasy newspapers did not have the right to address political issues and the only meetings allowed were religious, friendly society and mutual association gatherings. This formed a breeding ground for the development of the first anticolonial organisations. In 1913, the secret society VVS[28] was founded recruiting civil servants, commercial workers and most importantly student youth from the Medical School and Le Myre de Vilers School. This secret society was accused of revolt and incitement to revolt and was dismantled in 1916 with a large number of its members sentenced to hard labour. Yet there was a resurgence of this rallying of meritocratic elites in the interwar period. Their demands, expressed in a newspaper run by Paul Dussac, a French settler, and then by the repressed protest of 19 May 1929, did not yet concern independence, but the axing of the French Code of Indigenous Status and full French citizenship, i.e. assimilation (Lahiniriko, 2012). Here again, the movement was crushed by the colonial authorities: the main communist affiliated leaders, Joseph Ravoahangy[29] and Jean Ralaimongo,[30] were put under house arrest and Dussac was imprisoned following a 1930 decree establishing a press offence.

After World War II, the nationalist movement grew as it institutionalised. The Popular Front's 1936 arrival in power in France had already ushered in a first wave of civil rights in the colony. Union rights were

[28] *Vy*: iron; *Vato*: stone; *Sakelika*: network.

[29] Doctor Ravoahangy, one of the founders of VVS, had joined Ralaimongo in 1926 after he was granted amnesty.

[30] *Betsileo* primary school teacher who, as a volunteer serving in World War I, had come into contact with the left-wing parties in France.

granted to literate Malagasy, the press offence was repealed and the SMOTIG was scrapped. Following the war, the new French Constitution establishing the French Union scaled up this trend by extending the possibilities for political participation to an electorate, albeit small.[31] From July 1945 to March 1947, 12 elections and 2 referendums were held. Three Malagasy representatives were elected to the French National Assembly. Freedom of the press and freedom of association then enabled political parties to form. The first separatist nationalist party, the MDRM, founded in Paris at the initiative of the three MPs, was politically organised in Madagascar essentially by members of the *Merina* elite (Spacensky, 1967; Lahiniriko, 2012). It was also funded, like the clandestine movements that gravitated around it,[32] by members of the former bourgeoisie whose economic interests had suffered at the hands of colonisation (Tronchon, 1974; Archer, 1976). Despite this dominantly *Merina* element, the party secured broad-based support in the country by encouraging the creation of cooperatives supposed to help the Malagasy 'help themselves' (Lahiniriko, 2012). The *Parti des Déshérités de Madagascar* (PADESM – Party of the Disinherited of Madagascar) was founded in response to the creation of the MDRM out of fear that the *Merina* high families would be the main winners of immediate independence (Randriamaro, 1997). It was an alliance of *Merina Mainty*, or descendants of slaves, and members of the *côtier* elites. Although the party had no real popular base, it was financially and politically supported by the colonial power, which saw in the MDRM an attempt to restore *Merina* power (Spacensky, 1967; Archer, 1976). It was in this politically tense environment that the uprising erupted on the eastern side of the island on 29 March 1947 and, despite ferocious repression by the colonial administration[33] (Tronchon, 1974; Koerner, 1994; Fremigacci, 1999, 2007b; Cole, 2001), continued pell-mell for 18 months in an expression of the colonial regime's unpopularity. The MDRM, regarded as the main instigator of the insurgency, was dismantled and its leaders sentenced

[31] Only citizens who had received a certain education and were landowners could vote (Deschamps, 1960).

[32] Secret society JINA (Nationalist Youth) working for the popular uprising was headed by one of the rare Malagasy manufacturers of the time, Samuel Rakotondrabe.

[33] The 1947 death count and assessment of the extent of the repression by French forces constitute an important facet of Madagascar's commemorative construct. Its elements have often been cited without being based on any real research. The opening of the Vincennes archives enabled J. Fremigacci to evaluate the number of deaths at over 30,000, including at least 20,000 civilians who died of starvation and disease because of their displacement by the conflict.

and then exiled, clearing the way for PADESM to monopolise political representation through to 1956 (Spacensky, 1967).

Despite the 1956 French Overseas Reform Act establishing universal suffrage, a single electoral college (ending the distinction between French and other citizens) and the principle of administrative decentralisation under the authority of an assembly elected in the colonies, the MDRM's successors in the shape of the *Union des Populations Malgaches* (UPM – Union of Malagasy Peoples) and then the *Antokon'ny Kongresin'ny Fahaleovantenan'i Madagasikara* (AKFM)[34] failed to return to the political forefront, except in Antananarivo Province. The Social Democratic Party of Madagascar (PSD) founded by Tsiranana,[35] former PADESM[36] leader, became the dominant party and, following its alliance with the UDSM (Union of Social Democrats of Fianarantsoa and Toliara founded by Norbert Zafimahova, himself a former PADESM leader), Tsiranana was elected Vice-President of the Central Government[37] of Madagascar in 1958.

From 1960 to 1972: The Dependent Independence of the First Republic

The colonial period and the political developments following World War II had divided the ruling elites into *Merina* (nationalist) and *côtier* (Francophile) factions, two categories[38] fuelled by the colonial administration's 'ethnic' policy (Archer, 1976). The dismantlement of the MDRM and resentment among the *côtier* populations, especially those on the east coast (on whom the rebellion had taken the heaviest toll[39]), ended up ensuring the dominance of the *côtier* political movements, in favour of independence without any radical break with the colonial power. The PSD hence quickly rose to a position of hegemony. The 1956 French Overseas Reform Act cleared a path for party leader, Philibert Tsiranana, to the vice-presidency of the Central Government of Madagascar. The 1958 referendum then endorsed his political alternative (autonomy for Madagascar

[34] Congress Party for the Independence of Madagascar.

[35] A primary school teacher from an influential *Tsimihety* family in northern Madagascar.

[36] This party's collaboration with the colonial power lost the people's esteem and it folded in the 1950s.

[37] Presided over by a French High Commissioner representing the French Republic and comprising a vice-president and eight Malagasy members.

[38] Which had very little to do with the realities of the 1947–8 uprising.

[39] The *Betsimisaraka, Bezanozano, Tanale* and *Zafisoro* had provided the majority of the MDRM fighters (Spacensky, 1967).

within the French Union) and the 1959 change of constitution swept him to the presidency of the Republic,[40] the position from which he ultimately negotiated independence in 1960. The Constitution, largely modelled on the Constitution of the Fifth French Republic, granted a remarkable amount of power to the president, as both head of state and head of government, especially since the legislature was entirely on his side with just three MPs not in the presidential party (Randriamihaingo, 2004).

Political Reorganisation of the State

Post-independence political rule gave the *côtier* elites a large representation, especially for their members from the civil service.[41] Yet independence did not mean the total ousting of France from political rule. The French ambassador was frequently consulted about major decisions (Razafimbelo, 2004), French ministers sat in government, French consuls remained members of the provincial assemblies (Randrianja & Ellis, 2009) and army officers were trained by French instructors at the military academy in Antsirabe (opened in 1965). The senior civil service also counted a large number of French technical assistants, who rivalled the former *Merina* administrative bourgeoisie for these positions.

Foreign control of the productive system meant that most of the labour competition in this period was for government positions – whether political, administrative or military – and often became a contest between *côtier* elites and *Merina* elites.[42] A large proportion of the political positions were snatched up by *côtier* elites, although the old *Merina* elites were not completely excluded. Tsiranana actually made a great deal of room in his governments and administrative management positions for *Merina* representatives.[43] These political positions gave their holders not-inconsiderable possibilities for personal gain. Many of the members of Tsiranana's government held management positions in Malagasy subsidiaries of foreign companies and Tsiranana himself was a shareholder in

40 He was elected by the members of the Constituent Assembly with 113 of the 114 votes.

41 For example, the PSD's landslide victory in the 1965 general election with 94% of the vote saw 60% of the seats going to civil servants and/or mayors or deputy mayors (Goguel, 2006).

42 However, this did not mean that the situation turned into a 'fundamental conflict' between *côtier* and *Merina* ethnic groups. The period's policies show no particular bias in favour of one region or another (Archer, 1976).

43 In the first Tsiranana cabinet, half of the ministers were *Merina* (Archer, 1976). At this time, Charles Andriantsitohaina, from a *Merina* high aristocratic family who was to become a heavyweight of the Malagasy economy, held the position of Private Secretary of the Ministry for the National Economy.

several colonial businesses and managing director of the Compagnie des Transports, one of the island's largest companies (Archer, 1976). Yet the actual administrative power remained essentially in the hands of an urban bourgeoisie in the shape of the *Merina* monarchy's former dominant status groups. In this rivalry between coast and *Merina* elites, foreign technical assistance was often used as a way of preventing too large an influx of educated individuals from the highlands into the administration.

From 1960 to 1972, the PSD maintained and even extended its hegemony in the country. In contrast to the many parties on the eve of independence, only two other parties fully survived this period: AKFM in the capital led by pastor Richard Andriamanjato (who served as mayor of the capital throughout the First Republic) defending a pro-Soviet political line and Monja Jaona's MONIMA (*MOuvement National pour l'Indépendance de Madagascar*; Madagascar for the Malagasy) in the south, a people's peasant, anti-imperialist party and, as such, an admirer of China. The members of the PSD held the main positions in the administration and the ministries, so much so that it was referred to by some as the PSD State. 'Party membership was a quick way to move up the social ladder' (Razafimbelo, 2004), but also a 'way of taking part in the all-powerful *fanjakana* and hence of being protected' (Raison-Jourde & Roy, 2010). The number of civil servants tripled in 12 years (Vérin, 1990) and the PSD State ultimately permeated every part of society. At the grassroots level, district heads were merely the authority's economic and social minions and 'elections became a rubber stamp formality' (Vérin, 1990). At the 1972 presidential election, just months before the events of 1972 that led to the setting up of a transitional government, Tsiranana was consequently re-elected by 99.8% of the turnout.

The First Republic was also a period of expansion for the Malagasy army, with a large increase in troop numbers (Ramasy, 2010). In 1960, the armed forces' field officers had all trained in France, at Saint-Cyr and l'Ecole de Guerre, and most of them, like Chief of Staff General Ramanantsoa, were from the former *Merina* oligarchy with its aristocratic mindset (Archer, 1976). The military hierarchy therefore mirrored in part the old status-based hierarchies. Tsiranana's government tried to curb this elite group's power as far as possible by furthering the promotion of *côtier* officers in the army and sharply hiking up paramilitary police force numbers (7,000 men in the gendarmerie in 1971 compared with 4,000 in the army; Archer, 1976) with officers from different ethnic groups and different regions. In 1966, he also set up the Antsirabe Military Academy (ACMIL – *Académie Militaire*), which offered a free education combined with a job to families that could not afford to send their children to university and whose articles of association reserved places for *côtier* groups (Ramasy, 2010), and created the Republican Security Forces (FRS – *Forces Républicaines de Sécurité*)[44] made up mainly of soldiers from the coastal regions.

The PSD State moreover prioritised investment in schools. Tsiranana, who despite coming from an influential family in northern Madagascar owed his rise to the expansion of schooling, put in place an ambitious education policy: a lower secondary school in each sub-prefecture and an upper secondary school in each prefecture, the creation of a university (1963), and cooperation agreements with France to give a large number of *baccalauréat* holders scholarships to study in France. The success of this educational promotion policy drove up the influx of skilled students on to an urban labour market, out of step with actual skilled job opportunities. These dashed hopes were behind the strike movements and student protests of the first half of 1972, including the demonstration of 13 May 1972 with its bloody crackdown[45] by the Republican Security Forces. The student strikes, initially held in Antananarivo under the leadership of the AKFM youth movement, quickly spread nationwide (Althabe, 1980; Goguel, 2006; Randrianja & Ellis, 2009). They ultimately precipitated the fall of the regime and the transfer of full powers to General Ramanantsoa, the highest ranking military officer and the longest standing in the rank of general.

Economic Developments

In spite of the PSD State's avowed purpose to work on the country's development, the period's economic organisation did not fundamentally change compared with the previous period. The five-year plan (actually extended through to 1972), defined as a tool to 'quickly and immediately change the island's socioeconomic fundamentals without a revolution, without damaging any interests and drawing on all the means . . ., as much the dynamics of the liberal, capitalist private sector as the stricter state enterprise set-ups',[46] was initially designed to drive forward development without fundamentally challenging the previous organisation. The plan was based partly on a 'belly policy'[47] (Hugon, 1989a) intended to raise

[44] Riot police. [45] Some 40 people were killed. [46] Statement by P. Tsiranana.

[47] This policy was designed to meet the people's basic needs. The expression here therefore has nothing to do with the term 'politics of the belly' popularised by J. F. Bayart (1993) in his analysis of the State in Africa, which referred to a concept of the state system perceived as a way in to wealth, privileges, power and prestige for oneself and the members of one's clan.

agricultural production and exports[48] and partly on import-substitution-based industrial development,[49] which took off essentially in 1966.

From 1960 to 1970, industrial production grew 13.5% per year in current Malagasy francs, raising the share of the industrial sector from 10% to 18% of gross domestic product (GDP) (Hugon, 1989a). Industries appeared such as the Paper Mill of Madagascar (PAPMAD – *Papèterie de Madagascar*) in Antananarivo in 1965, the Malagasy Refinery (SMR) in Toamasina in 1964 and 1965, the Mahajanga Textile Company (SOTEMA – *Société Textile de Mahajanga*) in 1968, and the Shipbuilding and Navy Armaments Division (DCAN – *Direction de la Construction et de l'Armement Naval*) in Antsiranana.[50] The geographical location of these different industrial units in some of the main towns in the provinces reflected an intention to develop the country in its entirety, even though the policy appears to have overlooked the provinces of Fianarantsoa and Toliara (*Expansion Madagascar*, 2010). A grocery chain called M was also developed to distribute these Malagasy products at the best price (Vérin, 1990).

This move to develop local industry created new opportunities for the emergence of a Malagasy industrial bourgeoisie over the period,[51] mainly in the shape of *Merina* high families.[52] Yet virtually all the industries were still owned by foreigners, as was indeed the case in the tertiary sector: the retail sector continued to be controlled by the three major import–export companies and Europeans remained in the majority of key positions in the banks and private companies (Archer, 1976). These modern sector businesses, which controlled two-thirds of the monetised part of national income, transferred abroad more than double the amount they invested in the country (Goguel, 2006). Tsiranana was re-elected in 1965. Tending toward authoritarianism and with his sights set on fast-track agricultural development, Tsiranana made

[48] Set up vanilla and banana cooperatives, municipal consortiums to harvest lima beans and state farms. See Vérin (1990).

[49] Approximately 50% taxation on imports, many facilities granted by the 1962 Investment Code (Hugon, 1989a), the 1962 establishment of a National Investment Company (NIC) to serve as a financial intermediary, and the 1963 establishment of the National Malagasy Development Bank.

[50] This company was established in 1945 but received substantial funds from the five-year plan.

[51] This was particularly the case with soap company Savonnerie Tropicale established in 1967–8 by André Ramaroson, member of the rich Antananarivo bourgeoisie and former nationalist activist.

[52] Although notable exceptions included Franco-Malagasy producers in the sisal sector, Indo-Pakistani families in the artisanal mining sector and local coastal elites in the vanilla sector (World Bank, 2010).

labour mandatory, sent the army out to plant trees, ordered the now-swollen numbers of civil servants (55,000 in 1965 as opposed to 6,000 before independence) to work in rotation in the highlands, and took a certain number of measures against the season's 'idle'.[53] However, this pressure on the people did not turn out as expected. The trading economy continued to be a dominant organisational arrangement and cash crops, though not very widespread, still accounted for three-quarters of exports. The foreign presence was considerable even in this sector, standing at one-third of all production. Food production, however, was at a clear disadvantage. Food produce prices, especially rice prices, were kept stable to hold down the cost of living in urban areas and support agribusiness (Hugon, 1989a; Vérin, 1990). Lastly, foreign dependency continued, despite the drop in imports of consumer goods, due to imports of raw materials and capital equipment.

***

Colonisation and the First Republic that succeeded it therefore altered the structure of power in Malagasy society to some extent. They put an end to the *Merina* political hegemony by taking over central power and giving back power to the *côtier* elites, thereby stirring up new rivalries. The emphasis on education and extending the state's reach gradually ushered in a new meritocratic elite recruited from among the different regions' wealthiest families. However, the official end to the caste system and the abolition of slavery did not profoundly change a society rooted in discriminatory principles. As F. Rajaonah (1996) puts it, quoting F. Braudel, the mentalities, these 'long-term prisons', persisted right through to behaviour. The *Andriana* continued to have their patron–client relationship with the *Mainty* (providing rice and lending land in return for domestic work) and to use appropriate strategies (military, educational and ecclesiastical) to keep themselves among the elites (Rajaonah, 1996). The 'development' policy spawned a trading economy based on the exploitation of products of the earth for export and the import of French products. Growth hovered at around 2.7% throughout the period, which, in view of demographic growth, only just maintained the average level of per capita wealth and further widened the gap between the vast rural majority (more than 80% of the population), whose actual per capita income fell an average 30% over the period, and the urban world however disparate. This deterioration in

[53] 'Every year, district heads embarked on manhunts, furious to find huts deserted by villagers who had gone to camp in the forest with cooking pots and rice,' (Raison-Jourde & Roy, 2010).

the rural standard of living hit especially hard as the tax burden, by means of direct taxes (the fiscal minimum tax had replaced the capitation tax), continued to weigh heavily on rural inhabitants.[54] The analysis that G. Roy calls a village 'Book of Grievances' from 1966 to 1967 (Raison-Jourde & Roy, 2010) clearly shows the extent of this malaise driven by the impression of the *fanjakana*'s loss of consideration for its subjects (non-respect for *fihavanana*). This is also one of the main reasons for the 1971 MONIMA-led farmer revolts[55] in the south of the country, which were violently suppressed by the paramilitary police force.[56]

The system's contradictions consequently brought the First Republic grinding to a halt in the early 1970s. The educational boom made for high demand for skilled jobs on a heavily saturated labour market and the privileges granted foreigners, as much in terms of technical positions as business dealings, compounded resentment among the former elites. It was these frustrated aspirations that triggered the strike movements and student protests of the first half of 1972, rallied by ZOAM,[57] an association of unemployed, marginal youth affiliated with Manandafy Rakotonirina's *Mpitolona ho amin'ny Fandrosoan'i Madagasikara* (MFM – Party for Proletarian Power), the first revolutionary Marxist political party.[58] The ruling power interpreted the farmer revolts and student protests as attempts at destabilisation. Instead of seeking a consensus solution, Tsiranana stuck staunchly to a repressive attitude, ordering the bloody crushing of the farmer uprisings by the paramilitary police force, imprisoning his Interior Minister Resampa, who had expressed his discontent with these responses, allowing the Republican Security Forces (FRS) to

[54] In 1966, 3.5 million of the 24 million Malagasy francs in taxes came from the rural world, a substantial amount in view of the low incomes in the area (Goguel, 2006).

[55] Refusal to pay tax and contribution to the PSD.

[56] The official figures reported 48 dead and 62 injured among the insurgents. Yet other sources estimate the number at more than 800 dead and as many arrested (Raison-Jourde & Roy, 2010).

[57] The eruption of ZOAM on the Malagasy political scene is extremely important. They appeared for the first time in April 1972, when unemployed youths entered the university campus wearing cowboy hats and demanding recognition of the opinions of ZWAM (*Zatovo Western Anivon'i Madagasikara*), i.e. Young Cowboys of Madagascar. Once it became an organisation, the name was changed to ZOAM (Unemployed Youth; *Zatovo Orin'asa*).

[58] This latter urban movement 'gave birth to a number of left-wing organisations coordinated by the KIM Committee (*Komity Iombonan'ny Mpitolona* – Committee for the Coordination of the Struggle), which managed to obtain concessions and the recognition of certain democratic principles under the new regime before they were dismantled by General Ramanantsoa,' (Archer, 1976; Althabe, 1980).

open fire on the crowd of student protesters in May 1972, and making inflammatory comments that were nothing short of incitement to ethnic conflict.[59] These events galvanised the unions, churches and civil society to call for a new organisation of power. Tsiranana was forced to hand over power to General Ramanantsoa.

Figure 2.1 shows the distribution of power among the groups of players (1960–72).

2.4 From 1972 to 1991: Malagasisation and Growth of State Rent

From 1972 to 1975: The Ramanantsoa Interlude

General Ramanantsoa was therefore swept to power by a coalition of contradictory interests (Spacensky, 1970). The referendum of 8 October 1972 brought him real popular endorsement and a five-year term, with 86% of voter turnout in favour of Ramanantsoa.[60] He then set about forming a technocratic-military government dissociated from any political party line. Parties were banned and a National Popular Council for Development (CNDP – *Conseil National pour le Développement Populaire*), supposed to represent the population, replaced the National Assembly and the Senate.

Economic Changes

This first military government launched the economic and social reforms that were to mark the Malagasy trajectory for two decades to come. Two ambitious programmes were put in place: one to secure Madagascar's independence from foreign interests, and the other to power up productive farming by reorganising the *fokonolona*.

Madagascar pursued economic independence by leaving the franc zone and signing new cooperation agreements with France. With France's approval, the government introduced an economic Malagasisation policy. It imposed the recruitment of Malagasy corporate managers and directors along with the partial reinvestment of profits and encouraged government-assisted takeovers of small businesses and share-farming operations by

[59] For example, equating the members of the AKFM with the old *Merina* monarchy (Saura, 2006).

[60] As will be seen in the following sections, [this use of the referendum.... This use of the referendum as a way for a ruler entering office unconventionally to gain popular endorsement is particularly common in Madagascar's history.

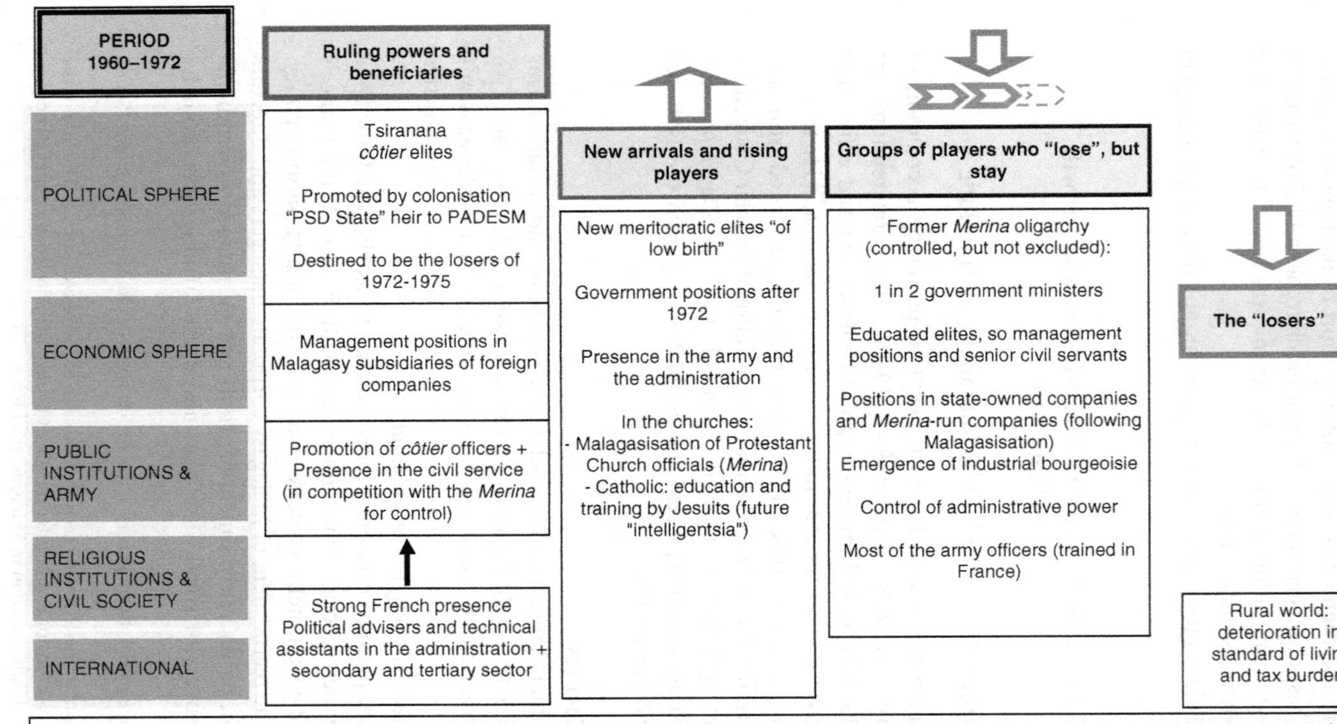

Figure 2.1 Distribution of power among the groups of players, 1960–1972.

nationals. The state also took control of the key economic sectors (banks, insurance, foreign trade and foreign and domestic transport), acquiring majority shareholdings or acting through representatives. This move created major national corporations such as SONACO (*Société Nationale du Commerce Extérieur*; National Foreign Trade Company) and SINPA (*Société d'Intérêt National de Comercialisation des Produits Agricoles*; National Farm Produce Marketing Board). These virtual monopolies enjoyed astounding privileges (Hugon, 1989a). The new state-controlled capitalism augmented the state's power and encouraged the formation of a technocratic and administrative elite. The main positions of economic control were held by members of the former *Merina* elite, *Andriana* and *Hova*, suspected of forming a secret society dubbed the 'Club of 48'. Although there is nothing to suggest that such a club ever existed as an indisputably established organisation, there may have been an informal alliance of high families connected by networks of friends and family[61] and economic interests. Its alleged members did indeed exercise oligarchic control over the economy during the period by directly investing in production activities and forming alliances with often-foreign entrepreneurs and traders in the provinces, such as the directors of the Compagnie Marseillaise de Madagascar, the Barday brothers in Mahajanga, Lam-Sek in Fianarantsoa and Sam-Kan in Toliara (Archer, 1976).

The Malagasisation policy in actual fact reduced economic activity and employment with it, in turn fuelling urban social unrest. Many Europeans, Chinese and Indo-Pakistanis left the island (Razafimbelo, 2004) during the period and foreign majors tended to reduce their capital expenditure in the country, afraid they might not later be able to repatriate their profits. GDP plunged some 4% and recession hit textiles and clothing, the mechanical engineering and metal industries and construction and civil engineering full on. It affected commodities and energy upstream and transport and trade downstream (Hugon, 1989a). The exit from the franc zone and global economic recession further added to the country's economic decline. As P. Hugon reports, Madagascar was in effect among the countries hardest hit by the recession, which weighed on the price of commodities and imported manufactured products (for the same volume of petroleum products, the value of imports shot up from MGF 6.2 billion in 1972 to MGF 19.5 billion in 1974). This drove up imported inflation which, combined with monetary inflation

[61] The meaning of the figure 48 is not clear. It could stand for either the date of the supposed formation or the number of families in the club. For more information on the Club of 48, see Archer (1976), pp. 77–92.

brought about by the increase in treasury financing, reached 12% in 1973 and nearly 23% in 1974 (Hugon, 1989a), thus slashing the purchasing power of the vast majority of Malagasy households by as much again.

The second strand of the development policy focused on reforming the rural structures. This direction was the brainchild of Colonel Richard Ratsimandrava, Interior Minister, to promote economic development. It was based on a form of decentralisation that gave the traditional rural communities (*fokonolona*) more freedom of choice and organisation (mainly by granting them control over unfarmed land[62]) and restructured the administration from the bottom up, from the basic units up to national level. The first step of this policy was to scrap the fiscal minimum tax and cattle tax to enable the decentralised communities to conduct certain development operations (Hugon, 1989a). This agricultural development policy was underpinned by a price policy (paddy price guarantee to producers and fertiliser subsidy) and inspection of the rice marketing channels by SINPA. The axing of the fiscal minimum tax and the increase in agricultural prices raised rural incomes, especially for landed farmers. However, the economic situation prevented these farmers from stepping up their rice production and they even cut back the share they sent to market (11.2% compared with 16.6%), precipitating a surge in rice imports. Moreover, the increase in agricultural prices drove up the urban cost of living even further and spelled trouble for some small businesses that were intensive users of local agricultural products and manpower (Hugon, 1989a, 336).

Political Developments

General Ramanantsoa's government presented itself as apolitical and a guardian of national unity. The cabinet comprised six military officers from the different army and paramilitary police corps and six civilians renowned for their expertise. The cabinet also guaranteed in principle the representation of the six provinces of Madagascar. Yet the individuals' career paths and social backgrounds meant that they had different sympathies, which fuelled the period's political instability.

Being from the Antantanarivian haute bourgeoisie, General Ramanantsoa was naturally inclined to give preference to the interests of members of the *Merina* aristocratic elite. Under his and Colonel Rabetafika's[63] influence, the

[62] The *fokonolona* were also equipped with an economic committee, the *vatoeka*, with extended decision-making powers.

[63] 'Member of one of Imerina's most illustrious families, Rabetafika's grandfather had been a pastor in Antananarivo, while his younger brother was an ambassador in New York and his cousin was an English professor at the University of Madagascar and also married to

main economic governance positions went to members of this elite,[64] feeding into the public's belief in the existence of a Club of 48 (mentioned earlier), especially because the technicians who replaced the French were generally also from this background (with their higher-quality technical and intellectual education provided by the highlands' superior education infrastructure).

Gendarmerie Commanding Officer R. Ratsimandrava and Lieutenant Commander D. Ratsiraka owed their careers and social advancement to the official extinction of the status group system and introduction of meritocratic principles. Ratsimandrava, son of a PADESM activist primary school teacher from Antananarivo, was a *Merina* of *Andevo* origin (Randrianja & Ellis, 2009; Ramasy, 2010). Ratsiraka, of *Betsimisaraka* origin, came from a modest family in the eastern region of Madagascar where his father was a 'writer interpreter'.[65] Both men arguably represented a left-wing tendency within the government, even though D. Ratsiraka, who worked closely as Foreign Affairs Minister on negotiating the cooperation agreements with France and the country's exit from the franc zone, kept a careful distance from domestic affairs at the time. Yet it was R. Ratsimandrava who launched the *fokonolona* reform that challenged the traditional power structures[66] and who, in late 1974, ordered the investigations into embezzlement by National Investment Company directors that were to destabilise the Ramanantsoa government.

The major losers of this political reorganisation were the former PSD members and the *côtier* elites. Ousted from the leading political and economic posts, some of them founded the Malagasy Socialist Union, which openly declared itself to be acting in the interests of the *côtier* people and organised anti-*Merina* and anti-government demonstrations in coastal towns and cities (Razafimbelo, 2004). From December 1972 to

Dr Ranjeva, himself a lecturer at the University and descended from the royal family of Imerina' (Archer, 1976, p. 71).

64 For example, Minister for the Economy and Finance, Treasury Director, Director of the Finance Department, Governor of the Central Bank and Head of the Tax Department (Archer, 1976, p. 82).

65 Writer interpreters interpreted for the French administrators. Some sources present Ratsiraka as a descendent of emancipated slaves and his father as a PADESM sympathiser. In his memoires, however, the former president denies these claims (Lavrad-Meyer, 2015).

66 The reform was designed to introduce 'management of development by the people'. In the *fokonolona*, anyone over 18 had to be granted the right to represent the people. The *fokonolona* were empowered to manage their own budgets and enact their own by-laws (*dina*) governing local security. Their members were entitled to decide how to organise agriculture, trade and civil justice (see Archer, 1976).

January 1973, a series of riots erupted in Toamasina, Mahajanga, Antsiranana and other urban centres. At the same time, dissension became manifest in the army between senior officers, who had trained at Saint-Cyr and l'Ecole de Guerre and were generally *Merina* of aristocratic origin, and those mostly non-*Merina* officers who had risen through the ranks and were excluded from political representation. One of them, Colonel Brechard Rajaonarison of *Antesaka* origin, a former non-commissioned officer promoted following independence (Archer, 1976), was to be accused of backing a coup attempt in 1975. Following this accusation, the GPM[67] (heir to the FRS) rebelled (B. Rajaonarison took refuge in the GPM barracks and the GPM refused to hand him over to the authorities). This rebellion, backed by Resampa, Tsiranana and the government's *côtier* ministers, triggered the fall of Ramanantsoa's government. Ramanantsoa – caught between the political demands of the *côtier* elites lined up behind the Malagasy Socialist Party (PSM, Parti Socialiste Malgache) and Tsiranana, his loyalty to the *Merina* economico-political oligarchy and pressure from the MFM and MONIMA for economic and political reforms – was ultimately driven to hand over power to R. Ratsimandrava (who was threatening to expose members of the corrupt regime in scandals) on 5 February 1975. Six days later, Ratsimandrava was assassinated in what has to this day remained a murder case that history has never managed to entirely solve.[68] A military directorate was promptly formed and set about restoring order with an armed repression of the GPM rebellion and declaration of martial law.

From 1975 to 1991: The Second Republic and Growth of State Rent

D. Ratsiraka ended up gaining the most influence in the military directorate owing to his purported ability to meet the different groups' contradictory demands and his image of firmness with the former colonial power, built up during his time as foreign affairs minister under Ramanantsoa's government. In accordance with a constitutional provision provided for by the referendum of 1972, he was duly elected head of state by the members

[67] Mobile Police Group/ Groupement de Police Mobile.

[68] The 'Trial of the Century' held from March to June 1975 tried a multitude of defendants, including Resampa and Tsiranana, but only handed down minor sentences. The records of the trial were burnt in late 1975, greatly reducing the chances of the truth ever surfacing one day. Yet this has not prevented researchers from coming up with their own lines of inquiry (see, for example, Archer, 1976; Raison-Jourde & Roy, 2010).

of the directorate on 15 June 1975. The directorate was then replaced by a Supreme Revolutionary Council (CSR) and Didier Ratsiraka swiftly launched a first wave of nationalisation of banks, insurance firms, cinemas, the Société des Transports Maritimes (SMTM) shipping company, the Société Malgache de Raffinage oil refinery and the Compagnie Marseillaise de Madagascar.[69] Then, on 21 December 1975, he held a referendum[70] to adopt the *Boky Mena*,[71] the Charter of the Malagasy Socialist Revolution, and a new constitution making him President of the Second Republic for a seven-year term. He therein reinstated the practice of popular endorsement by referendum initiated by G. Ramanantsoa a few years earlier.

The *Boky Mena* and the constitution established a highly centralised and personalised system based on socialist principles, very similar to the system put in place in Tanzania (Déléris, 1986). The executive and especially the president of the republic dominated the system (Rabetafika, 1990).[72] The legislative body now had just one house. MPs, elected by universal suffrage for five years, had to be members of the National Front for the Defence of the Revolution (FNDR – *Front National pour la Défense de la Révolution*),[73] defined in articles 8 and 9 of the constitution as the political body in place to 'lead and guide the revolution in its commitment to the construction of socialism, and inspire the activity of the state'. MPs hence served merely to rubber stamp the bills tabled. Yet the charter was also designed to reorganise the provinces, to the advantage of the coastal provinces. To this end, decentralised local administrative divisions were set up that were supposed to guarantee better representation for the provinces and give the people more power: *faritany*, *fivondronana-pokonolona* (*fivondrana*), *firaisam-pokonolona* (*firaisana*) and *fokontany*.[74] In actual fact, political centralism grew in this period compared with the First Republic. First, the

[69] The state took 51% ownership in these companies, but left their management to the former owners, with the exception of the Compagnie Marseillaise de Madagascar, which was totally nationalised.

[70] This referendum brought him comfortable popular support with 95% of voter turnout voting 'yes'.

[71] Red Book.

[72] The president is 'the supreme body of state power'. He chairs the Supreme Revolutionary Council (SRC) and the government in the Council of Ministers. He appoints two-thirds of the members of the SRC and chooses the other third from a list submitted by the National People's Assembly (NPA).

[73] As too did the president.

[74] Respectively: Province, Prefecture, Sub-Prefecture and Village or District.

system was designed as a hierarchical pyramid.[75] Second, despite being endowed with financial and executive autonomy, the *fokontany* continued to be kept on a very tight rein by ideological and technical assistance structures, and political control of their elected representatives, who were required to be members of the FNDR. AREMA (*Avant-garde de la Révolution Malgache*; Vanguard of the Malagasy Revolution), the party founded by the President in 1976, quickly became predominant in this Front (made up of AREMA, the four parties that called for a 'yes' vote in the December 1975 referendum – AKFM, MONIMA, VITM[76] and UDECMA[77] – and the MFM[78]). AREMA was virtually always in a monopoly position in the main elections held during this period (Pierre Bernard *et al.*, 1998; Randriamihaingo, 2004).[79] From this point of view, then, the political organisation was very similar to the previous situation.[80]

Economic and Social Change

Ratsimandrava had set out to turn round the agricultural policy to the peasantry's advantage by doubling the rice producer price, axing the fiscal minimum tax and cattle tax and making the *fokonolona* the self-governing 'base of the rural world's structure for the management of development by the people'.[81] The Second Republic's decentralisation and land reform, however, bore but a passing resemblance to these goals. Although the *fokontany* (comprising the members of the *fokonolona*) had broad powers,[82] it was ultimately no more than a 'cog in the wheel passing on

[75] Each local government body was directly in charge of the next level down and the entire system was under the government's administrative and financial control (Rajaonesy, 2008).

[76] *Vonjy Iray Tsy Mivaky* (Popular Movement for the Unity of Madagascar). PSD offshoot that joined the FNDR.

[77] Union of Christian Democrats.

[78] Joined the FNDR after 1977.

[79] AREMA won 90% of the 73,000 seats in the *fokontany* elections held in March 1977. In June 1977, AREMA won 220 of the 232 seats in the elections for the six provincial general assemblies, and 112 of the 137 seats in the National People's Assembly.

[80] This happened again under Ravalomanana when TIM, the president's party, also gained a dominant position (See the Ravalomanana period, from 2002 to 2009).

[81] Ordinance of 24 March 1973 (see Andriamirado, 1977).

[82] 'On the administrative level, it had public services; on the legislative level, it drafted binding *dina*; on the judicial level, it wielded its own powers assigned it by the laws on judicial organisation; in terms of defence, it took part in the defence of the territory and public security; on the economic level, it worked for the development of the socialist economy by organising cooperatives; on the political level, it elected and dismissed its representatives; and socially, it conducted all activities that contributed to the social welfare and sociocultural development of its members' (Randriamihaingo, 2004).

revolutionary directives from the top to the bottom of society' (Raison, 2007). Neither did the land reform, designed to encourage the development of a collective production and distribution system with the creation of socialist cooperatives, subsidies and access to credit, give the rural populations autonomy in their decisions and initiatives. They were in fact closely watched over by the armed forces for development,[83] whose role it was to educate, organise and supervise the farmers in keeping with the guidelines of the economic plan prepared by the central authority.

The prime objective of the land reform was to establish food self-sufficiency by developing food crops. Staple goods prices and distribution channels were controlled, while export crops were taxed with the establishment of commodities marketing boards bringing in fiscal resources for central government.[84] This policy in effect drove down the production of coffee, cloves, vanilla and pepper with a correlative reduction in export revenues, while the drop in actual producer prices for food products prompted rationing and the development of a black market (Blanc-Pamard, 1985; Raison J.-P., 1991). Production of rice for market consequently stagnated from 1975 to 1983 (while the population grew 30%) and rice imports rose fivefold to account for more than 80% of marketed output by 1983 (Hugon, 1986). The early 1980s were hence marked by recurrent shortages.

State control of the means of production was also supposed to generate industrial development. The first wave of nationalisation in 1975 had already gotten the state takeover of the production apparatus well underway. By the end of 1976, the state already controlled 100% of the banking and insurance system and the electricity and water boards, three-quarters of exports and 60% of imports (respectively 30% and 20% previously), one-third of industry and 14% of shipping (Rabetafika, 1990; Vérin, 1990). In 1976, strategic industries were in turn placed under direct military control. This move saw the establishment of the National Military Agency for Strategic Industries (OMNIS; *Office Militaire National pour les Industries Stratégiques*), the idea for which had already been put forward by D. Ratsiraka when he was foreign affairs minister under Ramanantsoa's government. This body, with D. Ratsiraka as its appointed chair, was tasked with managing heavy industry (Antsiranana Shipyard, etc.) and

[83] D. Ratsiraka merged the army and gendarmerie into a single force called first the people's army and then the development army in order to eliminate the sources of conflict within the forces of order, which had formed obstacles in the previous period (Archer, 1976).

[84] From 1975 to 1983, coffee producers received just 40% of the world price while vanilla and clove producers were paid just 25% (IFPRI, 1998).

strategic ore mines (Ravaloson, 2000). State economic control was further scaled up following the publication of the *Charter of Socialist Enterprises* in 1977 and nationalisation of other businesses such as SOSUMAV sugar company, Denis Frères and COROI trading company (Vérin, 1990). In the agricultural sector, lands still owned by settlers on the east coast were nationalised and entrusted to Malagasy families with a cooperative management set-up. Last but not least, a central staple commodities store called Koparema–Procoops was set up for farmers and managed by AREMA.

In 1978, the government launched what was known as an 'all-out investment' policy (71 billion Malagasy francs in 1978 and approximately 150 billion in each of the three following years) in a move to step up economic development on the back of the short-term balance of trade surpluses. This policy, also designed to foster the economic development of the regions, drove the acquisition of means of transport and ploughing machinery, the development of infrastructures and the construction of community colleges in the provinces. However, it also saw often outsized or poorly located[85] industrial structures set up, which generally proved unprofitable if not inoperable[86] due to a poor assessment of needs, poor equipment maintenance, supply problems, the small domestic market and the system of administered prices with its strong rigidities (Andrianarison, 1996). Moreover, coming as it did in the middle of a world recession, this investment strategy had seriously adverse economic and financial effects: deterioration in the balance of trade as commodity exports fell and the oil bill tripled, surging debt (from 18% of GDP in 1978 to 52% in 1982) and a new hike in inflation. From 1974 to 1978, prices had risen 7.5% on average per year. Yet from 1979 to 1982, the rate of inflation leapt from 11.3% to 28.6% (Hugon, 1986; Vérin 1990; Randriamihaingo, 2004).

Lastly, the education policy was a key aspect of the period's reforms. The school system's inequalities, inherited from the colonial system, continued under the First Republic despite the spread of education. This had the effect of marginalising rural inhabitants and coastal regions. The Second Republic introduced three measures intended to solve the problem: the

[85] For example, Zema, a fertiliser plant in Ambovombe, was located in a drought-ridden area with little agriculture, no port for exports and a road in very bad condition that did nothing to help transport (*Expansion Madagascar*, 2011).

[86] To give some extreme examples, the Zeren chemical fertiliser factory in Toamasina, the Toly farm tool-making complexes and the Lalasoa soya processing plant never got off the ground. The Kobama flourmill established in the region of Vakinankaratra and FAMAMA (*Famokarana Mahabibo Malagasy*) in Mahajanga never did more than tick over.

Malagasisation of education (previously taught in French), the further spread of education and the decentralisation of higher education. An official form of Malagasy (actually the form spoken in the Central Highlands) gradually became the language of education in primary and secondary school, and students who passed their *baccalauréat* were requisitioned for national education service without receiving any real teacher training. The decentralisation of higher education was designed to balance out the regions and bring higher education within everyone's reach. The number of grant holders quadrupled from 1974 to 1979 and MGF 30 billion were invested to build the Regional Community Colleges (RCCs).[87] Here again, the results were disappointing. In practice, 'education for all' was just a way of making it easier to graduate through the school years, enter secondary school and pass the *baccalauréat*. Without adequate resources in terms of teachers, premises and school materials, the end result of decentralisation was to disrupt the normal sequence of education and bring about a sharp drop in level (Randriamarotsimba, 2005).

The decade's development policy was therefore a virtually unmitigated failure. From 1974 to 1983, the situation in the industrial sector deteriorated dramatically with output lower in 1974 than in 1967 (Razafindrakoto, 1996). The number of jobs halved (Vérin, 1990) while agricultural production stagnated. In a climate of high demographic growth, purchasing power and household consumption ultimately tumbled (Ravelosoa & Roubaud, 1998; Fremigacci, 2007a).

In the 1980s, the country came under donor pressure to change its economic course. It implemented the structural adjustment programmes proposed by the IMF, exceeding even the donors' expectations (Hugon, 1986; Leymarie, 1989a; Willame, 1994)[88] and setting the country on the market-based reform road: gradual liberalisation of prices and free movement of goods,[89] repeated devaluations, winding-up of unprofitable companies, privatisation of the nationalised banks, massive public expenditure

[87] Antananarivo for law, economics, management, sociology, arts and humanities, medicine and sciences; Antsiranana for electromechanical engineering; Fianarantsoa for mathematics, physics and the third level of teacher training; Mahajanga for medical and dental studies; Toamasina for management; and Toliara for arts, sciences, teacher training and philosophy.

[88] At the World Bank, the programme was presented as one of the most remarkable on the African continent (Willame, 1994).

[89] Liberalisation of rice prices in 1985, total liberalisation of exports with the exception of coffee, vanilla and cloves, rescission of the pepper export tax, closure of the pepper marketing board in 1987, closure of the coffee and clove marketing board, liberalisation

cutbacks (freeze on civil servant wages and recruitment) and creation of export processing zones in 1980 (Razafindratandra, 1993; Willame, 1994; Andrianarison, 1996). In return, the country benefited from huge financial facilities and an extraordinary repayment of its debt by the Paris Club in 1988.

Although structural adjustment made for a marked recovery in the public finance situation, it brought only a relatively small increase in foreign trade and no clear economic upswing. Structural adjustment placed a particularly heavy burden on middle and working class wage earners. From 1980 to 1988, actual civil service wages nosedived 56% and actual agricultural and urban wages slid back 22%[90] (Willame, 1994). The measures taken were also powerless to solve the shortage and price surge problems. Following a slight downturn, inflation again hit 18% in 1987 and leapt to 26.6% in 1988. In addition, these measures considerably widened the inequality gap as the liberalisation of prices and trade channels for food products fostered speculation and an increase in middlemen margins (Hugon, 1989b; Araujo Bonjean & Azam, 1996). However, they did improve farmers' earnings: 20% for rice producers, 7.9% for vanilla producers and 1.9% for clove producers (with only coffee producers suffering a 22.5% drop) (Willame, 1994). Per capita GDP did not see positive growth again until 1988. The 1980s were also marked by a severe health crisis: as child health indicators improved on the African continent, mortality rose in Madagascar, cutting life expectancy at birth by 13 years for men and 8 years for women between 1975 and 1986 (Gastineau *et al.*, 2010).

Socio-political Developments

What is known as D. Ratsiraka's socialist period – more accurately a state-controlled capitalist economy like that found in Côte d'Ivoire – was a continuation of the previous period. Extreme political centralisation and expansion of the state's reach from 1975 to 1993 fostered the rise to power and wealth of a new generation of high-flyers who had lacked the symbolic or material capital to secure positions in the previous republic (Galibert, 2011a). Membership of AREMA became key to social advancement, even more so than in the previous period under the PSD. Yet this new political elite did not monopolise all the positions of responsibility. Although the *côtier* elites were

of domestic and foreign trade with the exception of vanilla, and end of the state monopoly over exports in 1988.

90 One day's agricultural wage bought approximately 1 kg of white rice in 1991 compared with over 3 kg in the early 1970s (J. P. Raison, 1991).

the period's major losers, members of the *Merina* high families, while excluded from the highest positions, did regain some of the prerogatives they had lost under the First Republic. The upshot was that *Merina* cabinet representation rose from 18% under the First Republic to 36% under the Second Republic (Pryor, 1990). It was also during this period that 'state rent' developed the most (Galibert, 2011a). The military, to whom President D. Ratsiraka owed his rise to head of state, were among the major winners in this area. In addition to their being largely represented on the Supreme Revolutionary Council (CSR) and in the government, the establishment of OMNIS gave them wealth accumulation opportunities managing strategic companies (Galibert, 2011a). The growth of the public sector also opened up many wealth accumulation possibilities for senior AREMA officials, especially those closest to President Ratsiraka who were assigned the leading public enterprise management positions. And the proliferation of administrative positions in the new local authorities gave those holding these jobs prerogatives that gave them all sorts of opportunities to draw on the wealth generated (Fanomezantsoa, 1993). Ethnic group or caste counted less in these appointments and assignments than political allegiance and/or family ties.

Political control and economic control therefore held the power of the former elites in check (whether the *côtier* oligarchy that had risen to power under the First Republic or the *Merina* high families of the Central Highlands) and paved the way for the development of a class of nouveaux riches. Yet the importance of this system lock-out is not as straightforward as it seems. Politically speaking, the strict control of political activity, repression of opponents and ban on certain parties may well have cut down the number of legal parties and made for one-sided election results: the FNDR's single list won 96% of the vote in the 1976 general election while AREMA scooped 117 of the 137 seats in the 1983 election. After winning a 95% 'yes' vote in the 1975 referendum, D. Ratsiraka was re-elected president a first time in 1982 with 80.1% of the vote against Monja Jaona, the only authorised candidate. Yet the Malagasy economy's downward spiral and political upheavals on the international scene (fall of the Berlin Wall, the La Baule speech, etc.) marked the onset of political dissent first seen in the urban and farmer movements of the mid-1980s, especially the bloody clashes between Kung-Fu fighters and the TTS (*Tanora Tonga Saina*[91]) in late 1984 (Rakotomanga Mijoro, 1998; Raison-Jourde, 2002).[92]

[91] Young and aware of the future and their place in society.

[92] The Kung-Fu fighters were middle and upper class individuals, mainly sons of the families of prominent civilian and military figures, who were members of a highly structured martial arts

Also important was the new weight of the churches on the political stage. There are no full data available on the proportion of Christians in Madagascar. However, one estimate based on the Demographic and Health Survey (1997 EDS) puts the figure at nearly 75%. We know that Christians top 90% of the population in urban areas and that the number of practising Christians is extremely high. In Antananarivo, for example, two-thirds of the inhabitants attended a place of worship at least once a week in 1997 (Roubaud, 2000). This shows the influence these places of worship and the sermons they preach can have on people's behaviour. In 1972, the historical Christian churches of Madagascar – i.e. the Protestant Reformed Church (Calvinist) and the Anglican, Lutheran and Catholic churches – had very little indeed to do with the political crisis. Under the Second Republic, however, they became much more closely involved. A Malagasy Council of Christian Churches (FFKM – *Fikambanan'ny Fiangonana Kristianina eto Madagasikara*), an ecumenical council of the four historical churches, was formed in November 1979. From its first national conference in 1982, the Council set itself the task of contributing to the Nation's recovery. From 1989 to 1991, the FFKM's public positions[93] and major liturgical gatherings, 'where homilies focused largely on freedom and human rights' (Tronchon, 1995), made it a vehicle for political opposition and the emergence of civil society. For example, the National Election Observation Committee (KMF/CNOE; Komity Mpanaramaso ny Fifidianana/Comité National d'Observation des Elections) was set up in its footsteps in 1989 (Galibert, 2011a).

Economic Power and Political Power

On the economic scene, the vast majority of nationalisations were of foreign firms, leaving free rein to companies owned by nationals. The scale of nationalisation did not therefore prevent a large private sector from existing, even before the free-market about-turn. In 1991, the public sector may well have accounted for less than a third of formal GDP and just 3% of all jobs (World Bank, 1995).[94] This enabled members of the *Merina* high families to

club and tended to be opposed to the regime. The TTS, members of an informal organisation of unemployed youths who were distant cousins of the 1972 ZWAM, made it their business to infiltrate and disrupt opposition demonstrations by looting and committing other offences to enable the forces of law and order to legally intervene.

93 For example, a public statement made in 1982 said, 'It is as if one group were cornering the power and decisions and making off with outrageous benefits' (Jacquier Dubourdieu, 2002).

94 Very few industrial data are available on this period, let alone data that differentiate between the public sector and the private sector (Razafindrakoto, 1994). Where some publications give the figure of 60% of output produced by public enterprises, they never quote specific studies.

continue to profitably run their businesses in the socialist period without being party to the regime. Such was the case, for example, with C. Andriantsitohaina and his firms Viro and Prochimad, and with A. Ramaroson and his soap company Savonnerie Tropicale (World Bank, 1995). Others may even have benefited from this period, gaining monopoly positions for their products. Raison-Jourde (1993) mentions the case of the monopoly in medicinal drug imports by Cofarma, a company headed by pharmacist G. W. Razanamasy.[95] Over this period, then, there was no head-on opposition between the regime's supporters and these formal elites, some of whose members incidentally also continued to hold political positions (Colonel Rabetafika, for example, was appointed Inspector General of the Army after being found not guilty in the Trial of the Century).

The free-market watershed of the early 1980s brought a relative remodelling of the economic landscape by opening up economic opportunities. Privatisation formed a new source of private wealth for the *Merina* high families owing to 'their better knowledge of the Anglo-Saxon world, crucial in discussions with international bodies' (Raison-Jourde, 1993). The first wave of privatisations therefore tended to concentrate capital in the highlands sector (Jütersonke & Kartas, 2010). In the coastal regions, a small bourgeois oligarchy had already taken advantage of central government shortcomings to build efficient public investment misappropriation systems (Fauroux, 1999). Trade liberalisation gave them more power over the local economy (e.g. the Rajabaly, Kaleta and Solo Dollar families; Rakotondrabe, 1993). New entrepreneurs also sprang up on the back of foreign finance. This was particularly the case with M. Ravalomanana, a *Merina* from a farming family who secured a World Bank loan to set up dairy firm Tiko, which grew into a veritable empire in the space of a few years (Randrianja, 2005; Vivier, 2007). Lastly, companies owned by non-Malagasy were once again able to set up and win back market shares. This was seen especially in the commercial sector with Chinese and Indo-Pakistani firms whose owners, like the Barday and Ismail families, had often long been established in Madagascar. Some French groups (Bolloré and Fraise) also took advantage of the privatisation programme to position themselves in such areas as the production and sale of agricultural products (tobacco, sisal, etc.), drinks production and distribution and mining (World Bank, 1995).

Yet this did not mean that the leaders of the dominant party were ousted from the economic positions. Three million dollars in gifts given to

[95] On this point, see the discussion in the readers' letters (*Courrier des Lecteurs*) section of *Politique Africaine*, no. 53 (1993).

D. Ratsiraka by Colonel Gaddafi and Saddam Hussein, for example, were ploughed into Procoops managed by his sister-in-law and wife to defence minister H. Raveloson-Mahasampo. This business, turned into a limited company, grew into a sprawling corporation and developed highly profitable operations in all areas: trade in zebu, plantations (rice and cassava), cheap housing construction, import–export, mining, etc. (Leymarie 1989a, 1989b).

***

The period that opened in 1972 and continued with the Second Republic did break with the previous period in some respects. It was marked by the Malagasisation of the economy and society, a source of restored pride for the Malagasy people, with the firm purpose of creating a new social order in which the old hierarchical and geographical distinctions would be abolished. These points hammered home in the official speeches most certainly guaranteed the ruling party strong popular support, at least in the early years. Yet the fact remains that the political order continued to be highly centralised and personalised, in the tradition of the previous ruling powers. From this point of view, the period is more a continuation of than departure from the previous political formulas. The former elites were restricted in their access to the economic and political power that they had previously virtually monopolised, while a new ruling clan grew up around the president and his party. However, failure of the country's reforms set in motion the 1980s' economic openness that was to re-stimulate competition and the gradual political liberalisation that would enable the rise of dissent and popular expression of frustrations, especially by the middle classes (abstention from the 1989 presidential and general elections, protests in urban centres, student strikes, etc.). In fact, neither the socialist period nor the structural adjustment period lived up to the stated ambitions of reducing inequalities, whether between regions (especially between highlands and coastal regions), urban and rural areas, or between hereditary elites and lower classes. This phase actually saw the gap widening between farmers (and informal sector workers to a lesser extent) and state and the capitalist system since the scrapping of the fiscal minimum tax, the failure of the *fokonolona* reform and the impression of having been abandoned by the *fanjakana* now made them 'uncaptured' players.[96]

Figure 2.2 shows the distribution of power among the groups of players (1972–91).

[96] In his 1980 book on Tanzanian socialism, G. Hyden shows that the peasantry was not 'captured' by the capitalist market economy and the state and that it retained its exit option by withdrawing into a subsistence economy.

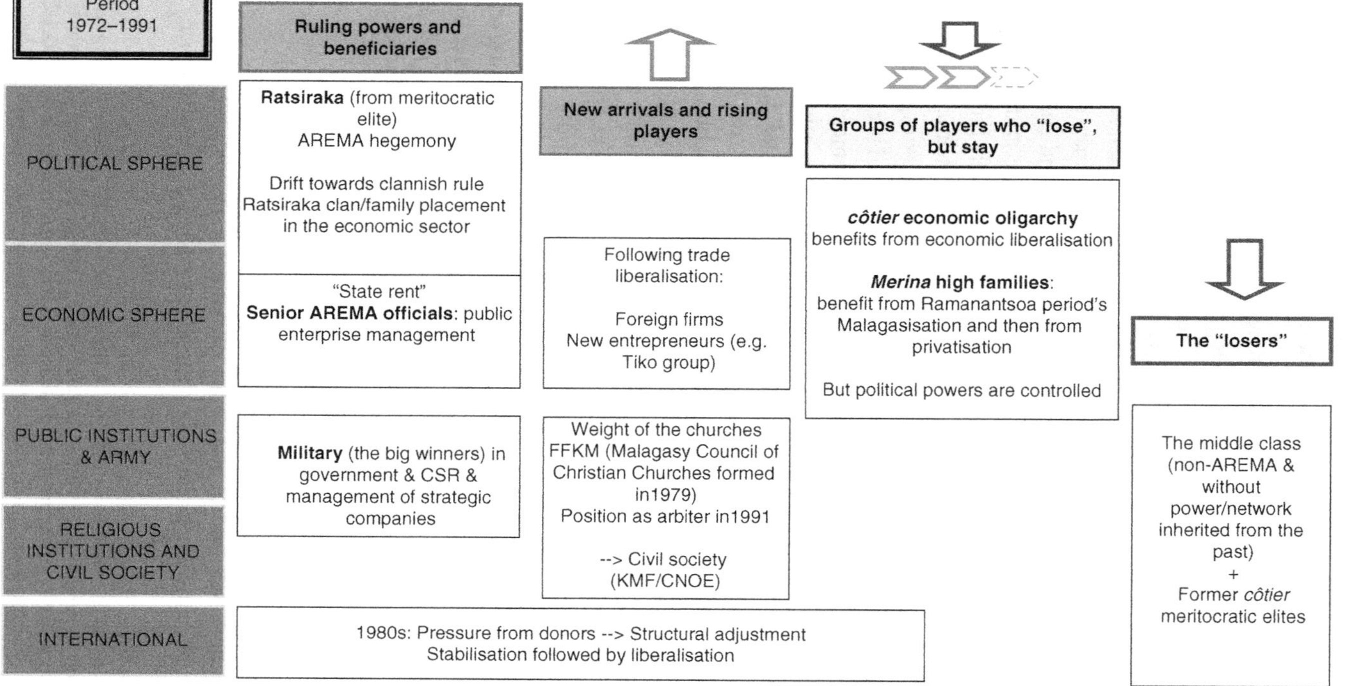

Figure 2.2 Distribution of power among the groups of players, 1972–1991.

2.5 From 1991 to 2002: The Ups and Downs of Economic and Political Openness

The disputed outcome of the March 1989 presidential election marked the start of a massive protest movement.[97] Under pressure to liberalise politics, the president wound up the FNDR in 1989 and reinstated the freedom of establishment of political parties in 1990. Yet this did not stop the movement, which united under the name of Forces Vives (Active Forces) and, following daily demonstrations and its launch of a general strike, formed an insurrectionary government in June 1991. The bloody crackdown (30 dead and 203 injured) on a demonstration in August 1991 and the attempt to play the 'ethnic' card[98] (Rakotondrabe, 1993; Leymarie, 1995; Fauroux, 1999) ultimately undermined D. Ratsiraka's credibility. He was forced to appoint G. W. Razanamasy, mayor of Antananarivo and eminent member of the *Merina* haute bourgeoisie, as prime minister and enter into negotiations with Forces Vives. These talks led to the Panorama Convention in October, sealing an agreement to form a transitional government to which A. Zafy, Forces Vives representative and former health minister under Ramanantsoa's government, was appointed President of the High State Authority and G. W. Razanamasy Head of Government while D. Ratsiraka remained President of the Republic.

The churches played a distinct role in leading the movement of 1991 with their peaceful revolution, punctuated by chants and prayers, a far cry from the events of 1972 (Urfer, 1993; Raison-Jourde, 1995; Tronchon, 1995; Ralibera, 2008). Having set itself up as a political arbiter back in 1990, the FFKM helped resolve the conflict by organising a number of national consultative forums, the last of which culminated in the signing of the Panorama Convention. Following this, the FFKM was made partner to the new government whose institutions (High State Authority [HAE] and Committee for Economic and Social Recovery [CRES]) were set up 'under its responsibility and management' (Galibert, 2009).

The Ebb and Flow of Democratisation

Democratisation was one of the main demands of the 1990–1 protest movement. The interim government therefore passed a constitution by

[97] D. Ratsiraka won the election with 62.7% of the vote (against 19.3% for MFM leader Rakotonirina Manandafy, 14.9% for M. Razanabahiny (VITM) and 3% for Monja Jaona.

[98] For example, the drive for the provincial assemblies to set themselves up as 'federal states' triggered a certain number of violent anti-*Merina* and anti-government actions in Toliara and Antsiranana, which raised fears of civil war.

referendum restoring the two-chamber system and establishing a parliamentary system in which the National Assembly had the power to control the executive by appointing the prime minister and to remove the president from office. The head of state's term of office, referred to by the constitution as *Ray amandreny*, guardian more of moral authority than executive power, was also reduced to five years renewable once. The state's new political organisation was therefore designed to put an end to the extreme concentration and personalisation of power found in the previous periods (Cadoux, 1993). In February 1993, northerner A. Zafy, a former Ramanantsoa government minister married into the Zafimahova family, one of the *côtier* high families, was consequently elected President of the Republic by direct universal suffrage (with two-thirds of the vote to D. Ratsiraka's one-third).

Yet this new balance of political power was a key source of political fragility. The March 1990 reinstatement of the freedom of establishment of political parties had already seen a proliferation of new political parties, representing individual interests more than social groups or political ideas. The June 1993 general election consequently had 121 political parties and organisations in the running,[99] encouraged by the proportional representation system.[100] A total of 26 of them were ultimately represented at the National Assembly (Pierre Bernard *et al.*, 1998). Although this multiplicity did not initially prevent A. Zafy from obtaining majority support, it undermined the development of a consistent economic policy and propelled Madagascar into a period of serious instability. A. Zafy's four years in the presidency saw a string of three different prime ministers and five governments. The policy-related conflict between A. Zafy and his Prime Minister M. Ravony, supported by a majority of MPs, led the president to call a constitutional referendum in September 1995[101] to give back the president the power to appoint his prime minister. This political coup replaced M. Ravony with N. Ratsirahonana as prime minister and recentralised power, but it did not prevent MPs from passing a vote of no confidence in the government eight months later followed by a motion to

[99] The number of parties has been on the rise ever since. There were more than 180 parties in 2009 and more than 340 in August 2012. Source: Act 2009-002 on Political Parties and Madagascar Interior Ministry website in August 2012.

[100] The choice of this voting system had been endorsed as much by pro-Ratsirakas as by Forces Vives supporters because neither of the two 'configurations' was sure to win the majority in the event of an election on a majority basis (Rakotoarisoa, 2002).

[101] Just over 70% of registered electors went to the polling stations, with 64% of them voting for the constitutional amendment.

impeach the president for violation of the constitution (Pierre Bernard *et al.*, 1998; Roubaud, 2000).

So following a few months during which the prime minister was appointed acting president, Madagascar held a free, transparent presidential election in late 1996 for the second time since the popular events of 1991. However, the dispersion of political parties meant that the run-off pitted the same two candidates, A. Zafy and D. Ratsiraka, against each other as in 1993. Victory ultimately went to the latter. Yet a record number of voters stayed away from the polls (50.3%), reflecting the people's disenchantment with democracy and rejection by part of the urban middle classes of the choice they had been given (Roubaud, 1997a). At the end of the day, Ratsiraka was elected by just one-quarter of the potential electorate. D. Ratsiraka hence returned to power, but having this time dropped any reference to socialism and now flying the flag of liberalism. In March 1998, he in turn had a new constitutional reform passed by referendum,[102] considerably consolidating the presidential powers (appointment and dismissal of the prime minister; appointment of the highest judicial authorities, namely the President of the High Constitutional Court and the First President and General Prosecutor of the Supreme Court; and dissolution of the National Assembly) and at the same time limiting the power of parliament (which could now only call for temporary impediment of the president solely for reasons of physical or mental incapacity).

The constitutional reform also provided for the creation of autonomous provinces (Antananarivo, Antsiranana, Fianarantsoa, Mahajanga, Toamasina and Toliara), as legal entities with administrative autonomy, in a logical extension of what had been conceived in 1991 to save the Second Republic. The public protests of 1990–1 had been particularly marked in Antananarivo, inhabited mainly by highlanders who were 80% *Merina*. D. Ratsiraka had endeavoured at the time to uphold his regime by playing on ethnic sentiments and old anti-*Merina* resentment. To this end, he had rallied the support of 'traditional' provincial authorities (*tangalamena*) in a blaze of publicity and pushed for the creation of a federalist movement. These moves had given rise to a National Conference of Federated States in his home city of Toamisina and a certain number of violent incidents in September 1991 (Delval, 1994; Fauroux, 1999).

The 1998 referendum's creation of the autonomous provinces therefore had less to do with democratic decentralisation than with a strategy to consolidate

[102] 'Yes' won with 51% of the votes cast by the 70% of electors who turned out.

presidential power with the support of provincial authorities supposed to represent their constituents. In fact, the autonomous provinces remained largely under the authority of the head of the executive, who appointed a Government Delegate General for the Devolved Administration in each province and had the constitutional right to dissolve the provincial council (the local elected parliamentary assembly) for 'assignable causes'. Moreover, although the autonomous provinces were effectively created by an Act of 22 August 2000, the majority voting system and the fact that other parties were thin on the ground in the provinces gave the upper hand to AREMA[103] in the provincial elections to largely dominate the provincial councils and thereby control the provincial executives: the six elected governors were all members of AREMA (Rakotoarisoa, 2002). This political lock-out, combined with a new 'AREMAisation' of the administration and upbeat macroeconomic performance, ushered in relative political stability for six years. It brought a time when those close to the regime, first and foremost the president and his family, were again able to use their political positions for personal gain (Randrianja, 2005; Randrianja & Ellis, 2009). However, democratic disenchantment subsequently grew as already seen from the rising number of voters staying away from the polls in the different elections. A 1997 survey found, for example, that the vast majority of the public were highly critical of the political class (84.9% said it did not reflect their concerns) and of democratic governance in general (Razafindrakoto & Roubaud, 2003a).

Entry into Free Market 'Modernity'

As seen earlier, the many liberalisation and state divestiture measures taken in the 1980s following the country's disastrous closure in the 1970s failed to curb the downward trend that had started in the previous decade. It was not until 1988 that per capita GDP started to show a glimmer of improvement. Yet the popular events of 1991 compromised this upward path and the civil unrest and political instability from 1991 to 1993 triggered a slump that sent per capita GDP tumbling 8.9% (Paternostro *et al.*, 2001). Political dissension also had direct repercussions on the economy in the period that followed. It created a climate of confusion that discouraged private investors and held up negotiations with international donors at a time when the country was financially strangulated and highly dependent on foreign aid. In 1994, as Madagascar's economy continued to slide, infighting broke out between the prime minister in

[103] Which became the Association for the Rebirth of Madagascar in 1997.

support of the austerity measures recommended by the multilateral organisations and the head of state in favour of 'parallel financing' of dubious origin to escape the Bretton Woods institutions' oversight. This political battle saw the suspension of international aid payments, which resumed only after A. Zafy was replaced as head of state in late 1996. The country's macroeconomic growth echoed this political instability and the fears it spawned, staying extremely low at 0.1% per year from 1991 to 1997. At the same time, the introduction of a floating exchange rate in 1994 saw a 300% depreciation of the Malagasy franc and a new inflationary surge[104] (Razafindrakoto & Roubaud, 2002b; Dorosh *et al.*, 2003; Gastineau *et al.*, 2010).

D. Ratsiraka's return to power, despite his slim electoral victory, brought a temporary end to the political instability and ushered in a new growth cycle, which lasted through to the political crisis of 2002. For the first time since the beginning of the 1980s (aside from the brief upswing in 1988 and 1989), per capita GDP resumed what proved to be an increasingly sharp growth path. D. Ratsiraka applied the liberal formulas advocated by the IMF and embarked on a new wave of privatisation. As with the first wave of privatisation, undertakings were sold off at a much undervalued price enabling those well-informed, financially empowered individuals close to the power base to buy them for a song (World Bank, 2009). The agreement signed with the Bretton Woods institution prompted the other multilateral and bilateral donors to resume their activities in the country and gave Madagascar the benefit of the cancellation and treatment of part of its external debt by the Paris Club. The improved socio-political environment was hence clearly one of the reasons for the positive momentum in this period for the first time in three decades. Growth was driven first by an upturn in domestic demand owing to an increase in consumption enabled by shrinking inflation and a rise in wages, especially in the public sector, but also to recovering public and private investment. A certain number of foreign investors, for example, mounted operations in the country to take advantage of the upbeat business climate, some of the world's cheapest manpower, export processing zone status and the new possibility to buy land on 99-year leaseholds. Yet this growth was also the result of an extensive change to the country's economic organisation in the 1980s. Industrial exports became a key driver in this, replacing traditional agricultural products with their slow-growing demand on the world market. This industrialisation movement was manifest in the remarkable increase

[104] 36.9% in 1994 and 48.4% in 1995.

in the weight of industrial export processing zone exports, from 2% in the early 1990s to nearly 40% of all exports in 2000 (Cling *et al.*, 2005). At the same time, traditional products (coffee, vanilla, cloves, pepper and cocoa) shrank from 38% of the total value of exports in 1990 to just 14% of export earnings in 2000. This wholly exceptional state of affairs for sub-Saharan Africa, with its rather poor trade performance over the period (Gros *et al.*, 2001), hence reflected Madagascar's capacity to move in modern economic circles (Razafindrakoto & Roubaud, 2002b).

However, this growth further widened the country's historical spatial and social inequalities. Growth was essentially urban, if not entirely Antananarivian. Competitive industries and export processing zones developed mainly in and around the capital (Radert, 2008), while rural and coastal output posted much lower growth. So although urban poverty fell sharply from 63% to 44% (and from 39% to 19% in the capital) over the period, poverty held steady in the rural areas at around 77% (Gubert & Robilliard, 2010). This mediocre performance by the agricultural sector may have been partly due to often-negative climate conditions, but it was also a sign of the great divide in the country. Many rural areas were lacking in infrastructure and small producers were fragmented with little contact with the market economy. These factors stood as a barrier to growth in food production despite price liberalisation, which should have stimulated food output (Roubaud, 1997b). In addition, catastrophic government intervention policies (trade regulation, price fixing, taxation, etc.) in the traditional export sectors, particularly cash crops (vanilla, coffee, cloves, etc.), made at best for stagnation in these sectors and at worst for an outright collapse in export earnings (vanilla) even as they locally secured 'inordinate profits for the local potentates who monopolised their trade' (Raison-Jourde & Raison, 2002). The urban world also remained deeply divided itself with the poor gaining little or nothing from the economic upturn (Razafindrakoto & Roubaud, 1999).

***

The 1990s marked a certain number of changes in Madagascar's socio-political organisation. Democratisation empowered the expression of new aspirations, but also generated a high level of political instability. The ebb and flow of political liberalisation saw the spread of new forms of collective mobilisation by the old and new churches – especially those founded on Pentecostalism and the Revivalist Movement (Gingembre, 2011) – and by non-governmental organisations to a lesser extent (Droy, 1996). These NGOs may well have often been set up 'at the initiative of foreign entities . . . to capture development rent', but a certain number of them really were nascent civil society organisations. Such is the case, in particular, with the National Election Observation Committee (KMF/CNOE) created in 1989 and later with SeFaFi (*Sehatra Fanaraha-maso ny Fiainampirenena* – Public Life Observatory) set up in February 2001. However, these civil society bodies generally remained top-down organisations headed by a few key figures (generally women) from the upper classes of Malagasy society. For example, Madeleine Ramaholimihaso, member of a *Merina* high family,[105] was (and still is) Honorary President of both the KMF/CNOE and SeFaFi. The country's 'liberal modernity' also contributed to the spread of economic individualism, which ran right through Malagasy society as seen from the development of corruption at all levels, the appearance of the '4'mis' (homeless in Antananarivo; Andrianarivo-Razafimanjato, 2000) and, in an extreme example, the proliferation of ancestral tomb raiding for bone peddling (Randrianja & Ellis, 2009). Yet these changes still did not prevent the persistence of characteristics inherited from the previous periods: strong discord between elites, tendency towards the concentration and personalisation of power, and the rural world overlooked if not passed over altogether.

Figures 2.3 and 2.4 summarize the distribution of power among the groups of players (1991–2002).

2.6 From 2002 to 2009: The Ravalomanana Era or the Fusion of Political, Economic and Religious Powers

The 2002 Crisis

The political stability of the 1996–2002 period was really merely skin-deep. It was based on a 'reconcentration' of political power and a positive economic climate in which political competition may have seemed less important to uphold and extend the former elites' positions. Yet behind it lay two other phenomena whose roots reached further back: the rise of new business players in the modern sectors most integrated into the global economic system and

[105] 'Daughter of Joseph Ramanandraibe, the industrial merchant (collection, import–export and chocolate maker) who made his fortune in the colonial period at the head of one of the leading Malagasy import–export companies and a number of rice-processing factories, she is from one of the *Merina* high families of *Andriana* origin. Founder and head of a chartered accountant's, she is married to Rahaga Ramaholimihaso, publisher of *La Tribune*. A devout Catholic, she is also one of the lay representatives of the Church in Madagascar with privileged access to the Vatican (*The Indian Ocean Newsletter*, 2002).

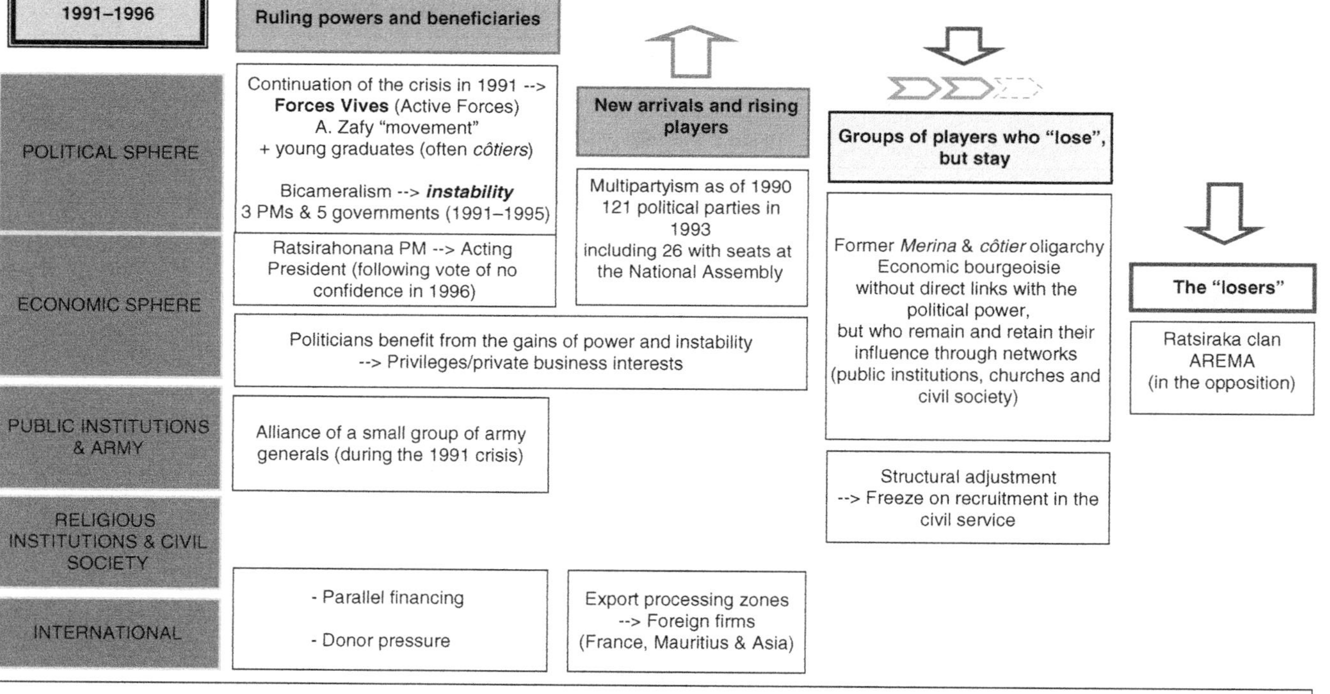

Figure 2.3 Distribution of power among the groups of players, 1991–1996.

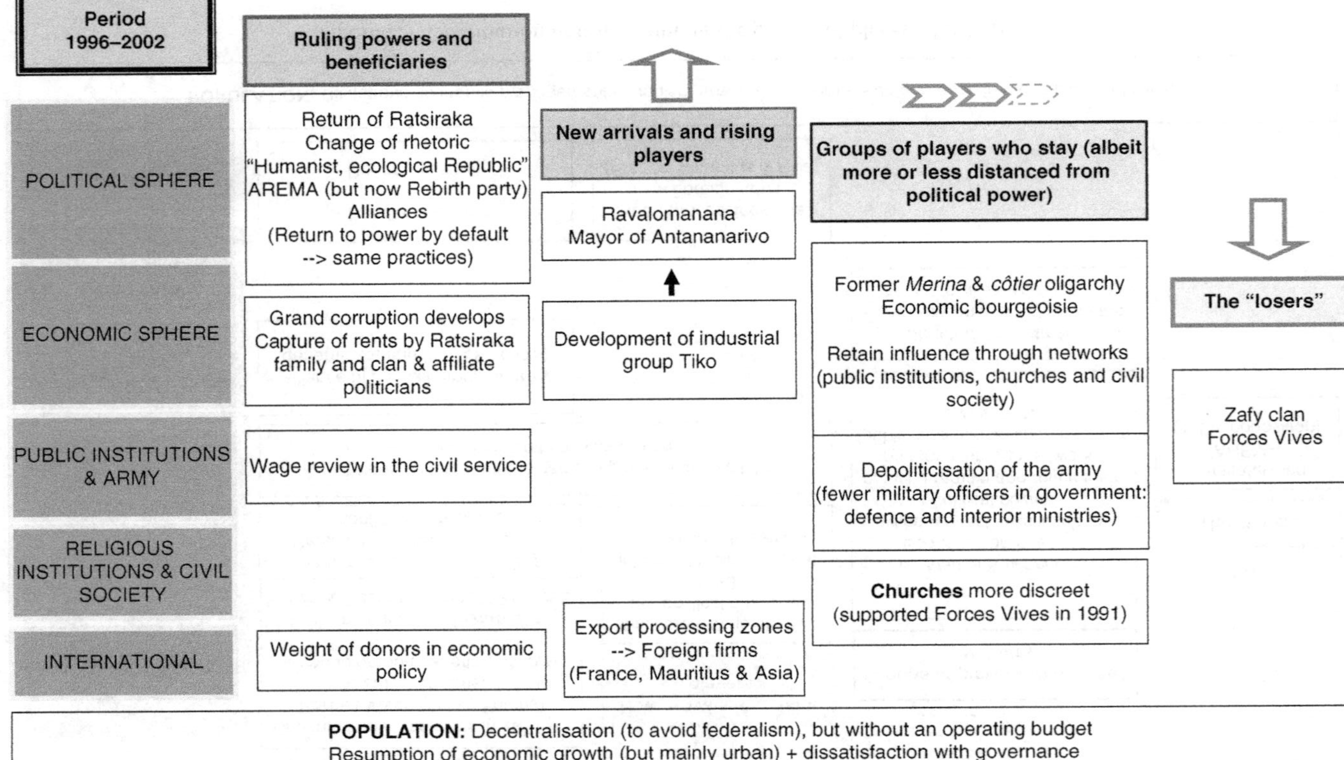

Figure 2.4 Distribution of power among the groups of players, 1996–2002.

the population's simmering profound rejection of the political class. This is the context in which to situate M. Ravalomanana's appearance on the political scene and understand the events of 2002.

The 1980s drove the emergence of a new generation of entrepreneurs, who 'cashed in on light industry, riding the wave of global economic liberalisation and supported by the international financial institutions' (Randrianja, 2012b). Some of them entered politics in this period (such as M. Ravalomanana and Herizo Razafimahaleo), seeking to impose a new economic order to grow their businesses. As mentioned above, M. Ravalomanana is a *Merina* businessman from a farming family that made its fortune from the economic openness of the 1980s. During this decade, as the politico-economic elites' increasingly patent corruption and nepotism brought them into disrepute with the population, his career path embodied the dream of social change that could make individual merit and integrity pay. Consequently, entering politics under the banner of 'Tiako Iarivo'[106] with a powerful communication campaign, he won the 1999 Antananarivo mayoral election by a large majority against a political insider, son of Pastor Andriamanjato (former leader of the AKFM and mayor of the capital from 1959 to 1975). Yet his aura and popular political support emanated from more than just his extraordinary, meteoric rise in business relatively independently of the political power.[107] They also came from his religious observance, seen from his deep devotion to the Church of Jesus Christ in Madagascar (FJKM), Madagascar's leading Protestant church of which he was to become vice-president in 2000.[108] This commitment, in a general climate of religious revival and expansion, was seen as a guarantee of moral standards and personal disinterestedness, a far cry from the alleged amorality of the old political elites.

Riding high on his success in the Antananarivo local elections, he stood in the presidential election on 16 December 2001, drawing on considerable financial resources (his campaign had the use of an airplane and several helicopters) and numerous support committees often steered by FJKM pastors. His fresh political rhetoric based on an all-out business start-up and growth campaign combined with his

[106] 'I love the thousand.' Antananarivo is etymologically the city of the thousand. Opinions differ as to where this name comes from.

[107] There is more to this last point than meets the eye. He owes his take-off to a loan from the World Bank whose representative in Madagascar, José Broffman, subsequently became a shareholder in Tiko. M. Ravalomanana also largely benefited from various tax breaks and customs relief under Zafy's government (Raison-Jourde & Raison, 2002; Randrianja, 2005).

[108] He was again re-elected to this office in the 2004, 2008 and 2012 elections.

message of newfound unity in religious faith spoke to a young electorate in search of justice. Voter turnout, galvanised by the nature of this election, was relatively high in the first round compared with the previous presidential election (nearly 70% as opposed to 50% in 1996). Yet a dispute over the results was to spark a political crisis that virtually split the country in two. Whereas the Interior Ministry announced a probable run-off between M. Ravalomanana and D. Ratsiraka, Ravalomanana's support committee (which had used its extensive logistical means to collect the results directly from a large share of the polling stations) and the Independent Election Observation Consortium (which notably included the KMF/CNOE) both considered that M. Ravalomanana had won the election in the first round. More than six months of political conflict followed. Mass protests involving thousands of demonstrators were held in the cities and especially in Antananarivo. These in turn set in motion a general strike that ended up convincing M. Ravalomanana to declare himself president two months later (22 February) and set up a parallel government. D. Ratsiraka responded by moving his government to Toamasina, decreed the new capital by the governors of the five coastal provinces, and his troops set up barricades on the main roads to choke Antananarivo (Rakotoarisoa, 2002). The country was only really freed from its paralysis once the High Constitutional Court had pronounced M. Ravalomanana the winner of the election on 29 April 2002. This announcement was followed by international recognition of Ravalomanana's government in June, the former president's departure from the country in July (to the Seychelles and then France) and, lastly, the regular armed forces' entry into 'liberated' Toamasina (Pesle, 2006).

Who were the political and social forces in this crisis? The country's geographical divide during the crisis might point to an ethnic division between *côtiers* and highlanders. Yet this notion does not stand up to scrutiny, as shown by a 2002 study on the results of the election of 16 December 2001 (Razafindrakoto & Roubaud, 2002a). It makes it clear that although there was definitely some regional voting (the candidates won more votes in their home regions), it was in no way enough to explain the distribution of scores. By extension, the hypothesis of an ethnic choice evaporates, confirming what one of the authors had already found in previous elections (Roubaud, 2000). In Antananarivo, for example, D. Ratsiraka won 20% of the vote, which is much higher than the *Betsimisaraka* electorate (1% of the capital's inhabitants). Conversely, M. Ravalomanana won 41% of the vote in Toamasina, which is twice the proportion of *Merina* living in the city. Yet the study revealed other dividing lines. The Ravalomanana vote by *fivondronana* (prefecture) was found to rise with level of education and where turnout was higher and had grown the most since the previous elections. The authors therefore concluded that a vote for M. Ravalomanana expressed a rejection of the previous regimes by the most critical segments, those most disenchanted with the political world.

Yet if there was no regional or ethnic divide between the two candidates, what was the country's deep geographical rift from February to June 2002 all about? Aside from what may have to do with specifically Malagasy cultural traits, the relatively low level of violence observed (it is estimated that the crisis claimed fewer than 100 lives), given what might have happened in a country that looked on the verge of civil war, reveals the partially fabricated nature of this split. The blockades set up by D. Ratsiraka supporters on the roads to the capital were actually manned by paid militia[109] armed with military hardware supplied by Algeria (Randrianja & Ellis, 2009). They rarely saw any large-scale violent confrontations,[110] although they did make substantial profits for those operating them.[111] Meanwhile, the deeply divided army kept its distance from the events pending the High Constitutional Court's announcement in April 2002 when it ultimately swore allegiance to the victor (Rabenirainy, 2002). Only a handful of officers and non-commissioned officers openly sided with D. Ratsiraka out of loyalty, appearing in some regions 'as veritable warlords alongside some of the regime's barons' (Randrianja, 2005).

Note, however, the role played by the regional governors put in place by D. Ratsiraka and whom he had tasked with organising the resistance. Seeing this as an unprecedented opportunity to boost their political and economic clout, four of them dealt a particular blow to the social climate by declaring their provinces independent in May 2002.[112] These independences were driven mainly by a provincial oligarchy's hunger for power. They had no real

[109] D. Ratsiraka also tried to use foreign mercenaries, but the French Foreign Ministry intervened to have the airplane flying them to Madagascar return to France just a few hours after take-off (Ramasy, 2010).

[110] History remembers especially the attempt by young Kung-Fu fighters from the capital to blow up the Brickaville barricade in mid-March.

[111] The blockades were actually quite porous, representing more than anything a source of financial gain for their operators (Raison, 2002).

[112] These were the provinces of Antsiranana, Toamasina, Toliara and Mahajanga. The other two provinces, Antananarivo and Fianarantsoa, the country's most populated provinces, remained under the control of M. Ravalomanana's self-proclaimed government.

economic basis (Toamasina, for example, had its port bringing in large tax revenues from customs duties and charges, but most exports and imports were to and from Antananarivo) and hardly reflected the people's aspirations.[113] However, as with the federalist movement in the second half of 1991 (Rakotondrabe, 1993; Fauroux, 1999), they bore the seeds of a certain number of ethnic crystallisation and political criminalisation phenomena (Raison-Jourde & Raison, 2002). The churches, among the main architects of the political resolution to the 1991–2 crisis, did not play a role of mediator this time round because most of their members apparently stood behind M. Ravalomanana, including the Catholic Church. Many priests and nuns in cornets joined top EKAR (Roman Catholic Church) dignitaries to parade before M. Ravalomanana in 13 May Square, proclaiming his slogan from the Gospel according to Saint . . . Mark, 'Don't be afraid, just have faith!'[114]

Last but not least, there is the question of the importance of the protests and the length of the general strike in Antananarivo, Mahajanga and Fianarantsoa. The general strike was called in 13 May Square in late January and was not lifted until two months later. Such a long strike in a country where most households live on the breadline could well point to the extent of popular support for the Ravalomanana candidate, but the length of the strike was also due to the fact that many strikers continued to receive their wages during the period. Such was the case, for example, with the civil servants for whom a special organisation was put in place to enable the Treasury to pay their wages.[115] Yet it was also the case with employees of firms in employers' organisations such as *Groupement des Entreprises de Madagascar* (GEM – Confederation of Trade Organisations of Madagascar, headed by Charles Andriantsitohaina). Back at the start of February, GEM struck an agreement with the main Malagasy trade unions to rapidly resolve the economic crisis and protect business interests against acts of vandalism in return for continuing to pay the strikers' wages.[116]

113 In Antsiranana, Toliara and Mahajanga, M. Ravalomanana had won a large majority of the vote in the first round of the presidential election (AFP, 2002).

114 *Aza matahotra fa minoa fotsiny ihany*. This slogan was also blazoned on all the Tiko lorries.

115 On 18 February, the Central Bank and the primary banks of Antananarivo opened their doors to this effect, giving rise to long queues and the lifting of some roadblocks.

116 Also indirectly marking its opposition to D. Ratsiraka, GEM moreover objected to the transfer of the Central Bank's prerogatives to the provinces and criticised barriers to the movement of goods and persons.

The Ravalomanana Period: Fusion of Political, Economic and Religious Powers

M. Ravalomanana's election manifesto promised rapid economic growth based on industrial development in compliance with the Washington Consensus prescriptions on stabilisation, privatisation and liberalisation. From this point of view, the political agenda, even with its poverty reduction window dressing, was no different from the previous government's programme. A first massive wave of investment was ploughed into public infrastructure (particularly improvements to ports and main roads linking the country's capital with the six provincial capitals[117]). This was followed by an economic strategy (Madagascar Action Plan – MAP) to develop the private sector and encourage foreign investors to set up operations in natural resource-rich regions (creation of the integrated growth poles of Fort Dauphin, Nosy Be, Antsirabe and Toamasina during his second term). These moves secured the country a growth rate of nearly 5% per year from 2006 to 2009. The free market transition set the economy bounding further forward. The number of days required to establish a company, for example, was slashed from 67 in 2000 to 7 in 2007 (Randrianja, 2012b).

The Ravalomanana era was also marked by a significant improvement in the country's international governance indicators: public financial management, control of corruption, public procurement regulation, control of financial fraud and money laundering, independence of the justice system, and the role of civil society and the media. The creation of an Anti-Corruption High Council (CSLCC) in 2003 and an Independent Anti-Corruption Bureau (BIANCO – *Bureau Indépendant Anti-Corruption*) in 2004 substantially rolled back petty corruption in the country (Razafindrakoto & Roubaud, 2003b; Razafindrakoto *et al.*, 2009a). In terms of freedom of expression too, the period saw growing numbers of newspapers and radio stations, often speaking very freely. All of this made the Madagascar of the 2000s a real model of success in the eyes of the international community and donors, warranting their full attention and support.

Yet these economic and political performances appear in a different light when considering the characteristics of the growth in question and delving more into the political order. Growth in the first presidential term was driven less by the expansion of the private sector than by public

[117] 'In seven years, the regime built 9,000 km of tarmacked roads, much more than all the governments put together since Independence' (Randrianja, 2012b).

expenditure, financed in good part by foreign aid. Note here the considerable weight of foreign aid in Madagascar in the 2000s. It accounted for, '40% of public spending and two-thirds of government revenue, twice the amount in Tanzania, Mozambique and Senegal' (World Bank, 2009). Moreover, tax breaks on many industrial inputs intended to support national industry did not stimulate exports but widened the trade gap due to the increase in import volumes. The ensuing currency depreciation was flanked by a sharp surge in inflation (22% in 2004 and 11.4% in 2005). The price of imported rice, a staple of the Malagasy diet, shot up 2.5-fold from 2003 to 2005. In the second term, private and foreign investment was strongly concentrated in a small number of projects, especially those in titanic iron ore and nickel mining (Sheritt and QMM/Rio Tinto projects). This kind of international specialisation was a step backwards compared with the previous decade (whose productive vibrancy had been driven largely by the boom in export processing firms), in that it made for an enclave economy poor in jobs and disconnected from the local productive fabric (Gastineau *et al.*, 2010b). The upshot was a geographical concentration of growth, which, given the 'absence of government fiscal equalisation and migratory problems due to the remoteness of certain regions', actually widened inequalities and failed to significantly reduce the poverty rate, contrary to the Poverty Reduction Strategy Paper goals (in 2006, more than 85% of Malagasy were still living on less than $2 a day; World Bank, 2009).

Turning to governance, anti-petty corruption and pro-press freedom success stories glossed over an underlying tendency towards power concentration and presidential autocracy. The president was using his position at the head of state to restrict competition with his company's products (see later) and roll back political dissent (mainly with spot tax audits). Freedom of expression was effectively fettered as seen from a number of political measures ranging from the closure of private radio stations in Toamasina and Toliara in 2004, the non-renewal of the French RFI correspondent's visa in 2005, and the expulsion of Christian Chadefaux, founder of the *L'Express* newspaper and editor-in-chief of the *Les Nouvelles* newspaper, through to the closure of the Viva TV station in 2008 (which was to spark the subsequent crisis).

***

M. Ravalomanana's arrival in office marked a decisive change in the way political elites were elected. Ravalomanana was neither a descendent of a high family, part of the academic elite (having left school very early and with a poor command of French) nor a member of the military elite. His rise to power was based solely on his meteoric business career and his religious devotion. Yet he did not break with the Malagasy political mould. In fact, he accentuated the system's main traits: political control by a hegemonic party, extreme presidentialisation and the clannish seizure of power. As soon as he took presidential office, like Ratsiraka with AREMA and Tsiranana with the PSD before him, he founded his own party, *Tiako i Madagasikara* (TIM),[118] in a nod to his agribusiness group Tiko. TIM won a huge majority in the 2003 general election (106 of the 160 seats) and local elections against a weak, divided opposition[119] and further strengthened its hegemony in the 2007 general election (105 of the 127 seats), not least because an amendment to the elections act reduced the weight of the most densely populated regions where opposition strongholds were traditionally found (World Bank, 2009). Hence during M. Ravalomanana's terms of office, the National Assembly once again became more of an executive decision registry office and endorsement body than an independent source of legislative proposals.[120] Presidentialisation can also be seen from the considerable growth in the number of presidential aides and the tenfold increase in the presidency's budget from 2003 to 2008 (World Bank, 2009). Political centralisation was stepped up again following the 2007 adoption by referendum[121] of a new constitutional amendment. This amendment replaced the autonomous provinces with regions (numbering 22) for which M. Ravalomanana directly chose the regional leaders, enabling the president to rule by decree 'according to extraordinary circumstances of which he remained the sole judge, without clearly defined time limits,' and reducing the number of MPs from 160 to 127. Centralisation also took shape with the late 2007 change to the status of the *Fokontany*, whose heads were no longer elected, but 'appointed by the district head, as the government's representative reporting to the interior minister' (Galibert, 2009).

This extreme political concentration also gave the president the means to expand his economic power. His food (dairy, oil and flour) and drink production and distribution companies benefited from tariff protection measures (taxes of some 20% on imported products that were identical to those they produced) and tax breaks on their inputs, giving them a virtual

[118] I Love Madagascar.

[119] AREMA lay decapitated: a large number of its leaders, in exile abroad, were judged in absentia and given prison sentences, dissuading them from returning to the country.

[120] From 2003 to 2006, the National Assembly tabled only 8 bills as opposed to 218 from the executive (Jütersonke & Kartas, 2010).

[121] The 'yes' won 75% of the vote, but with just a 44% turnout.

monopoly position[122] and huge business growth. Over the 2002–9 period, the president's Tiko group expanded its business beyond agribusiness moving into the media, construction, publishing and even oil sectors, and quadrupling its turnover (Randrianja, 2005; D'Ersu, 2009; Pellerin, 2009; World Bank, 2009). The blurring of the dividing line between economic and political powers and their strong concentration in the hands of a small group of people hence attained a record level. 'TIM headquarters were on the premises of Magro (Tiko's agrifood distribution subsidiary) just like the Tiko group company Alma long had its head office in one of the public works ministry annexes' (Pellerin, 2009). Those who ended up being dubbed the 'Tiko Boys', i.e. Tiko group company directors, were more than often found on ministers' staff, heading state agencies and managing public enterprise.[123]

In addition to this fusion of political and economic powers came President M. Ravalomanana's ambition to reinforce his power in the religious sphere. His accession to power owed a great deal to his religious activism and support for the FJKM. Following his March 2006 announcement of his intention to transform the Malagasy regime into a theocracy, he proceeded to remove the constitution's reference to secularism in the 2007 constitutional amendment. Prior to this, he was re-elected vice-president of the FJKM in 2004,[124] while the president of the National Assembly and TIM member, Jean Lahiniriko, became its treasurer. Over the same period, he was also the most generous donor to the highly powerful Malagasy Council of Christian Churches (FFKM), thereby supporting many of its eminent members, both Protestant and Catholic. Incidentally, Jacques Sylla, a Catholic, was appointed prime minister at Cardinal A. Razafindratandra's suggestion (Pigeaud, 2006).

Figure 2.5 summarizes the distribution of power among the groups of players, 2002–9.

122 Tiko also developed other strategies to win market share. For example, 'In 2008, Tiko managed to get the American firm Seaboard Corp., partner to the Malagasy Prey group in Les Moulins de Madagascar, to withdraw from Madagascar by means of flour price dumping. Prey subsequently went bankrupt, resulting in 600 direct-job losses, and tax harassment forced Prey's CEO, Edgard Razafindravahy, into exile' (D'Ersu, 2009).

123 Although the government pursued its privatisation programme, it kept holdings in numerous non-strategic companies. It remained a shareholder, for example, in the hotel business (Carlton), fisheries (Pêcherie de Nosy Be), textiles (Cotona and FITIM), timber (Fanalamanga), drinks production and distribution (Star), the airline, the telecommunications company, and granite and marble quarrying (World Bank, 2009).

124 He was re-elected in 2010.

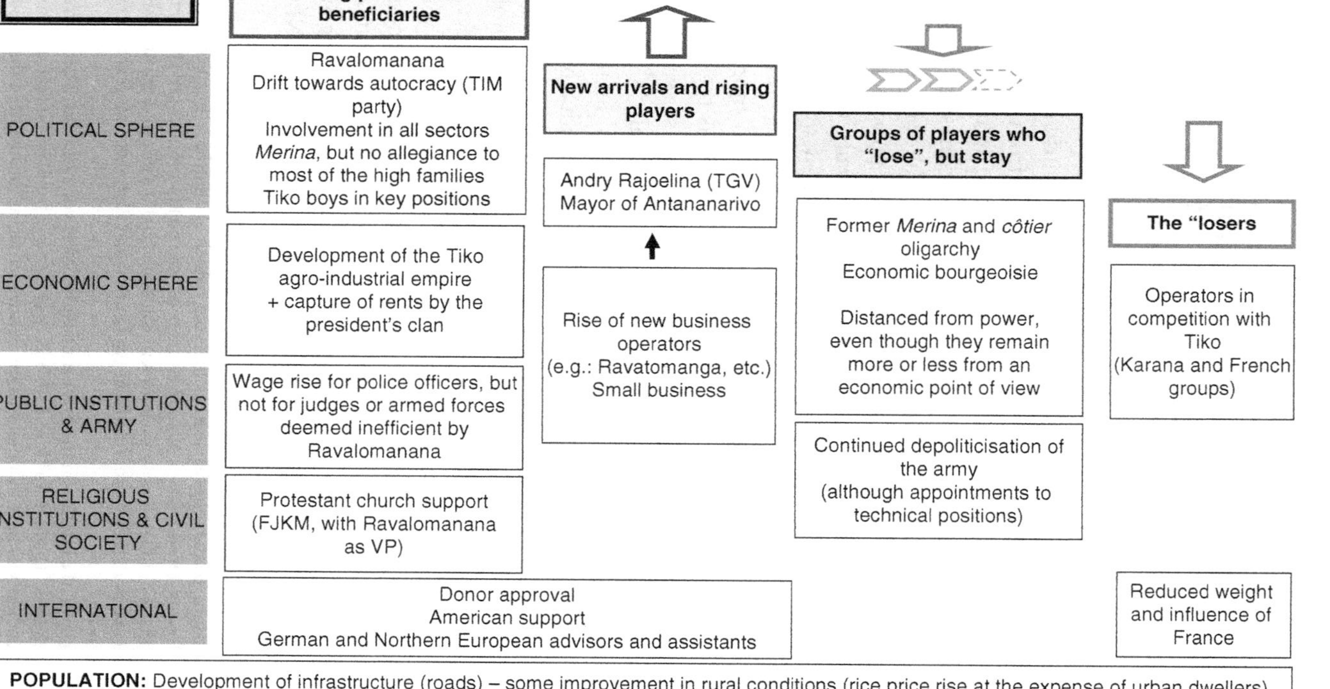

Figure 2.5 Distribution of power among the groups of players, 2002–2009.

2.7 From 2009 to the Present Day: State Decline

M. Ravalomanana enjoyed strong popular support, as seen from the results of the first round of the presidential election in 2001,[125] his re-election in 2006[126] and, to a lesser extent, the adoption by referendum of the 2007 constitutional reform.[127] The 2005 and 2008 Afrobarometer surveys also clearly show his popularity: nearly 65% of Malagasy said they had confidence in the president at the very time when the mood was rather one of distrust of the political world. Yet his support waned in urban areas (from 60% to 52%) and among the most educated Malagasy (from 67% to 44%) from 2005 to 2008. In 2008, more than one-third of individuals with a secondary education or higher felt that freedom of expression was not respected and more than 65% were not satisfied with the way democracy was working (Razafindrakoto *et al.*, 2009b). The ruling power's monopolisation of the public and economic arenas was actually fuelling deep resentment and discontent in some segments of Malagasy society.

Some therefore shifted gradually towards dissent. Such was the case with the members of the politico-economic oligarchy who had more or less managed to maintain their positions under all the previous regimes and whom the ruling power was quick to tackle head on. It was also seen among the *Merina* politico-administrative elite who had dynastically[128] held the most important positions (central bank, commercial banks, finance ministry, etc.) in the past and who had found themselves gradually dispossessed of their prerogatives. It was the case, too, for economic operators (including some members of the historical 'high families') whose profits had been undercut either by free market transition reducing the protection they had enjoyed in their trading activities or by the government's anti-competitive practices in areas touching on the Tiko group's businesses (D'Ersu, 2009; Pellerin, 2009). As early as 2003, SIM (*Syndicat des Industries Malgaches*; Federation of Malagasy Industries) spoke out against the policy of tax breaks on imports and, in November 2008, CONECS

125 The first count placed him at 46% of the vote, which should have guaranteed him election if a run-off had taken place. Although he was finally pronounced the winner after months of conflict, Razafindrakoto and Roubaud (2002) show in close analysis of the official results of the first round that he could not actually have won more than 50% of voter turnout.

126 In 2006, he won the election in the first round with 55% of voter turnout. There were 13 other candidates. Turnout was low, with 38% staying away from the polling stations.

127 The referendum was held in a highly impromptu manner at the height of the flooding (Galibert, 2009b). In addition, turnout was just 44%.

128 The same names went back to the First Republic (Galibert, 2009; Randrianja, 2012b).

(National Economic and Social Council; *Conseil National Economique et Social*) chaired by André Ramaroson (also CEO of soap company Savonnerie Tropicale) organised a demonstration of more than 800 people in Antananarivo (Pellerin, 2009).

The relative decline in the importance of the army in society was also a source of concern and discontent. As mentioned earlier, the army had been closely involved in political affairs since 1972. The government sought its unfailing support with highly political promotions, making the Malagasy army one of the most star-studded in the world (one general for 100 soldiers; Rabenirainy, 2002; SeFaFi, 2003; Ramasy, 2010). The period starting in 1991 had driven a demilitarisation of government (especially under the Zafy governments, which counted no more than two military officers). This had contributed to the army's expulsion from the political arena, as seen from its refusal to take a stand in 2002 (albeit also the mark of its internal wrangling). This movement continued in part under M. Ravalomanana. Although he was careful to assign government posts to representatives from each of the armed forces (gendarmerie, police, army and navy), he launched a depoliticisation and demilitarisation policy in 2003. In 2004, he appointed a civilian defence minister for the first time ever in Malagasy history. At the same time, he set out to weaken the army's power by increasing central government control over pay and pensions management, promoting colonels instead of generals to positions of command in the army (with no regard for previously prevailing rank and seniority hierarchies), announcing his intention to downsize the army (retirement of generals, recurrent bids to close the Antsirabe Military Academy, etc.), confining the army to a humanitarian rural security role and giving precedence to the paramilitary police force (gendarmerie) over the army. All these elements were instrumental in creating 'strong resentment within the armed forces' (Randrianja, 2005; Ramasy, 2010, 2012).

Lastly, the churches, which had appeared to unanimously back M. Ravalomanana (against D. Ratsiraka) in 2002, also ended up deeply divided. Religious rivalry weakened the previous consensus. This caused a rift among the Protestant churches (Gingembre, 2011) and set in part the Catholic Church, more involved in civil society associations and refusing to support the head of state's increasingly authoritarian rule, against the leading Protestant church (the FJKM), which felt duty-bound to support the regime by dint of the head of state's involvement within it. So the Catholic Church ended up in a way on the side of the opposition and was consequently subject to state harassment (deportation of Jesuit Father S. Urfer, ban on broadcasts, etc.; Galibert, 2009; D'Ersu, 2009). In the conflict that followed, the Catholic Church, in the person of Cardinal Odon Razanakolona, moreover openly supported A. Rajoelina against M. Ravalomanana (Gingembre, 2012).

The 2009 Crisis

These are the opposition forces that led to M. Ravalomanana's overthrow in 2009. A challenge to his rule had already been expressed in the capital in October 2007 when the population abstained en masse from the general election following the constitutional reform: 75% of the capital's electorate stayed away from the polls. This discontent was aired again with the first-round election[129] of Andry Rajoelina as Mayor of Antananarivo in December 2007 against the TIM party candidate and PDS (Chairman of the Special Delegation) of Antananarivo. Even though the scale of abstention from this election (57%) is a clear indication that he was swept to power less for his personal qualities than as an anti-government protest, Andry Rajoelina nevertheless had two assets that were to attract support from a population desirous of change: he was young (33 years old at the time) and a stranger to the world of politics. Born into a modest middle-class *Merina* family, he amassed a small fortune with his printing and advertising company Injet. The company, linked to major advertising agency Domapub, owned by his wife's family, quickly cornered the market in billboard advertising in Antananarivo. It has been alleged that Andry Rajoelina chose to stand for mayor primarily to defend his company's business interests (D'Ersu, 2009). In 1994, he also organised his first Live concert, a major annual concert attracting tens of thousands of young people 'in a social mix rarely seen in Antananarivo' (Galibert, 2009). These young people also formed a sizeable pool of support.

Andry Rajoelina's ascension was a positive threat to the president of the republic, who did everything in his power to foil him. The decisive catalyst was the government's closure of Viva TV (purchased by the young mayor in 2007) in December 2008. In response, A. Rajoelina led a series of rallies in January 2009 targeting freedom of expression and protesting against the government's political practices (including the purchase of a second presidential airplane and plans to provide 1.3 million hectares of land to a South Korean company on a free 99-year leasehold). These rallies were attended by 15,000 to 30,000 people at a time, mainly young people from the 'lower parts' of town who saw

[129] He won 63% of the vote.

them as an outlet to voice their dissatisfaction. Rajoelina was supported in his struggle by some leading figures who saw it as an opportunity to put an end to M. Ravalomanana's rule. He received more or less explicit support from eminent members of civil society such as Madeleine Ramaholimihaso and Nadine Ramaroson (also members of 'high families'), political figures such as Roland Ratsiraka (D. Ratsiraka's nephew, mayor and member for Toamasina and 2006 presidential candidate), Alain Ramaroson (leader of the Masters political party and André Ramaroson's brother) and Monja Roindefo (leader of MONIMA and son of its founder Jaona Monja, himself also a 2006 presidential candidate), members of the Catholic Church and even Christian fundamentalist FJKM dissidents (D'Ersu, 2009; Gingembre, 2011).

In late January 2009, in an echo of the events of 1991, A. Rajoelina formed and assumed the leadership of a High Transitional Authority (HTA). A demonstration degenerated into looting. The national television and president's MBS TV buildings were looted along with Tiko group warehouses. On 7 February, the presidential guard opened fire on demonstrators marching on the presidential palace, killing more than 30 people. It was this event, breaking the taboo of resorting to violence, which lost M. Ravalomanana his credibility and finally made him 'agree' to relinquish power. On 17 March, he signed an order transferring full powers to a military directorate of senior army personnel. Yet these top-ranking officers were captured by officers from the Army Corps of Personnel and Administrative and Technical Services (CAPSAT – *Corps d'Administration des Personnels et Services de l'Armée de Terre*) following their mutiny a few days earlier. They handed power back over to Andry Rajoelina while M. Ravalomanana fled to South Africa.

From Rajoelina to Rajaonarimampianina

A. Rajoelina set up a High Transitional Authority and assumed its leadership. What was supposed to be merely an interim government ended up as a fixture in the Malagasy landscape. Ad hoc institutions were formed (Transitional Congress – CT, *Congrès de la Transition* – and High Transitional Council – CST, *Conseil Supérieur de la transition*) and their members appointed to give the illusion of national representation. Seats were assigned to each party and civil society organisation according to their presumed weight and in such a way as to guarantee national coverage. However, the regime only managed to stay in power at the cost of a veritable merry-go-round of cabinet reshuffles, a surge in MP numbers (from 160 before the crisis to 356 in November 2010 and 526 in December 2011) and gagging freedom of speech including myriad forms of intimidation, demonstration bans and restricted demonstration possibilities,[130] convictions of journalists,[131] and trials and threats of proceedings for defamation.[132] The opposition was weak and failed to rally the masses or form a truly united front. The army, cosseted by the new regime, which showered promotions and financial perks on NCOs and officers alike, kept largely to the sidelines despite five mutinies and/or attempts to foment a coup d'état.[133] A freeze on a large part of international aid seriously cut back the regime's budget revenues until it signed a roadmap in September 2011 setting out the steps for a return to political normalcy. This drying up of international aid prompted the authorities to seek new sources of funding such as rosewood exports (Randriamalala & Liu, 2010), mining exploration contracts signed with foreign companies and financial support from private sector businesses. The lack of any real control over these operations opened the floodgates for large-scale trafficking, rising corruption and massive embezzlement within the administration. The disappearance of public investment and slowdown of economic activities weighed on growth. Roads and healthcare infrastructure deteriorated while poverty grew and education waned. Crime shot up in the cities and also some rural areas where *Dahalo* (cattle rustlers) terrorised the population and ran circles around the security forces.

The return to free and fair elections in 2014 did nothing to stem the decay. President H. Rajaonarimampianina was elected with very little support winning, like D. Ratsiraka in 1996, just over one-quarter of the potential electorate's vote. He was unable to rally enough political and economic players around him to govern

[130] This was not just symbolic: the new City Hall inaugurated in December 2010 (City Hall had been destroyed on 13 May 1972 during the Malagasy Republic's first political crisis) now took up most of 13 May Square (renamed Love Square), seriously limiting its capacity to assemble angry crowds.

[131] In January 2013, two opposition journalists were sentenced to three years' imprisonment for 'Affront to the public institutions and law enforcement forces, unauthorised demonstration and destruction of property.'

[132] Including against Raymond Ranjeva, a major opposition figure, for aiding and abetting the November 2010 mutiny attempt, *Tangalamena* P. Zakariasy for speaking out against a rosewood mafia in late 2012, and against Alain Ramaroson.

[133] March 2009, May 2010, November 2010, March 2012 and July 2012. These 'mutinies' do not appear to have been the expression of political forces. They never involved more than 30 or so soldiers, only saw low-level fighting if any (two dead in May 2010 and three dead in July 2012) and were often driven purely by sectional demands (May 2010 and March 2012).

properly. The semi-parliamentary system reintroduced by the 2010 constitutional reform showed cracks from the outset, just as the 1991 movement's system had, with the National Assembly's inability to clear a stable majority. First, it took over three months to propose a prime minister. Then, the head of state had to reshuffle the cabinet four times in four years, including appointing a new prime minister, and only much wheeling and dealing and changes of political affiliation within parliament kept him in power. He had to cope with a motion by MPs to remove him from office for constitutional violation in June 2015, which was rejected by the High Constitutional Court, followed by a narrowly rejected vote of no confidence just a few days later.[134] In May 2016, the National Assembly moved to impeach the president for high treason, but the move was rejected by the HCC in June of that year. His fragile rule ended with Hery Rajaonarimampianina defeated in the first round of the 2018 presidential elections winning just 8.8% of the votes cast, a particularly low rate in a country where the legitimacy associated with the position generally makes for a high level of popular support.

Far from disappearing, the trafficking in natural resources symptomatic of a mafia economy, if not 'criminal governance' to use the term coined by J. Ramasy (Bat, 2016), thrived[135] and the government proved powerless to control the violence and insecurity created by zebu rustling in particular (Pellerin, 2014, 2017). The social climate took a turn for the worse with a growing sense of insecurity, the spread of mob justice[136] often leading to clashes with the police,[137] a rise in land disputes and other socio-political signs of simmering social discontent,[138] and even the 'micro' military

[134] The motion was not passed only because of MPs' high absenteeism: it was approved by 95 votes as opposed to the 102 votes required. Just 17 MPs voted against it.

[135] In June 2014, 3,000 tons of rosewood from Madagascar were seized by the Singapore authorities, a higher volume than all seizures worldwide in the previous decade. The cargo was returned to its Chinese 'owners' a year later (Butler, 2014, 2015).

[136] The High Commissioner for Human Rights reported 108 cases of mob justice leaving 152 dead and 61 injured from July 2016 to August 2018 (OHCHR, 2018).

[137] Destruction of part of the Sucoma factory, looting and clashes with the paramilitary police in Morondava during a conflict between factory workers and management at a Chinese-run plant in 2014, a riot in Sambava in November 2015; rioting in Mampikony and Vatomandry in November 2016; and *Dahalo* rustlers lynched by a mob in Betafo in November 2016.

[138] Soamahamanina is a typical example of the growing land disputes. From May to October 2016, local residents protested violently against a Chinese company's permit to mine gold there, finally forcing the company to pull out (Pigeaud, 2017).

insurrection of November 2016.[139] On the economic front, political normalisation drove renewed economic growth in 2016 (the growth rate, estimated at 4.2% in 2017 and forecast at 5.0% in 2018, was higher than the average rate of 2.6 percent observed over the 2011–15 period and was ahead of the demographic growth rate). This growth driven by industrial production and exports (of a very small number of products) was accompanied by a downturn in the agricultural sector, meaning that the majority of the population did not benefit from the bonanza (World Bank, 2018).

The presidential elections at the end of 2018 saw 36 candidates in the first round, including the previous four presidents of the Republic. However, 33 candidates won less than 1.3% of the vote. The race was headed by the three most recent presidents: Hery Rajaonarimampianina (8.8% of the vote), Marc Ravalomanana (35.3%) and Andry Rajoelina (39.2%). The run-off was a ballot box repeat of the 2009 duel in the street and media between the latter two candidates. Andry Rajoelina was elected with 55.6% of the votes cast.

Although these elections were held in relative calm (Marc Ravalomanana supporter attempts to challenge the results in the street quickly died down), they nonetheless betrayed the fragility of the social balance. First, the exceptionally high abstention rate compared with previous elections (46% in the first round and 52% in the run-off) reflected the disaffection of a significant portion of voters. Second, the geographical distribution of votes revealed that they were highly polarised (see Map 2.1). Marc Ravalomanana got most of his support from the highlands, especially the region of Analamanga, while Andry Rajoelina achieved his best scores in the coastal regions. Although the two candidates were Merina and from the highlands (both had been mayors of Antananarivo, as is Marc Ravalomanana's wife, the current incumbent) and although Madagascar's different ethnic groups are highly unevenly distributed, this polarisation cannot be said to be the direct expression of an ethnic vote. However, it does clearly reflect differences in expectations between the less populated, poorer and more remote coastal regions and the more populated, more developed central regions. Marc Ravalomanana might therefore have appeared to stand for upholding regional inequalities and the domination of the central regions (or even 'Merina domination'),[140] while Andry

[139] On 10 November, Antananarivo City Hall was surrounded by armed soldiers for several hours following the arrest of one of their number by local police.

[140] His detractors often tried to portray him as racist ('*manavakavaka foko*') and he was forced to deny this claim on more than one occasion during the presidential campaign.

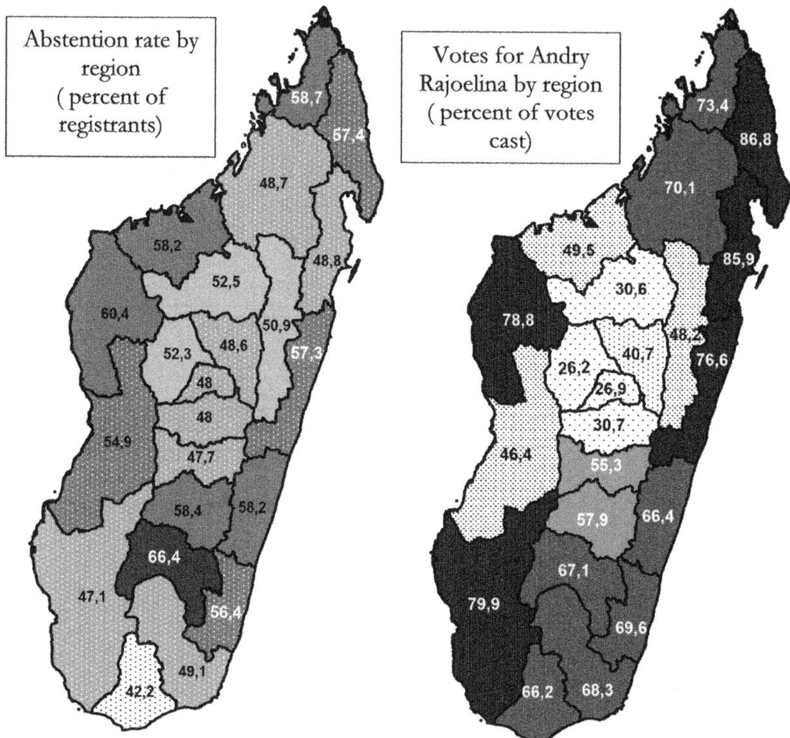

Map 2.1 Distribution of abstention and votes.
Source: HCC Madagascar (www.hcc.gov.mg); authors' calculations.

Rajoelina might have represented hopes of consideration and recognition of the coastal regions' interests. He certainly reaped the benefits of his many helicopter trips across the country, the plethora of resources deployed during the campaign (there is no legal ceiling on campaign spending), and the extravagant, all-out promises he made.[141]

Figures 2.6 and 2.7 summarize the distribution of powers among the players, 2009–18.

[141] Just some examples of his campaign promises are the construction of an Olympic swimming pool, a stadium with artificial turf and the largest power plant in Toliary; the transformation of the port city of Toamasina into Miami or the Malagasy 'Côte d'Azur'; cattle fitted with electronic chips to prevent zebu rustling and the use of drones to track thieves; an increase in the minimum wage to 200,000 Ariary; the construction of a vast six-lane avenue with suspended bridges in the capital; the construction of a new city to unclog the capital, etc.

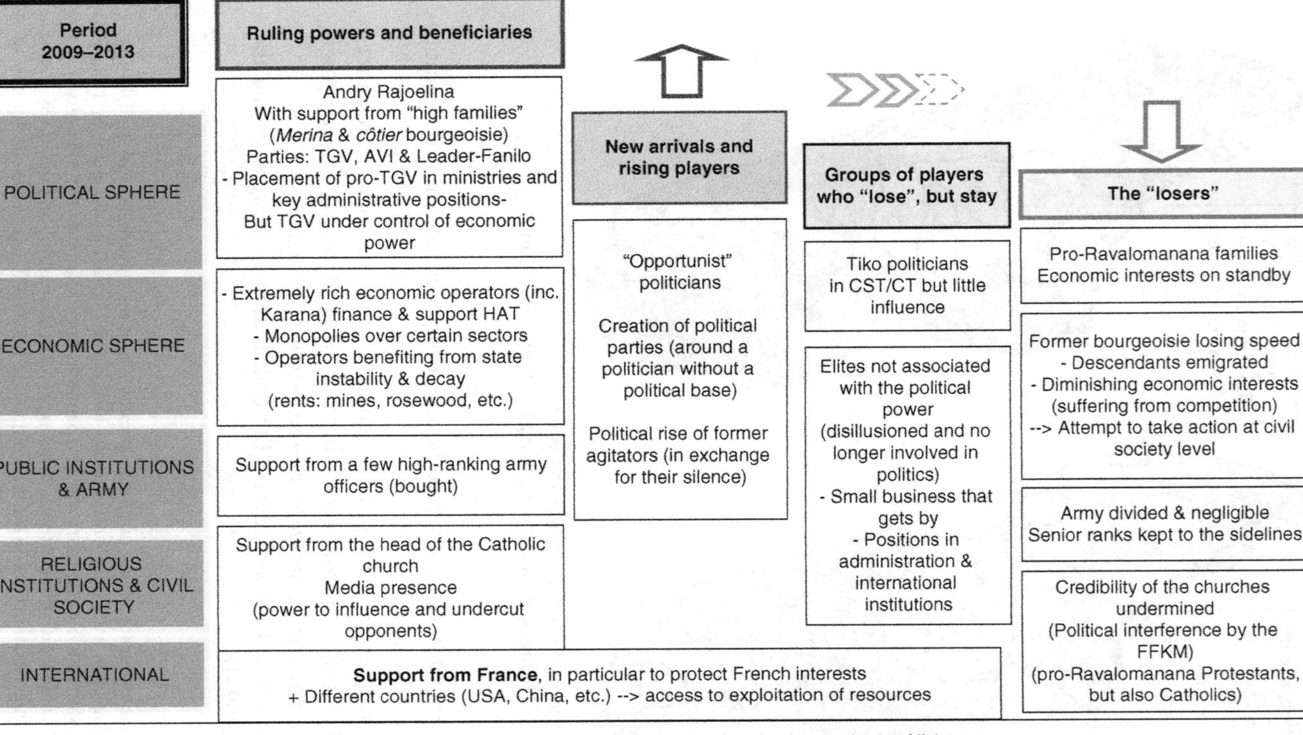

Figure 2.6 Distribution of powers among the groups of players, 2009–2013.

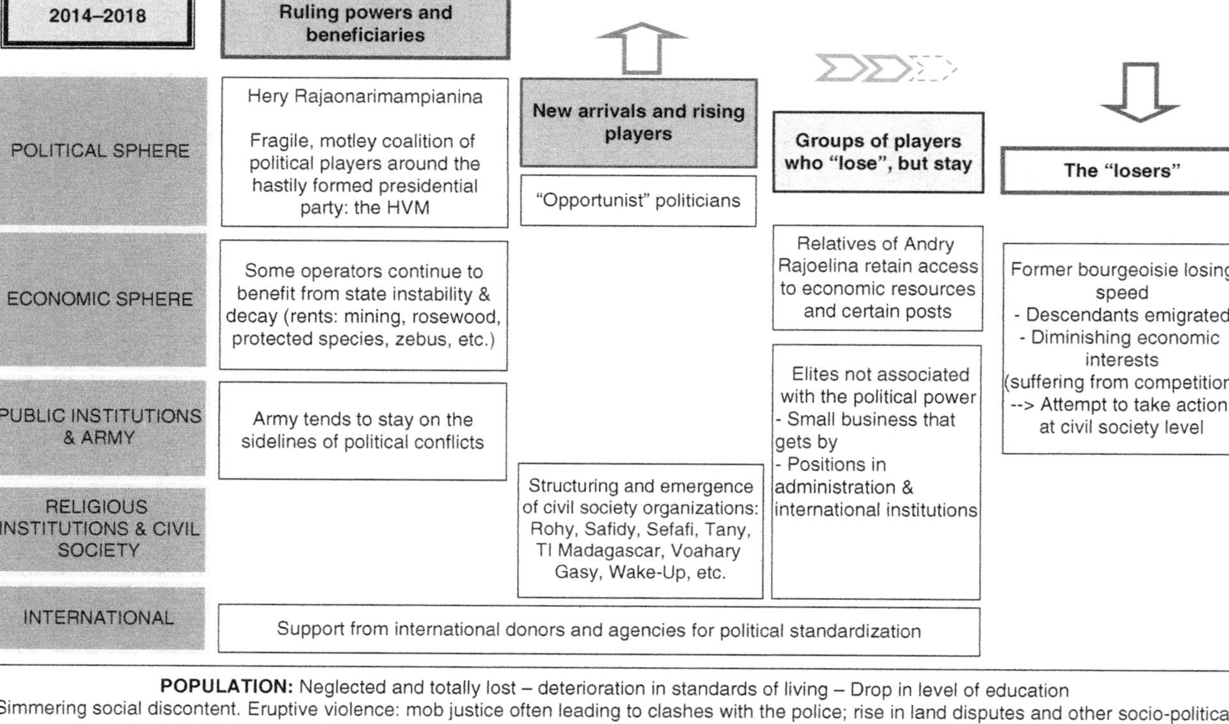

Figure 2.7 Distribution of powers among the groups of players, 2014–2018.

2.8 Conclusion

This review of Madagascar's history highlights the main developments in the island's economic and social regulation throughout its long history. Significant changes have taken place and we have seen the gradual expansion of the elite political and economic circle. The emergence of a meritocratic elite has been spawned by the institutionalisation of the state reaching as far back as the precolonial period, the abolition of slavery, the end to the status group system and the development of education. Similarly, political nepotism and the use of 'state rent' have driven the appearance of new political and economic players. At the same time, democratic aspirations have surfaced and found a voice to speak out against the different regimes' abuses and precipitate their fall. So the corridors of power do not appear to be impenetrable.

Yet the fact remains that behind the range of rhetoric and ideologies asserted over time, the system and practices at the highest levels of the state have barely changed. Neither the post-independence Malagasisation phase, the socialist years, the structural adjustment and liberalisation period, nor the coming to power of a self-made man from the rural world – let alone the 2009–13 so-called transition period or the subsequent period marked by the state's decline – has been able to uphold the principle of equity and reduce the inequalities between the hereditary elites and the lower classes, any more than between regions (especially between highlands and coastal regions) or between urban and rural areas. Irrespective of whether social position is by birthright or by merit in the rare cases of social advancement, the individuals concerned have generally used it to implement short-term strategies to manage and build their own economic and political power. No regime can claim to have enabled the country to really take off. In addition, in a mark of the elites' poor ability to form stable coalitions, 'all the heads of state since 1960 have been directly or indirectly brought to and/or divested of power by a political crisis' (Rabemananoro, 2014). The successive leaders since the First Republic have nearly always ascended to the head of state as the providential man, as the only possible alternative to end the previous regime. Each regime, fragile by nature, has systematically sought to increase its power by concentrating it, personalising it and securing the support of a small group of influential players (new *côtier* elites, party officials, church representatives, etc.). Unable to think outside of the short-term box, none has sought the support of the masses by trying to meet popular aspirations. Instead, neglect and exclusion of this vast, essentially rural, majority has been a constant throughout Madagascar's history. Yet it is precisely the accumulated discontents that have driven protest and regime overthrow every time, sometimes playing straight into the hands of political manipulation.

Economic rents in Madagascar have never been large, being small by nature or for lack of a growth strategy. However, for a country where poverty is preponderant and rents are shared among a very small number of players, whether hereditary elites or insiders, these revenues constitute both a goldmine and a source of major inequalities. Rents include those from the ownership of land and other real estate. The trading economy (coffee, vanilla, cloves and tea) that developed in the days of colonisation flourished for a time before stagnating and even declining in the 1980s and 1990s owing to the absence of suitable support policies and to international competition. However, the nationalisation of foreign businesses (in the 1970s) and subsequent privatisations (in the 1980s and 1990s) fostered the emergence of a small number of local entrepreneurs along with entrepreneurs from the *Karana* and *Zanatany* minorities. During this period, the better-informed individuals closest to the centre of power also sought to take advantage of the opportunities offered by free trade, possible exemptions, subsidies and large-scale public investments more or less legally appropriated. Despite the small size of the domestic market, the distribution of consumer goods is also a lucrative sector, in which the *Karana* are very present. The development of the export processing zone that began in the late 1990s has for the most part attracted foreign investors. There are very few nationals in this sector, as it is difficult to enter the highly competitive international market restricted to those with overseas networks. Yet the most easily accessible rents are those from foreign aid, which can be captured by means of public procurement contracts (civil engineering, institutional assistance, etc.). The appearance of new mining rents along with the illegal trade in precious woods could constitute a turning point in the 2000s in view of the sums involved, immeasurably higher than the aforementioned rents, and their potential source of destabilisation and major conflict. In short, rents in Madagascar have materialised mainly out of opportunities and benefits secured on a one-off basis (or over short periods) from inherited or acquired privileged positions in or connected with the corridors of power. These rents are beyond the reach of people outside the circle of power. Access and control are managed by individual or family strategies, not by group strategies.

3

Structural Assets

3.1 Introduction

Madagascar's long-term economy has displayed a virtually steady downward trend. None of the changes to either economic strategy or political system since the 1960s has managed to turn around this backslide. Classical development theories fail to explain this long-running economic underperformance. A review of the country's history finds a certain consistency of forms of power and governance along with the same groups of players in place over the years. Much like a jigsaw puzzle is pieced together, the following analyses seek to explain Madagascar's workings by singling out the society's main structural qualities.

In this chapter, we identify three strengths on which the country can depend: control of violence; its formal institutional capacities as shown by the dual economic (arrival of a class of new entrepreneurs) and political transition (democratic changes in power) as well as bureaucratic accomplishments, especially that of curbing corruption; and expression of the population's democratic aspirations.

Our approach draws on our knowledge of the terrain and existing analyses of Madagascar. It combines and compares an array of empirical material from quantitative surveys conducted from the mid-1990s to the present day with qualitative interviews of key figures in Malagasy society and findings from the analysis of the country's long history.

3.2 Social Order and Control of Violence

Control of violence forms the backbone of North, Wallis and Weingast's (NWW's) analysis. Stabilising the social order is seen as society's prime objective, and the state's ability to contain all forms of violence is a decisive feature as much of the different stages of natural states or limited access orders (fragile, basic and mature) as transition from the natural state to an open access order (see Box 1.1).

In open access social orders, the ability to form organisations with or without state consent ensures nonviolent competition in every area of society. Violence hence becomes illegitimate for use by any other than the state, in a way that is strictly governed by the legislative system. In natural states, they say, access to violence is open to anyone strong enough and well organised enough to use it, thereby forming a clear threat to stability. This is why a dominant coalition tends to form in these societies, with profitable compromises made between the most powerful groups as they restrict access to economic rents by other members of society. Moreover, most natural states also use patronage or clientage networks to extend certain forms of protection to non-elites. These form incentive systems that contain violence (by non-elites) and enable cooperation. Although NWW implicitly acknowledge the possibility of violence by non-elites, they claim that violence breaks out typically between elite factions trying to tip the previously made compromise in their favour. This is an inspiring theory, but it raises a number of questions when it comes to analysing Malagasy society's long-term workings.

Episodes of Violence: Flare-ups Rather than Deliberate Political Strategies

There seems to have been remarkably little political violence in the history of Madagascar since independence (see Box 3.1). The political crises and the changes of rule they have often entailed have occurred with very little physical violence to date. Unlike events in many other countries on the African continent, the conflicts have seen a relatively low number of cases of personal injury – whether in the form of loss of liberty, bodily harm or death – and they have been preceded, accompanied and/or followed by little political hardening (Figure 3.1).

Moreover, in times of unrest, the military have tended to keep a low profile and have sometimes even acted as mediators and peacemakers. Violence rarely transpires as a political resource in the hands of elite groups. Looking at the long history, the sporadic violence there has been neither controlled nor orchestrated by one or another elite group. No collective, concerted or really organised strategy to secure control and access to power appears to have been at work, considering that the popular uprisings of the first three crises in a way took the elites by surprise.

BOX 3.1 Portrait of Violence: A Review of Episodes of Instability over Half a Century

From independence to the end of the 1960s, the country experienced no marked episodes of violence. Violence emerged, on a small scale, in the early 1970s. In 1971, the farmers' revolt in the Toliara region led by MONIMA (*Mouvement national pour l'indépendance de Madagascar* – Madagascar for the Malagasy; Maoist political party) was joined by a mere thousand farmers attacking military posts and administrative centres with homemade weapons. This shows the feeble rallying capability of Monja Jaona's MONIMA. The movement was also kept in strict line by an oath to never kill, taken over a sacrificial cow. This made the rebellion not so much violent as threatening (Raison-Jourde & Roy, 2010). Yet repression by the political powers was brutal and violent nonetheless, reminiscent of the appalling methods employed by the colonial power in 1947. The authorities reported around 50 fatalities, though the figure was more probably in the region of 800 to 1,000 (Althabe, 1978; Raison-Jourde & Roy, 2010).

The general student strike of 1972 was essentially non-violent, even after the students were joined by ZWAM.[1] Lapses were indeed rare. Here again, the violence came from the government and not from the urban, student and proletarian youth. The arrest and incarceration of 395 students on Nosy Lava penal colony prompted a vast popular movement on 13 May (100,000 people in the streets of Antananarivo). It was then that the FRS (Republican Security Forces) opened fire on the crowd, triggering urban riots (cars ignited, barricades, pavements ripped up for use as missiles, an attack on the national radio station, City Hall burnt down, etc.). Despite Tsiranana's words, themselves particularly virulent,[2] 'only forty' were killed

[1] *Zatoyo Western Andevo Malagasy* (Malagasy Western Slave Youth) – *Zatovo* (youth), *Western* (due to their identification with cowboys), *Andevo* (slave), *Malagasy* – were an informal organisation of underprivileged youths from poor districts (the 'lower neighbourhoods'). They lived as outlaws and regularly clashed with the police. They marked their ascension in the political combat by becoming Zoam – Zatovo, Ory Asa (unemployed) eto Madagasikara – while maintaining a neighbourhood-based organisation (Raison-Jourde, 1972; Althabe, 1978; Randriamaro, 2009).

[2] 'If there have been many deaths, it's because you asked for it ... If you do not stop, your children will die. And so will you. It's as simple as that! I, the President, am telling you. Parents, workers, students, let me give you some advice. If you value your lives, do not join the strike ... If necessary, even if it takes 2,000 deaths, we will mow you down in one fell swoop! 2,000, 3,000 even! In one fell swoop! Blam! Now there's a death count. After that, even if there are 5,000, 6,000, 100,000 of you, we'll take you out! Blam! But that won't happen ... Do the right thing, eh? Walk away from this shady business' (quoted by Blum, 2011).

BOX 3.1 (cont.)

and 150 injured in these events, essentially on the side of the demonstrators (Blum, 2011). The elite groups remained very much on the sidelines of this conflict. Neither the police nor the army stepped in. The AKFM (political party with communist sympathies), representing the *Merina* elite ousted from political power, even took a stand against the unrest, which probably explains the torching of City Hall.[3]

However, the Malagasy economy's downward spiral under Ratsiraka in the 1980s saw something of a return[4] of social violence. In rural areas, the *Dahalo* phenomenon (cattle rustling in the Bara tradition) escalated and was met with a fierce crackdown by paramilitary police. In 1982, for example, on the pretext of flushing out the rustlers, gendarmes 'accidentally' killed a hundred peasants in the Toliara region. In 1989, a plethora of government strong-arm raids with a licence to shoot (Operation 'Tsy Mitsitsy', i.e. ruthless) reportedly left a further hundred dead. The unrest also spread to urban areas. A group called the TTS (*Tanora Tonga Saina*, i.e. aware youth) from working class neighbourhoods, like ZWAM before them, practised abductions, racketeering and black marketeering on the payroll of AREMA and D. Ratsiraka. In December 1984, more than a hundred members of the TTS were massacred by adherents of a Kung-Fu club. In this episode, the violence unleashed by the Kung-Fu fighters, as they were called, was not in principle in the service of any elite group (even though the Kung-Fu fighters acted as stewards at several MONIMA and MFM[5] demonstrations). Yet it did have political overtones in that the TTS covertly acted as the regime's shock troops. An attack on the TTS was therefore an open declaration of war on the government. So it was that, in July 1985, the regime retaliated and sent in tanks to destroy the Kung-Fu leader's villa. Dozens died and scores were arrested.

[3] The municipality of Antananarivo had been led by the party since independence. Generally speaking, the AKFM dominated the political scene in the province of Antananarivo.

[4] The term 'return' here alludes to the rebellion by the *Menalamba* who destabilised the French colonial state's establishment in Imerina from 1895 to 1898. This rebellion, often presented as an anti-French movement, was actually chiefly the mark of a sociopolitical implosion in a situation of Merina state decay. In this light, the Menalamba revolt may express a form of reaction to the domination of the *Hova* oligarchy and the Christian principles on which it was based (Campbell, 1991; Ellis, 1998).

[5] A Maoist party, like MONIMA, but urban and essentially Antananarivian, led by Manandafy Rakotonirina.

BOX 3.1 (cont.)

In March 1987, in the midst of an economic crisis, there was a spate of looting in shops owned by *Karana* (Indo-Pakistanis of Madagascar) in Antananarivo, Antsirabe, Toliara and Fianarantsoa. However, the systematic nature of these operations (known as OPKs or Anti-Karana Operations) cast suspicion on their real causes. Were they a kneejerk xenophobic reaction to the growing wealth of a stigmatised 'foreign' minority cashing in on the crisis or a manoeuvre to turn angry public opinion against the 'foreigners'?

In 1991, the social movement explicitly called for non-violence. This prevented the massive rallies on 13 May Square from ever getting out of hand. As in the early 1970s, the violence came from the government. A demonstration of 500,000 protesters marching on the presidential palace saw more than 30 killed and hundreds wounded, mown down by military gunfire on D. Ratsiraka's orders (Lavrard-Meyer, 2015). In these events, then, the political strength of the demonstrators, led by Forces Vives, was not in their potential violence, but in their sheer numbers. And it was indeed by such weight of numbers that they attempted to secure a solution negotiated with the government.

The 2001–2 crisis was also largely non-violent. Although some called it a civil war in the making as the country was apparently split in two, there were actually very few clashes and the death toll was 'only a hundred'. Nevertheless, the combatants in this case were clearly violent pawns in the pay of political groups: lumpenproletariat militia on D. Ratsiraka's side and army reservists on M. Ravalomanana's side.

However, the 2009 crisis marked if not a break, at least a deviation from the previous crises. The mass mobilisation was accompanied from the outset by roadblocks in the working class neighbourhoods and incidents of interpersonal violence (assaults). In the days that followed, reports came in from all over the country of the looting of Chinese and Indian shops, but especially Magro shops owned by the president. These events reported at least 68 fatalities, mostly due to the demonstrators' recklessness[6] (Vivier, 2010). A few days later, the presidential guard

[6] Some 40 charred bodies were found, for example, after the Magro shop in Antananarivo burnt down.

BOX 3.1 (cont.)

opened fire on unarmed demonstrators marching on the presidential palace, killing around 30 and wounding more than 200.[7] The president's attempt to resolve the crisis by handing over power to a military directorate (in a repeat of the events in 1972 and 1975) was also foiled by the actions of CAPSAT (*Corps d'Administration des Personnels et Services de l'Armée de Terre* – Army Corps of Personnel and Administrative and Technical Services) officers who placed A. Rajoelina in power in the first real coup d'état in Madagascar's history.[8] Yet, here again, the violence remained minor and power was handed over with virtually no shots fired or bloodshed.

The many army and paramilitary police mutinies under A. Rajoelina's leadership (in March 2009, May 2010, November 2010, March 2012 and July 2012) do not appear to have been the expression of political forces. In actual fact, the 'mutinies' never involved more than 30 or so soldiers, only saw low-level fighting if any (two fatalities in May 2010 and three fatalities in July 2012) and were often driven purely by sectional demands (May 2010 and March 2012). The election in late 2013 also went off with very few protests, and the problems governing under the Fourth Republic (the executive and legislative bodies fail to come to any agreement) have not triggered any violence. However, social violence is on the rise. In urban areas, insecurity has reached record levels and the press regularly reports on theft, robbery and assaults (sometimes fatal) and even bank heists. In the south of the country and remote areas, *Dahalo* (cattle rustlers), working in gangs of dozens of individuals sometimes armed with guns, steal herds and clash with villagers and security forces. The security forces often respond in a disproportionate manner, burning harvests and homes and carrying out summary executions.

7 Certain descriptions of the events developed since allege that the shots could in fact have come from the crowd first, as might have been evidenced by bullet marks on city signs had they not been changed.

8 M. Ravalomanana's self-proclamation as president following the first round of the 2001 presidential elections also bears a resemblance to a coup d'état, however, even though he would most probably have been elected by a 'transparent' run-off. Razafindrakoto and Roubaud (2002b) show in close analysis of the official results of the first round that he could not actually have won more than 50 percent of voter turnout.

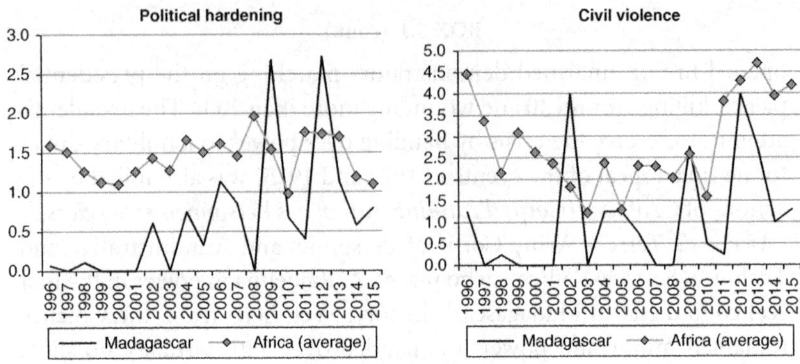

Figure 3.1 Political violence from 1996 to 2015.[9]
Source: Based on AfDB *et al.* (2016); authors' calculations.

Although this is an encouraging finding, it does raise questions about what is behind this political instability and, beyond, the nature of the Malagasy state itself. As elsewhere in Africa, conflicts may well appear to be a 'normal' form of political activity (Bach & Sindjoun, 1997). Yet, despite recent alarmist developments (Pellerin, 2014), allegiance to the state has virtually always been the rule nationwide and the use of political violence has remained essentially a state prerogative, hardly ever employed by the army. Political changes have always assumed a legalistic form, even when they have come prematurely. The Malagasy state therefore displays a paradoxical profile: fragile from the point of view of the instability of the governments that represent it, but sound considering its capacity to quell violence and sustain its institutions over time. It therefore sits uneasily with the analysis by North *et al.* of fragile natural states, which are described as incapable of controlling violence: it is always a delicate balance, as the possibility to contain violence depends on the dominant coalition's aptitude for making profitable compromises between the most powerful groups and developing patron–client networks.

[9] There is still a desperate lack of comparative statistical data available on violence over a long-run timeline. These charts have been put together from data recorded by the African Development Bank (AfDB), Organisation for Economic Co-operation and Development (OECD) and United Nations Development Programme (UNDP) starting in 1996. The second chart is an indicator based on the number of dead and injured during public unrest and violence. The first is a composite indicator of declarations of a state of emergency, political arrests and incarcerations, additional police resources and hardening of the political climate (expulsions, dismissals, curfews and dissolution of political parties).

Such a view could be deemed debatable, first and foremost by the Malagasy people themselves, especially given the situation since the 2008 crisis. Yet the events of soldiers opening fire on protesting crowds on 10 August 1991 and 9 February 2009, army mutinies grown frequent (albeit quickly contained, as started by small groups of isolated individuals), and growing insecurity epitomised by the reign of terror imposed by *Dahalo* (cattle rustlers) in the south of the island today, have made a particular impression on the population because these phenomena are at odds with the way the society works and the pacifism upheld as a Malagasy trait (see, for example, Ottino, 1996).

To underscore the low level of political violence in Madagascar, our argument also takes up the observation of the tremendous ability of the vast majority of inhabitants to accept daily hardships (widespread poverty, injustice, institutional decay, political wrangling, etc.) without rising up in organised rebellion against their leaders. Although the political crises and unrest might contradict this idea, the movements first have carried the banner of non-violence and second could be precisely the exceptions that prove the rule: crises are eruptions of long-suppressed frustrations.

In the light of the country's long history, then, no non-state organisation appears to have any real power to whip up violence. Although violence exists in Malagasy society, it is largely repressed and, when it does surface, it tends to take the form of infrapolitical eruptions expressing a discontent that does not clearly pinpoint its causes or directly designate those responsible. Granted, some political forces have tried to manipulate these discontents in support of their cause. This is particularly the case with D. Ratsiraka, who many a time used militia from poor neighbourhoods to secure the stability of his regime and tried to turn the dissatisfactions of underprivileged Malagasy to his advantage in the political crises. Similarly, certain elements suggest that the looting in 2009 (and also in 1987) may have been, if not masterminded, at least encouraged by the opposition to M. Ravalomanana (and supporters of D. Ratsiraka in 1987). Yet, in reality, these outbursts of violence have always outdone the political forces that seek to exploit them, but are unable to control them, as if violence were not or cannot be a legitimate strategic resource in Malagasy politics. It is often the very use of violence by the ruling power that precipitates its overthrow (P. Tsiranana in 1972, D. Ratsiraka in 1991 and M. Ravalomanana in 2009) and regime changes, even during crises, have always occurred with very little violence.

Aversion to Violence: A Reason for the Low Level of Political Violence?

Generally speaking, does the Red Island really display a low level of violence? The Global Peace Index, which ranks countries by level of peacefulness, places Madagascar among the top-rated countries in 2016: 38th of 162 countries worldwide and in third place of 44 sub-Saharan African countries (Institute for Economics and Peace, 2016).[10] This ranking has to do with more than just the fact that Madagascar is not subject to international conflicts. The country is rated 51st worldwide for its domestic safety and security indicators alone. Although the global indicators used by the institute have their limitations, these figures suggest that a relatively peaceful climate reigns in the country. In any case, no indicator points to any extreme or security situation in Madagascar today.

A comparative analysis of household survey data on some 20 African countries also confirms the relatively low level of political – and physical – violence in Madagascar (Figure 3.2). The island ranks among the two or three countries in which a clear majority of the population (80% or more as opposed to 40% on average in the 20 countries analysed) states that

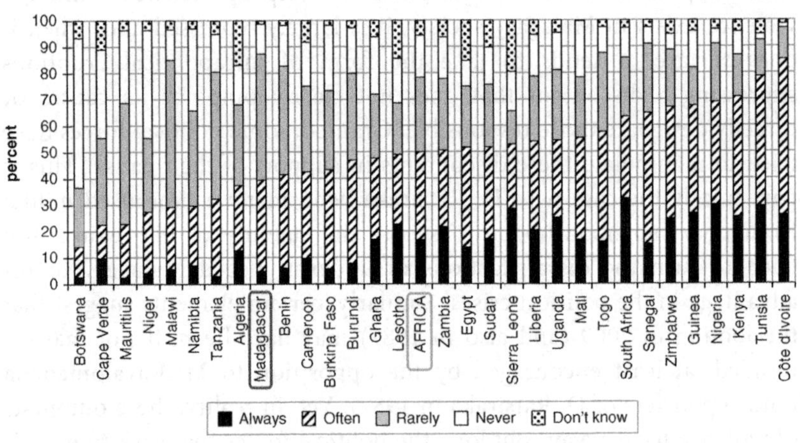

Figure 3.2 Violent conflict caused by competition between parties.
Source: Afrobarometer Survey, 2013/2014; authors'calculations.

[10] The Global Peace Index is composed of 23 indicators based on perceptions alongside data compiling people's experiences and behaviour in addition to objective facts on the countries. These indicators cover three areas: the countries' involvement in local and international conflicts, domestic safety and security and the degree of militarisation.

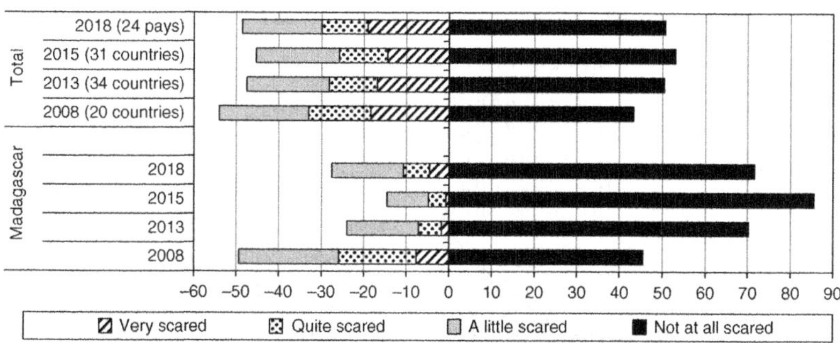

Figure 3.3 Fear of intimidation or political violence.
Source: Afrobarometer surveys, 2008, 2013, 2014/2015 and 2016/2018; authors' calculations.

political competition never or very rarely gives rise to violent conflict. Madagascar moreover stands out for the low level of physical violence experienced by the population in their everyday lives, with a very small percentage of victims of physical assault or burglaries at home compared with other countries (respectively 4% victims of physical violence and 11% victims of burglaries in Madagascar as opposed to 12% and 32% on average in the countries considered, i.e. approximately one-third the rate elsewhere).

Compared with the inhabitants of other African countries, the Malagasy people do not feel very threatened by the possibility of intimidation during election campaigns (Figure 3.3). Although feelings were mixed in 2008 (with one-quarter 'quite' or 'very' scared, 23% 'a little' scared and 46% 'not at all' scared, in percentages close to the average for the African countries considered), this situation was shown to be exceptional by the 2013 and 2015 figures, which leave no doubt as to the very low threat level. In 2015 (and to a lesser extent in 2018), the vast majority of Malagasy (85.5% and 72% respectively) said they were not worried at all about political violence during election periods (only Cape Verde and Niger post better rates among the 30 African countries studied in 2015).

Madagascar also stands out for a low level of physical violence experienced by the population in their everyday lives (Figure 3.4). The percentage of victims of physical assault or burglaries at home is very small compared with other countries (respectively 4% victims of physical assault and 18% of burglaries in Madagascar as opposed to 10% and 27% on average in the countries considered in 2014–15).

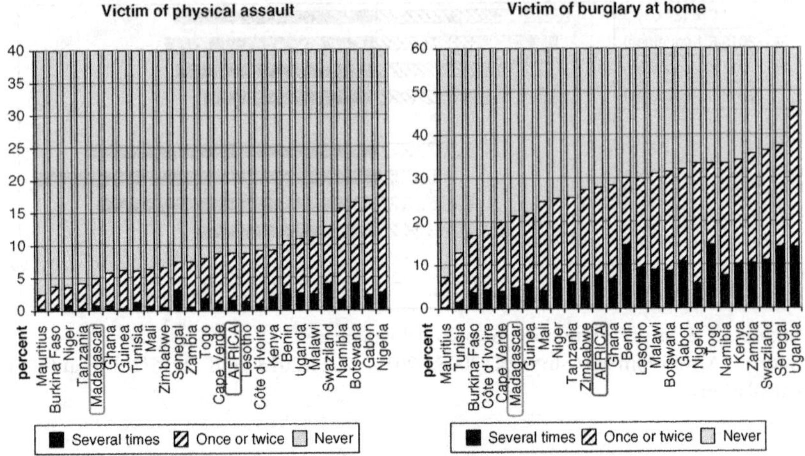

Figure 3.4 Victim of physical assault or burglary at home.
Source: Afrobarometer Survey Round 7, 2016/2018; authors' calculations.

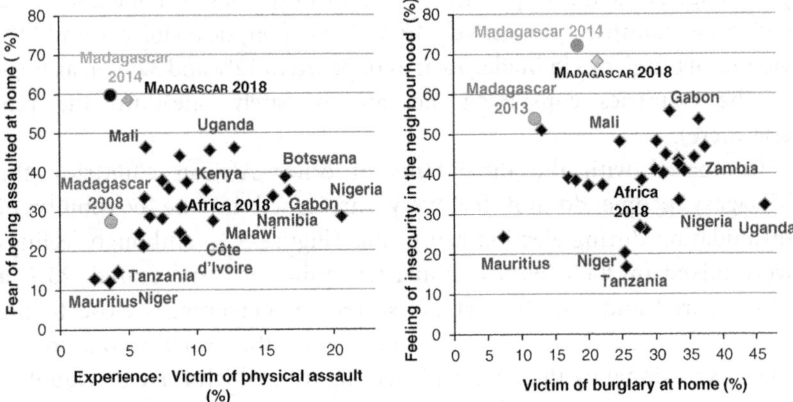

Figure 3.5 Feeling and experience of insecurity in Madagascar and Africa, 2008–2015.
Sources: Afrobarometer surveys, round 7, 2016/2018; for Madagascar, Afrobarometer, COEF Ressources/DIAL, 2008, 2013, 2014–15 and 2018; authors' calculations.
Key: The diamonds are the 2017/2018 data. The dot shows Madagascar's position in 2014 and in 2008 for the left-hand chart, in 2013 and 2014 for the right-hand chart.

An even more surprising finding is that Madagascar again proves to be a distinct case, unique among all the countries considered, when analysing the relationship between actual experience and perceptions of insecurity (Figure 3.5). Whereas the percentage of victims of insecurity was fairly low (18% of victims of burglaries at home and less than 4% of victims of physical assault), a large proportion of the population felt insecure in 2014 (72% did not feel safe in their neighbourhood and 60% were scared of being assaulted in their home). These percentages are much higher than in countries where insecurity is experienced three to four times more frequently (in Cameroon, 44% had been victims of burglaries, but 'only' 46% felt insecure; in Nigeria, 19% had been physically assaulted and 31% burgled at home, but 'only' 33% said they were scared of being assaulted at home).

So two factors stand out when comparing Madagascar with other African countries. The perceived level of insecurity is abnormally high in absolute terms, and even more so in view of the relatively low number of Malagasy who are actually victims of assault or burglary. Dynamically, although the number of burglaries at home rises (from 12% in 2013 to 18% of victims in 2014), this increase is accompanied by a disproportionate surge in the feeling of insecurity (the percentage of those who complain of feeling insecure rises from 54% in 2013 to 72% in 2014). This fear of violence, at odds with actual exposure to insecurity, demonstrates the Malagasy population's distinct relationship with violence.[11] The tendency to exaggerate the risk, impact and magnitude of violence could be driven by the population's particular aversion to violence.

Obviously, it would be tempting to see this as a specific cultural trait. Anthropologists have time and again raised the subject of *fihavanana*, a reputedly untranslatable term in that it covers so many different facets. This term is thought to constitute a common ethos for the Malagasy people as an ideal of harmony and social understanding which, through the way of life that is *fiaraha-monina* (social tact and living in harmony), imposes self-control and restraint from excessive expressions of disagreement (Ottino, 1996). Any form of conflict is therefore to be avoided. In debates, for example, Malagasy speakers endlessly apologise profusely for what they are about to say. The importance of taboos (*fady*) and fear of the wrath of ever-present ancestors (*tsiny*) further tighten this rein on

[11] Considering the same type of paradox in France in the 1980s, Lagrange (1984) draws on monthly series to show that the perception of insecurity increases when the media report on shocking, violent events whose victims are ordinary everyday people. He also observes a correlation between the level of concern and isolation or weak social links. Given that a high level of fear and distrust is one of the characteristics often put forward as a feature of Malagasy society, we examine these arguments later to elucidate the Malagasy relationship with violence and insecurity. More generally, the fear voiced by the population would appear to be an expression of their growing misgivings as to the ability of the collective form of organisation to keep the social peace. This phenomenon ties in with the country's recurring political instability.

violence. In an article written in 1981, however, J. Dez made the point that this non-violence in Malagasy society was an 'illusion'. He put it that the main regulator of violence in rural Madagascar was actually the risk of arousing jealousy (*fialonana*) and becoming a very real victim of witchcraft (*mosavy*) by fatal poisoning. He concluded that the hallmark of this type of regulation of violence among the Malagasy people was therefore more a feeling of insecurity than guilt. Yet this culturalist explanation is not totally convincing. The same forms of behavioural regulation by socialisation and sorcery have been described in many other societies, especially African societies (see Marie, 1997a, 1997b), which have sometimes proved particularly violent. Moreover, even though the *Dahalo* 'anti-social' violence in the southern countryside may not actually disprove this analysis, it at least does a great deal to temper it.

The relationship between culture and politics is really much less mechanical and one-directional than generally implied in reference to *fihavanana* in the political field. The most recent historiographical studies (Raison-Jourde & Randrianja, 2002; Galibert, 2004; Kneitz, 2014) clearly show that the 'morphing' of *fihavanana* since independence from a traditional neighbourhood and family code of social relations to a civic contract is not so much a product of a primary reality as an 'imaginary' Malagasy nation-building link. First theorised as such by P. Ramasindraibe (Rajaonah, 2014) back in the 1970s, *fihavanana* has since been regularly acclaimed by political rhetoric (and inscribed in the preamble to the Constitution of the Third Republic as an essential value of Malagasy society since 1992[12]) and circulated by the media and school curricula. These repeated references to *fihavanana* as a 'civic contract' sustain the fiction of a society where equal conditions reign, thereby influencing individuals' political representations and behaviour.

Yet observation of Malagasy society soon shows that this civic contract is imperfectly executed, to say the least. The standard conveyed by the notion does not work solely in a positive manner. In its condemnation of any act that jeopardises societal harmony, it is behind an invisible, structural violence that suppresses any opposition to the established order. In this way, *fihavanana* takes the form of the weak's consent to submission (Raison-Jourde, 2014).

[12] 'The sovereign Malagasy people, profoundly attached to their cultural and spiritual values, especially to *fihavanana*, the basis of national unity.'

Forms of Symbolic Violence: Rule of Social Order and Prevalence of a Hierarchical System

Another more socio-historical analysis could be made. Malagasy society is historically highly hierarchical, endlessly differentiating and ranking individuals by a hereditary inegalitarian order that has lost none of its symbolism over time, despite the country's politico-social changes. The status group system, in particular, remains rooted in the minds and souls of the people, assigning unequal values to individuals. M. Ravalomanana, for example, bolstered his political credibility by spreading the rumour that he was of noble descent. His successor occasionally sought to take on the appearance of royalty.[13] The principles of differentiation and rank also continue to have great resonance within the higher status groups themselves. However, social differentiation has tended to become more streamlined over time between a vast majority of *mainty* and a small minority of *fotsy*, creating a covert system rarely alluded to in the open, but one that strongly conditions their behaviour (especially marital). So this symbolic hierarchy is also a real hierarchy in that the *mainty* are 'confined by marriage taboos to the social reproduction of poverty [and] often excluded from rural land tenure and urban property ownership' (Galy, 2009). Seen from this angle, it could be said that social relations are based on symbolic violence that upholds the long-term domination of a small group of individuals over the masses. The main threat to social order in such a configuration could consequently come from the masses' rejection of this long-standing yoke of inequality.[14] One of the reasons for the refusal of, if not taboo on, the elites' use of violence in politics could ultimately be fear of sparking social disorder from which they, as a group, stand to lose so much. This is borne out by the following excerpt from an interview with a representative of the Malagasy intellectual elite:

I have never been to 13 May Square,[15] not in 1991, nor in 2002 or 2009, and I don't think I would go now, not even if it all got too much. Maybe, more than the mess of

[13] One example is the Fourth Republic's promulgation and new City Hall inauguration ceremony on 11 December 2010. A. Rajoelina, in traditional dress reminiscent of the country's kings and accompanied by his wife dressed in red like the princesses of old, with a parasol to shade her from the sun, walked the distance from the Queen's Palace to 13 May square flanked by ritual bodyguards, *mpiantsa* (royal singers) and a thousand warriors in a reconstruction of a fragment of the legend of Radama I (Carayol, 2010).

[14] PADESM in the 1950s was one such attempt to form a political force against the dominant elites by uniting the poor. Yet it was an artificial edifice and the party was in reality the product of a *côtier* elite, which stood more to lose than to gain from the emergence of awareness among the subjugated masses.

[15] The square where the main popular demonstrations took place.

it all, more than the scandals, I'm too scared of instability, upheaval, anarchy. . . . I'm too scared of a 14th of July 1789, of a storming of the Bastille. I see myself in a sort of Bastille (8 February 2012).

Keeping such a system in place assumes that everyone in some way accepts these principles of differentiation that ascribe unequal values to individuals. This is the mentality that makes political leaders often think they can do as they please without having to refer to anyone. It is also what enables some descendants of aristocratic families, especially in times of crisis, to make themselves self-proclaimed *raiamandreny*[16] and take part in the political debate as such. Political leaders therefore take advantage of Malagasy society's in-built inequality to take action with scant regard for their constituents. The kings had absolute power as to how they used their subjects, but also over their life and death. Kings coolly punctuated their speeches (*kabary*) with, 'If not, I will kill you all', 'I alone have the power of life and death over the people', and 'Should you disobey my orders, I will put you to death' (Galy, 2009). This contempt for life re-emerges in a way in the post-independence regimes. The frequent death tolls from the crackdowns on farmer riots and *Dahalo* raids, for example, did not meet with any strong expression of feeling from the elites or the urban world in general. Tsiranana's words reported in Box 3.1 also reflect in some ways how little value the ruling classes place on the lives of the common people.

The importance of this symbolic domination over the *mainty* could also explain why the violence sometimes seen in the wake of political crises generally takes the form of eruptions releasing frustrations that are never clearly expressed in political terms. This was the case with the *Menalamba* uprising in the nineteenth century, the farmer riots in the early 1970s (despite their being led by MONIMA), the urban *rotaka* and the OPKs (Anti-Karana

[16] In 2010, 37 prominent figures set up a group called *Raiamandreny Mijoro*. The power of the *Raiamandreny* to intervene in society was also laid down in articles 1 and 2 of the first chapter of the Draft Constitution of the Fourth Republic. 'Article 1 – Malagasy society inherits the ancestral wisdom based on the *"fanahy malagasy"* which gives precedence to *"fihavanana"*, a way of life for all to "live in harmony" irrespective of region, origin, ethnic group, religion or gender. Article 2 – 1 – The Circle for the Preservation of *Fihavanana* (*Seha-piahiana ny Fihavanana*) shall watch over the prevention of crises and conflicts of any sort liable to undermine the virtues of the ancestral values between Malagasy with a view to preserving national unity. 2 – The Circle for the Preservation of Fihavanana is composed of *Raiamandreny* or *Olobe*, in equal numbers of men and women, representing the traditional and socioprofessional associations and organisations of all the autonomous provinces of the Republic. The *Raiamandreny* or *Olobe* are chosen for their moral reputation and their expertise in the management of culture and traditional assets and in the prevention and settlement of crises and conflicts.' However, these articles were not retained in the adopted constitution.

Operations) in the 1980s. Similarly, today's organisation of *Dahalo* as armed gangs could be a form of reaction to the inequalities and the central administration's perpetual blind eye to the poor. However, the country's cultural opening in the 1980s built public awareness driven mainly by pop groups such as Mahaleo and, to a lesser extent, Rossy. This emerging awareness of the inequalities could explain the gradual rise in violent outbursts and outbreaks, observed especially during the 2009 crisis and at other times since.[17]

3.3 The Formal Institutions' Operational Capacities

In NWW's conceptual framework, the transition of countries defined as natural states (limited access orders [LAOs]) to open access orders (OAOs) is a long, risky business (wherein only a handful of countries successfully make the transition). In the typology of natural states, Madagascar appears at the bottom of the ladder (fragile natural state) based on its recurring socio-political crises and the prevailing situation since 2009 that places the country in danger daily of lapsing into a 'failed state'. Yet there is a problem with this proposed typology of natural states (fragile natural states, basic natural states and mature natural states), which are supposed to follow one another in an evolutionary progression.[18] The situation seems to be rather more complex than that. Depending on the period, Madagascar posts capacities and achievements that could place it at a more advanced stage of natural state in all three economic, bureaucratic and political arenas. Three examples illustrate this: the success of the export processing zones, significant results in the fight against bureaucratic corruption, and the process of democratic transition. Ultimately, the decisive factor appears to be the country's failure to enduringly build and consolidate its institutional capacities, rather than the possibility of achieving certain (local and temporary) performances characteristic of more mature orders in a relatively short space of time.

An Outstanding Continental Success: The Export Processing Zones

If there is one economic sector where the demands of competitiveness for growth are acute and hardly compatible with a social order built on the

[17] See Razafindrakoto *et al.* (2017b) for a more in-depth analysis of violence in Madagascar.

[18] In a recent version of their thesis, North *et al.* (2012) acknowledge that relapses are possible ('LAOs often exhibit episodic crises and regression rather than continuously moving forward').

extraction of unproductive rents, it is clearly the export processing zone sector. Free-zone companies need more than factor inputs and the ability to combine them efficiently if they are to stand a chance of sustaining or increasing their share on the global market, where they have to compete with the world's leading companies[19] (see Chapter 1 on this point). They also need a sufficiently developed institutional environment (property rights, public business services, human capital, etc.), without which their only comparative advantage in terms of labour cost would flounder. Madagascar has pulled off this challenge in a feat unparalleled in Africa or any country with a similar level of development. Scores of African countries have set up free trade zones (Bost, 2010, reports 133 countries worldwide), yet none has posted significant results.[20] In fact, aside from Madagascar, the only other success story in sub-Saharan Africa is Mauritius, which is a far more developed country.

The introduction of this exceptional scheme in 1990 followed the decision to develop an export-driven growth model, as promoted by the Bretton Woods institutions in the structural adjustment programmes (SAPs). Tax breaks combined with low wages alongside preferential trade arrangements with Europe (Everything But Arms [EBA] initiative) and the United States (African Growth and Opportunity Act [AGOA]) brought steady, outstanding growth to the Malagasy export processing zones compared with the rest of the country. The Madagascar Export Processing Zone Association (GEFP – *Groupement des Entreprises Franches et Partenaires*) reported that 180 firms employing some 100,000 staff were operating under this scheme by the end of 2004.

The spectacular success of the Malagasy export processing zones has been clearly documented by Razafindrakoto and Roubaud (1997) and Cling *et al.* (2005, 2009). It has had many positive repercussions on the Malagasy economy. First, in terms of export growth, the share of export processing zones in total exports rose from a negligible level to nearly 50% in 2005–6, a proportion unequalled by any other poor country (Figure 3.6). It also changed the nature of exports in what could be called a real structural transformation in the space of a few years. Whereas Madagascar exported essentially agricultural products in the early 1990s, nearly 50% of exports were manufactured products by the mid-2000s; and this, despite the disastrous effect of the 2002 political crisis.

[19] Unless they specialise in niche markets, which is not the case with the Malagasy export processing zone, specialised in the apparel industry.

[20] With the exception of Kenya, on a much smaller scale.

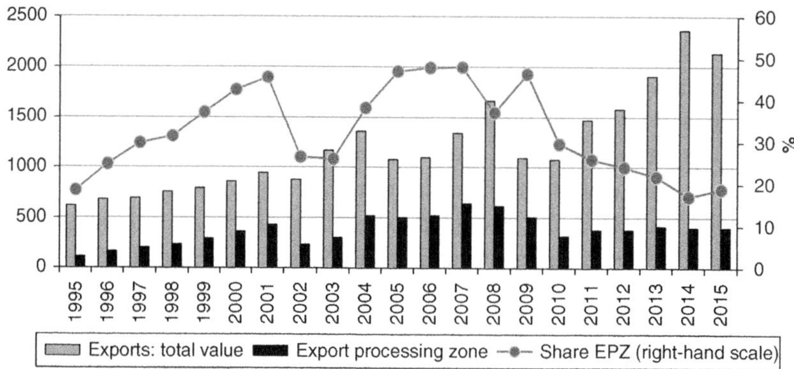

Figure 3.6 The boom in export processing zone exports: 1995–2015.
Sources: International Trade Centre PC-TAS database for total exports; Otexa and Eurostat for *Export Processing Zone* exports (clothing products); authors' calculations.
Note: in millions of dollars.

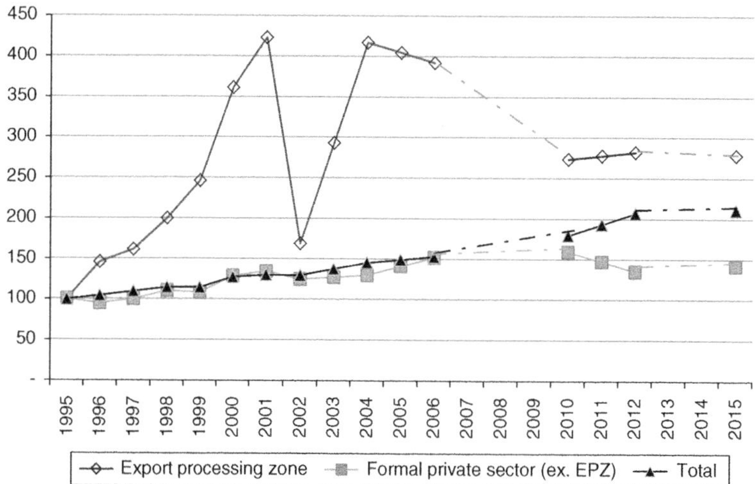

Figure 3.7 Formal employment dynamics in and outside the export processing zones, 1995–2015.
Source: *1-2-3 Surveys*, 1995–2015, MADIO, DIAL/INSTAT; authors' calculations.
Note: The dotted lines indicate an absence of available data for the period.

Second, export processing zone business growth brought a real boom in employment (Figure 3.7). Export processing zone job creations rose four times more sharply than jobs created by the formal private sector or the economy as a whole through to 2001. Employment collapsed with the 2002 crisis but bounced back extremely quickly.

Export processing zone firms also come out ahead across all other job quality indicators (labour standards, industrial safety, etc.). Not only have they gradually formalised their labour relations, but they have probably been the main factor in spreading these new contract-based labour standards more in keeping with international standards to other businesses in Madagascar.

The dismantlement of the Multifibre Arrangement (2005) and the scheduled end of AGOA, extended extraordinarily through to 2009, later broke the positive momentum, and the 2009 crisis further exacerbated the situation. Since 2010, export processing firm zone growth has been at a standstill, but job and export levels have held steady.[21]

The success of the export processing zones in Madagascar clearly shows that the country is capable of engaging in a dynamic of wealth creation, generated by real value creation (jobs and revenue) driven by a new class of entrepreneurs (nationals and foreigners), thereby boosting development – a distinctive feature of OAOs (Ould Aoudia, 2011) – rather than by interests cashing in on their connections with the corridors of power to make profits on their rents due to their membership of the dominant coalition of elites in place (characteristic of natural states). Excluding external factors (end of the Multifibre Arrangement [MFA] and [22] AGOA in 2009 due to political sanctions), which bear out the ambiguous role of the international community (see Chapter 4), this success was effectively interrupted twice by bouts of socio-political violence and it was only by bringing the violence under control that the momentum generated could be consolidated. Yet there is nothing to suggest that the episodes of violence in question were driven either by an elite group excluded from the profits of this new manna or by the ruling power because it was not reaping its benefits. The reason for the breaks is to be found elsewhere and the losses caused are purely collateral.

Significant Progress with the Fight against Bureaucratic Corruption

Widespread corruption is seen as one of the structural, constituent features of natural states such as Madagascar. This is evidenced by the correlation

[21] This raises the question as to whether Madagascar has reached an equilibrium level, which will no longer change significantly even if the socio-political climate were to improve, or whether a new take-off is possible if the climate of confidence were to return, bringing new investors with it. Currently, no data are available to draw one conclusion or the other.

[22] Act passed by the US Congress in 2000 to support the economies of African countries by enhancing their access to the American market.

between levels of development and corruption observed in all the quantitative studies based on the leading international databases. It is virtually impossible to reduce corruption to any significant extent when institutions and their associated organisations are weak, and there are precious few examples of policies that have had a lasting positive impact in these circumstances, especially in the most precarious natural states (fragile and basic), of which Madagascar is one. This intrinsic difficulty in fighting corruption is exacerbated by the presumption that the level of everyday corruption in Africa is all the higher because it is a socially accepted phenomenon, based on fundamentally different values and beliefs to those found in OAOs. This theory ties in with a line of interpretation based on culturalist premises as to how Africa 'works'. In this interpretation, corruption in a 'moral economy of corruption' (Chabal & Daloz, 1999) is made a natural social practice accepted by all by patrimonialism and clientelism, the straddling of public and private spheres, the primacy of community and ethnic ties, and informal redistribution functions. As modern descendants of traditional chiefdoms, civil servants are legitimately authorised to accept 'gifts' from constituents as a mark of their allegiance to the new holders of power. The impunity they enjoy is largely granted by the people, who consequently collude in maintaining these practices. Even when anthropological studies depart from this commonly held version, they ultimately enter a grey area bound up with the culturalist approach. Olivier de Sardan (1999), for example, asserts the idea of a form of collusion at all levels of the social ladder in the shape of sociocultural rationales that support the 'corruption complex' (logics of negotiation, gift-giving, solidarity networks, predatory authority and redistributive accumulation). However, this does not prevent him from pointing out the extent to which relations between the administration and users are tarnished with distrust, uncertainty and humiliation (Blundo & Olivier de Sardan, 2001).

No support can be found for these assumptions in the empirical data drawn from a series of multiround surveys covering some 20 years (the longest to date, to our knowledge, in a developing country).[23] On the corruption front, the findings show a steady, significant decrease in the incidence of petty corruption from 1995 to 2001. The percentage of corruption victims plummeted from 42% to 10% of the population in the

[23] Note that, unlike most of the work in this area, our measurement of corruption is based on actual experience (objective variable) rather than on perception of the phenomenon (subjective variable).

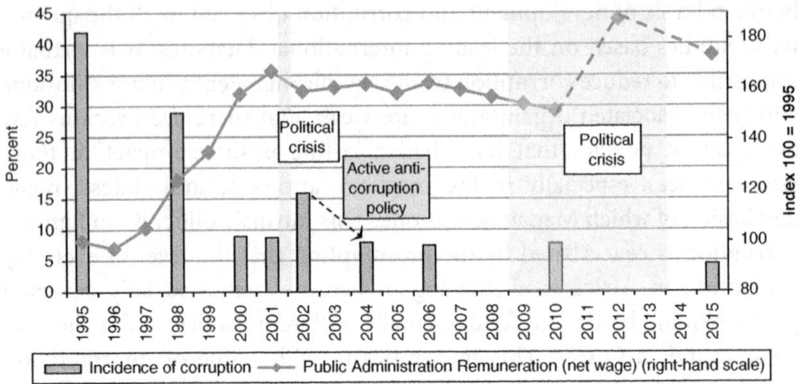

Figure 3.8 Civil service wages, crisis and incidence of corruption in Madagascar, 1995–2015.

Source: Razafindrakoto & Roubaud (2003) and *1-2-3 Surveys*, 1995–2015, MADIO, DIAL/INSTAT; authors' calculations.

Note: The corruption 'module' was not included in the survey in 1996, 1997 or 1999. The corruption indicator is an objective indicator (Percent of the population affected by corruption over the year). The data cover the agglomeration of Antananarivo. The dotted lines indicate the absence of data.

space of five years (Figure 3.8). This development can be compared with the growth in public servants' remuneration, also captured by the survey. There is a strong negative correlation between the level of corruption and civil servants' wages, which grew more than 60% in real terms over the same period (Razafindrakoto & Roubaud, 2003). Although the causality cannot be formally tested – the series is not long enough – and other factors may also have affected the level of corruption (such as inflation, political stability, etc.), it does corroborate the presumption of a positive link between public officials' pay and control of corruption, if not the administration's performance in general (for example, multiple jobholding by public servants also decreased over the same period).

On this controversial question, a certain number of studies based on aggregate data have found no significant link between the perception of corruption and civil servants' (relative) wages (Treisman, 2000; Swamy *et al.*, 2001). Our findings tend to lend support to the converse hypothesis of a significant association, as obtained by Van Rijckeghem and Weder (2001) from a sample of some 30 countries and also by Di Tella and Schardgrodsky (2003). This link would have major implications for public service reform in developing countries. In particular, it could go some way to explaining the virtually systematic failure of the first generation of civil service reforms in sub-Saharan Africa in the 1980s and 1990s, when severe cuts were made to public servants' wages (Lindauer & Nunberg, 1994; Lienert & Modi, 1997; see Chapter 4 on the ambiguous role of the donors).

Second, the findings establish a direct connection between institutional quality and corruption. Madagascar's severe political and institutional crisis following the contested presidential election of December 2001 (Roubaud, 2002) immediately saw a dramatic rise in corruption with incidence doubling in the space of one year. Institutional chaos (strike, power vacuum and confrontations), rapid inflation and the subsequent drop in civil servants' real wages all formed serious incentives for corrupt practices. In the same way, restored order, institutional stabilisation and renewed growth in public wages had the opposite effect. From 2002 to 2004, the incidence of corruption halved, dropping to a lower level than before the crisis (8%). The burden of corruption on household budgets also fell. In 2004, the total amount spent on corruption stood at just 1.2% of annual household income (as opposed to 3.3% in 2002).

In addition to the aforementioned factors, note that in 2002 the new administration made active anti-corruption and pro-transparency policies a major thrust of its action. The Anti-Corruption High Council (CSLCC) was established in 2003 to launch information campaigns and implement targeted strategies. An Independent Anti-Corruption Bureau (BIANCO) was set up in 2004 to monitor and enforce concrete measures. Once again, although the nature of the data rules out any formal evaluation of the impact of these measures, the reduction in actual corruption implies that they played a not-inconsiderable role in improving the situation. However, the positive momentum probably has more to do with the credibility of the government's anti-corruption commitment than the actual measures (legal action, disciplinary action against corrupt civil servants, etc.), which had not yet taken effect at the time of the survey. The perception indicators tally with the objective indicators in corroborating this positive climate. The population considers that the situation has clearly improved on this front: in 2004, the balance of opinion on growth in corruption presented a highly positive swing at +50 points for both petty and grand corruption. The period from 2004 to 2006 reveals that the recovery in growth and perseverance with the anti-corruption campaign stabilised bureaucratic corruption at the relatively low level (by local standards) of some 8%.

The absence of regular data on subsequent years makes it hard to analyse later developments. Only two points are available after 2006. In 2010, more than a year after the start of the crisis, the incidence of corruption stood at the same level overall as in 2006 (8%). However, there is no information available on the trend between these two dates. By 2015, incidence had dropped significantly (to less than 5%). Yet this downturn should be interpreted with care as it could be partially due to the increase in wages. Now this far from means that the situation has necessarily improved: a certain number of indicators point to a steady decline in the public institutions and the percentage of the population in contact with state institutions displays a sharp drop (from 74% in 2010 to 63% in 2015). It cannot therefore be ruled out that growing distrust of public officials and possibly fear of being a victim of corruption may have driven some members of the public to adjust and reduce their contact with public services. The reduction in the extent of corruption over this period may also derive from a drop in contact by those who are the most likely to be hit by the phenomenon.

The second assumption, broadly applied to natural states, that corruption is a socially accepted phenomenon is also demolished by the findings of surveys comparing general public and international expert opinions (Table 3.1) of the same questions (see Razafindrakoto & Roubaud, 2010a, for a presentation of the mirror survey). Nearly all the Malagasy people (90%) see corrupt practices as criminal, socially unacceptable behaviour. Yet the experts have an entirely different view, in keeping with the above-mentioned academic theses. They massively overestimate the extent to which corruption is culturally embedded and underestimate the importance that the population attaches to the anti-corruption campaign. And this feature is not idiosyncratic, as the same discrepancy is found by similar studies conducted in West Africa. The population's submission to corruption would appear to have less to do with any tacit acceptance than with their lack of means to resist and speak out against corruption. This impotence in the face of the state's predatory approach and everyday oppression by government officials is directly associated with the structural weakness of the opposition groups and civil society supposed in both cases to impose accountability on the state. Corruption is actually just one manifestation among others of the poor treatment suffered by the population at the hands of their administration (civil servant absenteeism, widespread contempt for users, etc.; Blundo and Olivier de Sardan, 2001).

Democratic Transition and Consolidation: The Case of the 1990s

The last example is drawn squarely from the political field to show that certain features of the social orders in Madagascar can bear OAO traits and

Table 3.1 *Tolerance of corruption as seen by the population and the 'experts'*

Percentage	Madagascar	Benin	Burkina Faso	Côte d'Ivoire	Mali	Niger	Senegal	Togo	Weighted average
Considers a bribe acceptable									
Population survey	11.1	4.2	7.7	5.1	4.0	3.2	2.4	3.9	4.5
Mirror survey (experts' estimation)	33.5	32.9	27.1	28.8	33.8	36.6	34.5	29.2	31.9
Corruption = major problem									
Population survey	96.9	94.2	87.8	91.0	88.4	91.6	87.9	82.2	90.3
Mirror survey (experts' estimation)	74.4	83.6	68.4	70.5	63.9	61.8	69.4	81.5	71.2
Mirror survey (experts' opinion)	84.1	96.7	67.7	90.3	82.0	71.4	82.5	95.7	84.7

Source: *1-2-3 Surveys* and *Mirror Survey* (346 observations); authors' calculations.

that the idea of there being no bridge between natural states and OAOs, or at best a bridge over a centuries-long time scale, does not seem to be workable for this country. In their definition of natural states, NWW (2009) identify the presence of 'polities without generalized consent of the governed' as one of their three founding characteristics. In addition, they consider that the transition from one order to another by means of the reforms traditionally put in place (land registry, civil registration, electoral register, tax and pension system and banking institutions) stands every chance of being doomed to failure as these reforms bring into play much more than project engineering and public policies: they touch on the very anthropological foundations of the social orders (Dufernez, Meisel & Ould Aoudia, 2010). Many formal rules and institutions directly imported from the Northern countries could exist only on paper, such is the vast difference in the values and beliefs underpinning their 'normal' functioning in the countries where they were historically developed.

Madagascar's electoral and democratic experience shows that this reading is not as cut-and-dried as it professes to be. The sequence of elections in the 1990s is broadly in line with the stylised democratic functioning of OAOs. If democratic transition is defined as a shift from an authoritarian regime to the institutionalisation of liberal procedures of government (open political competition, a multiparty system, universal suffrage, freedom to vote, election transparency and freedom of the press), it could be said that this phase actually occurred with the 1992 election. Even using the most restrictive and widely recognised yardstick whereby power needs to rotate twice with two successive free elections (Bratton & Van de Walle, 1997), Madagascar is a member of the exclusive club of African countries that have met this criterion (see the 1993 and 1996 presidential elections; see Chapter 2). The successive presidencies of A. Zafy and D. Ratsiraka do not stand in opposition to one another. They actually form a continuum with the second conserving the achievements of the first. The first decade of the Third Republic therefore clearly marks a fundamental change from the Second Republic.

On a more general note, our analyses of the democratic transition in the 1990s (Roubaud, 2000, 2001) rejected the premise of a Malagasy (and more broadly 'African') exception. Not only is sectarianism far from the main driver of electoral behaviour, but this aspect of identity is neither irreconcilable nor incompatible with democratic principles. Although sectarian feeling can definitely be found, due to ethnic and religious tension, it is not the main explanatory factor for voting behaviour. A comparison with developed countries' electoral patterns ascertains that the structural, sectarian component of voting has no more weight in Madagascar than in these developed countries. Alternation of power by election alongside the diversification of electoral preferences show that universal suffrage fulfils its role of rewarding/rejecting the policies implemented by those in power. The absence of a captive electorate, the low weight of lobbying led by rigid corporatism and the range of preferences and reasons for the choice of candidate all confirm that both election results and public opinion are closely associated with the candidates' actual or expected performances, which is a key characteristic of the electoral principle. This all goes to demystify 'what voting means', which all too often tends to be seen as radically and 'fundamentally' different in exotic settings, such as the Red Island, consequently discrediting democratic advances.

The second point concerns the question of the underlying core values upstream of the democratic institutions, set against the backdrop of the implicit idea of there being a divide between the two in countries such as Madagascar. Our analysis focuses on what the people want, their political practices, their values, their perceptions and their expectations. Generally speaking, is the population in favour of democracy and the principles on which it is based? Upstream, does the very concept of democracy mean the same thing in Madagascar as it does in historical democracies? The short answer to these questions is that, contrary to common belief, the Malagasy are ultimately not so different to Western citizens, as democracy is clearly a universal concept (Sen, 2005) unduly appropriated by Europe and its 'neo-colonies' in its attempt to 'steal history' (Goody, 2010).

When asked about the extent of their support for democracy, 9 in 10 people said they were in favour of this type of political system (Table 3.2). Barely 1% of the Antananarivians unequivocally reject democracy. This result is especially remarkable considering the political climate in which this opinion was expressed (in 2003). The serious political and economic unrest that followed the 2002 crisis might reasonably have been expected to undercut the pro-democratic feeling. In fact, quite the opposite was the case. It was a thirst for democracy that actually drove the 2002 protest movement as the population refused to see themselves defrauded of the choice freely made at the polls in the presidential election of December 2001 (see Chapter 2).

Not only does support for democracy in general ring loud and clear, but this type of political system is more appreciated by far than any other form of government. Three other types of political systems, in addition to democracy, were put forward for the respondents' consideration: they were all largely rejected. The Malagasy people show themselves to be

Table 3.2 *Assessment of the different forms of political system by income levels*

	Total	Per capita income quartiles			
		1st quartile	2nd quartile	3rd quartile	4th quartile
A. Have a strong man as leader who does not have to worry about parliament or elections	13.7	18.0	17.2	11.6	10.4
B. The army governs the country	13.6	15.7	15.9	13.1	11.2
C. The experts, and not a government, decide what is good for the country	36.1	38.3	34.2	36.4	35.8
D. Have a democratic political system	88.1	85.5	85.9	90.9	88.9

Source: 1–2–3 *Survey*, *Democracy* module, 2003, DIAL/INSTAT/MADIO; authors' calculations.

Note: The quartiles represent one-quarter of the ordered per capital incomes. The first quartile contains the 25% poorest and the fourth quartile the 25% richest.

fundamentally opposed to any form of authoritarian regime, whether headed by a strong man or by the army. Nearly 14% see these regimes in a positive light and fewer than 5% are very much in favour of them. They neither succumb to the authoritarian temptation nor want experts, rather than a democratically elected government, to decide what is good for the country. Although 36% are prepared to accept this type of leadership, the option comes in way behind democracy, which picks up more than 88% of the votes. Even more surprising, when gauged against popular belief, is that the findings contradict the theory that the poor's own values and economic situation make them recalcitrant about the establishment of democratic regimes.[24] So democracy, understood as a political process of appointing leaders by the ballot box, is therefore clearly seen as the best system of government when compared with other types of political systems, i.e. from a comparative stance.[25]

[24] See Razafindrakoto and Roubaud (2005) for a more detailed analysis on this subject.

[25] The national surveys (notably Afrobarometer) confirm this observation even though miscarriages of the democratic process have raised doubts as to its effectiveness and drove up the number of 'don't know' answers in 2008 and 2013.

Table 3.3 *The meaning of democracy by income levels*

The following characteristics are fundamental for democracy:	Total	Per capita income quartiles			
		1st quartile	2nd quartile	3rd quartile	4th quartile
1. Free and transparent elections	97.3	98.0	96.8	96.6	97.9
2. Freedom of speech and the press	95.9	96.5	94.9	96.1	96.0
3. Equality before the law	95.0	94.9	95.2	94.2	95.5
4. Freedom of worship	94.8	94.1	96.3	94.5	94.3
5. Freedom to travel	94.6	94.4	95.6	93.6	94.8
6. Political freedom (choice of political party)	91.0	91.6	88.9	92.3	91.2
All six characteristics	81.8	80.2	81.5	83.0	82.0

Source: *1–2–3 Survey*, *Democracy* module, 2003, DIAL/INSTAT/MADIO: authors' calculations.

Note: See Table 3.2 for the definition of quartiles.

Now that we have shown the general view of the concept of democracy and established how it measures up against other political systems, the question arises as to what exactly democracy means to the population. What hides behind the word 'democracy'? This question is key in that an entire school of thought based on culturalist theories considers that democracy is a Western value and that it means something different in other historical and cultural contexts. Therefore, a definition is needed here as to what 'democracy' means to the Malagasy people. To do so, survey respondents were given a list of features traditionally associated with democracy and asked if they considered them to be essential and integral to this notion.

Here again, the findings are unequivocal: the Malagasy people have the same idea of democracy as that which prevails in historical democracies. This suggests that there is a universalist concept of democracy in Madagascar as in the North. More than 90% of Antananarivians consider all six of the elements on the list to be essential (Table 3.3). At the top of the list comes the holding of 'free and transparent elections', fundamental for more than 97% of respondents. Next in order come 'freedom of speech and the press' (96%), 'equality before the law' (95%), 'freedom of worship' (95%), 'freedom to travel' (95%) and 'political freedom (choice of political party)' (91%). Here, too, the poor's understanding of democracy is no different than that of the rest of the population, despite their particularly precarious economic situation. They share the 'academic' and universalist view of it.

This consensus over the definition of democracy is not a Malagasy exception (no more than is the preference for democratic systems). Surveys conducted in other African countries show that it holds everywhere (Table 3.4). In all cases, more than 80% of the population consider that every one of the six properties is fundamental for democracy. Only Mali and partially Burkina Faso do not completely join this fine chorus. Yet even this difference is relatively slim as agreement over the fundamental importance of any given property never comes to less than 85% of the population.

To conclude, the intention is not to indulge in a blissful reading of the success stories in Madagascar's history. None of the examples given were lasting successes. The export processing zones' momentum was broken by external and especially internal factors (the crises of 2002 and 2009) and does not appear to have taken off again since. Petty bureaucratic corruption may have been substantially rolled back, but there is nothing to suggest that this improvement has had any impact on grand corruption (even though figures are not available to underpin the diagnosis). Although democratic transition has taken place historically, the transition to democratic consolidation has not. Each time, these advances have been undermined by outbreaks of violence (1991, 2002 and 2009) which, though limited, have been enough to overturn the regimes in place with the resulting political instability. However, the fact remains that this violence has been low intensity and cannot always be interpreted negatively (take the example of the 1991 mass movements, which led to the establishment of a democratic regime). Despite their limitations, the structural capacities discussed earlier show that the distance between natural states and OAOs is not unbridgeable and that certain fundamental OAO characteristics can be attained temporarily and partially, but relatively quickly, even in a country as poor and as far down the social order ranking as Madagascar.

3.4 The People Matter

The Role Played by the Population

The people are background figures in NWW's analyses (2009, 2012). Any development process, any change of social order appears to play out within the elites who are broken down into more or less fluid fractions, forming

Table 3.4 *The meaning of democracy in eight African cities*

The following characteristics are fundamental for democracy (% of adults):	Benin 2015	Burundi 2014	Cameroon 2014	Cape Verde 2016	Côte d'Ivoire 2015	Madagascar 2015	Malawi 2015	Mali 2015	Uganda 2013
Freedom of speech	79.9	97.9	86.6	97.3	85.6	93.5	93.5	90.8	91.1
Freedom of press	80.1	97.3	83.8	93.4	83.1	88.3	89.6	90.8	80.7
Equality before the law	82.8	97.7	72.5	97.3	83.9	93.5	*N/A*	72.9	79.9
Political freedom (choice of political party)	83.2	97.3	94.6	98.2	93.2	84.9	92.2	95.1	92.8
Free and transparent elections	83.3	98.5	90.3	97.7	91.9	93.5	92.81	94.2	91.1
Freedom to travel	84.2	98.7	89.5	98.1	91.0	91.7	88.73	93.3	90.8
Freedom of worship	85.1	98.6	94.7	98.9	92.2	91.8	92.0	93.6	97.2
Freedom of association	84.9	97.3	92.0	98.3	90.9	89.0	87.8	94.3	88.1
Absence of discrimination	83.3	98.0	76.9	98.6	83.4	92.2	85.8	75.8	77.1
First seven characteristics	68.9	94.4	60.6	87.4	69.1	77.8	76.5	65.7	64.9
All nine characteristics	67.2	93.9	56.6	86.2	66.8	77.1	72.9	63.0	58.5

Source: *GPS-ShaSA module*, National Statistics Offices; authors' calculations.

coalitions to channel violence and control the rents they can extract for their benefit. We believe this to be somewhat of a blind spot in their theory. The 'masses' and their representatives are at best manipulated by elites who pull all the strings leading (or not) to development and, at worst, are totally absent. This problem has already been raised by Vahabi (2011) in his critique of NWW's theories: 'From this point of view, history is the work of the elites and social conflicts, especially those led by the masses, have no impact on institutional change . . . Unlike Acemoglu and Robinson (2005), the authors believe that such change is not brought about by pressure from social conflicts (revolutions or riots), but by a deliberate choice by the elites themselves . . . [Yet] social conflicts and especially pressure from non-elites have played a key role in institutional innovation.'

Note, incidentally, that the Annales School historically based its scientific project precisely on improving on the historiography of kings, courts and elites that informed the discipline. Long before, Marxist authors and writers of other persuasions had taken an interest in the peasant world, social unrest, the working classes, revolutions and social movements as driving forces of history (Hobsbawm, 1966).[26] In Africa, advocates of 'bottom-up politics' (Bayart *et al.*, 1992) have endeavoured to escape this 'nobility lens' and 'its palace revolutions', to paraphrase (in a twist) the title of a book (Dezalay & Garth, 2002). In short, this subsection shows that the people matter, even in a country with deeply entrenched power imbalances where ordinary citizens have very little empowerment (education, information, representation, voice, etc.) in the way their counterparts in developed countries do (see Chapter 4). We even believe this to be a key trait in Madagascar's case, especially when it comes to explaining the Malagasy paradox. Changes of government have often been driven by large-scale movements:

- *In 1972*, popular movements decried inequalities and non-inclusive development, even though political motives were also on the agenda: new aspirations reminiscent of the May 1968 French student revolt and condemnation of France's political and economic stranglehold (Althabe, 1978; Raison-Jourde & Roy, 2010). The main players were marginalised farmers in the south of the country and students.

[26] Although the Annales School and NWW's analytic framework have a number of points in common (long-term history, focus on the economic dimension, role of beliefs, etc.), where the former's aim is to expand beyond just political, military and diplomatic aspects, NWW's broader global perspective falls somewhat short of fully capturing social history and the role of non-elite social groups.

- *In 1991*, the country was on an economic growth path, but unfulfilled democratic aspirations associated with gradual political liberalisation triggered a popular uprising, especially among the middle classes.
- *In 2002*, the economy had never had it so good, but perception of corruption and electoral fraud at a time when democratic aspirations were high (with the appearance of a 'new man') prompted a popular uprising (Razafindrakoto & Roubaud, 2002b).
- *In 2009*, the scenario was the same as in 2002 (governance and corruption discontents) with a relatively positive economic situation (at a macro level at least), but the economic model was less inclusive as it was largely based on mining rents and official development assistance with their much lower multiplier effects. The macroeconomic momentum did nothing to reduce inequalities and poverty. Yet popular support for the coup d'état was much thinner on the ground than in 2001.

The Importance of Aspirations to Explain the Paradox

Our first point of entry concerns the role of civic aspirations in the country's economic dynamics and especially in triggering crises in Madagascar. We have already advanced discursively that the farmer revolts in the south in 1971 were rooted in the pro-urban policy and neglect of rural areas under President P. Tsiranana. The 1972 crisis that led to the fall of the First Republic was related to the disconnect between education policy and skilled job openings, exacerbated by nationalist aspirations (a good number of the most highly skilled jobs were held by French nationals). Similarly, the popular dissent and mass demonstrations that toppled the Second Republic in 1991 can justifiably be put down to the population's unfulfilled democratic aspirations. More controversially (and disputably), it could even be argued that the 2009 crisis was fuelled by a will for change from President M. Ravalomanana's excesses even though popular dissent, largely limited to the capital, was on a much smaller scale than in the previous episodes.

The aim here is to empirically support these interpretations, which remain hypothetical or conjecture in the absence of conclusive evidence. This entails using data collected by the authors over the 2000–10 decade, thereby covering the last two crises in 2002 and 2009. To our knowledge, this type of approach has never been conducted owing to a lack of adequate information. This, then, is its main originality. The results show that, despite favourable economic

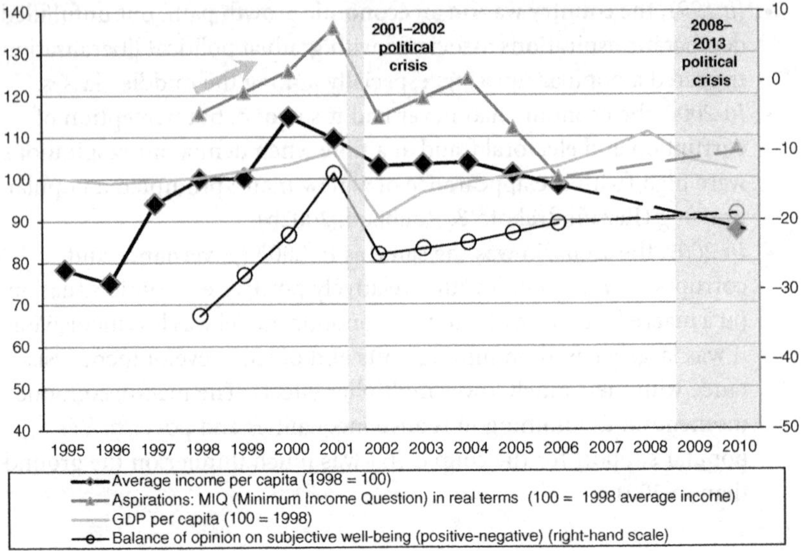

Figure 3.9 Changes in GDP, household income, aspirations and subjective well-being, 1995–2010.
Source: *1-2-3 Surveys*, 1995 to 2010, MADIO Project, INSTAT and DIAL; authors' calculations.

conditions (which was also the case with the aforementioned crises), aspirations outstripped actual performance. This gap is a direct source of popular discontent and dissatisfaction. As such, it forms a breeding ground for crises. This would suggest that the people are not merely manipulated by politicians to overthrow the ruling regimes (even though they may be used by politicians who do not care about the people's interests).[27]

Economic Aspirations

Escalating economic aspirations are a major source of potential discontent. The second half of the 1990s saw a phase of growth in household incomes unequalled in the country's history (Figure 3.9). Such growth can potentially have two opposite effects: either individuals are satisfied with this real and somewhat unexpected material improvement, or the boom releases long-contained aspirations and creates a mismatch between ambitions and fulfilment.

[27] This raises the question as to the conditions for the transition from discontent to mobilisation. There is clearly no popular movement without discontent, but not all discontent results in mobilisation.

This issue can be addressed by comparing income actually earned with the stated minimum income required to make ends meet (*Minimum Income Question* [MIQ]). The answer is clear with respect to the late 1990s. Although incomes grew 10% from 1998 to 2001, individual income aspirations rose nearly twice as fast (18%). Similarly, the gap widened in the economic recovery phase after Marc Ravalomanana took office following the 2002 crisis. A further upturn in income aspirations came from 2002 to 2004, when incomes stagnated (although GDP was trending upwards). It can therefore be concluded that growth phases whet appetites and consequently potential frustration.

Nonetheless, aspirations are not entirely out of touch with reality. The 2002 recession (and its catastrophic impact on incomes) drove down aspirations. Likewise, the downward trend in incomes that started in 2004 also saw a significant downturn in answers to the MIQ. Here is a phenomenon with which union demand analysts are very familiar: demands are usually higher in upbeat economic periods.

A lack of data makes the subsequent years harder to interpret. From 2006 to 2010, incomes fell as aspirations rose. This counterintuitive reading is probably inaccurate, as information is available on the situation in 2006 and then in 2010, i.e. a year after the start of the crisis, but there is no information available between these two dates. Taking the previously observed model, it could be assumed that the observed GDP growth ended up filtering down to the households (at least partially) through to 2008 (the peak of this boom period), and that aspirations picked up more sharply, widening the gap between the two. The 2009 crisis might then have stalled this divergent trend and, as in 2002, reduced real incomes (as seen from the drop in GDP, while aspirations would have come crashing down).

What Figure 3.9 also shows is the huge difference between the two growth phases of 1995–2001 and 2002–8 in terms of the pace of accumulation. Whereas the first phase driven by growth in the labour-intensive sectors (primarily the export processing zones) brought an objective and subjective improvement in the population's economic situation, the second proved on the whole neutral, as much in terms of incomes as of perceived well-being.

Beyond the Economic Field: Democratic Governance Aspirations

Perhaps even more than economic aspirations, unfulfilled democratic governance aspirations appear to be a key driver of popular frustration. The figures available for the 2002 crisis are incomplete, but nonetheless convergent with the more qualitative assessments that we can make. As we have seen, never before had the Malagasy people posted such substantial improvements in their

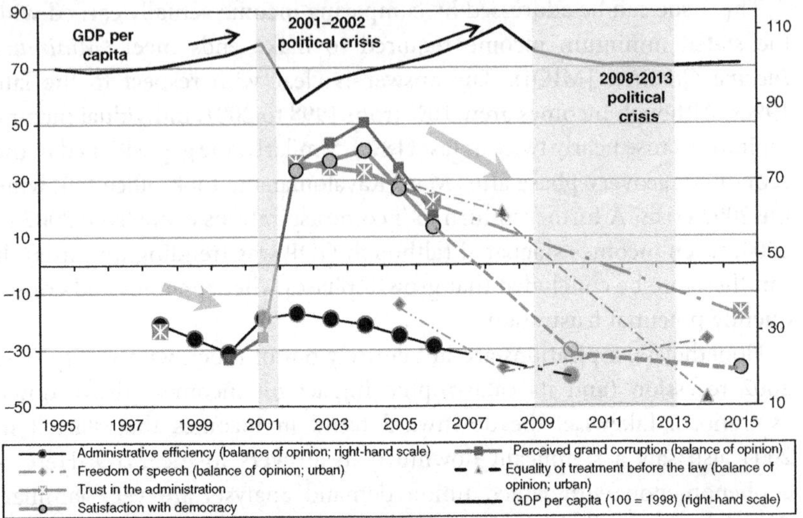

Figure 3.10 Changes in GDP and selected governance indicators, 1995–2015.
Source: *1-2-3 Surveys*, 1995 to 2015, Antananarivo, MADIO Project, INSTAT & DIAL; Afrobarometer surveys, 2005, 2008, 2013 and 2014; authors' calculations. (The AB curves concern the urban population.)

living conditions. Moreover, the indicators available clearly show that growth benefited all the population strata, at least in urban areas, ruling out the question of inequalities and exclusion as a factor of potential unrest.[28]

This leaves less strictly economic explanations for consideration. We believe that two factors played a decisive role. The first is the Malagasy attachment to democratic values, in no way inhibited by their poor material living conditions, and their hunger for and refusal to be robbed of their civil liberties. After turning out en masse to vote, the Malagasy people peacefully took to the streets to condemn the electoral fraud and defend their choice. The second factor is the rejection of a distant, arrogant style of government wherein the upper echelons of power, first and foremost the presidential family, grew openly and shamelessly more corrupt by the day. In support of this theory, there is a marked drop in opinions of the administration's efficiency in the late 1990s along with a sharp upswing in perceived petty and grand corruption (Figure 3.10), despite a real improvement on the corruption front due to the increase in civil service wages (see earlier).

28 Although inegalitarian tendencies loomed, they crystallised mainly between town and country, whereas the protest movement was primarily urban, especially in the capital, the foremost beneficiary of growth.

This diagnosis is borne out by the subsequent Ravalomanana government period, on which the surveys provide much better empirical support. M. Ravalomanana inspired great hopes as shown by the spectacular upturn in all the institutional perception indicators (better control of grand and petty corruption, trust in the administration, satisfaction with democratic governance, etc.). Yet although these hopes lived on for a while (at least through to 2004), they were quickly dashed.

From 2004–5, all the aforementioned indicators trend downwards. The Afrobarometer surveys confirm this picture through to 2008, taking different indicators trending in the same vein. The balance of opinion regarding freedom of speech fell 15 points while the balance of opinion concerning equality of treatment before the law plummeted nearly 25 points. So despite economic performances presented as success stories both within the country and to the outside world, the popular discontent that had been visible since 2008 crystallised the portents of the impending crisis.

The data available on subsequent years show the needles still in the red. Despite the election in late 2013, formally marking the end of the crisis with the arrival of a legitimate government, no change can be detected. The different governance indicators continue their inexorable slide. To take just a few examples, where 58% of the capital's inhabitants said they were satisfied with democracy in 2006, just 20% were left with this opinion in 2015. Similarly, those trusting in the administration shrank from 64% to 35% over the same period (Figure 3.10). So the return of government legitimacy did not turn around the opinion of governance. If this downward spiral continues, will the people resign themselves to it or will it bring a new popular movement?

To conclude, the 'Malagasy paradox' finds an explanation when the democratic governance dimension is considered alongside purely economic factors. This finding is in line with NWW's theories. However, the role played by the people, especially their aspirations, cannot be ruled out even in the most fragile natural states. Yet wasn't that precisely one of the main conclusions made by T. Gurr (1970) in his famous book *Why Men Rebel*, which is still relevant today, 40 years on?[29] And despite obvious differences (a unique event and more developed countries), an instructive parallel can also be drawn with the Arab Spring.

[29] 'I continue to think that people, with all their diverse identities, desires, and beliefs, should be central to our analyses of conflict ... It is not enough to point to big economic and social structures as the "explanation". We need to understand how people interpret the situations in which they find themselves' (Gurr, 2011).

Torn between Traditional Values and Democratic Principles

Given the observation that one of the explanatory factors for the recurrent crises is the lack of consideration of the people's aspirations, the reasons for this absence need to be explained. Various factors could be raised, including weak intermediary bodies that might otherwise voice the expectations of an isolated, fragmented, neglected population (see Chapter 4). The focus here, however, is on those factors associated with the Malagasy people's values. A crisis of values between the Malagasy people's relatively strong attachment to traditional values and 'modernisation' aspirations and/or constraints is sometimes put forward as one of the obstacles to development to explain the country's trajectory (Urfer, 2012a).[30] Malagasy society does indeed seem riddled with contradictions, one of which is the contrast between attachment to respect for authority – sacredness of power – and support for democratic principles.

Low Uptake of the Idea of Government Accountability

Data from the 2005 and 2008 Afrobarometer surveys, with their questions put differently from one year to the next, draw one and the same conclusion: compared with the citizens of other African countries, the Malagasy people are among the least inclined to question their leaders' actions or hold them accountable for their performance. The prevailing attitude tends to be one of respect for authority and crediting the country's rulers with the status of 'parents', i.e. looking after the people (see Figures 3.11 and 3.12).[31] Even though a higher percentage of the population in 2013 felt that the government should be accountable to the people (38% as opposed to 30% in 2008), this rate is still much lower than the average for other African countries in the same year (55%).

Explanatory factors can be put forward for these findings based on the qualitative interviews conducted for this study. The importance of *fiarahamonina* (or living in harmony) means that the Malagasy avoid direct confrontations or criticism, in particular with respect to authority (local or national). This is underpinned by the fact that the state in Malagasy translates as *fanjakana*, a term etymologically associated with royal power and hence sacred. This sacredness of power, found again in the status of *raiamandreny* (parents or elders) bestowed on leaders, is incompatible

[30] This tug of war between traditional values and 'modernity' is among the reasons most frequently brought up in the interviews conducted for this study.

[31] The same observation is made by the Governance, Peace and Security survey conducted in 2015 (Rakotomanana *et al.*, 2016).

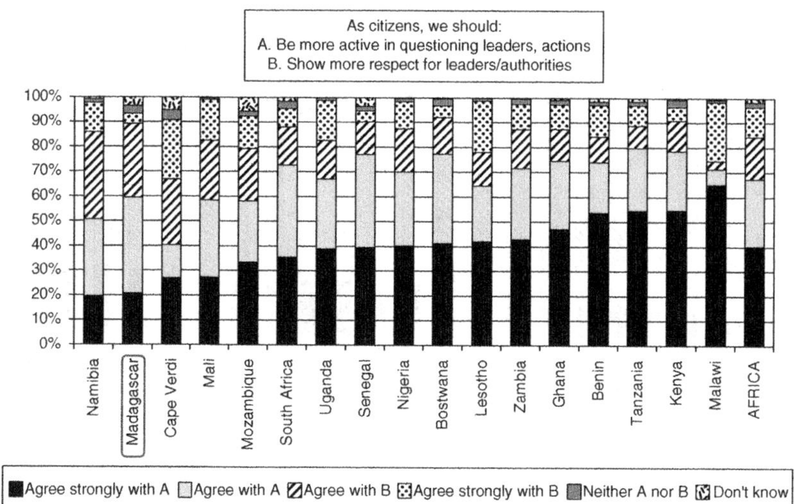

Figure 3.11 Control of leaders' actions and respect for authority.
Source: Afrobarometer surveys, COEF Ressources/DIAL, Madagascar, 2005; authors' calculations.

with the public's right of control in a democratic system (see Chapter 4 for a further discussion of these points).

A Strong Sense of Civic Participation

Taking the same survey data and compared with other African countries, however, the Malagasy people turn out to be the most convinced of the role they should play as citizens in overseeing that the president and parliamentary representatives carry out their duties to the best of their abilities (Figure 3.13).[32]

The figures speak for themselves on this score, placing Madagascar at the top of the 20 countries considered in 2008: 70% of Malagasy people consider that citizens should oversee MPs' actions once they are elected (as opposed to 38% on average overall) and 72% hold the same view with respect to the president (as opposed to 39% on average). This finding is especially noteworthy in that Madagascar's elites are less convinced of this idea: 'just' 54% (respectively 43%) of them rank the electorate as the main people in charge of ensuring that MPs (respectively the president) do their job (see Chapter 5).

This observation is bolstered by the fact that relatively fewer Malagasy say they experience any real problems making their voice heard (Figure 3.13).

[32] The same result is found for local councillors.

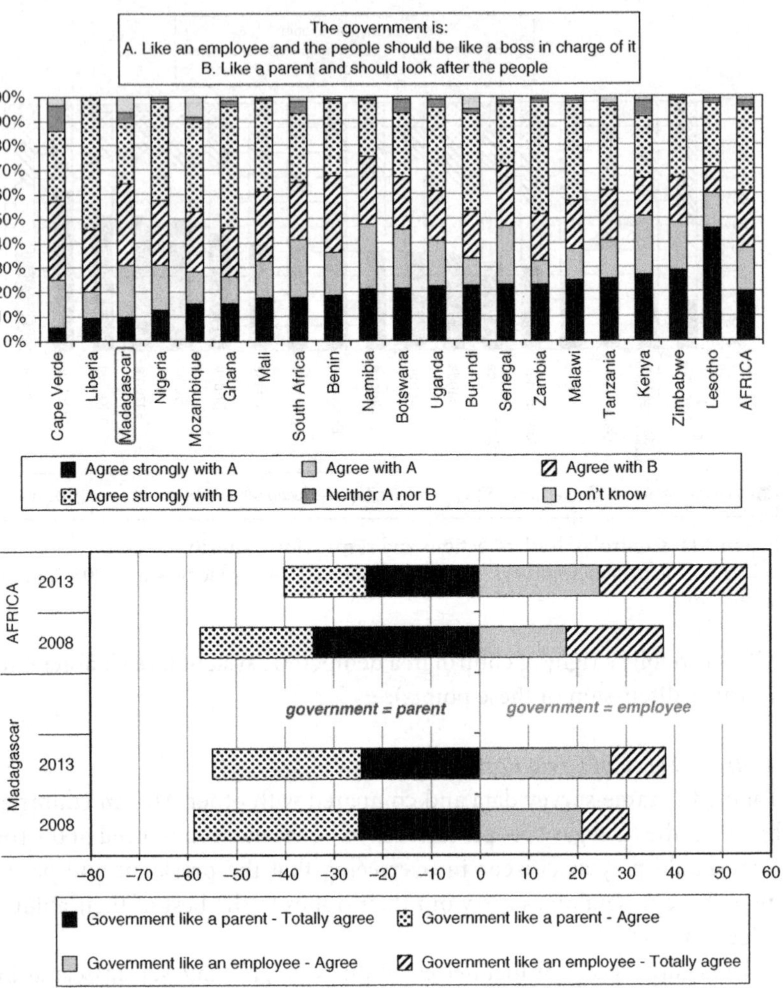

Figure 3.12 Leaders accountable for their actions or with parent status.
Source: Afrobarometer surveys, COEF Ressources/DIAL, Madagascar, 2008; authors' calculations.
Note: The question in 2013 was: 'Let's talk a little about the type of society you would like the country to have. Which of the following statements do you agree with most? Statement 1: The government is like a parent and should decide what is good for us. Statement 2: The government is like our employee, the people are its boss and should tell the government what to do.'

Madagascar is again top of the ranking of the 20 countries classed by the people's perceptions of the possibility to voice their expectations and points of view: a mere 17% of Malagasy see this as 'very hard' compared with 43% on

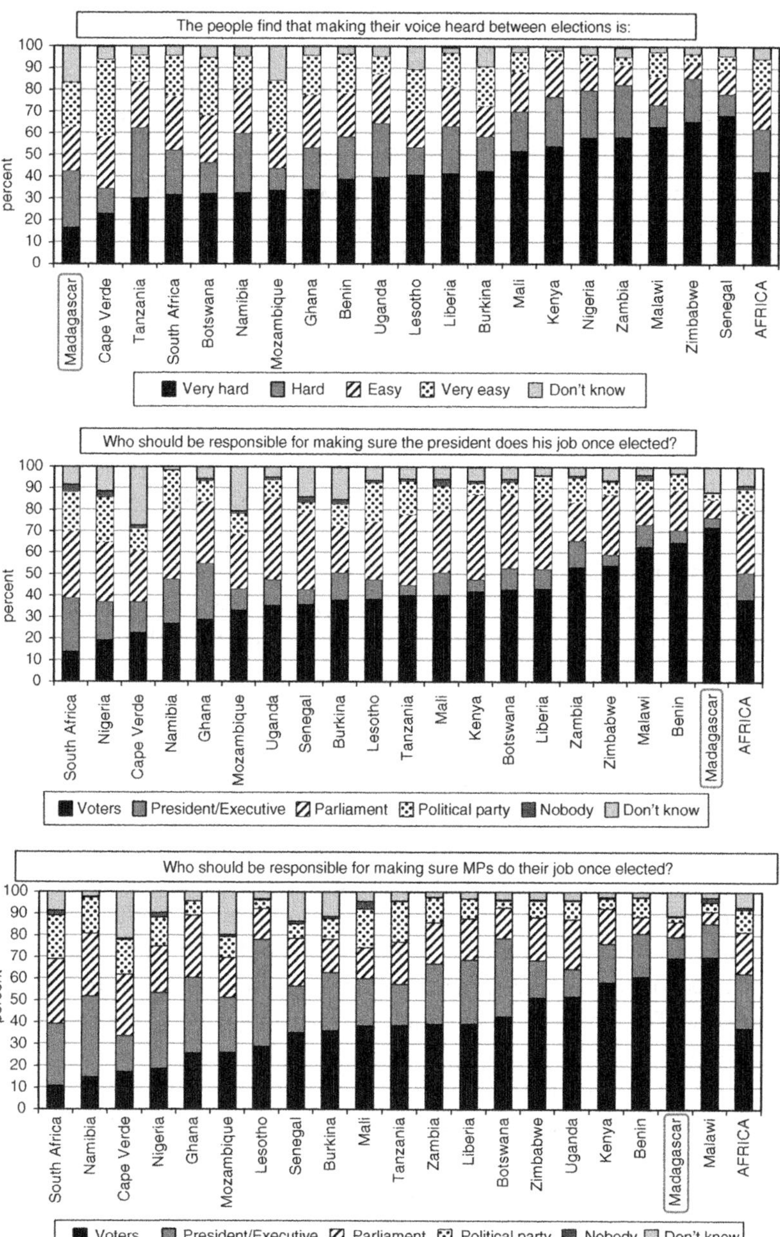

Figure 3.13 Role and voice of the people.
Source: Afrobarometer surveys, COEF Ressources/DIAL, Madagascar, 2008; authors' calculations.

average across all the countries (and 43% of Malagasy say it is 'very hard' or 'hard' as opposed to 63% on average).

These results seem at odds with the previous findings on the duty to respect authority and what could be called the 'citizen's duty to exercise restraint' with respect to the authority's actions (the people should refrain from criticising given that the ruling power is sacred and/or leaders are equated with parents). This contradiction points up how hard it is for the Malagasy people to find their place in the ongoing process: midway between tradition and modernity, the people are torn between the past (respect for the *fanjakana*, 'royal power') and their democratic aspirations (demand for the people's power of oversight).

3.5 Conclusion

Despite the largely negative picture of Madagascar's trajectory in Chapters 1 and 2, the country has a certain number of structural assets that go towards explaining how it works. In fact, the Red Island displays especially outstanding transformative capacities considering that it is mired in a long-term economic recession. Yet in seeking to highlight Malagasy society's strengths, this chapter has also unearthed some intrinsic historical and structural weaknesses.

Among the main assets, control of violence is key. There have been few episodes of violence in Madagascar's history since independence. Conflicts have been low in intensity and have never degenerated into mass carnage. On the Malagasy political scene, the ruling power has never been able to resort to violence without being condemned and more often than not ousted for it. The use of state violence is never deemed a justifiable strategy in any circumstances. Although this taboo on political violence is clearly an asset, its downside is inertia when it comes to enduring forms of symbolic violence. The aversion to any violence that might be sparked by social unrest supports the perpetuation of an inegalitarian hierarchical system that has become entrenched over the years.

Second, Madagascar's formal institutions appear to have a real operational capacity. The institutional system was relatively sounder at independence than in other comparable developing countries, and Madagascar has demonstrated its institutional capacity for regulation on a number of occasions: the exceptional continental success of the export processing zones; significant results in the fight against bureaucratic corruption from 1995 to 2005; and power rotating twice in two successive free elections (1993 and 1996), bringing the Red Island into the exclusive club of

African countries meeting this democratic transition criterion in the 1990s. However, the country has failed to consolidate these achievements and has even lost ground as some institutions have gradually slipped into decline.

Last but not least, the role of the people is key to understanding the country's economic and socio-political history. Civic aspirations clearly play a role in the country's economic dynamics and especially in triggering crises. Aspirations to democratic governance are manifestly a major driver of popular frustration. Expression of the population's dissatisfaction by popular, even eruptive, movements has to date never engendered an enduringly more inclusive, more democratic society. It has, however, always stood as a corrective force putting a stop to the autocratic excesses of the governments in place. In this respect, its role appears to be highly positive. Yet despite the people's democratic agenda, they are torn between civic aspirations for democracy and meritocracy and the traditional values that demand respect for the objective and symbolic hierarchies inherited from the past. The dilemma then is how to make the sacred status of power, seen in the *raiamandreny* status (parents or elders) bestowed upon leaders, compatible with the idea that these same leaders should be accountable to the people for their actions in a democratic system.

It may seem surprising to find structural societal qualities in Madagascar's past experiences given its steady downhill slide. Yet the idea could be put that the positive and negative dynamics observed are ultimately two sides of the same coin: the virtuous circle can rapidly turn into a vicious cycle when a certain number of criteria or conditions are not met, and vice versa. Consequently, explaining the mechanisms behind the deterioration in the island's social, political and economic situation can help identify the conditions, the potential levers needed, to define suitable policies able to turn around the long-standing recessive trend and set Madagascar on a positive path.

4

Obstacles

4.1 Introduction

The previous chapter discussed Madagascar's structural assets. Yet these qualities have failed to prevent its long-term downward slide, as a combination of powerful obstacles stands in the country's way. This chapter looks into the nature of these impediments: atomisation of the population, which restricts interaction and possibilities for the collective expression of aspirations and discontents; weak intermediary bodies between the people and leaders; a long-standing political theology that assumes the legitimacy of the 'traditional' leader; elite individualism wherein the elites are incapable of creating sound organisations and forming stable coalitions; a strong urban–rural divide; and the ambiguous role of donors and the international community. This chapter will first show that an atomised rural population, weak intermediary bodies, the elites' organisational flaws and strong social segmentation are salient features of Malagasy society. It will go on to explain how these social structure characteristics play a part in the recurring political instability and long-term social inertia by fostering the system's reproduction over time. Lastly, it presents the external factors that need to be taken into consideration: weight of the donors and, more generally, the international community.

4.2 Population Atomisation and Increasingly Individualistic Elites

An Atomised Population

An Uncaptured Rural Class

The atomisation of the population is a first defining feature of the way Malagasy society works. In keeping with what G. Hyden (1980) has analysed in many African countries (and potentially more so than in these other countries), Madagascar's rural world has not really been 'captured' by either the political system or the economic system. The fact that there is no real structural pressure on the land or on the means of subsistence enables the rural class to live on their territories virtually self-sufficiently. Madagascar still has a very low population density (42 people per km^2 in 2015 as opposed to 49 in Cameroon, 66 in Burkina Faso, 71 in Côte d'Ivoire, 78 in Senegal, 97 in Benin and 622 in Mauritius), even though the country has no real desert areas[1] ruling out human settlement. Although the south of Madagascar has often been hit by drought, cyclones and locust infestations that repeatedly cause serious food shortages among the people living there, these events have never triggered any massive population displacement to other areas, rural or urban. This is an important feature of Madagascar. The country has a particularly low level of rural exodus compared with other African countries, and the vast majority of migrants who do head for the capital are 'well-educated' individuals from secondary towns.[2] So the rural world still accounts for 78% of the Malagasy population today (INSTAT, 2013).

There is a low level of rural capture by the political system, because the state merely scrapes the surface of a good part of the Malagasy countryside. Rural public infrastructures are often substandard if not absent altogether.[3] The so-called decentralisation policies have in reality done little to connect local government bodies with the central administration. There is moreover some suggestion that certain laws – such as the 2001 domestic security act giving back power to the *fokonolona* – promote a somewhat remote organisation of government, particularly given the possibility of enacting security *dina*.[4] And then there is the fact that government organisation

[1] Madagascar ranks eighteenth of the least densely populated countries in sub-Saharan Africa. Among the countries with significantly lower density are Namibia, Mauritania, Botswana, Chad, Niger, Mali and Somalia.

[2] 'In 2012, only 15% of the inhabitants were migrants (not born in the *fokontany* in which they live). They were essentially local migrants, with 56% from another *fokontany* in the same commune and 24% from another commune in the same district. Inter-district migration stood at 5.3%. Inter-province migration accounted for 14.5% of migration' (INSTAT, 2013).

[3] In 2012, for example, 28% of country-dwellers were still illiterate as opposed to 11% of urban residents, reflecting the inadequacies of state education in this respect.

[4] The *fokonolona* has the power to enact its own rules called *dina*. 'The dina decrees those measures that the population concerned deems necessary for the harmonisation of social and economic life ... in a structure based on popular self-government of security ... and establishes a collective disciplinary arrangement to keep order and public security' (Act 2001–004 on the general regulations covering public security *dina*). In the event of

around a dominant party, which provided a form of integration under the first and second republics, has gradually unravelled over time. The upshot of all these factors is that the legitimacy the rural population is supposed to confer on the holder of the *fanjakana* is often mere lip service (Fauroux, 1999; Raison-Jourde & Roy, 2010). Distanced as they are from the central power, the rural people show little interest in public affairs.[5]

There is also a low level of rural capture by the economic system, as there is still little monetisation in the countryside. Economic integration is limited on the rural markets. For example, the average earned income in rural areas was 34,000 ariary in 2012 (INSTAT, 2013), or approximately 11 euros per month at the exchange rate at the time. These earnings of less than half a dollar per day per worker employed in agriculture[6] clearly show that the vast majority of the rural population's consumption comes from their own production.[7]

The rural population's mutual economic situation could well act as an incentive to join forces, but two elements stand in the way. First, their aspirations are constrained by their knowledge of and access to a world that far transcends the local level and which they may see as out of reach, but where decisions that affect them are made. Cut off as they are in the back of beyond,[8] their hardships are not always associated with dissatisfaction (Gurr, 1970). And even when they do express discontent, the political arena does not easily spring to mind as holding the solutions (fatalism). Second, fragmentation and geographical isolation are not conducive to the development of the kind of networked sociability (Tilly, 1976) liable to spread awareness and support or drive collective action.[9] This phenomenon is reinforced by a lack of interpersonal trust (see Box 4.1).

a breach of a *dina*, the *vonodina* is enforced stating the damages, pecuniary or in kind, owing to the victim and the *fokonolona*.

5 The Afrobarometer surveys clearly show this lack of interest in public affairs. In 2013, for example, 60% of the rural population said they were not very (29%) or not at all interested (31%) in public affairs, compared with 40% on average in the 33 countries taking part in the survey. Only the Ivoirians displayed a higher rate (65%).

6 The fact that not all the members of the rural households are gainfully employed places Madagascar way below the World Bank's extreme poverty line of $1.25 a day (even though this threshold is calculated in purchasing power parity terms).

7 The phasing out of the fiscal minimum tax in 1972 paradoxically added to this distancing of the countryside by constraining entry to a market system (see Chapter 2).

8 Their isolation is exacerbated by poor television coverage. The 2013 Afrobarometer survey found that 77% of country-dwellers had never watched the news on television (compared with 57% of rural Africans on average). See also Wachsberger (2007).

9 Even though the spread of mobile phones may change things slightly.

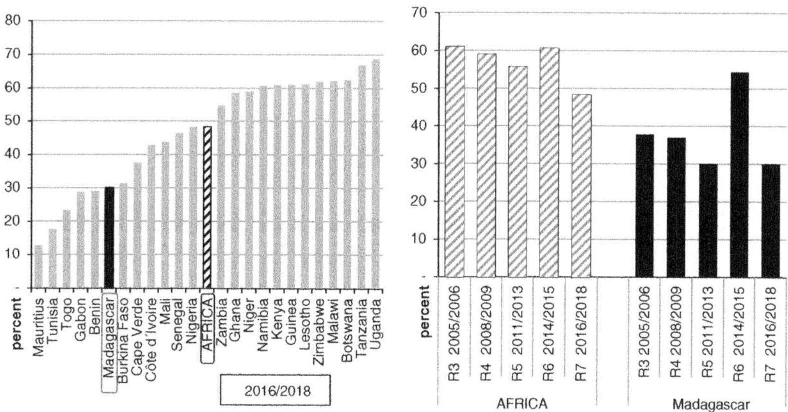

Figure 4.1 Partisanship.
Sources: Afrobarometer surveys for Madagascar, COEF Ressources/DIAL; authors' calculations.
Note: The figure on the left reports on data from the seventh wave (R7) of the Afrobarometer surveys (2016/2018).

Weak Intermediary Bodies

The population's isolation reinforces and is reinforced by the weakness of the formal and informal intermediary bodies. Intermediary bodies (political parties, unions, pressure groups, community-based groups, etc.) are independent, autonomous social groups that can provide the link and interactions between individuals and the state. These intermediary bodies are particularly weak in Madagascar. The number of political parties has risen considerably since the 1990s, but their number is inversely proportional to their popular representation. The 2013 Afrobarometer survey reveals that just 30% of Malagasy identify with a political party (as opposed to 56% on average in Africa), making Madagascar one of the African countries where parties are least representative of the people. Moreover, this rate of partisanship has declined over time: from 38% in 2005 to 37% in 2008 and 30% in 2013 (Figure 4.1).

Associative involvement is also sporadic. The rate of association membership in 2014 was one of the lowest of all the African countries surveyed: 77% of Malagasy said they were not a member of an association (and 17% said they were a passive member). Excluding the small islands (Cape Verde and Mauritius) and the countries in the north, association membership is the lowest in sub-Saharan Africa. In addition, considering active members only, Madagascar has the lowest level of the entire continent. This particular Malagasy situation is clearly borne out by other statistical sources,

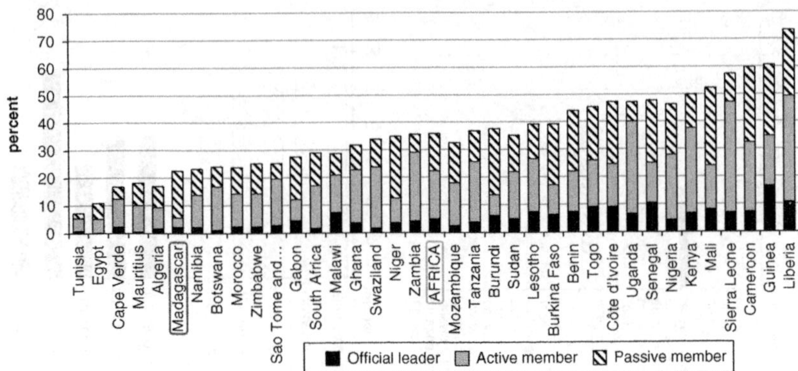

Figure 4.2 Membership of associations. (a) Member of an association or a community-based group.
Sources: Afrobarometer survey 2014; authors' calculations.

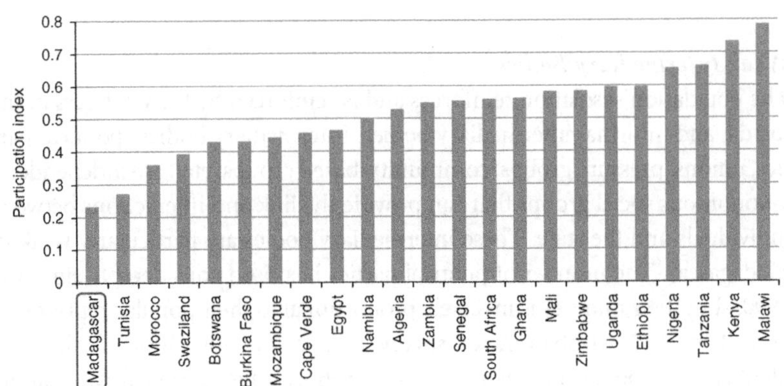

Figure 4.2 Membership of associations. (b) Involvement in or membership of a club or association.
Sources: *Indices of Social Development* (ISD), June 2013, International Institute of Social Studies (ISS) in the Hague, Erasmus University Rotterdam. www.indsocdev.org/; authors' calculations.
Note: The index used here is an aggregate of indicators from different sources.

such as those produced by the International Institute of Social Studies in the Hague (Figure 4.2). Lastly, even on a local level, individuals have little contact with political representatives. More than 70% of Malagasy never get in contact with a local councillor.

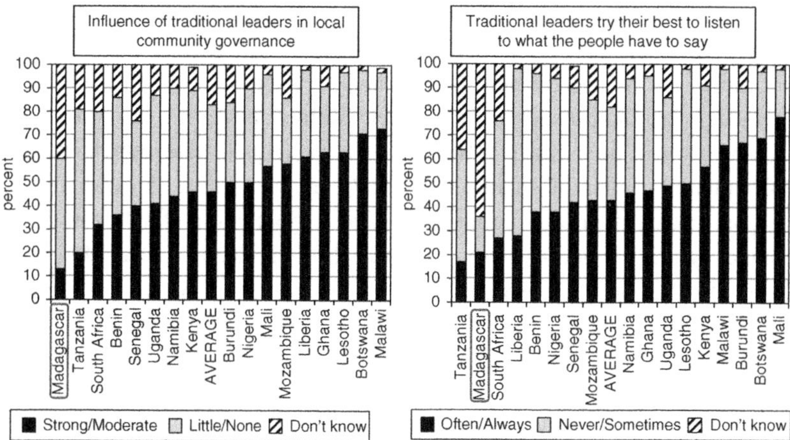

Figure 4.3 Informal intermediary bodies: Weak or non-existent influence of traditional leaders.
Sources: Afrobarometer survey 2008; COEF Ressources/DIAL; authors' calculations.

It would therefore seem that neither local authorities nor political parties and civil society organisations have any real power. They hold no sway with the population and their lack of influence means that the people do not feel the need to approach them.

Neither is the weakness of formal intermediary bodies offset by the existence of informal structures. The pre-eminence of informal forms of organisation, especially the role and weight conferred on traditional leaders, is frequently put forward to explain the workings of developing societies, particularly in Africa. However, traditional leaders have little influence in Madagascar which, once again, stands out as the country where they are the most disconnected from public life in Africa (Figure 4.3). Traditional leaders are confined to an entirely secondary role. Not only do they have little influence (just 13% of the people consider they influence governance in their local area compared with 46% on average in the sub-Saharan countries), but they are also criticised for their poor capacity to give the people a voice (a mere 20% say the traditional leaders do their best to listen to the population, compared with 43% on average for the other countries). Although their symbolic power is mentioned in certain circumstances (more out of respect for elders, and therefore 'traditions' than recognition of their role), traditional leaders suffer on the whole from the same disrepute as formal authorities in Madagascar. The reasons for this can be found in the country's history, especially in the colonial strategies that undermined the traditional authorities.

BOX 4.1 Lack of Interpersonal Trust

'Culture' is often advanced to explain development. In the case of Madagascar, the population's mind-set features among the obstacles regularly brought up in the quantitative surveys and qualitative interviews (see Chapter 5). Different characteristic traits are mentioned (individualism, self-centredness and/or family-centredness, no notion of the common good, inability to set up a group project, short-sightedness, etc.), although they are not substantiated by any real evidence. Yet what is especially striking about these statements is that they are ostensibly at odds with '*fiaraha-monina*' ('living in harmony'), supposedly a Malagasy cultural value (Urfer, 2012b).

Individualism and a sense of community at a societal level tie in with the question of interpersonal trust put forward by a vast body of literature, building on Fukuyama (1995), to explain a country's organisational efficiency. We take the population survey findings to shed some light on this question in Madagascar's case.

Distrust of others could form one of the explanatory factors for Malagasy society's instability and development impasse. The suggestion is that lack or loss of trust is behind individualism and failure to set up and see through collective projects in the long run. Politicians' short-term, shifting alliances of convenience (see later) could be a result of this.

The Afrobarometer surveys provide the means to empirically support this theory and identify any Malagasy particularities. The Malagasy people do not stand apart from other nationals in terms of kinship trust (the circle comprising the extended family), where they are more or less in line with the African average (Figure 4.4). This finding is consistent with the country's ranking among the traditional societies that attach a great deal of importance to the family.

However, the Malagasy clearly differ with respect to their level of trust in people outside the family circle. In 2008, a year for which detailed data are available, the island had one of the lowest levels of interpersonal trust: 39% of Malagasy said other people they knew were fairly or entirely trustworthy (as opposed to 56% on average for the 18 countries studied, with a maximum of 84% for Uganda); 23% of Malagasy said people they did not know were fairly or entirely trustworthy (compared with 40% on average, with Uganda again in first place with a 77% level of trust). In 2013, when a larger number of

BOX 4.1 (cont.)

countries were surveyed,[10] Madagascar's position looked less extreme. Yet the island still ranked among the countries where apprehension of acquaintances (outside the family circle) predominated: only 35% of the population placed some extent of trust in the people they knew (as opposed to 39% in 2008) and just 6% said they trusted them entirely (as opposed to 13% in 2008).

These findings raise the question as to the reasons for this distrust and whether it is structural or cyclical. Although the wording of the survey questionnaires has changed slightly, dynamic comparisons reveal a decline in interpersonal trust. This trend could be due to the population's impoverishment and a survival strategy set in motion by a climate of insecurity and a weakening state. At the same time, annual variations aside, Madagascar's history may also explain the low level of trust found in the country. The divisions created during the colonial period, especially with the events of 1947, may be behind still-festering resentment (Wantchekon *et al.*, 2011; Chadefaux, 2012; Lahiniriko, 2018). Mention might also be made of the effect that dysfunctional institutions (discussed later in the analysis) can have on interpersonal trust. Yet whatever the reasons, this predominant mood of distrust among the people cannot fail to have an impact.

Individualistic Elites Cut Off from the People

Weak Elite Organisations

Elites and coalitions of elites are central to North, Wallis and Weingast (NWW)'s framework. Yet analysis of Malagasy society finds that social atomisation is also manifest in the shape of extensive individual ranking and differentiation, including, if not primarily, within the elites for whom these principles of distinction and hierarchical rank tend to be more important than principles of resemblance. This explains why there are more families – sometimes full-blown clans – than there are organisations.

Chapter 2 paints a picture of the country's elite groups based on a reinterpretation of Madagascar's history through the political economy lens. It defines six periods revealing several power strata. Each of the periods is marked by a balance-of-power game change and relative renewal

[10] However, the interpersonal trust questions were less detailed. In particular, no information is available on the level of trust in people the respondents do not know.

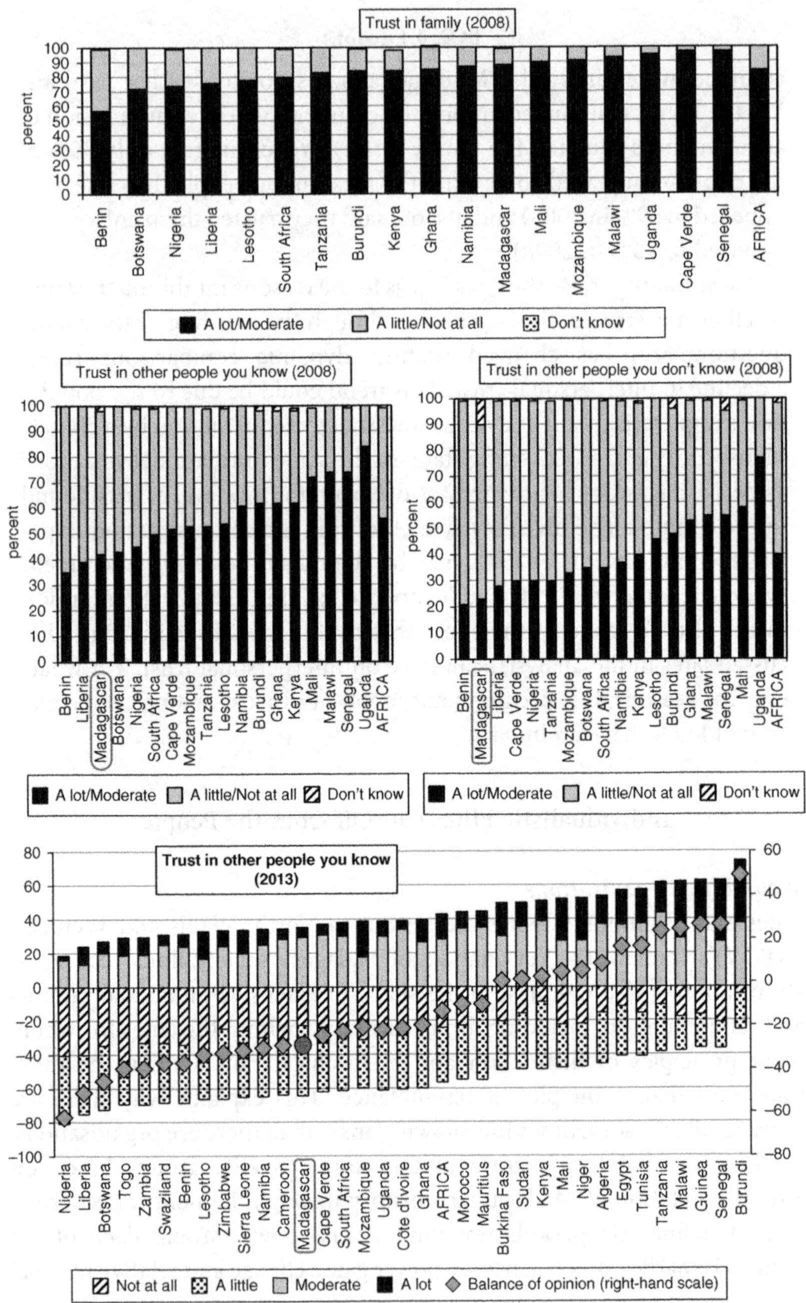

Figure 4.4 Level of interpersonal trust.
Sources: Afrobarometer survey, COEF Ressources/DIAL for Madagascar, 2008, 2013; authors' calculations.

of the dominant coalition. At the same time, the defined power 'groups' are also found to have porous borders. Individual strategies to stay on top (education and marriage strategies, conversion from one type of power to another and switching allegiances) resemble reciprocal elite assimilation in part (Bayart, 1993; Galibert, 2011a). The elite sphere in Madagascar hence remains very contained, as discussed in Chapter 5: elite members are marked by strong social birthright, which grows stronger over time. Consequently, neither ethnic group, geographical proximity or membership of the same status group, nor similar economic, religious or political activities can establish sound enough interpersonal solidarities to draw set lines between groups. Madagascar hence has no real non-state organisations or at best extremely weak organisations. The political and economic sphere is historically dominated by a small number of families, but none of them appears to have enough power to organise society (Galibert, 2011a; Fremigacci, 2014b).

Given their small number considering the sources of power and wealth, conflicts are generally minor and do not involve the formation of any real long-term coalitions. They take less the shape of a struggle between firmly established elite groups than a jockeying for position (*ady seza*) among individuals, families or clans.

When conflicts do occur, temporary arrangements may emerge as assorted flexible alliances of convenience (Forces Vives, Trois Mouvances, etc.; see Chapter 2). They cannot last as they are arrived at by negotiations binding on individuals only (they are not inclusive and do not commit the credibility of organisations). In a way, since independence, the elites have not felt the need to organise as they have not faced any real conflicts with well-identified enemy groups, whether from outside the country (see the case of South Korea; You, 2012) or from within the country (in the case of ethnic conflicts, which do not hold much currency in Madagascar; see Chapter 2). Paradoxically, then, Madagascar looks today to be a country suffering from both its national cultural unity and its situation, as remote both geographically and from the point of view of the economic interests behind the sources of international conflicts.[11] No group forms or needs to consolidate because there have never been any conflicts on a large enough scale to warrant their organisation. Alternatively, the lack of any division into set, long-standing groups with which individuals identify might itself explain the lack of conflicts.

[11] See later for the impact of this situation on the donors' position.

Social and Spatial Segmentation

The atomisation of the population, and the elites to a lesser extent, combines with strong social segmentation as seen from the importance of position by birthright and urban–rural divides alongside a profound disconnection between the elites and the rest of the population.

A recent economic history study comparing social mobility in five African countries (Bossuroy & Cogneau, 2013) from the 1930s to the late 1960s reveals that social mobility was particularly low in Madagascar during this period. Malagasy farmers' children remained farmers much more frequently than in the other four countries considered (Côte d'Ivoire, Ghana, Guinea and Uganda). This phenomenon cannot be explained by fundamentally different changes in occupational structure. The authors believe that strong occupational inheritance in Madagascar is due mainly to educational inheritance, as (rural) farmers have much less access to schooling.

Low social mobility also combines with very low spatial mobility. This is evidenced by domestic migration, between provinces and areas of residence, where Madagascar posts the lowest rate of the five countries considered in the study. Yet it is also true of international migration. While Madagascar's actual rate of emigration (Table 4.1) is lower than the average for sub-Saharan Africa (1% vs. 1.7% in 2010), the Malagasy people's spectacular immobility can be seen above all from their emigration aspirations. Whereas nearly one in three Africans (32%) expresses a hope of emigrating one day, just one in ten (11%) aspire to emigration in Madagascar (OECD & AFD, 2015). Not only did the Malagasy consider

Table 4.1 *Emigration and international emigration aspirations*

(%)	Madagascar	Sub-Saharan Africa	Benin	Burkina Faso	Côte d'Ivoire	Cameroon
Would like to migrate (2007–13)	11	32	23	30	25	34
• permanently and in the next 12 months	9	13	14	17	39	14
• have started making arrangements	8	30	12	28	28	20
Rate of emigration (2010–11)	1.0	1.7	0.6	0.7	4.4	1.5

Sources: OECD, AFD, 2015; authors' calculations.

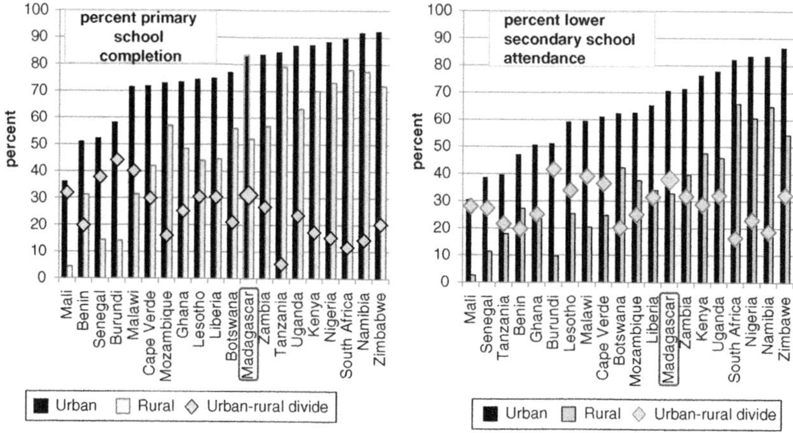

Figure 4.5 Urban–rural educational divide.
Sources: Afrobarometer survey, COEF Ressources/DIAL, Madagascar, 2008; authors' calculations.

the idea of leaving the country less often over the period, but proportionally four times fewer considered leaving for good and in that particular year, while only a minute proportion said they had started making arrangements to do so (0.07%, twenty times less than their African counterparts). The Malagasy have the least desire to emigrate of our four comparison countries, and the least motivation by far of the entire continent (the next countries down the list being Rwanda and Burundi).

This low spatial and social mobility, two self-reinforcing phenomena, is a definite long-run characteristic among the Malagasy population. Both hierarchical structures and geographical divides persist. The gap between urban and rural areas (where 78% of the population live) remains today. Education indicators show that the cities have taken precedence, with a particular drive enabling more than 80% of city dwellers to complete at least primary school and more than 70% to attend secondary education, both highly satisfactory rates compared with many African countries (Figure 4.5). The countryside, however, has been left to fend for itself and posts much lower results (52% and 33% respectively). Madagascar displays the largest gap between town and country of all the countries that can boast a relatively educated urban population. This observation speaks volumes about the policymakers' neglect of rural areas.[12]

[12] The urbanists' censure of what they call the 'anti-urban bias' of development assistance (Guilloux, 2010; Helluin, 2010) in no way counters this observation. First, the political leaders' positions on which these studies are based do not necessarily reflect the realities of

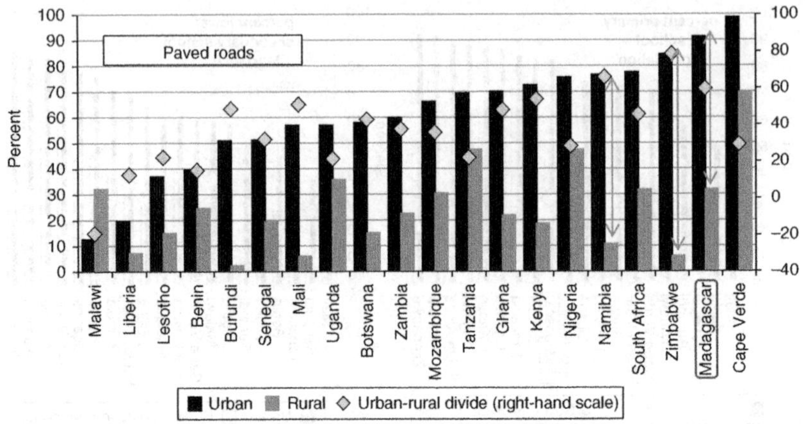

Figure 4.6 Percentage of paved roads in urban and rural areas.
Sources: Afrobarometer survey, COEF Ressources/DIAL, Madagascar, 2008; authors' calculations.

The same observation can be made with respect to certain infrastructure development indicators (Figure 4.6). In a comparison of twenty African countries, Madagascar is well placed in terms of urban road infrastructures with a high rate of surfaced roads (90%). Yet the rate in rural areas barely tops 30%.

The island ranks among the countries with the widest urban–rural divide (in third place behind Zimbabwe and Namibia). This may well be directly due to the sheer expanse of the countryside which, although justifiable, demonstrates the magnitude of the town–country inequalities.

Another example that clearly illustrates this divide between town and country (and the even wider divide between the capital and the countryside) concerns the people's interest in public affairs. Figure 4.7 shows that Madagascar had the widest urban–rural divide in this area in 2008 (ahead of Kenya and Côte d'Ivoire). More than 70% of urban dwellers said they were interested in public affairs as opposed to just 55% in rural areas. This finding reflects a feeling of exclusion (or self-exclusion) that certainly has an effect on political participation.

One last striking feature of Malagasy society is the disconnect between the elites – a tiny minority of 'educated' individuals directly or indirectly associated with the ruling power (see Chapter 5) – and the majority of the

the policies conducted (as seen, for example, from the very low level of actual decentralisation and the education figures discussed earlier). Second, the donor 'urbanophobia' reviled by these authors has hardly made any significant change to date to the balance between urban and rural worlds.

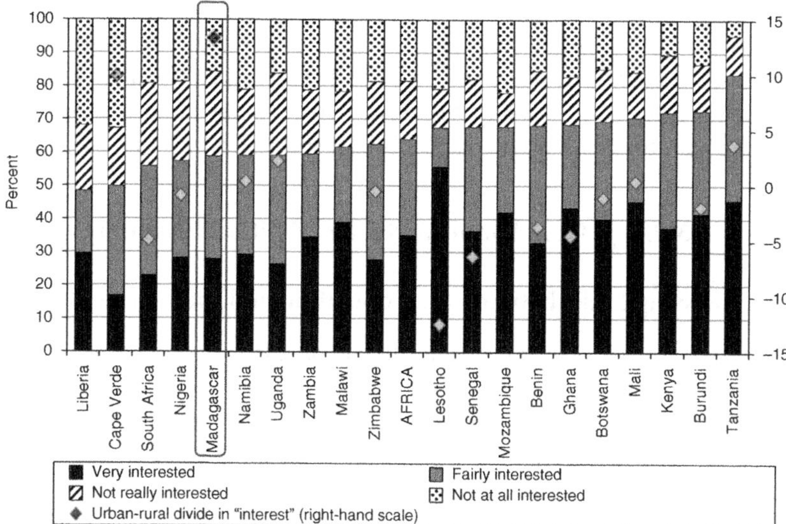

Figure 4.7 Urban–rural divide in interest in public affairs.
Sources: Afrobarometer survey, COEF Ressources/DIAL, Madagascar, 2008; authors' calculations.

population. This disconnect, a source of exclusion and disaffection, hinders democratic consolidation. It also allows for a poorly informed population to be manipulated and used, thereby adding to political instability. The high levels of some of the indicators on urban dwellers – with the potential to place Madagascar among the African achievers, if not the highest African achievers – make the inequalities between these elites and the rest of the population even more problematic. It might indeed seem surprising that a privileged few enjoy conditions similar to developed country nationals while no effort is made to improve the situation of the vast majority of the population locked in poverty traps.

The dynamics at work at the international level further accentuate the domestic inequalities. The presence of 'globalised elites' who manage to align their standard of living with developed countries widens the gap with the masses who are shackled to the domestic growth rate (stagnation and recession).[13] Moreover, these elites frequently place a good part of their savings outside of the country either because of misgivings about the country's future or quite simply out of economic self-interest. Cogneau (2015)

[13] In November 2015, *Forbes* magazine published the first ranking of the wealthiest people and families in French-speaking sub-Saharan Africa: four families in Madagascar featured in this ranking in fifth, sixth, eleventh and twenty-third place.

finds from a file of Swiss HSBC subsidiary bank accounts that Malagasy investments from 2006 to 2007 were among the thirty highest as a ratio of the GDP of the country from which they came. They represented 2.9% of the country's 2005 GDP, making Madagascar the number four sub-Saharan African country (behind Liberia, Zimbabwe and Kenya) for this indicator.

4.3 Long-Term Social Inertia and Political Instability

Missing Links between the Population and the President

Malagasy society's weak intermediary bodies have left the country with a lack of echelons able to act as go-betweens in negotiations between the people and their leaders. From this point of view, Malagasy rural dwellers and urban informal workers resemble the small-holding peasants described by Marx in his study of the social classes in France from 1848 to 1851.[14] The same political inference could also be drawn from this as that observed by Marx in 1851. Unable to defend their interests, the Malagasy working classes cannot represent themselves and must themselves be represented. 'Their representative must at the same time appear as their master, as an authority over them, an unlimited governmental power which … sends them rain and sunshine from above,' (Marx, 2005). In Madagascar, it is always the rural dwellers who make the election (and the urban dwellers who break it) by choosing the person who best embodies these characteristics.

The country's leadership is personalised by the president, flanked by his family and a few affiliates who have forged ephemeral alliances with him. Outside of his small family clan, the president chooses (or has to choose) the figures in his entourage for contingent political reasons. Allies can therefore turn coat in a blink, as they are not constrained by any solid, lasting bond such as membership of a given political family or any other group (ethnic groups, for example, in other countries).

The model proposed by NWW, whereby vertical organisations structured into patron–client networks enable an informal redistribution of wealth from rents, is not applicable to Madagascar. Although the country clearly displays some forms of clientelism, their reach is limited in time (to a given period) and space (to a very small number of people). There cannot

[14] 'The small-holding peasants form a vast mass, the members of which live in similar conditions but without entering into manifold relations with one another. Their mode of production isolates them from one another instead of bringing them into mutual intercourse. The isolation is increased by France's poor means of communication and by the poverty of the peasants' (Marx, 2005).

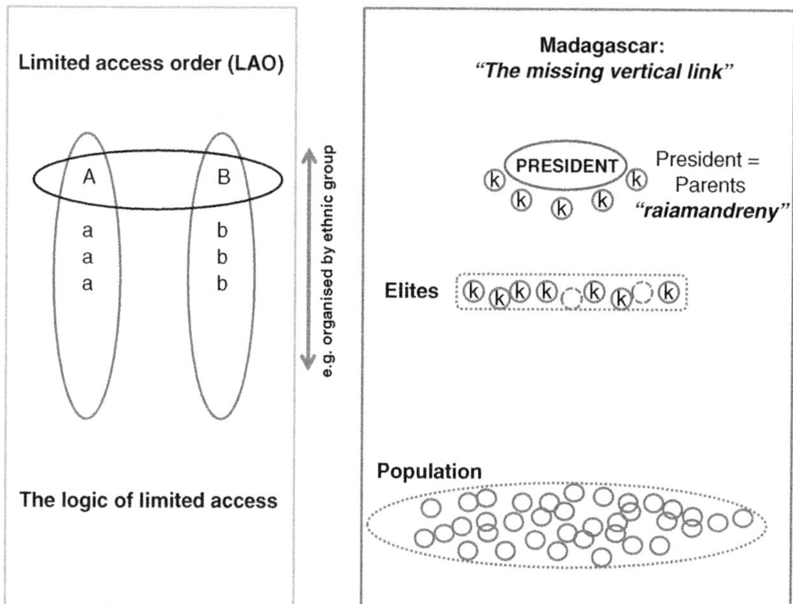

Figure 4.8 Missing links between the population and the president.
Source: Authors.

be said to be either a network or a system linking the interests at the top to those at the base of a well-established organisation (Figure 4.8). There have been attempts in Madagascar's past to set up this type of pyramid system (e.g. with the proliferation of Vanguard of the Malagasy Revolution [AREMA] in the 1970s and 1980s, and Tiko in the 2000s), but these systems could not endure because their existence hung upon a direct link with one man, the president in office.

Personalisation of power and 'excessive presidentialisation' stand the president alone before the people. This phenomenon is accentuated by the still-pervasive traditional belief (that leaders exploit, if not sustain) in the exceptional nature of the *fanjakana*[15] (the state) and the *raiamandreny* status (the duly respected father and mother of their subjects) of those who embody it. This reveals a certain relationship with politicians inherited from the way the Malagasy state formed and constituting what, in keeping with Kantorowicz (1981), could be called a political theology. As already

[15] *Fanjakana* means the state, but is etymologically associated with *manjaka* (to reign) and *mpanjaka* (the king). So the president could in a way be considered 'King of the Republic', as illustrated by photographs of Andry Rajoelina and his wife dressed in the royal colours descending the steps of the Queen's Palace in December 2010.

seen, this relationship with politicians tends to place a particular value on the 'traditional' leader whose position is based on his dynastic roots, making him a *raiamandreny*. In that peasants cannot represent themselves and that they adhere to this political theology, they feel politically represented by the leader who manages to fit this traditional description[16] (see Box 4.2). This state of play is often demonstrated by the referendums (Weber, 2003) regularly held by the different heads of state.

This missing vertical link between the population and the president not only suffers from a lack of safeguards, but it is also behind the president's extreme fragility. The popular support the president seeks to win, particularly at the ballot box, is always quite tenuous in reality. It rests solely on a symbolic dimension that is either accepted (*raiamandreny* status) or imposed (the presidential party's network within the administration), rather than on patron–client relationships that anchor affiliations to the ruling power. The president cannot count on structurally sound forces to organise, negotiate, support and guarantee the stability of his power. So any popular discontent, be it from a minority or shared by a majority, can be used by people with a minimum of rallying capacities to destabilise the regime. Aware of this risk, the president in turn seeks to strengthen his power even further and becomes increasingly autocratic.

The Role of Religion and the Churches in Structuring Society

Churches and religion have decisive weight on the national scene in Madagascar (Map 4.1). Two recent nationwide surveys (2012 National Survey on Employment and the Informal Sector and 2015 Employment Survey, INSTAT) both show the influence of Christianity, with just over 70% of the Malagasy population claiming to be practising Christians (31% Catholic, 21% Protestant FJKM, 13% Malagasy Lutheran Church, 1% Anglican, 1% Adventist and 5% other Protestant).[17] This religiosity is not just a popular phenomenon. It is strongly represented at the highest level of the nation, as Madagascar is a secular republic whose constitution asserts the

[16] This echoes one of the elements developed by Mannoni (1948) in his day. Nonetheless, we do not subscribe to his essentially psycho-culturalist explanation of Malagasy society or, in particular, his theory of a dependency complex, which has often come under severe criticism (Bloch, 1990).

[17] Previous estimates finding the rate of conversion to Christianity to be approximately 45% nationwide (Hübsch, 1993) underestimated the weight of Christianity. The two latest official surveys moreover report that 19% of the population say they practise the religion of the ancestors (*fivavahana nentin-drazana*) while fewer than 2% say they are Muslim.

BOX 4.2 Form of Access to Power and Political Theology

The changes of heads of state display a certain continuity from 1960 through to the early 1990s. Access to power is grounded, at least in part, in a sort of political tradition. Tsiranana was vice-president of the national executive council under colonisation (following the French Overseas Reform Act), before becoming its president. He was elected President of the Republic by parliamentary vote. The first presidential election by universal suffrage was held in 1965, when he won 97% of the vote. Ramanantsoa received his power from Tsiranana before his popular endorsement by referendum in 1972 (86% of voter turnout). The military directorate headed by Ratsiraka did not take power, but had it handed over by Ramanantsoa. Ratsiraka then gained popular endorsement from the 1975 referendum (95% of the vote). Just like the medieval European kings, the head of state here personifies something of an immortal political entity.

The rural world's adhesion to this political theology helps keep the political power in place without a patron–client network to shore it up. The rural areas in effect have been left out in the cold by all the policies conducted since independence, with the possible exception of the measures introduced by Ratsimandrava before his assassination in 1975.

However, this political theology has lost ground since the late 1980s. Although the countryside re-elected Ratsiraka in the 1989 presidential election, the cities – including Toamasina, the president's stronghold – voted massively for the opposition candidates and D. Ratsiraka won only 63% of the vote. In 1991, power changed hands for the first time in a break of continuity driven by the urban middle and working classes. Two years later, A. Zafy was elected by universal suffrage, but with 'just' two-thirds of the electoral vote and made an abortive attempt to extensively change the country's political organisation. And even though the return of Ratsiraka in 1996 restored the president's virtually monarchic power, he was elected only by a very small number of votes. All of these elements reflect a certain flagging of the political theology that supported the previous social order.

However, M. Ravalomanana's 'election' marked a return of this political symbolism in a new shape, with the transition from traditional leader to charismatic leader: the providential man. He was effectively 'elected' in good part for his remarkable attributes. This particularity meant he could uphold the monarchic form of the state with new

BOX 4.2 (cont.)

legitimacy (albeit endeavouring to give his rule tradition roots by hinting at being of noble extraction). These elements were behind his re-election in the first round of the 2006 presidential election and his strong popularity ratings (Razafindrakoto *et al.*, 2009b).

A. Rajoelina was brought to power by a coup d'état. This not-uncharismatic figure's assumption of power supported by a disillusioned urban youth party was based on no form of legitimacy. Yet once in office, he made incessant use of royal symbols to gain popular support. As to Hery Rajaonarimampianina, his election to the head of state had more to do with game theory (Rabemananoro, 2014) than any sort of legitimacy. The previous government's finance minister was not a favourite in the first round and picked up just 15.8% of the vote (across 33 candidates). He was finally elected in the run-off only because of a sharp drop in turnout (from 61.6% to 50.7%). His win with 53.5% of the votes cast therefore meant that he was actually elected by just 27% of registered voters.

So despite the waning influence of political theology since the end of the 1980s, elements of it still remain. Most of today's political players moreover continue to be recruited from among the ranks of the descendants of the former political leaders (see Chapter 5). A. Rajoelina's opponents, for example, organised themselves into movements associated with extant former heads of state. Descendants of high families continue to take part in the public debate as *raiamandreny*. And political leaders have continued to act as monarchs, making unilateral decisions, not accounting for their actions and sometimes using violence on the lower classes (see Chapter 3 on violence).

principle of the separation of church and state, but states in its preamble that 'The sovereign Malagasy people ... affirm their belief in God the Creator.'

In addition to the role of religion as a regulator of individual behaviour in everyday life, its predominant role is apparent in the influence that ecclesiastical bodies exert over the country's political scene through their public statements.[18] Down through the different periods and events, the

[18] For just some of the references available on the role of the churches and how religious circles have influenced Madagascar's socio-political path, see Raison-Jourde (1991), Urfer (1993), Roubaud (1999, 2000), Rabearimanana (2001) and Rafitoson (2014).

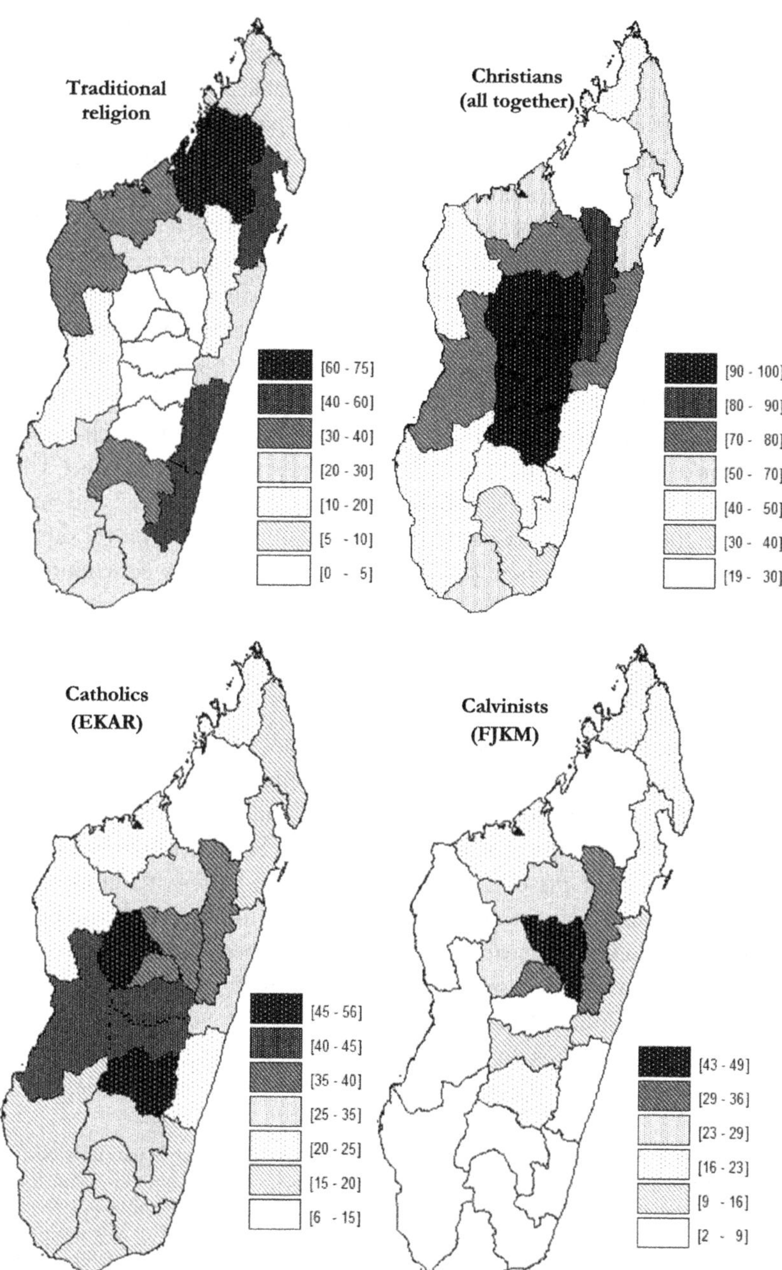

Map 4.1 Distribution of main religions by region (%).
Sources: ENEMPSI (2012), INSTAT; authors' calculations.

churches have been at times wanted and approved (if not acclaimed) and at others condemned by the people.[19] Second, given that churches are seen by the people as potential countervailing forces, or at least as moral authorities serving as guardians of ethics and social justice, politicians seek to win their favour and support. So among the strategies used by leaders to gain the people's support are including explicit religious references in their speeches and, directly or indirectly, bringing on board certain church representatives in national affairs to underpin their legitimacy.

This strong influence of religion raises the question as to its role in the workings of society in general. The question is particularly apposite given the aforementioned absence of a vertical organisation capable of acting as an intermediary and advancing the dialogue between the Malagasy people and their leaders. Does the churches' pivotal presence at all levels nationwide make them the cement that holds Malagasy society together? Their contribution to the island's stability and development is clear and vindicated by the population (Chapter 5) in such areas as their moral support (Wachsberger, 2009), their participation in the people's education and public awareness and even some of their positions that have helped settle crisis situations at key moments in the country's history (Urfer, 1993). Nevertheless, they do not play an unequivocal role in the hierarchical structuring of Malagasy society.

First, the weight of religion can be used to reinforce the previously mentioned political theology that elevates the president, the ultimate incarnation of secular power, to a symbolic and virtually divine station (keeper of *Hasina*[20], the providential man, etc.). So rather than working in favour of the principle of popularly accountable leaders, religion can be manipulated and play an ambiguous role. For a large part of the poorly informed population in search of guidance and steeped in religious credulity, any reference to or association with the churches can bestow a special status on leaders that places them beyond democratic control.

Second, the churches do not escape the principles of differentiation and rank inherited from the past and still rooted in society (Chapter 3).

[19] The population clearly wants the religious authorities to take an active part in public life, in particular by showing the way with respect to major societal questions, but it also considers that the churches should not interfere directly in politics (Roubaud, 1999). For example, churchgoers were incensed at Archbishop Odon Razanakolona's position in support of Andry Rajoelina during the 2009 crisis and the approval of his office as President of the High Transitional Authority by the bishops of the Episcopal Conference of Madagascar (Rafitoson, 2014).

[20] The monarchs' supposed invisible essence of power, which could be passed on to their descendent and formed the basis of their political legitimacy.

Differential statuses are conferred by denomination with, for example, generally higher social standing (in terms of assets, income, access to employment, etc.) for FJKM households (Roubaud, 1999). At the same time, there is an implicit hierarchy of parishes ranked by parishioner family status. These observations may be merely the consequence of the aforementioned phenomenon of social reproduction from one generation to the next. Yet they nonetheless stand as evidence of structuring that, instead of placing all the people on an equal footing, actually appears to entrench the hierarchies and secure the social pyramid.

The Effects of Social Structure

The upside of the atrophy of non-state organisations and absence of any real coalitions between groups holding political and/or economic power is that the political system is not a closed shop. The question could therefore be put as to why Madagascar exhibits such pervasive inertia, aside from short episodes of political unrest in protest at the ruling power (even though these have become chronic, recurring with increasing frequency). For example, it is surprising to find that the political crisis starting in 2009 lasted five years. Amid rising popular discontent, economic and social indicators in the red, and a president of the High Transitional Authority supported only by alliances with individuals who may well have been powerful, but were void of a base, no national non-state organisation emerged to break the deadlock in a situation so often judged potentially explosive. In reality, most of the players involved in politics, counting essentially on international pressure, were waiting for the two protagonists responsible for the crisis (Andry Rajoelina and Marc Ravalomanana, president and ex-president) to make the decisions (Châtaigner, 2014). So we need to try and understand the reasons for society's general inertia. The country's economic path of ongoing recession since the early 1970s has obviously left a mark on the population's capacity to react, organise and mobilise. Economic recession generally tends to inhibit aspirations.[21] Yet the absence of forces pushing for change can also be explained by Madagascar's social structure.

At the top of the structure (Figure 4.9) is the president and his affiliates who tend to monopolise the power and rents. Just beneath them are the other members of the elites. They tend to be in favour of the status quo and are likely to fear disruption of the established order, which could lead to

[21] Even though aspirations increase in growth periods (as shown in Chapter 3).

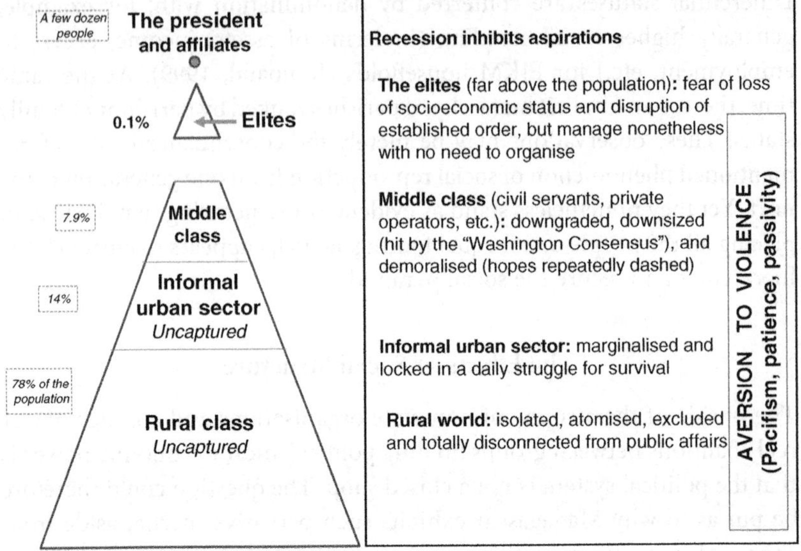

Figure 4.9 Social structure and factors behind inertia in Madagascar.
Source: Authors.

a loss of socioeconomic status and privileges. They have the benefit of economic rents (their family legacy, level of education and network),[22] which secure them a much higher standard of living than the vast majority of the population without the need to organise or mobilise. We could go so far as to raise the idea of an implicit pact between elites and the ruling power, given that the majority of the members of the elite take part in ruling or are associated with prominent figures in power. Only those members of the elite out to capture large-scale rents (or above a certain threshold) and those who start out lower down the ladder (newcomers on the public scene) need to engage in a minimum of organisation, or rather seek allies (short-term allies until they gain the power), and create a climate of agitation to access the rents. Yet these are mere individuals acting alone or in small groups. They do not seek or manage to rally any real formal organisations (parties, civil society organisations, etc.) or informal organisations (militia, service associations, pressure groups, etc.) in their support.

Nor does the middle class form a force capable of galvanising mobilisation. With their formal urban players (private and public), they have

[22] An analysis of the elite reproduction process and the scale of their networks is presented in Chapter 5.

already suffered a downgrade as their situation has massively deteriorated with the recession. In addition to their relative impoverishment at the hands of the 'Washington Consensus' and adjustment policies, the class has also been downsized by a reduction in civil servant numbers. The long line of dashed hopes and fear of further downgrading in a divided society can but make for demoralisation.

Ranking beneath the middle class, in urban areas, come the informal urban workers. Their very status spells their marginalisation. Unable to count on support from the authorities, they feel excluded and their exclusion from the system is exacerbated by their informal situation, which places them on the fringe of the legal system, beyond all state control. They are caught up in a daily struggle for individual survival in an environment that is hardly conducive to starting their own social movements. The rural masses at the bottom of the pyramid are even less likely to make their voice heard. As discussed earlier, they are geographically isolated, atomised, excluded and totally disconnected from public affairs. They therefore have no way of organising or forming a force for change.

This social stratification supports a form of passiveness, which in turn reinforces the stratification itself. This imposed, albeit probably acquiescent, passiveness is clearly revealed when the population are asked about the nature and their extent of acceptance of extreme inequalities between rich and poor in Madagascar (Table 4.2). Half of the population see this situation as normal: 26% think it is 'normal because that's fate', while a similar proportion (25%) say that it is 'normal because it's the fruit of

Table 4.2 *Perception of the nature and legitimacy of inequalities*

Percentage	Urban	Rural	Male	Female	Total
In Madagascar, there are people who are extremely rich and others who are extremely poor. It is:					
Normal because that's fate	25.8	26.1	25.6	26.4	26.0
Normal, because it's the fruit of their labours	20.3	27.2	25.4	25.6	25.5
Not normal, but nothing can be done about it	25.5	22.7	22.9	23.9	23.4
Not normal and something should be done about it	28.4	24.0	26.1	24.1	25.1
Total	100	100	100	100	100

Source: 2015 *1-2-3 Survey*, Power and the People module, INSTAT-Katsaka; authors' calculations.

their labours'. Among the other half concerned about the inequalities, 23% say that it is 'not normal, but nothing can be done about it.' Just one-quarter (25%) believe that it is 'not normal and something should be done about it'. These findings tie in with the symbolic violence discussed earlier (see Chapter 3), which silently suppresses any thought of challenging society's enduring hierarchical system. The vast majority are divided between fatalism, internalisation of domination and resignation: three-quarters of the population accept the glaring inequalities either because they find them natural, or because they find them legitimate or because they think they can do nothing about them (Wachsberger *et al.*, 2016).

4.4 External Factors

The lack of economic development and the recurrent political and economic crises appear to be largely endogenous. First of all, Madagascar is outperformed by many countries subject to a similar international environment, especially in sub-Saharan Africa, for the most part less well endowed with factors of production such as natural resources and human capital (see the case of Burkina Faso; Koussoubé *et al.*, 2015). Second, these internal factors are massively perceived as the prime cause of Madagascar's downfall, as shown by Chapter 5. However, external factors also play a significant role in the country's trajectory, as discussed here.

The Ambiguous Role of the Donors

The NWW framework regards external factors as exogenous shocks. Yet in a country such as Madagascar, external factors are not limited to shocks. They also take the form of enduring elements with long-term repercussions: the arrival of foreign firms with the onset of globalisation, and the influence of donors with a permanent presence in the country and the political choices they impose (in the absence of a strong state with the wherewithal to propose alternative solutions; see the case of Vietnam analysed by Cling *et al.*, 2013).

The 'orthodox' literature points out the positive aspects of external factors. Yet where external players seek to promote general guidelines and 'best practices' drawn from developed countries, i.e. in NWW's terms, where they endeavour to mechanically transpose the (supposed) characteristics of open access orders (OAOs; competitive markets, property rights, liberal democracy, separation of powers, etc.) to limited access orders (LAOs), these external players, first and foremost the donors, generate perverse effects that can prove more negative than positive. In a word, market and democracy do not come to order.

To take just a few examples, on the economic front, it is commonly held that the strategy of export-led growth and exposure to global competition is the best way to exert pressure for economic efficiency via a productive standards replication or imitation effect. The resulting modernisation is supposed to generate the power to support competitive firms and a shift away from the rent-seeking companies often associated with businesses that are socially well-connected or prepared to pay bribes. This type of virtuous cycle can be found (You, 2012) in the case of South Korea, for example. It has also played a direct role in the case of Madagascar, as discussed earlier. A similar analysis could be made of the privatisation policies (introducing competition between foreign and national firms, deemed naturally more efficient than public enterprise). On the political front, consider the global pressure for democratisation during the third wave of democratisation (Huntington, 1991), the La Baule speech by President F. Mitterrand (1990) to French-speaking sub-Saharan African countries, and other external factors characteristic of certain environments (such as the competition with communist North Korea also raised by You to explain the end of the authoritarian regimes in South Korea).

Although some of these external factors can have a positive impact, it is important to consider their often seriously underestimated negative aspects. The following examples are taken from studies that we have conducted on Madagascar, focusing mainly on donor action.

The Structural Adjustment Programmes

The first example, and probably one of the most important, concerns the long-term consequences of the structural adjustment programmes (SAPs). These programmes formed the cornerstone of all economic policies implemented in Madagascar for nearly two decades, from the first half of the 1980s through to their official burial at the end of the 1990s. The question could incidentally be raised as to whether the poverty reduction strategies launched in the early 2000s (Poverty Reduction Strategy Paper [PRSP], Heavily Indebted Poor Countries Initiative [HIPC] and Millennium Development Goals [MDG] initiatives, with local version the Madagascar Action Plan [MAP] put in place by President Marc Ravalomanana) were not a way of pursuing the SAPs by other means. This discussion leaves aside the SAP agenda (the famous Washington Consensus: domestic and foreign liberalisation, and privatisation; Williamson, 1990) to concentrate on the programmes' harmful repercussions.

In addition to the SAPs' underwhelming growth record (see Chapter 2), their most damaging long-term impact – for economic, financial and ideological reasons not detailed here (see Raffinot & Roubaud, 2001) – was the destabilisation and loss of credibility of public institutions and action, and the civil servants in charge of implementation. Civil servants were largely criticised: overstaffed, overpaid, overcautious, privileged, unproductive, clientelistic, tribalistic, corrupt, etc. They found themselves transformed from development spearhead into parasites; scapegoats for the failure of the adjustment policies. To add to this symbolic stigmatisation, their social status was sometimes dramatically undermined by the freeze on hiring, if not firings, and budget cutbacks. The 'better state' window dressing merely served as a smokescreen for the more classic 'less state' slogan. From a strictly economic standpoint, this policy had three direct repercussions: the number of civil servants was cut, the purchasing power of civil service wages plummeted, and young people were crowded out from civil service jobs.

Most analyses of the reforms in Africa take civil service overstaffing as a premise (Lindauer & Nunberg, 1994; Lienert & Modi, 1997; World Bank, 2000). Yet the notion of optimal administration size is a subject of much debate. In reality, Madagascar, like the rest of the continent, suffers from chronic under-administration rather than over-administration (Razafindrakoto & Roubaud, 2001b). Although incomplete, the data available on both the 1990s, during SAP implementation, and the 2010s show this to be the case (see Table 4.3). In the mid-1990s, the ratio of the number of civil servants to the labour force stood at 2% to 3% in Madagascar compared with 24% for France; and things have gotten steadily worse since (the rate of public jobs halved from 1996 to 2010). The last time France had a ratio of two public servants to 100 working individuals was back in 1886 (de Singly & Thélot, 1988). This makes the relative size of Madagascar's administration one of the smallest in the world. More recent data merely serve to confirm this diagnosis: the rate of government employment[23] stands at 7% for Madagascar, slightly lower than but fairly similar to the level found in many African countries (albeit the only rate that is falling) and much lower than the rates observed for the European countries (from 50% to 100%).

Second, the wage–price de-indexation policy launched in the late 1970s stayed in place through to the mid-1990s. The resulting plunge was

[23] The rate of government employment, which is the ratio of civil service staff to the total population, is the indicator generally used for international comparisons.

Table 4.3 *Comparison of the rate of government employment in Africa and Europe (1990–2015)*

Percentage	1990	2015		1990	2011
Benin	(1995) 0.6	0.9	Sweden	(1995) 12.0	11.8
Burkina Faso	(1995) 0.4	0.8	France	(1996) 7.5	8.6
Cameroon	(1995) 1.6	1.3	Germany	(1995) 7.0	5.7
Côte d'Ivoire	(1995) 0.7	0.8	United Kingdom	(1998) 6.5	8.9
Madagascar	(1996) 0.8	0.7	Italy	(1997) 6.0	5.8

Sources: African Civil Services Observatory (OFPA), OECD/Public Management: Public Sector Pay and Employment (PSPE), 2015 Budget Act for the franc zone countries and Madagascar; authors' calculations.
Note: Some caution is called for when comparing the figures in view of the differences in structure and classification between countries. The rate of government employment is the percentage ratio of the civil service to the total population.

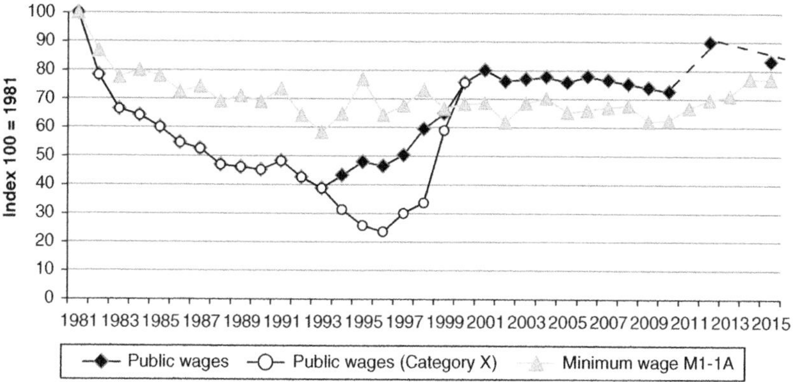

Figure 4.10 Public sector wages in real terms, 1980–2015.
Sources: Ministry for the Civil Service, Labour and Social Legislation; authors' calculations.
Note: Civil service wage category X is the highest category.

dizzying. From 1978 to 1996, average public service wages tumbled 74% in real terms (Figure 4.10). Despite a subsequent trend reversal, civil service wages in 2000 remained at 46% below their 1978 level. By 2010, they still had not moved from their level at the start of the decade. Although wage adjustments have tended to raise wages in recent years, the question is whether this trend will last. Civil servants are still far from recovering from the collapse of the early 1980s.

Lastly, the reduction in public sector recruitment over the last three decades has affected young graduates disproportionately. With the formal private sector failing to take up the slack, young graduates have suffered the most acute loss of socioeconomic status. Their downgrading is moreover social and financial: in the late 1990s, the starting wage for young civil servants nosedived 70% compared with the 1975–81 period when civil service wages peaked under the Second Republic's socialist regime (Antoine *et al.*, 2000). Contrary to observed trends in the developed world, the intra-generational gaps narrowed between those who managed or were able to pursue their studies and those shut out from school and school dropouts. Although such a trend tends to be inequality reducing, it comes as part of an overall race to the bottom for all.

This human resources shrinkage applies to all facets of public action, to the extent that a recent study on the state's economic performance finds it has 'one of the weakest public sectors in the world' (Naudet & Rua, 2018), as much in terms of its expenditure as its revenue (domestic and foreign). For example, per capita public expenditure has fallen two-thirds in volume since 1980, at twice the rate of per capita GDP. The diagnosis is the same for government revenue, mainly in the form of tax receipts, which are among the world's lowest, with an average long-run tax burden of approximately 10% fluctuating between 8% and 12% since the late 1990s. These figures are most probably lower in reality due to the underestimation of GDP.

State Weakening

The second example that we have chosen to discuss more briefly concerns the donors' ongoing operational actions, which have tended to weaken the state (and not just shrink it) since the early 1980s, with disastrous consequences (Urfer, 2012b; World Bank, 2012). Three illustrations of this can be put forward here. First, the promotion – blind to local conditions – of a market and private sector strategy saw the liberalisation of the rice sector and dismantlement of large-scale irrigation in the 1980s to offset the early-1980s' explosion in imports. This policy was an unmitigated failure in terms of growth in production and yields (Roubaud, 1997b). These shot down and are now among the lowest in the world (one to two tonnes per hectare compared with around five for Vietnam, with its similar starting point), when Madagascar was historically known for being a net exporter of luxury varieties. In the absence of a private sector able to lift the constraints on growth in production (irrigation, extension, access to improved seeds, inputs and credit and regional disconnection) and in the face of weak farmers' associations, any sector modernisation would call for regulations and public intervention to support the long process of building market institutions. The Vietnamese counterexample is particularly enlightening in this respect.

Examples abound of this naïve, dogmatic, heavy-handed approach. It was applied to the two waves of privatisation (1980s and 1990s), wherein private monopolies that went to players close to the ruling power all too often replaced the old public monopolies, while none of the targeted reform benefits materialised conclusively. In both cases, the government made huge financial losses by allowing public enterprises to be bought for largely undervalued prices, while the donors readily granted loans to these 'entrepreneurs' whose chief quality was their connections (Zafimahova, 1998; Jütersonke & Kartas, 2010). It is worth mentioning that one of the entrepreneurs to emerge from the first wave of privatisation was none other than M. Ravalomanana. Another example is the abortive decentralisation attempt (stopped by the 2009 crisis), which was promoted in the name of a better local service and supposed 'accountability' between local authorities and constituents. The rent capture mechanisms, far from being eradicated, shifted from the national authorities to the subnational levels on a wave of nepotism and capture of local public services by local elites (Bardhan, 2006).

Official Development Assistance

The third point worth highlighting has less to do with the actual content of the donors' recommended policies than their dominant methods of intervention and implementation. These have two main shortcomings: no long-run capitalisation on successes, even fragile and partial, and the adverse effects of the official development assistance (ODA) allocation principles. These two aspects are closely linked.

In the first place, the 'disbursement culture',[24] the short project cycle (a few years) and inevitably short-lived fashionable trends (innovation at all costs with, for example, the promotion of the user's contribution to education costs introduced in the mid-1990s as the ultimate solution to improve the quality of education, followed by its equally sudden scrapping in the 2000s to raise school enrolment rates among the poor) do nothing to encourage long-term investment in programmes, even those that have proved fairly successful. This

[24] Already criticised by the Wapenhans report (1992) with reference to the World Bank twenty years ago, this culture has neither disappeared nor even receded (Cling *et al.*, 2013).

culture is fuelled by the leading donors' system of incentives for their 'line managers', encouraging them to spend no matter what, knowing full well that the job rotation system will relieve them of all responsibility since they will no longer be in the job once project impact actually becomes clear. In addition, the constant quest for national models as examples (the famous front runners and other poster children) inevitably takes the focus away from a certain number of dysfunctions, especially governance related, despite the touted principles.

The international community's culpable forbearance towards M. Ravalomanana during his second term (2006–9) is a typical example of this: the upturn in growth over the period justified the blind eye turned to crumbling democratic and market principles. Yet attention had long been drawn to his methods to constantly expand his industrial empire by systematically grabbing economic resources for his own benefit (or the benefit of his entourage) and to his political authoritarian excesses (Razafindrakoto *et al.*, 2009b; Pellerin, 2009). Given that like causes produce like effects, growth in the late 1990s under D. Ratsiraka's presidency (1997–2001) gave rise to a similar state of play despite shamelessly open high-level state corruption. In the end, the international institutions' modus operandi had the opposite effect to the official development policy line: creation of monopolies to the detriment of a more open, competitive productive structure, and personalisation of power rather than institution-building.

Second, the ODA selectivity principle adopted by the donors from the late 1990s aggravated their inability to capitalise on their own experiences. Some studies taking the line of pioneering work by Burnside and Dollar (2000, 2004) endeavoured to show that aid effectiveness increased when recipient countries were well governed. Although this question remains much debated by researchers as the causal relation is hard to establish in any robust manner, the idea, better known under the name of *aid selectivity*, gained ground (see Amprou & Chauvet, 2004, for a review of the literature on this issue). The World Bank recommended applying the principle in its *Assessing Aid* report back in 1998.[25] Many donors today more or less directly apply this idea as a guiding principle, as can be seen

[25] The report's authors asserted that a $10 billion increase in aid to well-governed countries could lift 25 million people out of poverty as opposed to just 7 million people in the case of untargeted aid.

from a string of empirical studies on aid allocation criteria (Berthélemy & Tichit, 2004; Burnside & Dollar, 2004; Dollar & Levine, 2004).

Therefore, despite the empirical weakness of the studies underlying this principle (Banerjee *et al.*, 2006), the donor countries formally adopted it in the Monterrey Consensus in 2002 with most of them using more or less esoteric formulas (Kanbur, 2005, calls them voodoo formulas) to allocate their aid based on a mix of needs (poverty) and governance. Aside from the ethical problem raised by a policy that effectively punishes the oppressed populations of poor countries by reducing, if not altogether axing, the aid they so cruelly need (as was the case with Madagascar following the 2009 coup), recent 'fragility trap' studies show that the repercussions of aid selectivity can be disastrous. It can have a negative resilience effect: a country that has experienced one political crisis is more likely to experience another (Collier & Hoeffler, 2004). And once a country has become a fragile state, the chances are it will stay that way (what Andrimihaja *et al.* [2011] call a low-growth-poor-governance equilibrium trap).

These authors take a model, partly inspired by Madagascar's current case, to develop a theoretical model in which the combination of political instability and violence, insecure property rights and corruption creates an equilibrium of low growth and poor governance, characteristic of fragile (or failed) states, from which the states cannot extricate themselves. The only way to break out of this 'fragility trap' is to treat all three failings at the same time. In these circumstances, and contrary to the selectivity conclusions, ODA can be highly productive and play a decisive role in preventing a country's collapse. For this to be the case, however, ODA needs to be maintained, if not increased, rather than reduced, as a reduction could well hasten the onset of a failed state situation,[26] with lasting adverse effects. This analysis is, in our view, highly relevant to Madagascar, where aid was frozen following the 2009 coup d'état when it could have actively helped the country out of its impasse.

It is especially worth looking into the donors' share of responsibility in Madagascar's downward spiral, in that the island is among the countries where ODA is structurally low (Naudet & Rua, 2018). Madagascar was the one African country (given comparable population size) that received the least aid in 2013, at just 21 dollars per capita (Figure 4.11). Only Angola was worse off. The volume of aid as a percentage of GDP was particularly low, at approximately 5% in 2013. This poor score was not

[26] The authors' calculations estimate the probability of a 'fragile' state in 2001 still being fragile in 2009 at 0.95.

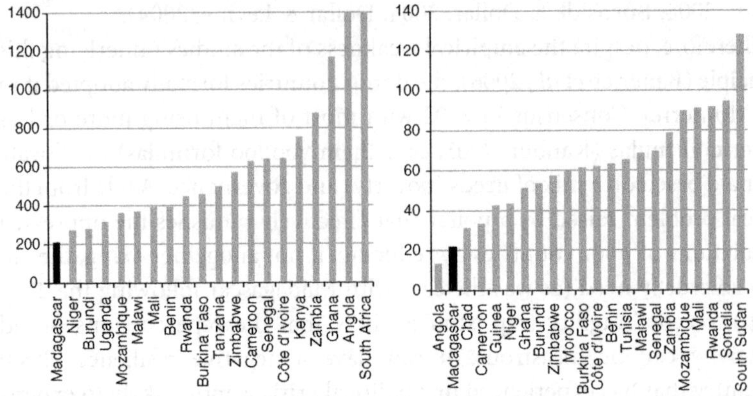

Tax revenue per capita in 2013 (2011 dollars, PPP) Tax burden in 2013 (tax revenue in percent GDP)

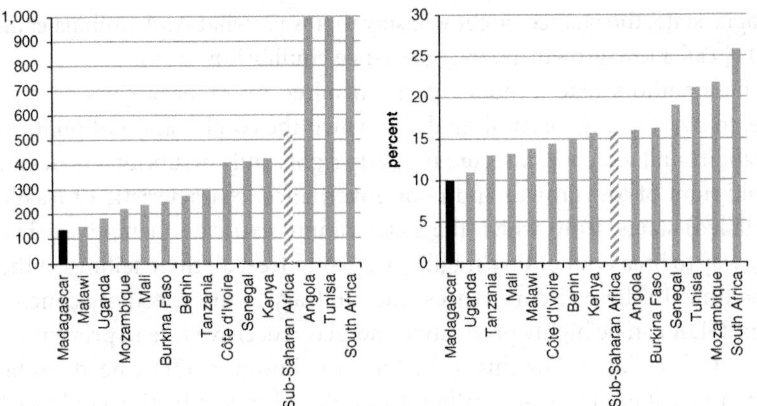

Figure 4.11 Official development assistance, government revenue and public expenditure per capita.
Source: Naudet and Rua (2017), data from DAC-OECD, IMF, World Economic Outlook Database; authors' calculations.
Note: The countries considered here have 10 million to 30 million inhabitants.

due solely to the crisis, as the ratio was even lower (4%) throughout the 2000–11 period and the few African countries with even less aid were all much wealthier. In fact, the weight of the volume of ODA cannot be evaluated solely on the basis of the country's population (more populated countries receive less on average). Poverty and governance also need to be considered, as explained above. An OECD study (2013) conducted just this exercise systematically. It came to the conclusion that Madagascar was an 'under-aided' country irrespective of the criteria taken to define the 'ODA benchmark'.[27] Madagascar even stood alone, alongside Malawi, as 'under-aided' across all four benchmarks. Even then, Malawi, comparable from many points of view, had received more than double Madagascar's per capita ODA (48 dollars as opposed to 18 dollars in 2011).

This situation is due in part to 'supply' factors. Madagascar does not attract donors because, unlike other countries (such as the Maghreb and the Sahelian countries for Europe), it is not deemed a sensitive or geostrategically important country that could become a source of instability for the Northern countries. In addition, the economic tragedy playing out in Madagascar is a long-run drama, which means it is not spectacular. It is therefore less likely to stir public opinion than acute humanitarian crises or bloody conflicts.

However, the aid deficit is also due to 'demand' factors. This makes it largely endogenous. The mobilisation to increase the country's aid attractiveness, the lack of proactive donor prospecting, and poor absorption and disbursement capacities all suggest that the low level of ODA may well be largely intentional. In the first place, the government and the political elites are behind this implicit will to refrain from foreign aid (while proclaiming it is insufficient) and avoid taxation and investment in public goods. Yet this arrangement also seems to suit the other elite groups, which are not seen to apply any pressure to change the situation and, in the case of taxes, benefit directly from it with a low rate of taxation. Nonetheless, there seems to be even more to it than that, as seen from Figure 4.12. Despite being manifestly under-aided, Madagascar counts among those African countries whose people believe they receive the most aid. A new paradox hence pops up in the Malagasy equation of a collective choice involving the elites and the population to the severe disadvantage of the people (and maybe even the elites).

Generally speaking on this issue of ODA, the country would in all probability gain from a strategy to increase the volume of aid and keep it at a stable level, rather than having the 'stop and start' situation induced by the principle of aid selectivity. This obviously means having to find new intervention modalities. Although the most obvious route is via non-state entities, targeted programmes also need to be designed to sustain the country's institutional capacities without condoning any illegitimate regime in place. This is a major challenge that depends primarily on

[27] Four benchmarks were chosen based on the aforementioned parameters of population, poverty and governance.

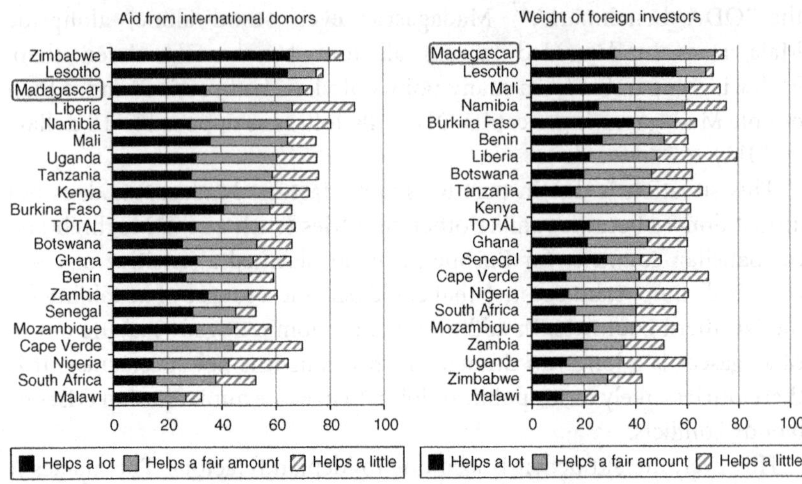

Figure 4.12 The people's perceptions of foreign assistance in Africa.
Sources: Afrobarometer survey. COEF Ressources (Madagascar), 2014; authors' calculations.

changing Malagasy society's political economy in terms of interactions between different elite groups and the social contract between the elites and the rest of the population. This issue is explored in Chapter 5.

Although there is no escaping the donors' role in diminishing public services and the low level of aid, they cannot be held the prime culprits for this situation. Such is the conclusion of the two authors of the above-mentioned study: the withdrawal of public services is essentially a political and economic organisational choice, the result of a form of consensus between elites who are indifferent to the pursuit of the common good and collective action. This conclusion stands as an illustration of the theories developed in this book. The same holds true for the case of ODA, which epitomises this view.

Institutional Deterioration and Loss of Legitimacy

We have seen that there are positive points in favour of Madagascar's institutions (see Chapter 3). These elements demonstrate their operational and organisational capacities when the political will exists and when the resources are there to run them. Today, however, the overall failure of the institutions is clear to see from the findings of qualitative interviews with key Malagasy figures, who disparage their shortcomings and dysfunctions.

We have sought to test the relevance of these assertions based on statistical survey data for the population *that specifically address these questions* (*Afrobarometer*, 2008). Here again, the surveys reveal a 'Malagasy exception'. Of the 18 countries where the same questions were asked, Madagascar is the country where institutional legitimacy (justice, police and tax administration) is the most problematic (see Figure 4.13). Just 39% of Malagasy consider that the population should always abide by court rulings (as opposed to 69% on average in the 18 countries). A small majority (51%) agree with the statement that *the tax administration always has the right to make people pay their taxes* (as opposed to 65% on average). Lastly, 60% (compared with 74% on average) agree with the assertion that *the police always has the right to enforce the law*.

The literature puts forward two theories with respect to trust in the institutions. First, the 'institutional' theory states that trust is determined endogenously depending on institutional performance (North, 1990). The 'cultural' theory, on the other hand, posits that trust is built exogenously (Inglehart, 1997). In the case of Madagascar, the question could be put as to whether this weak institutional legitimacy compared with the other African countries studied is due to cultural (and hence structural) characteristics or whether it is the result of gradual institutional deterioration. The population surveys provide some answers to this question. The opinion of the people in the capital (on which medium-run data are available) reveals a clear decline in the situation since the early 2000s: decreasing numbers of people believe the administration is efficient and place their trust in it (Figure 4.14).

This diagnosis is confirmed by the Afrobarometer surveys of a representative national sample. The data show that institutional legitimacy, already relatively weak in 2005, has dwindled over time:[28] The percentages fall respectively from 57% in 2005 to 39% in 2008 for justice, from 55% to 51% for the tax administration, and from 67% to 60% for the police.

A comparison of the indices of trust (taken from the question, 'Do you trust the following institutions?') also shows what appears to be an inexorable slide for the army, the justice system and the police from 2005 to 2014 (Figure 4.15). These observations suggest that the lack of trust might have more to do with the institutions' failings than a specific feature of Malagasy culture.

[28] The questions chosen to measure the legitimacy of the institutions are presented in Figure 4.13.

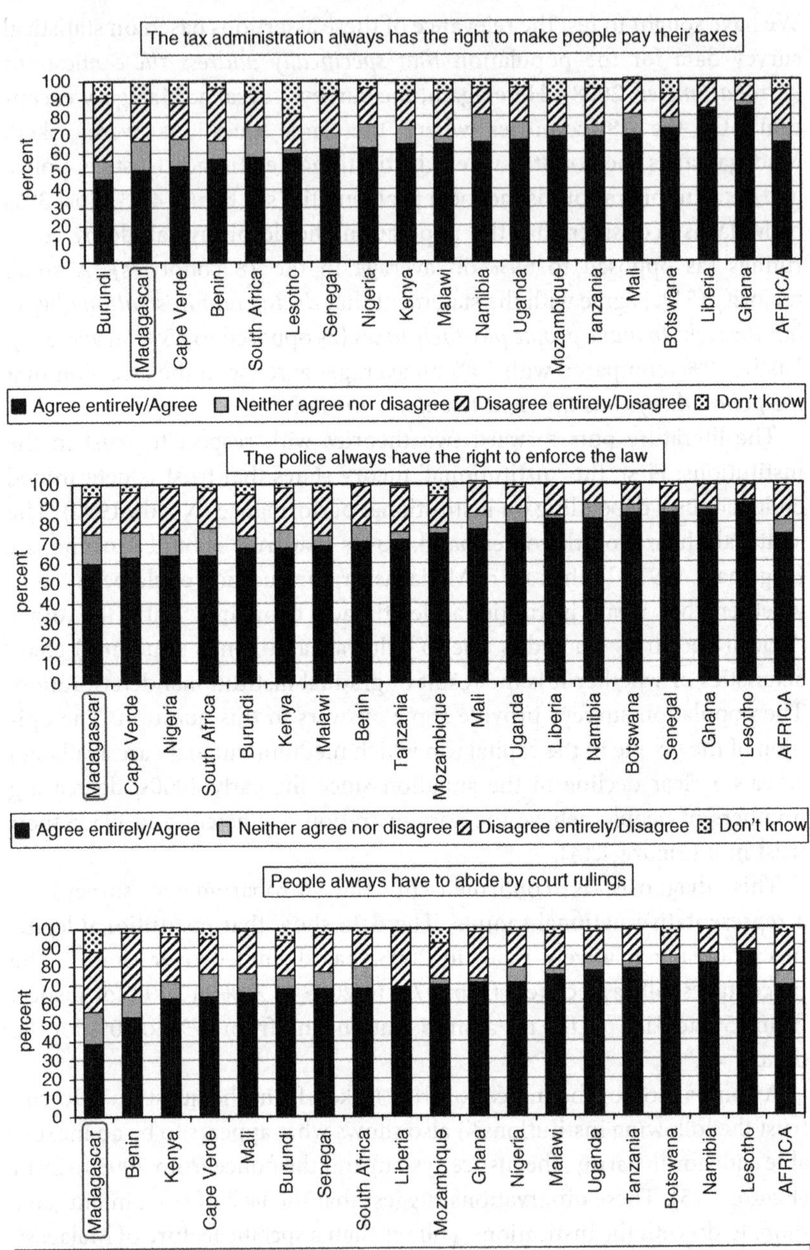

Figure 4.13 Institutional legitimacy (justice, police and tax administration).
Source: Afrobarometer survey, COEF Ressources/DIAL, Madagascar, 2008; authors' calculations.

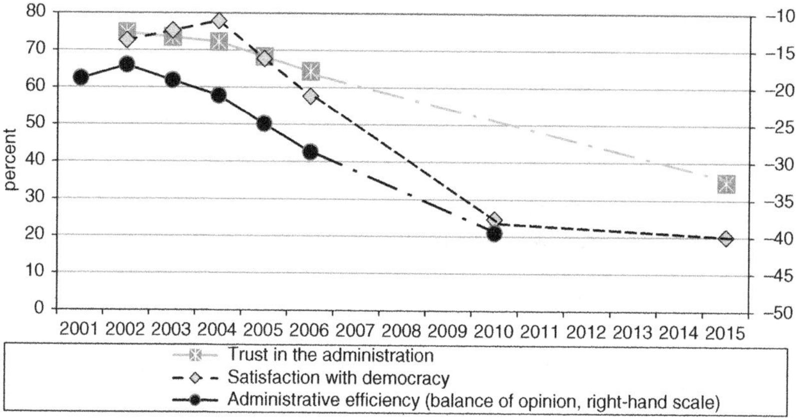

Figure 4.14 Gradual institutional decline.
Sources: *1-2-3 Surveys*, Antananarivo, 1995 to 2010, MADIO Project, INSTAT and DIAL, authors' calculations.
Note: The dotted lines indicate an absence of data for the period.

It could be speculated here that the state institutions inherited from colonisation and transplanted without necessarily taking account of local contexts (Badie, 1992) should gradually acquire real legitimacy. Unfortunately, there is no data available to measure the population's level of trust in the institutions in the 1970s and 1980s. Yet in the Malagasy case, the impact of the structural adjustment and 'less state' policies was particularly damaging to the effectiveness of the state institutions, which most probably undercut their legitimacy.

The institutions' weakness also ties in with the loss of a sense of community decried by the people. Institutional evasion tactics have gradually taken root and spiralled into a vicious circle. As avoidance behaviour grows to engulf more of the population, so it undermines the institutions' effectiveness and legitimacy. In the face of this institutional decay and the everyday difficulties that lock the population into survival strategies, individuals feel they only have themselves to count on. The above-mentioned poor interpersonal trust in Madagascar might therefore be interpreted as a consequence of distrust in the institutions.

Generally speaking, the institutions' loss of legitimacy when they are supposed to guarantee common principles and rules appears to have knocked out a frame of reference. This state of affairs gives free rein to all manner of individual survival strategies by the people and strategies to take and hold onto power by those who want to gain power or already

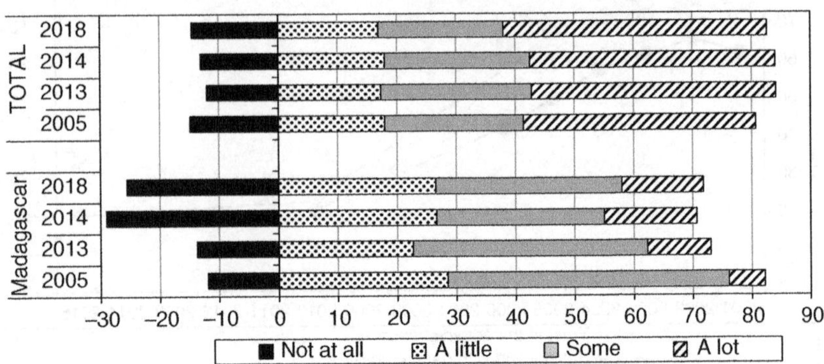

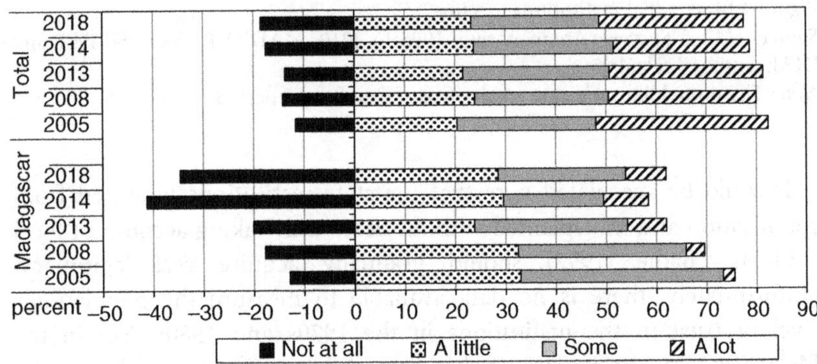

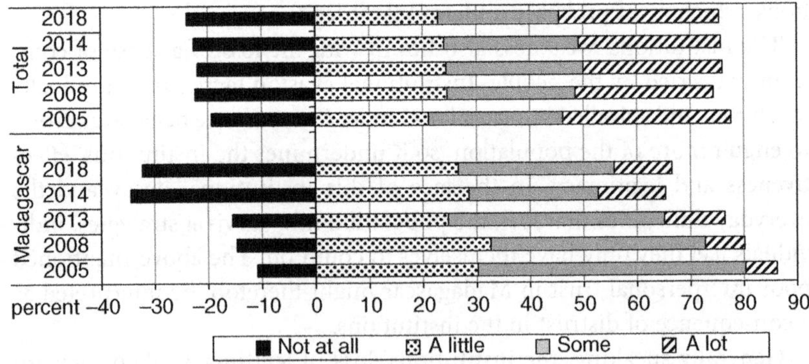

Figure 4.15 Decline in trust in the institutions.
Sources: Afrobarometer survey, COEF Ressources/DIAL, Madagascar, authors' calculations.
Note: 'Total' refers to the average for all the countries considered by the Afrobarometer network.

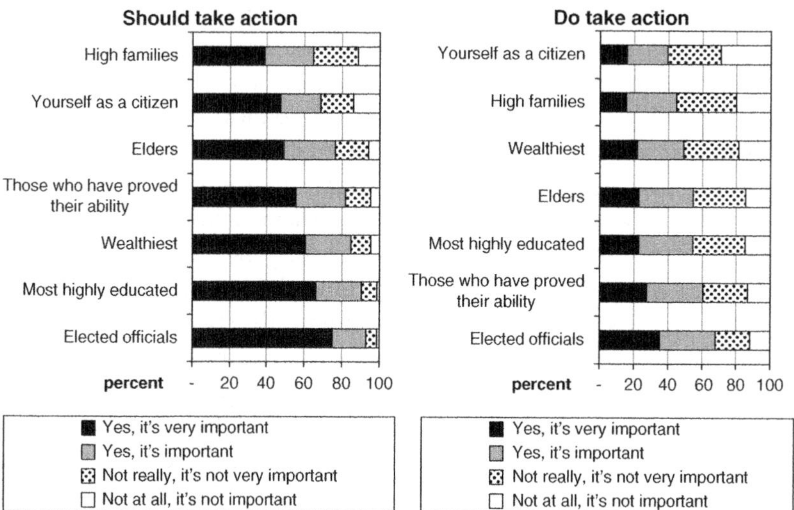

Figure 4.16 Role for the common good.
Sources: 2015 *1-2-3 Survey* in Madagascar, Power and the People module, INSTAT, Katsaka manga; authors' calculations.

have it. This change of standards has shattered the sense of public interest, damaging interpersonal trust with it. With individual actions and short-term games of alliance uncontrollable, distrust has grown among individuals and driven another vicious cycle as it makes collective actions impossible.

The question could be raised as to whether there is a deliberate formal institution avoidance strategy at work here for the purpose of applying informal rules, as put by the theoretical framework proposed by Khan (2010). Yet what we are seeing in the case of Madagascar is more the authorities' inability to stop the institutional rot (formal and informal). Some elites look on and make the best they can of this state of decay, while a very small group actually takes advantage of it. No one really feels responsible. The economic operators consider *it is not their job to deal with the country's affairs.* The bourgeois elite, operating behind the scenes, can argue that they are not directly involved in political rule. The leaders in government, aside from their main aim to secure their economic and political power, can wash their hands by claiming pressure from economic groups, prominent families and the international community. And the people, dissatisfied but disempowered, continue to leave matters in the hands of their leaders or, more broadly, the elites (see Figure 4.16).

For example, when asked who should take action for the common good (Wachsberger *et al.*, 2016), the Malagasy place elected officials top of the list with 93% saying it is their role to take action and 75% saying it is very important they do so. Other elements of political legitimacy seen as important in addition to the status of elected official are education, wealth and past engagement. Two-thirds of Malagasy think it is very important for the most highly educated individuals to participate in public affairs, followed by 61% and 56% respectively designating the wealthiest and those who have previously proved their ability to work for the community.[29] Yet it is the comparison of expectations of action with actual action that really shows the lack of action taken by both elites and the people. Action is systematically judged inadequate (20 to 40 percentage points below expectations). For example, although the vast majority of the population expect elected officials to take action, barely over two-thirds believe they actually do and just 35% say they take a great deal of action. The gap is even wider when it comes to the most highly educated: two-thirds of adults feel that action by these individuals could do a great deal for the country, but just 23% think that this is really the case. Dissatisfaction is also clear from the population's extent of involvement, although there is no telling from the survey data whether this is out of choice or constraint. Whereas two-thirds would like to take action, a mere 40% actually do (and just 16% in a significant manner). This gulf between expectations and taking responsibility reflects a widespread sense of not knowing which way to turn.

4.5 Conclusion

Malagasy society's obstacles are first and foremost internal. They have a good deal to do with the long-run perpetuation of a deeply unequal social order in which status and place of birth still strongly condition the individual's lot in life. These inequalities are firstly spatial, with a growing divide between urban and rural worlds. Rural dwellers, overlooked if not despised by the ruling elites, are atomised and have poor rallying capacities. Locked in the fallacy of *fihavanana* as a civic contract, they remain dominated by a political theology that will normally make them accept authority figures as legitimate and put up with their lot. Yet the principles of differentiation

[29] Taking M. Weber's classification of authority, political legitimacy is a combination of 'legal-rational' (based on the leaders' skills and the legal way they have come to power), 'traditional' (power is granted certain individuals according to their social status) and 'charismatic' (power is bestowed on certain individuals based on their extraordinary characteristics).

and rank also affect the elites, preventing them from organising themselves as a group. Although members of the ruling elites form alliances, they are generally coalitions of convenience to put a stop to one person, family or clan becoming too influential or to prevent a newcomer from entering the inner circle. They are dissolved once they have achieved their aim. These factors hence explain as much the country's political instability as its long-term social inertia. Political instability is a consequence of this inability among elites to form stable organisations and sound coalitions while the deep divide between elites and the rest of the population supports the long-term reproduction of a status quo. However, this is not to overlook the importance of external factors, especially the donors' role. The structural adjustment programmes of the 1980s and the free market policies spawned since have exacerbated the inequalities and shrunk and weakened the state, thereby adding to its loss of legitimacy. And the structurally low level of ODA combined with the effects of the principle of aid selectivity are not devoid of their own adverse effects when they help keep in place an authoritarian regime or when they hasten the decline of an illegitimate government and the entire country in its wake.

5

Elites in Madagascar: A Sociography

5.1 Introduction

Elites are central to North, Wallis and Weingast's subject matter and, more broadly, to all studies of institutions and organisations, given that they are fashioned and controlled by individuals and social groups or coalitions whose most influential players are elites. Most of the recent studies on elites in Southern countries are concerned with how these elites affect the development process in general (based on the generic opposition between rent-seeking elites and developmental elites; see, for example, Amsden *et al.*, 2012) more than with who they are and what they actually do. Yet can a satisfactory answer really be found to the first question without addressing the second?

The frequency of research bringing into play the concept of elites is inversely proportional to the empirical material available to studies on the subject. In most cases, elites are either referred to in a loose, abstract manner (predatory, rent-seeking, mafia, enlightened elites, etc.), or are addressed by more thematic approaches (political, economic, bureaucratic, religious elites, etc.), or are approached in isolation by case studies (examples of individuals, families, lineages, etc.). There is good reason for this. The first of the three major challenges facing the academic community in its quest to advance in its research on elites is precisely how to define them and identify who they are in concrete terms based on sound empirical data.[1]

[1] 'The first and most fundamental impediment facing both scholars and policy makers seeking to understand the role elites play in the process of economic development is the absence of a commonly agreed way to identify who constitutes a member of the elite' (DiCaprio, 2012).

This particular challenge is not exclusive to the field of the elites, as similar debate surrounds the concept of the middle class (see Darbon & Toulabor, 2011; and Jacquemot, 2013, in the case of Africa), but it is felt more keenly here. From the point of view of sources, although biographical databases in the Northern countries (like *Who's Who*) provide statistical information on the elites, they are by nature incomplete (an often-opaque selection procedure determines directory inclusion) and they differ in quality from one country to another. In addition, they more often cover political or administrative elites than business elites (Genieys, 2011). In the Southern countries, and in Madagascar in particular, such databases are much thinner on the ground and are even more incomplete. However, it has been possible to use some of them (*Official Journal* and biographical directories: Verdier 1995, 2000, 2002). Traditional quantitative data sources (mainly household surveys) can more or less outline the shape and profile of the middle class, whatever its definition. Yet there are no equivalent sources on the elites, who are by nature absent from these data. They are too few and far between to appear in sufficient numbers in the usual samples. Moreover, they generally refuse to answer this kind of survey for reasons of prestige or availability.

In addition to the intrinsic elite 'measurement' problems, the last decade's international development agenda has played a part in sidelining thinking on this group. Its virtually exclusive focus on poverty reduction (Millennium Development Goals [MDGs], Poverty Reduction Strategy Papers [PRSPs], Heavily Indebted Poor Country [HIPC] initiatives, etc.) has placed the poor and poverty eradication strategies at the top of the research and policy agenda, while the study of the 'top of the distribution' (of incomes, wealth or, more broadly, power) has been shifted offstage and into the wings in developing countries. Granted, the question of the reconfiguration of inequalities (national and global) has prompted many studies (see Bourguignon, 2015, for a short summary). In the developed countries, some studies have focused on analysing the top quantiles drawing on the most detailed level of tax data available (i.e. a level of detail that can capture elites in terms of income; Piketty & Saez, 2006; Piketty, 2014). Unfortunately, such sources do not exist in developing countries (especially the poorest). So not only do the elites remain unexplored territory, but the inequalities they create are massively underestimated (Guénard & Mesple-Somps, 2007).

The purpose of this chapter is twofold. The first ties in directly with the purpose of this book as to the role(s) played by the elites in the regulation of Malagasy society and especially in its trials and tribulations; in a word, on its development impasse. For want of being able to tackle this problem head on, beyond the general and stylised analyses of the previous two chapters, this chapter looks into the process of elite reproduction from both angles: objective (player strategies) and subjective (value systems). Upstream of this question, the chapter draws up as accurate a sociography as is possible of the elites in Madagascar. This is a fundamental first step before any more detailed analytical undertaking on the subject: how can we explore these social players we call 'elites' without first defining their contours and describing their internal structure? This taxonomic (species description) step is especially important because, to our knowledge, it has never been done in Madagascar or elsewhere, at least not in the terms we propose here.

Indeed the main originality of this chapter is that the results presented are drawn from a first-hand statistical survey designed to be representative of the elites in Madagascar since independence – the first of its kind to our knowledge. The survey of 'elites' in Madagascar (ELIMAD) is designed to capture the pathways, social networks and values of a representative sample of members of the different types of 'elites'. It poses a triple methodological challenge: definition of scope (who is or are the elites?), representativeness (where to find a comprehensive list of the sphere in question?) and reliability of the information collected (how to guarantee honest, in-depth answers?). The sheer magnitude of these methodological questions probably explains why no one has managed (if indeed undertaken) to conduct an operation of this kind before. Not wishing to go into the technical details, which is not the point of this book, we believe we have risen to the challenge by providing some 'satisfactory' answers to the methodological questions raised earlier. This research interviewed a total of 1,000 people considered to be part of the elites in Madagascar in at least one of the nine spheres covered (political [governmental, elective and partisan], economic, religious, military, civil society, international organisation and public institution) from 2012 to 2014. Although we have absolutely no intention of side-stepping valid questions (a certain number of technical details on ELIMAD are presented in Boxes 5.1 to 5.4),[2] we prefer to focus here on the survey findings to give this book's readers the exclusive first. A special supplementary survey directly connected with ELIMAD was conducted in 2013 on a sample of 1,200 people representative of the adult population living in Madagascar (CITMAD survey). This mirror survey

[2] More detailed methodological presentations are (and will be) made in individual scientific papers (Razafindrakoto *et al.*, 2012).

put a set of common questions to elites and the rest of the population to compare their opinions and values. It takes up the principle already tried and tested by the authors in the area of governance and corruption in French-speaking Africa, to wit comparing experts' points of view with those of the public at large (Razafindrakoto & Roubaud, 2010).

This chapter is in three parts. The first section starts with a tentative estimation of elite group size before presenting a detailed outline of their socio-demographic profile. With the scene thus set, we consider the strategies used to access and remain in the spheres of power, in their different dimensions. The second section focuses on the elite reproduction process from its many angles. It maps out the elites' social pathways, focusing on intergenerational and intragenerational mobility (vertically) and matrimonial alliances (horizontally). Yet elite strategies also take the form of branching out simultaneously into different areas of the social space – political and economic, public and private – in a phenomenon well known and defined in the Africanist literature as *straddling*. Then there is associative involvement, especially building, maintaining and drawing on individual networks. This section also measures the level of this associative involvement and analyses the structure of these egocentric elite networks. The last section addresses the question of values. Lifestyle and means of reproduction are not the only elements that differentiate elites from the rest of the population. They are also set apart by a system of representations, which may be more or less antagonistic with the other social groups' representations and more or less conducive to development. Here, we take the aforementioned mirror survey to compare the elites' answers with the rest of the population in order to measure and interpret the distance between the two groups.

5.2 Who Are the Elite Groups in Madagascar?

Who holds the power (political, economic, military, religious, etc.) in Madagascar? Is it a homogeneous group, which reproduces itself over time? Does the process of elite reproduction work on a family basis and/or by means of group strategies (ethnic or status groups)? Is the ethnic or status group aspect relevant? Is the power in Madagascar '*Merina* power' or '*Andriana* power'? What are the overlaps between the different dimensions of power in Madagascar? These are the questions addressed based on the initial findings of the survey of the elites.

Looking at the sociodemographic characteristics of the elites as a whole in Madagascar, all spheres combined, note first that this is a mature, graduate, male population (Table 5.1). Their average age is fifty-two

BOX 5.1 Survey Scope: Definition of the 'Elite' Concept

Given the debate and lack of consensus over the notion of elite in the literature, we need to specify the definition we have adopted. We define 'elite' in its broadest sense as *any person with or potentially with power and/or influence over the decisions and running of society in Madagascar.*

These are people who hold or have held 'important' positions and/or have a level of responsibility in different spheres:

1. Government (minister, principal private secretary or permanent secretary)
2. Elected office (national assembly, senate, city hall, etc.)
3. Political party
4. Public institution (administration; non-political position)
5. The army (paramilitary police, police, army, etc.)
6. Large corporation (public or private)
7. Civil society, including the media; consortiums such as *Groupement des Entreprises de Madagascar* (GEM – Confederation of Trade Organisations of Madagascar) and *Jery sy Paikady ho an`i Madagsikara* (JPM – Young Business Heads of Madagascar), unions and associations or committees such as CNOE, *Sehatra Fanarahamaso ny Fiainam-pirenena* (SeFaFi – Public Life Observatory) and Consortium of Solidarity with Madagascar (CNOSC – *Coordination Nationale des Organisations de la Société Civile*)
8. Religious institution
9. International organisation (including the large international non-governmental organisations [NGOs])

These conceptual choices call for two comments. First, the power (to be measured) held by the 'elites' is not a binary variable (has or has not), but a continuous variable (has more or less). Although this definition does not pose a ceiling problem (e.g. the President of the Republic in the political field is necessarily a member of the elite), a floor needs to be set below which an individual is no longer considered part of the elites. This threshold is arbitrary by definition. In ELIMAD, we chose a separate floor for each sphere set at a relatively high level, as seen from the distribution of posts/positions in our sample. Second, our breakdown into nine spheres (and their aggregation into four fields) is designed to cover all the elites in Madagascar with power at the national level. This field in principle excludes three groups that can be considered as elite at

BOX 5.1 (cont.)

their level: local elites, diaspora elites and international elites who influence Madagascar from the outside (e.g. President of the French Republic, President of the World Bank and the head of a global industrial group with operations in Madagascar). These groups are evidently excluded for reasons of technical difficulties (access, in particular), but they can also be legitimately considered as extensions to our scope and subsequently worth surveying. However, the main foreign communities (Indo-Pakistani – *Karana*, Chinese – *Sinoa*, and descendants of settlers – *Zanatany*) long established in the country are part of the survey's scope.

Categories of elites: classification of elites in the different fields of power

For the needs of the analysis, we have to identify the spheres of power to which the elites belong. As we will see later, elites are active in different spheres ('straddling'). We have therefore assigned the survey respondents to a main field as follows:

- **Political field (27.7%):** This category is designed to capture political responsibilities by including all individuals who have held (or currently hold) a position in government or elected office (members of the National Assembly or the Senate, including members of the High Transitional Council (CST) and Transitional Congress (CT) in the transitional period) and senior political party leaders
- **Economic field (23.9%):** Classed in this category are business elites who have never held a position of political responsibility
- **Public institutions (28.1%):** The elites who have held (or currently hold) senior positions in public institutions or in the army, but have not had either political responsibilities or responsibilities in large corporations
- **Civil society and others (20.3%):** The elites who cannot be classed in the above three categories are classified in this category. They are leading figures in religious institutions, civil society and international organisations who have not held a position of political responsibility or responsibility in a large corporation or public institution. More than two-thirds of them head civil society organisations.

Table 5.1 *The elites' main socio-demographic characteristics*

	Status group				
	Andriana and equivalent	*Hova* and equivalent	Others (incl. don't knows)	Total	
Elites	51.5	12.3	36.2	100	
Population[3]	1.5	2.6	95.9[4]	100	
	Ethnic group				
	Merina	*Betsileo*	Others	Total	
Elites	63.9	10.7	25.4	100	
Population	32.4	19.0	58.6	100	
	Religion				
	Catholics	FJKM (Calvinist)	Others	Total	
Elites	38.1	37.2	23.1	100	
Population	30.6	19.6	49.8	100	
	Age, gender and education				
	Under 45 years	46 to 60 years	Over 60 years	Women	Higher education
Elites	28.1	51.5	20.4	20.5	96.7
Population	63.8	24.2	12.0	49.7	3.0

Sources: ELIMAD survey 2012–14, Afrobarometer survey 2013 (ethnic group) and 2008 (status group), COEF Ressources and IRD-DIAL; ENEMPSI (ethnic group) 2012, INSTAT; authors' calculations.
Note: All figures are percentages of the total population aged 25 years and over.

[3] The survey questionnaire contained more detailed categories, but some categories have been clustered (mainly under the 'civil society and others' category) for the quantitative analysis (where groups need to have large enough numbers). Caution is called for when analysing the results derived from these aggregates because their relevance could be debatable. For the breakdown by ethnic group, given that the available information was on the respondents' parents, individuals with one *Merina* parent were classed as '*Merina*'.

[4] This high percentage actually reflects the low number of Afrobarometer survey respondents who claimed to be of 'high' status origin. Note that the 2008 Afrobarometer survey interviewed 1,200 people sampled by stratified random sampling by gender and (former) province for a total of 78% country dwellers and 22% urban dwellers. Hardly any of the respondents answered this question, either because there were no status groups in their parents' ethnic group or because they did not know what status group their parents belonged to or even because they did not wish to divulge this information.

BOX 5.2 Sampling Strategy for the Representativeness of the Elite Universe

In the absence of any pre-existent sampling frame, we used a two-step strategy.

1. Purposive Sampling

A first survey wave (around thirty questionnaires) was launched with the selection of some 30 'super-interviewers' (themselves members of the elite; see later) from as wide a range of backgrounds as possible. Chosen from among the team members' connections (the team also being members of the elite), they interviewed respondents in their own network (after validation by the central team). Taking this base as the launch pad, a 'snowball' technique was then used whereby the 'elite' network of these first respondents was asked at the end of the ELIMAD questionnaire to fill in a table suggesting eight people to be contacted to take part in the survey in turn. Following a mid-term qualitative evaluation (400 questionnaires) to identify shortcomings, a second wave was launched targeting the main areas of underrepresentation (e.g. the Indo-Pakistani community, Catholic religious elites, etc.) to be reached 'by all means'. At this stage, the second strategy was launched.

2. Building a Sampling Frame

Alongside the first survey wave, we set out to develop a comprehensive elite sampling frame. We drew on a wide range of sources for this, some common and others specific to each elite sphere. They included the *Official Journal*, the different official directories and registers, websites, the press and direct interviews. Wherever possible, we also went through these sources' archives for the 1960–2012 period. This gave us a list of nearly 10,000 names (9,357), or some 7,000 after eliminating doubles (individuals identified in more than one sphere).

This sampling frame is obviously imperfect, but it constitutes a reasonable preliminary approximation of the elite universe. As partial elements of validation, virtually all the first 400 ELIMAD respondents checked out as being in the frame. In the same vein, our examination of the press checked that the prominent people cited by our respondents were in the frame. Any who were not were added in. The frame's other

BOX 5.2 (cont.)

limitation is that often only the name is available without any other information on the person in question, which rules out any possibility of ex ante stratification of the sample. This sampling frame serves two purposes. The first is to align (during the survey) the ELIMAD sample with the frame structure (e.g. proportion of women). From this point of view, ELIMAD could be considered to be a stratified survey based on two criteria: gender and sphere. The frame's second purpose is longer term. This long-term investment should be able to be used as a sampling frame for all future surveys on the elites once updated and enriched by individual characteristics.

years and 55% are over fifty. Just 20% are women and 96% have graduated from higher education. Their religious breakdown is relatively balanced between Protestants (FJKM) and Catholics, with the other churches representing approximately a quarter of the total. The *Merina* ethnic group (ethnic group from the region around the capital) is predominant (64%), followed a long way behind by the *Betsileo* (another Central Highlands ethnic group). Nevertheless, one-quarter of the elites are from coastal (*côtier*) regions. Lastly, most (52%) of the elite population are descendants of the *Andriana* (nobility in the days of the kingdom).

A comparison of the composition of the elite population with the population of Madagascar in general gives a more precise idea of the elites' particularity in terms of their composition.[5] Elites are 2.5 times less likely to be female or under forty-five years old. In terms of religion, whereas Catholics are overrepresented among the elites (38% vs. 31%), this bias is even greater for FJKM followers (37% vs. 20%) to the disadvantage of the other persuasions. The elites are also twice as likely to be from the Central Highlands. Yet what sets them apart much more is that they are thirty-one times more likely to be higher education graduates than the rest of the population and up to thirty-four times more likely to claim to be of *Andriana* descent or assimilated.[6]

[5] Given that elite members are all over twenty-five years old, we compare them with the general population over twenty-five years old.

[6] The social stratification into status groups described in Chapter 2 was a characteristic common to a number of ethnic groups, but the terms used to refer to them differed from one ethnic group to the next. The *Andriana* (nobility) and *Hova* designations applied essentially to the *Merina* (ethnic group from the Antananarivo region). At the same time,

Table 5.2 *Elite demographic characteristics by sphere of power*

	Men	Women	25–44 years	45–60 years	Over 60 years	Total
Political sphere	85.6	14.4	18.8	50.9	30.3	100
Economic sphere	78.2	21.8	33.9	52.7	13.4	100
Public institutions	81.5	18.5	24.6	55.2	20.3	100
Civil society and others	70.0	30.1	38.9	45.8	15.3	100
Total	79.5	20.5	28.1	51.5	20.4	100

Sources: ELIMAD survey 2012–14, COEF Ressources and IRD-DIAL, authors' calculations.
Note: Although no age limit was set, all members of the elite are at least 25 years old.

Behind these averages for the elite universe as a whole lay large differences by elite sphere and field. The political sphere is by far the most male and mature, with 86% of men and 30% of over-sixties (Table 5.2). This characteristic is also found in the senior public administration, albeit less pronounced. The members of the economic sphere and especially 'civil society and others' are younger and more female. However, the proportion of women never tops 30% in any sphere.

The question of education is obviously central to the elite issue. Overall, 97% of the elites report having a level of higher education. Yet this indicator provides but a highly imperfect measurement of their 'over-education'. Whereas the population's rate of higher education attendance by level (undergraduate, graduate and postgraduate) forms a logical pyramid shape, the pyramid is inversed for the elites (Table 5.3). Over 40% of elites say they attended university for more than five years and 80% for more than three years. A member of the elites is approximately fifty times more likely than the rest of the adult population to have attended university at master's level and 200 times more likely to have gone on to postgraduate level. In addition, the proportion of those who have studied abroad is far higher than the percentage of 'ordinary' people who have

the *Hova* actually included commoners as much as clans who enjoyed the same privileges as the nobility. The question asked (for both parents) in the ELIMAD and Afrobarometer surveys was, 'If the ethnic group of your father (mother) had castes or status groups, do you know which caste or status group his (her) family belonged to?' The analysis classified the answers to these questions into three categories in order of frequency of answer: *Andriana* or assimilated, *Hova* or assimilated and a last category covering all the other answers, including 'don't knows'. This necessary statistical clustering has the disadvantage of obscuring each status group's subtle internal distinctions.

Table 5.3 *Elite level of education by sphere of power*

	Secondary or less	Higher (1–3 years)	Higher (4–5 years)	Higher (over 5 years)	Total
Political sphere	4.0	12.9	37.5	49.6	100
Economic sphere	3.2	18.1	49.1	29.6	100
Public institutions	2.3	20.2	31.6	46.0	100
Civil society & others	3.9	13.3	42.2	40.6	100
Total Elites	3.3	16.3	39.5	40.9	100
Total Population	97.0	2.0	0.8	0.2	100

Sources: ELIMAD survey, 2012–14, COEF Ressources and IRD-DIAL; ENEMPSI, 2012, INSTAT; authors' calculations.
Note: Population aged 25 years and over.

Table 5.4 *Elite ethnic and status groups of origin by sphere*

	Ethnic group			Status group			*Total*
	Merina	*Betsileo*	Others	*Andriana*	*Hova*	Others	
Political sphere	46.9	12.3	40.8	52.7	7.6	39.7	100
Economic sphere	76.1	8.4	15.5	54.4	15.9	29.7	100
Public institutions	66.6	11.4	22.1	47.7	16.4	35.9	100
Civil society & others	69.0	10.3	20.7	51.7	8.9	39.4	100
Total	63.9	10.7	25.4	51.5	12.3	36.2	100

Sources: ELIMAD survey 2012–14, COEF Ressources and IRD-DIAL; authors' calculations.

attended higher education. The same holds true for their knowledge and command of the French language, and even other foreign languages although these are still relatively rare. All the elite spheres exhibit this overqualified characteristic, with the political and public institution elites in first place in this respect. So even though the respondents have probably inflated their academic record, there is no doubt that access to higher education is a necessary (albeit not sufficient) condition for integration into the elite world.

Although the different spheres display similar curves by their members' religion, this is not the case when looking at ethnic and status groups. The *Merina* are relatively more numerous in the economic sphere, which they massively dominate (76%; Table 5.4). They are also found in large numbers in the 'civil society and others' sphere and in the public institutions, where they represent two in three civil servants. Their weight is lowest, and even in the minority (47%), in the political sphere. The status groups present less variation in their distributions by fields of power. Descendants of the *Andriana* are in the majority everywhere except in public institutions, where they nonetheless corner 48% of the positions. Descendants of the *Hova* tend to favour the economic sphere and public institutions. The rate of 'castes' is ultimately highest among the business heads, where it exceeds 70%.

The elite universe is, by definition, profoundly inegalitarian. In this chapter, we have defined the elite by their power of action in society. However, if members of the elites are differentiated from other members of society by their 'holding' power, their own universe is necessarily differentiated from this point of view. Everyone in it holds more or less power. So a valid line of inquiry is to analyse the elites' social breakdown by the power they hold. Differentiation by level of power is important to build an accurate picture of the elites.

We have developed a scale of power with four levels (Box 5.3). The oldest are more often found at the top of the scale of power (respectively 83% of over-sixties, 73% of forty-six- to sixty-year-olds and 63% of under-forty-fives are ranked at the highest level; Table 5.5). Although there is an automatic aspect to this link between age and level of power, as the oldest have already had the time to reach the peak of their career, a purely gerontocratic factor could also be at work whereby age, as such, takes precedence. From the point of view of gender, not only are women under-represented within the elites, but their numbers dwindle as the scale rises. They fall from a share of nearly half at the lower levels (3 and 4) to just 18% at the highest level of the ladder.

BOX 5.3 Inequalities in the Elite Universe: Development of a Scale of 'Power'

In a population survey, the observation units are considered to be equivalent, are weighted in the same way and can be substituted for one another. This statistical principle echoes the democratic principle of 'one man, one vote' and reflects relative homogeneity. Yet unlike the rest of the population, the elites are profoundly and intrinsically heterogeneous from the very viewpoint of what defines them; that is their power. It stands to reason that the President of the Republic has an infinitely greater power of action and influence than a director-general in the

BOX 5.3 (cont.)

central administration, president of a producer's association or a prelate. This heterogeneity is both internal (between the elites themselves) and external (between the group of elites and the rest of the population). From this point of view, a survey of the elites is more like a business survey than a household survey: where businesses need to be differentiated by size (in staff numbers or turnover), elites need to be able to be identified according to the power they hold.

However, measuring an individual's power is a tricky exercise. First, the sources of power (status position, charisma, expertise and tradition) and the instruments of power (law, force and influence) are many and varied. It is very hard not only to capture them all, but also to determine a system of measurement whereby they can be compared. Second, power cannot be addressed solely by a substantialist approach like realisable, accumulative, disposable capital. An individual's power lies not solely in the individual's capacities for material or moral action, but also in the potential to 'impose one's own will within a social relationship, even in the face of resistance' (Weber, 2003). This approach defines power less as a stock than as a relationship, as its influence only really comes to bear in the interaction.

Power cannot be measured directly by the ELIMAD survey, either from its interactionist or its substantialist angle. Our approach therefore consists of making the reasonable assumption that it is essentially a function of the individuals' status position(s). The individuals have hence been classed according to their rank on a 'standard' hierarchical scale. Putting this theoretical metric into operation is no mean task. It calls for a double classification operation: first within each of the nine spheres (and sub-spheres) and then between the spheres. This was a painstaking task based on the survey's two main pieces of information: institutional affiliation and position held. Some auxiliary variables were also used (e.g. business size for the economic sphere) with a diagnostic conducted by manual processing, on a case-by-case basis, of qualitative information declared in full by respondents on their current status (e.g. business name, still in the economic sphere). This operation encoded more than 6,000 elite positions held by the 1,000 people interviewed and more than 15,000 links with their elite network. Three nested classifications were hence developed. For the purposes of this chapter's analysis, we use here only the most aggregated scale with its four levels of power.

Table 5.5 *Elite demographic characteristics by rank on the power scale*

	Men	Women	25–44 years	45–60 years	Over 60 years	Total
Level 1 (max)	82.0	18.0	24.6	51.9	23.6	100
Level 2	79.9	20.1	33.2	52.8	14.0	100
Level 3	48.1	51.9	51.9	44.2	3.9	100
Level 4 (min)	61.5	38.5	46.2	38.5	15.4	100
Total	79.5	20.5	28.1	51.5	20.4	100

Sources: ELIMAD survey 2012–14, COEF Ressources and IRD-DIAL; authors' calculations.

Table 5.6 *Elite ethnic and status groups of origin by sphere*

	Ethnic group			Status group			*Total*
	Merina	*Betsileo*	Others	*Andriana*	*Hova*	Others	
Level 1 (max)	63.8	9.7	26.5	53.3	12.2	34.5	100
Level 2	65.0	14.5	20.6	45.8	12.6	41.6	100
Level 3	63.5	9.6	26.9	53.9	11.5	34.6	100
Level 4 (min)	53.9	7.7	38.5	38.5	15.4	46.2	100
Total	63.9	10.7	25.4	51.5	12.3	36.2	100

Sources: ELIMAD survey 2012–14, COEF Ressources and IRD-DIAL; authors' calculations.

The analysis in terms of religious and ethnic groups does not return a very steep curve, since no category appears to have an advantage over the others (Table 5.6). Nonetheless, a few minor differences can be observed by status group. Slightly more *Andriana* are found at the top of the power scale, but the difference is slight (75% of *Andriana* are at Level 1 compared with 72% of all elites).

So the Malagasy elite, associated by definition with the ruling class, has remained the same on the whole in Madagascar since independence (see Chapter 2). It is made up largely of the *Andriana* and *Hova* bourgeoisie, which has inherited symbolic power (before colonisation for the *Andriana*, and before and during colonisation for the *Hova* who were responsible for managing public affairs). Members of the *côtier* high families have joined this group based on the place they have secured on the national scene as representatives of their region, among others, since the colonial period.

This role of ethnic groups and castes in Malagasy society (despite their late nineteenth century abolition) is a persistently nagging question in the country's history. The elites' point of view about the importance of the

Table 5.7 *Elite opinions of the importance of status groups*

Castes are important	Caste of origin			Religion			Gender		Age	Total
	Andriana	*Hova*	Others	Catholic	FJKM	Others	Men	Women	<45	
To you	39.4	19.5	18.0	25.5	29.3	34.8	27.6	35.6	24.9	**29.2**
To society	58.6	46.3	38.1	46.5	51.1	52.6	47.4	58.5	48.0	**49.7**

Sources: ELIMAD survey 2012–14, COEF Ressources and IRD-DIAL; authors' calculations.

status groups or castes sheds further light on the pre-eminence of origins in Malagasy society. Two questions were put to find out whether the people interviewed attached importance to these status groups – if they considered them important (in their life and career) – and whether they felt that these groups were important to Malagasy society in general.

More than a century after the abolition of the principle of status groups, nearly 30% of the members of the elites said status groups were still important to them personally and nearly 50% said they were still important to society (Table 5.7). These responses show that the symbolic ranking system still prevails, at least in the elites' minds, even though its importance diminishes slightly among the younger people. An analysis of responses by individual status origin hones this observation. Descendants of the *Andriana* in effect most frequently say that a system placing a higher value on them by birthright is important to them (39%) and to society (59%). Conversely, only 18% of the individuals who did not give their origin in terms of caste placed value on the status groups, even though 38% of them felt they were still important to society.

Alongside descendants of the *Andriana*, it is the socially dominated groups in the rest of the population (women, the oldest and minority church congregation members) who believe castes to be a defining principle of Malagasy society today, either as they personally see it or by virtue of their observing its effects. This paradox merits further exploration, but it could reflect the fact that the few rare elected representatives from these categories seek to make their mark by overrating caste attributes they did not initially have.

In general, although the elites' statements somewhat play down the importance of status groups (only a minority openly feel they still carry weight today), the strong presence of the *Andriana* in this group tends to suggest that the *Andriana*'s strategies to preserve their power or influence are not overt.[7]

[7] See, for example, the importance of things 'left unsaid' as highlighted by the qualitative interviews.

BOX 5.4 Highly Sensitive Questions: Minimise Non-responses and Guarantee Reliability

How can a satisfactory response rate and honest answers be obtained to such sensitive subjects when respondents at the top of the social ladder may feel they do not have time to waste on answering a statistical survey or may have good reason not to want to divulge their resources? Special strategies specific to the field of study had to be put in place to address these issues.

First, ELIMAD targets elites: only a 'horizontal' relationship is possible (elites talking to elites). Given that elites like to cultivate their own small world (as this chapter's network analysis clearly confirms), interviewers were chosen from among the members of the elite itself. This choice makes it harder for respondents to dismiss the interviewer out of hand, which would have been a natural tendency with an average interviewer. Second, the ELIMAD questionnaire is particularly long (two hours on average). The opportunity cost of the time spent answering the questions is very high. Consequently, despite all the respondents being connected, interviews can only be conducted face to face. The few attempts to proceed otherwise (submitting or e-mailing the questionnaire) came to nothing. Third, ELIMAD deals with highly sensitive questions, especially the question of network and social capital. Respondents are asked to provide a list of all their connections and a maximum of personal characteristics. Not only is such a procedure terribly intrusive, but it also bears a certain number of negative connotations. The idea of elite collusion via their networks is quite common. So a relationship of absolute trust is needed between interviewer and respondent. Only an interviewer who is not only a member of the elite, but also known (or recommended) to the respondent will be able to obtain honest answers.

These three main strategies were applied successfully to limit total and partial non-response rates. Other approaches were also used. For example, emphasis on the esteem of being chosen as part of the elite, akin to other public figures, made the survey a mark of elite membership. In addition, reference to the long-standing credibility of the team of researchers served as a guarantee of data confidentiality.

However, these instructions were not always applied to the letter. In a certain number of cases, the chosen strategies are double-edged and a choice has to be made. For example, some respondents find it easier to confide in a friend or relation than a stranger. In other cases, it is easier to talk to an anonymous stranger to prevent the family from finding out

BOX 5.4 (cont.)

certain personal details and possibly arousing jealousy. Intimate knowledge of the 'terrain' means the strategy can be adjusted on a case-by-case basis to the known or presumed circumstances. This meticulous high-end 'tailoring' obviously raises the question as to whether the survey can be replicated in other contexts.

5.3 Strategies to Access the Spheres of Power and Remain in Power

The elites' sociodemographic profile has already turned up certain particularities in their strategies to access the spheres of power. One of the pillars is investment in higher education, facilitated when parents have the financial and human resources. This mechanism already gives family origin and entourage a key role in access to the elite circle. Yet the group's formation in a relatively closed configuration does not channel through this path alone. The significant proportion of descendants of the *Andriana*, the highest status group in the day of the kingdoms, tends to point at the same time to an implicit or explicit social reproduction strategy. This status strategy applies from generation to generation, nurturing the persistence of hierarchical distinctions all the more sacred in that they are rooted in the past. Membership of a status group can therefore form a resource to control power by restricting access to birthright heirs.

The first part of this chapter sheds some light on the strategies that may have been used by the elite class to reach their high position on the power ladder. This second part sets out to explain the mechanisms behind them and measure their effects. Do the elites form a homogeneous self-reproducing group? Is the elite reproduction process really essentially family based? Can a particular career path explain elite access to the spheres of power? Do members of the elite have a large network of contacts or relations in the different spheres of power? And to what extent is this social capital used to climb the ladder? The answers to these questions will provide a gauge of social fluidity, of the nature and reach of elite practices for occupying different fields of power.

Elite Social Reproduction: A Growing Phenomenon?

First of all, access to elite status may stem more or less directly from parental lineage. In the case of Madagascar, there is clear evidence of

Table 5.8 *Elite reproduction and growth over time*

Percentage	At least one parent a member of the elites	Both parents members of the elites
Under 35 years	63.3	27.9
36–45 years	59.8	18.1
46–55 years	44.4	5.4
56–65 years	35.9	4.2
Over 65 years	38.7	2.8
Total	46.1	9.1

Sources: ELIMAD survey 2012–14, COEF Ressources and IRD-DIAL; authors' calculations.

a family-based elite social reproduction mechanism. Nearly half (46%) of the elites have at least one parent who is (or was) a member of the elites (Table 5.8). And note here that these figures are largely underestimated due to the way the survey put the question.[8] This phenomenon is more marked among the younger generations. Those whose parents are or were members of the elites represent respectively 44% of the forty-six- to fifty-five-year olds, 60% of the thirty-six- to forty-five-year olds and 63% of the under-thirty-fives. This observation can be interpreted in two potentially interrelated ways: either individuals with non-elite ascendants take more time to attain positions of responsibility or this reproduction phenomenon is growing over time.

Nevertheless, a comparison of the weight of 'hereditary elites' (descendants of the elite groups) among fifty-six to sixty-five- and forty-six to fifty-five-year olds (age brackets old enough to have reached positions of responsibility in their careers) suggests that the reproduction mechanism applies more to the younger category (36% among the fifty-six- to sixty-five -year olds as opposed to 44% among the forty-six- to fifty-five-year olds). This observation tends to lend support to the second hypothesis that the elite reproduction phenomenon is gaining ground with time. Yet whichever hypothesis is taken, access to power in each case proves easier for descendants of elites, corroborating that a family-based reproduction process is indeed at work.

8 The survey asked respondents for their parents' exact occupation. These occupations were coded and the coding used to calculate the column's figures. This calculation in principle underestimates the number of 'hereditary elites' due to the fact that occupation is not the only elite membership criterion, particularly among women.

Table 5.9 *Elite reproduction by category*

Elite spheres (%)	At least one elite parent	One elite parent (for < 46 years)
Public institution	45.1	60.4
Army	38.2	53.8
Civil society	46.2	55.3
Political party	48.7	57.1
Elected office	37.1	57.1
Government	43.8	55.6
Corporations	52.3	68.3
International organisations	53.6	64.3

Sources: ELIMAD survey 2012–14, COEF Ressources and IRD-DIAL; authors' calculations.

This phenomenon concerns all the spheres of power, even though descent has more of a hand in access to some than others. The reproduction mechanism plays a particular role in access to economic power (52% of elites in business circles are descendants of elites, with the percentage standing at 68% among the under-forty-sixes; Table 5.9). It is also pronounced among elites working in international organisations (respectively 54% descendants of elites and 64% among the under-forty-sixes).

With their investment in school and capacity for a level of education largely above the Malagasy average (including studying abroad), it is relatively easy for the children of elites to attain privileged positions in the different spheres of power. So it is not surprising to find the same family names since independence in the ruling class. There is no shortage of descendants of dignitaries of the First Republic in the political class. Granted, new names appear, but by and large an oligarchy made up of a bourgeois elite, including *côtier*, already in position following independence still holds an important place today (Fremigacci, 2014b; see also Chapter 2).

Straddling Positions of Power: A Strategy to Expand and Diversify the Spheres of Influence?

The hypothesis is that a strategy known as 'straddling' positions of power, as illustrated by Médard (1992), might be used to attain and remain in the highest social positions. The survey of elites in Madagascar can test this hypothesis in concrete terms. We take the elites' paths to analyse the extent

Table 5.10 *Concurrent positions in different spheres of power*

Concurrent positions in the past/career		Concurrent positions today	
Involved in past or present in	%	Involved in present in:	%
At least two spheres	84.4	At least two spheres	48.7
At least three spheres	64.5	At least three spheres	19.9
At least four spheres	40.7	At least four spheres	6.8
At least five spheres	21.7	*One sphere only*	*44.4*
At least six spheres	10.7	*No spheres*	*6.9*

Sources: ELIMAD survey 2012–14, COEF Ressources and IRD-DIAL; authors' calculations.

to which they simultaneously hold positions of responsibility in different spheres of power.

This straddling strategy is clearly in use among the members of the elite in Madagascar. Nearly half (49%) simultaneously held positions of responsibility in at least two different spheres at the time of the survey and 20% held positions of responsibility in three different spheres (Table 5.10). When the analysis is extended to entire careers starting with the first position of responsibility, the elites expand and diversify their power by means of their past and present involvement in different spheres: 84% have held high-ranking positions in at least two spheres, nearly two-thirds in at least three spheres and 41% in at least four different spheres. Hence concurrent positions or duties prove not only to be widespread practice, but also appear to go hand in hand with a strategy to diversify their footholds as time goes on.

Whether social capital is used to control, close doors or build solid bridgeheads, it guarantees advancement up the ladder to individuals, and friends and family alike. Use of this straddling strategy lends support to the hypothesis of at least partial elite capture of the spheres of influence. We measure the repercussions of such a strategy on the concentration of power. Its implications are far reaching in that it extends from the positions held by the elites themselves to those held by friends and family, as we will see in the following section. Figure 5.1 presents a stylised chart of these overlaps between elite spheres in the case of Madagascar.

Elite Network Structure and Size

The elites typically display a very high rate of participation in associative structures, as clearly shown by a comparison of membership rates across all associations combined. Whereas around just 20% of the population as

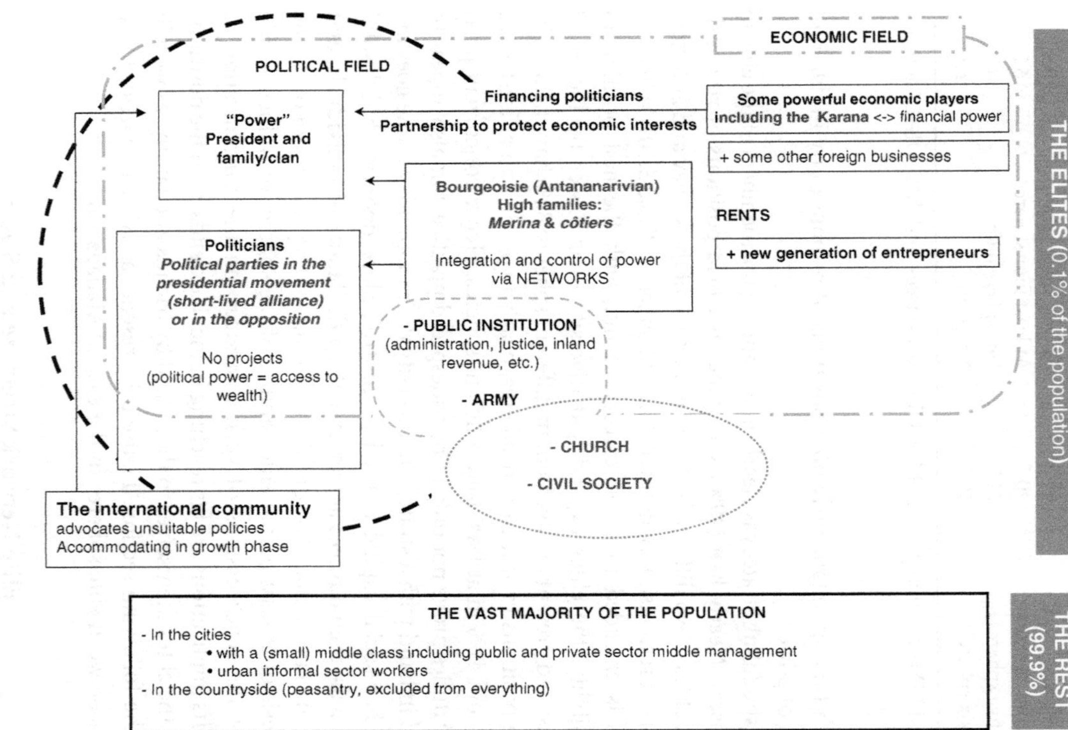

Figure 5.1 Distribution of power and interactions between different groups of players.
Source: Authors.

Table 5.11 *Associative involvement by status group, ethnic group of origin and gender*

	Status group of origin			Ethnic group			Gender		Total
Member of:	*Andriana*	*Hova*	Others	*Merina*	*Betsileo*	Others	Men	Women	
All associations	82.9	70.7	80.9	76.5	82.2	90.6	80.5	81.5	80.7
Service associations	20.0	18.9	17.7	18.2	19.8	20.9	18.3	22.1	19.1
Hometown associations	47.7	33.6	48.9	33.7	60.4	72.4	48.4	38.6	46.4
Freemasonry	13.9	5.7	7.8	10.8	9.3	11.1	10.4	11.8	10.7

Sources: ELIMAD survey 2012–14, COEF Ressources and IRD-DIAL; authors' calculations.

a whole say they are members of an association (see Chapter 4), the rate tops 80% among the elites (Table 5.11). Is this intensity of social activity a specific strategy to access and remain in power? The characteristics of the associations in which the elite class is involved shed some light on the stated and implicit objectives of membership. One-fifth of the elites are involved (or have been involved) in service associations (Lion's Club, Rotary Club, etc.), 46% are (or have been) in hometown associations[9] and 10% say that they belong (or have belonged) to a Masonic organisation.[10] Aside from their engagements and services, these elite choices to join associations are confined exclusively to a small circle of individuals – because members can only be co-opted – are not disinterested and exhibit a volition to cultivate their own small world.

Descendants of the *Andriana* stand out with a higher rate of associative participation (83%), especially in hometown associations. In particular, nearly twice as many join Masonic lodges, even though membership concerns only a minority (14% as opposed to less than 8% on average for the 'others'). The higher percentage of hometown association members among the 'others' may be due to the fact that the majority of these ethnic groups are based in the capital, far from their home regions. Yet this rate could also be an explanatory factor for their position among the elites. Participation in this type of association provides a ticket to approach members who might afford a way in to a position of power.

[9] Associations based on a shared geographical origin. This origin is generally a hill standing in veiled terms for a status position.

[10] In view of the fact that secrecy is the rule of Freemasonry, the elites who answered 'don't know' (rather than give a negative answer) to the question as to whether they belonged to a Masonic organisation implicitly acknowledged being members of one.

Table 5.12 *Associative involvement by sphere and level of power*

Elite sphere	Political sphere	Economic sphere	Public institution	Others	Total
All associations	86.6	77.0	76.2	83.3	80.7
Service associations	19.9	26.3	14.7	15.4	19.1
Hometown associations	67.2	33.5	41.0	41.3	46.4
Freemasonry	13.9	12.7	7.5	8.4	10.7
Level of power	Level 1 (max)	Level 2	Level 3	Level 4 (min)	Total
All associations	83.4	75.7	73.1	46.2	80.7
Service associations	20.4	17.4	11.8	0.0	19.1
Hometown associations	48.7	40.2	42.0	38.5	46.4
Freemasonry	12.6	7.0	0.0	7.7	10.7

Sources: ELIMAD survey 2012–14, COEF Ressources and IRD-DIAL; authors' calculations.

Associative enrolment, hence networking, strategies differ by gender. Female members of the elite are found relatively more in service associations (22% vs. 18% for the men) and less frequently in hometown associations (39% compared with 48%).

The elites who have (or have had) a role in the political sphere differ in terms of their much higher rate of involvement in associations in general (87% vs. 81% on average), in hometown associations (67% as opposed to 46% on average) and in Freemasonry (14% compared with 11% on average; Table 5.12). These findings tend to confirm that there is a specific link between associative participation and access to political power. The elites – especially political elites – consequently appear to be in a position to benefit from support and forms of legitimation by means of their membership in these circles.

The connection between social engagement and access to power is confirmed above all by the fact that extent of involvement in associations tends to rise with the level of power. A full 83% of the elites on the highest rung of the power ladder (Level 1) are or have been members of an association, while 49% are enrolled in a hometown association and 13% are involved in Freemasonry (compared with 46%, 29% and 8% respectively for those on the lowest rung of the ladder). The question could well be raised as to the direction of the causality, as a high-ranking position may smooth entry into the most exclusive associative circles. Yet given the constraints of associative involvement, it is more than probable that membership meets instrumental goals rather than simply altruistic ends. The associative environment

Table 5.13 *Network of elite contacts in different spheres of power*

Contacts, friends and family in the following spheres	At least one contact (%)
Government	84.5
Public institutions	82.1
Corporations	73.2
Army	67.7
International organisations	60.2
Civil society	59.9
Political parties	58.3
Elected office	54.3
Religious institutions	54.1
In at least one sphere	100

Sources: ELIMAD survey 2012–14, COEF Ressources and IRD-DIAL; authors' calculations.
Note: 85% of elites in general have contacts in government.

framework strengthens connections that can be used in strategies to get on, stay on and climb the power ladder.

Elite networks are not restricted to the network created by participation in the above-mentioned associations. They can be driven as much by individual, family and professional connections as by contacts made at school (alumni association or children's school), religious affiliations, sports, etc. This range of possible places where social capital can be created, sustained and cultivated gives an idea of the relationships on which elites can potentially draw. That is not to say that frequenting the same places necessarily creates a relationship of trust and assimilation of an acquaintance into a close-knit circle. The automatic development of connections is actually less evident here in that the Malagasy population appears to have a low level of interpersonal trust (see Chapter 4) and the elites, compared with the populace, are even more distrustful (19% of elites say that most people can be trusted, while the equivalent percentage is 26% for the population as a whole).

Is the climate of wariness of others an obstacle to building and cultivating networking connections? The structure and size of the elite networks leaves no doubt as to their actual reach. The elites have at least one elite contact (person in a position of responsibility whom they can potentially call directly) in one of the different spheres of power. For example, 82% have a contact in their phone book who has (or has had) responsibilities in a public institution. A total of 85% have acquaintances who hold or have

Table 5.14 *Importance of the elite network by sphere and level of power*

	Average number of connections in the elite network				
Spheres	Number of connections	No. close and very close	No. spheres	No. connections with at least weekly contact	No. connections who have helped at least once
Political sphere	16.2	14.6	6.4	3.2	12.7
Economic sphere	15.4	12.9	6.1	2.6	11.7
Public institution	13.4	12.1	5.5	2.6	11.3
Others	14.9	12.8	6.1	2.4	11.8
Level of power					
Level 1 (max)	15.8	13.8	6.2	3.1	12.5
Level 2	13.6	12.1	5.6	2.1	10.9
Level 3	10.9	9.5	5.2	1.3	8.3
Level 4 (min)	7.3	6.4	4.3	1.1	5.7
Total	15.0	13.1	6.0	2.7	11.9

Sources: ELIMAD survey 2012–14, COEF Ressources and IRD-DIAL; authors' calculations.

held a government position (Table 5.13) and 73% have contacts in the business world. The contacts in these three spheres are also called upon the most to request and obtain assistance, reflecting the potential use of this network for instrumental ends.

In keeping with the previous observation of the political elites' particular trait of associative involvement, they also have the densest network. The elites who have (or have had) a role in the political sphere differ from the other elite categories in that they have an even richer network. On average, they post a higher number of connections in the elite class, a higher number of close or very close relationships among these connections, a wider range of spheres to which the members of their network belong, more connections with whom they are very frequently in contact (at least weekly), and a higher number of connections who have assisted them at least once.

The importance of social capital in opening the door to the highest-ranking positions of power is also borne out. The higher an individual on the ladder of power, the richer his or her network as defined by the different chosen measurement criteria (number of connections, closeness, range of spheres to which network members belong, frequency of contacts, and assistance provided or not). The average number of connections cited hence increases from 7 on the lowest rung of the power ladder to 16 at the top, and the average number of connections who have provided assistance rises from 6 to 12.5 (Table 5.14).

Here again, the question arises as to the direction of the causality. Is it access to political power, or high-ranking positions, that provides the means to develop and enrich an elite network or is it the richness of the network that facilitates access to the political sphere and advancement on the power ladder? We do not endeavour to test these hypotheses as such (given the endogeneity constraints inherent in this type of question when using econometric models). However, as with the aforementioned question of associative involvement, we can venture that the most probable hypothesis is two-way causality. The network is both a cause and an effect in the process of getting on, staying on and climbing the power ladder.

5.4 A System of Values and Representations Conducive to Development?

The previous analyses clearly show that the elites in Madagascar form an extremely airtight world largely disconnected from the vast majority of the population. They use all the resources at their disposal to ensure their reproduction as a dominant group at the apex of the social hierarchy. If the system breathes at all, it is essentially internally (between the different spheres of power) as individuals juggle with a certain amount of give between one field and another. However, the elite world's borders are well guarded by strategies designed to limit and control newcomers' access to power. This modus operandi of preserving privilege is in itself already at odds with the principles of meritocracy and equal opportunities on which modern democratic societies are supposed to be founded. The question then is whether this exclusive club is driven by a system of specific, explicitly elitist values or whether it acts behind the scenes, under cover of more collectively shared representations. Basically, what are the elites' stated values in terms of organisation and goals for Madagascar and are they conducive to development?

In line with the previous analyses, here we compare the elites' opinions with the rest of the population on a certain number of key questions: adherence to democracy, the main development obstacles and priorities, and assessment of the different historical periods. This exercise naturally draws on the results of the ELIMAD survey, but compares them here with the CITMAD survey presented in the introduction. A number of identical questions, with exactly the same wording, were put in mirror fashion by both surveys to identify points of agreement and disagreement between elites and the general public in order to ascertain democratisation and development hindrances and potential drivers.

Mixed Attitudes to Democratic Principles

Attachment to democracy is far from massive even though it meets with the approval of the majority of the elites. A 'mere' 55% of elites consider that, 'Democracy is preferable to any other form of government.' The percentage even falls to 46% among the business elites (Table 5.15). A significant proportion feel that, 'A non-democratic system may be preferable in certain circumstances,' (36% of all elites and 45% of business elites).

The question as to whether the elites are more attached to democracy than the rest of the population is far from straightforward. On the one hand, 26% of the general public say that the type of government does not matter to them (as opposed to 6% of the elites). These people would appear to expect nothing (any longer) from government. On the other hand, 82% of those who believe the form of government is important look to democracy, which

Table 5.15 *Elite opinions of democratic principles and governance*

% of those who feel that:	Political sphere	Economic sphere	Public institution	Others	Total Elites	Rest of the population
Choice between the three statements						
Democracy is preferable to any other form of government	64.7	45.8	52.7	55.2	**54.9**	**41.4**
A non-democratic system may be preferable in certain circumstances	28.7	45.3	37.2	34.3	**36.2**	**9.3**
Type of government does not matter	5.1	5.9	6.5	8.5	**6.4**	**26.2**
Choice between the two statements						
A. People are like 'children' and the government should look after them like a parent (*raiamandreny*)	17.3	20.2	19.3	20.3	**19.2**	**54.3**
B. The government is like an employee and the people should be like a boss in charge of it	63.9	66.8	62.9	63.9	**64.3**	**39.3**
Neither A nor B	9.6	8.0	10.7	6.9	**9.0**	**1.7**

Sources: Surveys ELIMAD 2012–14 and Afrobarometer 2013, COEF Ressources and IRD-DIAL; authors' calculations.
Note: The total for each of the two questions does not add up to 100% as the 'don't knows' are not reported.

is the case with just 60% of the elites. This suggests that a higher proportion of the elites would be prepared to accept a non-democratic regime.

This general question on democracy actually reflects how much the population values the principle of electing the country's leaders. We have taken this question of democratic attachment further by also asking our respondents which type of relationship they think there should be between the government and the people. A full 54% of the general public agree with the statement, "People are like 'children' and the government should look after them like a parent." Yet this paternalistic view of the mode of political regulation, consistent with the concept of *raiamandreny* already largely analysed in previous chapters, is defended by just 19% of the elites. The principle of a *raiamandreny* government therefore paradoxically appears to be more acceptable to the public at large than the elites, who could benefit from this type of system. However, this finding is paradoxical in appearance alone. It may well partially reflect the influence of 'social desirability' behind the respondents' answers, tacitly acknowledging that the 'right' answer to the question is the people should be in charge of the government. It may also express the fact that the members of the elites, most of whom are not in a position to govern, do not want the government to make decisions that they cannot control.

Poor Leadership Is the Main Obstacle to Development: An Admission of Responsibility?

The central role of governance (whether defined narrowly as the management of public monies or broadly as all democratic governance), and upstream of 'developmental' (or 'inclusive') institutions, is a key tenet of the work developed by North, Wallis and Weingast (2009) and other authors examining the divergent paths of nations (Khan, 2010; Acemoglu & Robinson, 2012). This line of reasoning is largely shared by the Malagasy elites, all of whom consider (irrespective of their sphere) that 'poor leadership' is far and away the main obstacle to Madagascar's long-run development. A full 99% believe that it plays a significant role and 92% that it is decisive (Table 5.16). This finding merits two general comments.

First, it confirms that the governance theme is not imported from the West, as sometimes suggested. This spotlight might be seen as a mark of internalisation of a globalised discourse on the issue, at least for the fraction of 'Westernised' elites. Yet the fact that the population, including the most marginal groups, subscribe to this point of view lends support to the idea of

Table 5.16 *Elite opinions of the main obstacles to development*

The following situations form obstacles to development (%)	Political sphere	Economic sphere	Public institution	Others	Total Elites	Rest of the population
Poor leadership	98.5	98.7	98.5	99.0	**98.7**	**82.8**
Real obstacle	*89.8*	*94.1*	*89.4*	*93.6*	***91.5***	**46.2**
People's attitudes	81.8	87.9	86.6	86.7	**85.6**	**64.2**
Real obstacle	*55.8*	*57.7*	*56.9*	*54.7*	***56.4***	**18.4**
Weight of the past (colonisation)	65.1	61.9	64.3	71.8	**65.5**	**26.1**
Real obstacle	*28.4*	*25.9*	*23.1*	*33.2*	***27.3***	7.4
Foreign interventions	67.4	59.7	63.6	64.5	**63.9**	**32.2**
Real obstacle	*28.6*	*26.9*	*24.4*	*26.1*	***26.5***	**10.5**
Poor natural resources	28.8	27.7	27.4	24.9	**27.3**	**45.5**
Real obstacle	*15.9*	*13.2*	*12.0*	*11.9*	***13.4***	**18.3**

Sources: Surveys ELIMAD 2012–14 and CITMAD 2013, COEF Ressources and IRD-DIAL; authors' calculations.

a common and largely endogenous breeding ground. Certain donor denigrators (especially in the South) maintain that governance is advanced by an 'international community' struggling to explain the long-run failure of Africa's development. They accuse these same donors of making 'poor' governance a convenient scapegoat in order to deflect the blame from their own intervention strategies onto endogenous factors, i.e. the detrimental effect of rent-seeking elites who pervert the recommended 'good policies' (see Chapter 4 on this point).

Second, it is paradoxical that the elites would pile such a load of responsibility on their own heads for the failure of development in Madagascar, when it would have been so easy to point the finger at foreign interference, whether political (France's covert role in the 1972 and 2009 crises; Rakotomalala, 2014) or economic (failure of the structural adjustment policies imposed by the donors). It is then worth asking what is really behind this unanimous condemnation. Are the elites really taking the blame for a negative role in Madagascar's trajectory or does it reflect the implicit idea that 'poor leaders' are always the others, with everyone washing their hands of their own responsibility?

Although the elites see poor leadership as the main obstacle to development, other factors are also incriminated. The multiple-choice question put in the survey provides a gauge of these factors. First, 86% of the elites accuse 'people's attitudes' (with 56% of these citing it as a major cause). Although the questionnaire does not go into this aspect in detail, the qualitative interviews give an idea of what lies behind this catch-all term. A whole host of factors are mentioned, such as the weight of traditions, respect for taboos, poor time management, lack of entrepreneurship and lack of education. These opinions bear overtones of the 'culturalist' line of reasoning, with the elite seeing the failings of the masses as the second source of the country's maldevelopment.

The idea that the past and the present-day outside world both weigh negatively on Madagascar is not ruled out either. Far from it, in fact, as nearly two-thirds of the elites hold colonisation responsible (65%), while an equivalent proportion (64%) accuses the donors and foreign firms. The 'geographical' theory, however, tends to be dismissed: the prevailing idea is that Madagascar has a wealth of natural resources, and the risk of this wealth generating negative externalities (curse of natural and mineral resources: Dutch disease[11]) does not come into the picture.

It is particularly interesting to compare this elite point of view with the rest of the population. Although there are certain similarities in their answers, it is the differences that prove the most enlightening. The main point of agreement is the predominance of domestic causes and the role of human beings in the Malagasy tragedy – primarily the leaders, slated for negligence by 83% of the population – but also the preponderance of Malagasy attitudes as a source of the country's woes. This ties in with the observation at elite level: the people appear to be beating themselves up. Yet this phenomenon may also be a mark of a form of awareness (at both elite and population level) of the ambivalence and contradictions, as analysed in Chapters 3 and 4, with respect to democracy and 'modernity' in general (democratic demands alongside respect for hereditary hierarchies, rejection of state regulations, etc.).

Two significant differences are of note. First, more than twice as many elites see foreign interventions as a sticking point. This finding appears to confirm the North, Wallis and Weingast theory that external factors, by changing the rules of the game (change to the rules of accession to power, emergence of new players and capture of rents), tend to undermine the internal balances

[11] Dutch disease refers to the negative economic repercussions often triggered by a sudden surge in a country's exports of natural resources.

between the elites and the rest of the population or between different segments of elites. This is also a good way for the elites to play down their responsibilities, an assertion to which the rest of the population does not subscribe. Secondly, a larger percentage of the rest of the population thinks that poor resources are holding back Madagascar: 46% as opposed to just 25% of the elites. The discovery of mineral resources on a large scale and the launch of mining operations under M. Ravalomanana's presidency would appear to vindicate the elites' opinion.

Although no clear self-evident interpretation can be made of this difference, we can speculate as to some of the reasons. The difference between the elites' judgement and the rest of the population could stem from the way natural and mineral resources are managed in Madagascar. As mentioned in Chapter 2, these resources are mined by an enclave economy poor in jobs and disconnected from the local productive fabric. This makes mining relatively low profile. Note, moreover, that the majority of the population has very little access to information. This lack of awareness of the scale of Malagasy natural resources most likely works in favour of the population's acceptance of their situation. Another interpretation draws on the idea of the elites' system of representations. The elites might be clued-up as to Madagascar's potential wealth but believe that they are prevented from benefiting from it by the foreign powers' monopoly over the situation.

The opinion most shared by all in Madagascar, at all levels of the social ladder, is of the disastrous contribution made by the country's leaders. This casts doubt on the elites as a group. Yet it is a disparate group and so they are not necessarily all discredited in the same way. We have sought to find out precisely where the finger points by asking the population about the role of each segment of society in the country's steady downhill slide.[12]

The verdict is damning for the political elites, who are massively censured for their baneful role (Figure 5.1). Yet all the other groups are seen in a fairly positive light: the economic and military elites, but especially civil society leaders and above all the religious elites. It is interesting to note that the population also sees the general public's contribution as largely positive, an opinion that tempers the aforementioned negative role put down to people's attitudes. From 2013 to 2014, however, the overall situation improves. The changes are slight, with the exception of the political elites whose hugely negative contribution (with a negative balance of opinion

[12] Unfortunately, we did not ask the equivalent question in the ELIMAD survey (what the elite spheres think of each other).

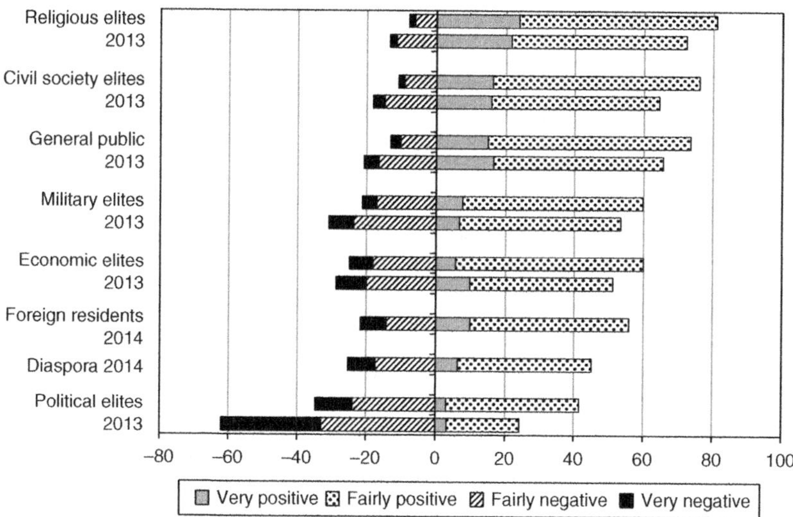

Figure 5.2 Contributions of the different groups to development.
Sources: Afrobarometer Survey 2013 and 2014 (specific questions), COEF Ressources and IRD-DIAL; authors' calculations.
Note: The question is worded as follows: How much do you think each of the following categories of people contributes to the country's development? Note that, in 2014, a neutral option (contribution neither positive nor negative) was added to the four response options presented here.

of −42 points) becomes slightly positive (+7 points). These results are highly coherent and a guarantee of the quality of the data. The year 2014 marks the end of the political crisis, with the accomplishment of the electoral cycle and a new democratically elected government. It is perfectly logical for the people to give more credit to the new political elites they have just chosen. Given, however, that the role of the other groups does not change as sharply over the period, it is equally logical that their contribution was similar over the two years. Despite this upturn in 2014, the political elites remain the most highly criticised and, unfortunately and predictably, they are once again discredited in 2015. The Governance, Peace and Security survey in effect finds that two-thirds of the general public consider that the members of the political class think only of their own interests (Rakotomanana *et al.*, 2016). This is a perfect illustration of our theories, where 'everything changes so that everything can stay the same'.

The 2014 survey introduces onto the scene a new player hitherto scarcely mentioned: the diaspora. The population perceives the diaspora's contribution to the Red Island's development as fairly positive (+20 points; Figure 5.2). Nevertheless, it is the least appreciated group, aside from the

Table 5.17 *Weight of the Malagasy diaspora compared with some other African countries*

	Stock of migrants and destination zones (2015)			Sum of international remittances received (2014)	
	Worldwide (thousands)	In France (thousands)	Percentage in developed countries	Remittances per capita (in current US$)	Remittances/ GDP (%)
Côte d'Ivoire	850	90	21	17.1	1.1
Cameroon	329	81	63	11.0	0.8
Mali	1,006	76	10	54.0	6.6
Senegal	587	118	54	112.0	10.8
Madagascar	170	143	92	18.3	4.0

Sources: For the migration data: United Nations, Department of Economic and Social Affairs (2015); for the personal remittances: World Development Indicators (2016); authors' calculations.

political elites of course. Even foreign residents are seen in a much better light (+34 points). The relationship between these two communities of Malagasy back home and their emigrant compatriots abroad is generally so complex, especially in the case of Madagascar, that it would naturally be absurd to take non-emigrant Malagasy opinions at face value. However, the elements available do show that the Malagasy diaspora, unlike other diasporas (Table 5.17), including from countries of massive emigration, takes a back seat in the island's long-run dynamics; which also explains why this book does not make it a central player in its analyses.

Two recent studies provide new, albeit as-yet sketchy, elements on the hitherto largely uncharted Malagasy diaspora (FORIM, 2016; Razafindrakoto *et al.*, 2017). With an international emigration rate estimated at 1%, Madagascar ranks twenty-eighth of the forty-eight sub-Saharan African countries for which data are available, largely behind the continent as a whole (1.7%) and far behind Mali and obviously Côte d'Ivoire (see Chapter 4). The Malagasy diaspora is small globally, which restricts its potential influence on the home country. In 2015, the number of emigrants was estimated at approximately 170,000 people (United Nations, Department of Economic and Social Affairs, 2015). However, the Malagasy diaspora displays two specific characteristics that have an inverse effect. First, it lives massively in rich countries: more than 90% of the diaspora have moved to an OECD country, 85% to France. By way of comparison, nearly 40% of sub-Saharan Africa's international emigration is to other Southern countries. Second, it is a particularly well-educated diaspora. One-third of the Malagasy diaspora have a higher education qualification and over 40% of those who have migrated to an OECD country (virtually the entire diaspora) work in a skilled profession. The corresponding figures are lower for the continent as a whole, especially for the diasporas from West Africa. These general characteristics make the Malagasy diaspora a potentially underestimated candidate for the elite world and a subject for further study in the future.

Basically, the Malagasy diaspora's high purchasing power compared with most of the other sub-Saharan African diasporas should have been a powerful factor in making it a major player on the Red Island. Yet this is not the case at all. The diaspora may be small in number, but most importantly seems to be less organised and less home country oriented. Further studies are needed to support and hone this diagnosis, as the information on this point is hazy. However, it can be said from the current information available that members of the Malagasy diaspora take a more individual view of assimilation into their host society. This can be gauged, among others, from the fact that diaspora members are much more frequently naturalised than those from other diasporas. They are also predominantly female, with marriage to host country nationals being an important motive for migration. The diaspora has a definite associative fabric, but it is less dense and relatively more engaged in ex-pat community activities (especially religious and . . . sporting events) than driven by a purpose to invest in the country and/or prepare for return migration. A certain number of Malagasy societal characteristics described in this book are found to a degree transplanted (uprooted) abroad, which on balance is not surprising. This also means that the diaspora has great mobilisation potential and initiatives have started to emerge (Collectif Tany, Zama, etc.[13]), but here again this is pure 'potential' and comes in addition to the other above-mentioned assets that the Red Island fails to harness (once again, a Malagasy characteristic).

Social Stability or Improvement to Living Conditions: What Are the Priorities?

How can the recurring crises be explained when such importance is placed on social peace in Madagascar? Is controlling violence the priority and/or

[13] Tany is a French non-profit association set up to combat Malagasy citizens and farmers' dispossession of their lands. Zama (*Zanak'i Madagasikara Ampielezana*) is a French association that organises diaspora actions in support of Madagascar's development.

should this take priority over improving living conditions and/or democracy? The same question was put to elites and to the rest of the population to find out their priority aspirations: more traditional ambitions for stability and improving material well-being or democratic aspirations in the form of giving people more say in government decisions and protecting freedom of speech.[14]

Of the four options proposed, the elites ranked respectively in first and second place 'maintaining order' in the country (37%) and 'improving living conditions for the poor' (28%). Only a small minority considered the other two options to be priorities: 12% of the elites opted for 'giving people more say in government decisions' while 16% selected 'protecting freedom of speech'. Although all the elite spheres share the same priorities as a whole, certain significant differences can be observed. The political sphere and senior management in public institutions pay the least attention to poverty reduction. However, senior administration is the most sensitive to maintaining order. Political and economic spheres are fairly similar at the end of the day, even though business leaders prove more focused on material values and, of these values, on improving the standard of living. All things considered, the most atypical profile is the 'civil society and others' category. These individuals are both the most sensitive to improving the population's living conditions and the most attached to the people's rights, political voice and also freedom of speech. Yet above and beyond these relative differences, the vast majority of elites are more focused on materialist values than on 'postmodern' values, which brings them more in line with their fellow citizens than the populations of developed countries to whom they are much closer in terms of living conditions.

In effect, 'improving living conditions for the poor' is unsurprisingly by far the top priority for the public at large at 52%, while 'maintaining order' comes in second at 28%, leaving little room for the other options proposed (Table 5.18). Yet aside from the predominance of these two categories as a whole, the two groups' respective positions are at odds with one another. Not only do the elites rank 'maintaining order' above

[14] This question on the main development priorities is borrowed from a standardised version used by modernisation and cultural change theory experts in the World Values Surveys (see Inglehart, 1997). Four categories of response are possible. Two of them – 'maintaining order' and 'fighting rising prices' are designed to represent the materialist values found in modernising, industrialising societies, while the other two – 'giving people more say in government decisions' and 'protecting freedom of speech' – stand for the post-materialist values found to be on the rise for decades in most developed countries, which these authors then call 'postmodern' societies.

Table 5.18 *Main priority for Madagascar as seen by elites and the rest of the population*

Percentage	Political sphere	Economic sphere	Public institution	Civil society and others	Total Elites	Rest of the population
Maintaining order	37.7	38.9	43.9	25.6	**37.3**	**27.9**
Improving conditions for the poor	25.7	32.6	23.6	33.5	**28.4**	**51.9**
Protecting rights and freedom of speech	18.1	15.5	11.8	19.2	**15.9**	**10.0**
Giving people more say in decisions	13.4	7.5	13.2	15.8	**12.4**	**7.4**
Civil society and others	5.1	5.4	8.1	5.9	**6.0**	**3.9**
Total	100	100	100	100	**100**	**100**

Sources: ELIMAD 2012–14 and CITMAD 2013 surveys, COEF Ressources & IRD-DIAL; authors' calculations.

all else, but they also appear to see no particular pressing need to place poverty reduction at the top of the country's political agenda. The proportion of those in favour of doing so is nearly half that of the general public (28% vs. 52%).

Assessment of the Different Periods of Madagascar's History

Among the points of view expressed by the elites, their perceptions and judgement of the different periods of history shed light on the systems of governance and episodes that have marked them the most negatively or positively. The analyses in Chapter 2 identify ten historical periods. This breakdown does not include the new term of office (starting in 2014), as the survey was conducted before the elections in late 2013. What is striking from this sweep of history is the absence of any golden age whatsoever in either the elites' collective consciousness (for the earliest periods) or the contemporary elites' experience (for the most recent periods) wherein Madagascar is seen as having clearly chosen a harmonious development path. No matter which period is considered, never more than one-quarter of the elites view it in a very positive light

Table 5.19 *Elite judgements of the different periods of Madagascar's history*

Very positive or positive judgement (%)	Political sphere	Econom-ic sphere	Public institution	Others	Total	Rest of the population
Kingdoms (before colonisation)	60.4	75.8	70.9	77.0	70.4	30.6
Very positive	*11.7*	*9.7*	*10.3*	*16.3*	*11.8*	*11.0*
Colonisation period	46.2	52.1	48.2	41.8	47.3	30.3
Very positive	*6.4*	*2.1*	*5.4*	*4.1*	*4.6*	*8.4*
Period under Tsiranana	90.0	85.8	88.4	82.1	87.0	55.6
Very positive	*30.6*	*18.5*	*25.4*	*21.0*	*24.3*	*18.2*
Period under Ramanantsoa	46.6	45.3	51.9	52.7	49.0	35.5
Very positive	*4.9*	*3.6*	*4.9*	*6.4*	*4.9*	*6.4*
Period 1 under Ratsiraka	45.0	27.2	35.5	24.8	33.9	62.1
Very positive	*6.7*	*3.0*	*4.0*	*2.5*	*4.2*	*16.7*
Period under Albert Zafy	35.5	21.0	28.9	25.9	28.2	28.2
Very positive	*3.4*	*1.7*	*0.4*	*1.0*	*1.7*	*5.2*
Period 2 under Ratsiraka	45.7	41.1	41.5	37.2	41.7	48.8
Very positive	7.8	2.1	3.3	2.0	4.0	*7.4*
Period 1 under Ravalomanana	70.3	83.8	79.4	84.4	79.0	79.4
Very positive	15.2	20.4	20.7	25.6	*20.1*	*30.9*
Period 2 under Ravalomanana	32.1	43.2	46.9	43.5	*41.3*	*57.7*
Very positive	5.6	3.9	8.9	9.4	*6.9*	*20.9*
Period under Andry Rajoelina	30.0	16.5	24.0	14.0	*21.8*	*40.3*
Very positive	2.3	0.4	1.5	0.0	*1.1*	*7.6*

Source: ELIMAD 2012–14 and CITMAD 2013 surveys, COEF Ressources and IRD-DIAL; authors' calculations.
Note: The wording of the question is: How do you judge the following periods for Madagascar's development, broadly speaking?

(Table 5.19). This relative disenchantment merely reflects the previously mentioned poor structural legitimacy of the rulers, irrespective of the regime considered.

Nevertheless, there are huge differences in how each separate period is rated. In order of preference, P. Tsiranana's First Republic is the clear leader (87% of the elites feel it had a positive effect on Madagascar's development). This period is followed by M. Ravalomanana's first presidency (70%) and the precolonial kingdoms (70%). These are seen as the three brightest periods for Madagascar. Yet opinions of M. Ravalomanana's rule plummet between the first term of office (2002–6) and the second term of office (2006–9), which receives a mere 41% of satisfactory ratings. This period ranks on the same level as D. Rastiraka's presidency in the late 1990s, with similar levels of discontent leading in both cases to the ousting of the presidents by force. The only periods that fare worse are D. Ratsiraka's long first rule (1975–90), A. Zafy's presidency and especially what is known as the transitional period (2009–13). This latter period is perceived as the worst the country has seen in nearly three centuries: just 22% of the elites feel it had a positive effect on the country's development. The fact that even the political elites, some of whom were members of the successive governments following A. Rajoelina's coming to power, take almost as critical a view of the situation clearly spotlights the disastrous nature of this transitional period.

In addition to the general finding, a certain number of significant traits are found when the data is broken down by the different elite spheres. The political elites are virtually systematically at one or the other extreme of the scale of opinions. They (relatively) overrate the Tsiranana, Ratsiraka (socialist and liberal), Zafy and Rajoelina periods and are more deprecating of the kingdoms and the Ramanantsoa and Ravalomanana periods. This picture reflects the political sphere's greater regional diversity and especially the (relative) overrepresentation of *côtier* elites in the field. These averages are therefore in part an optical illusion as this sphere is the most polarised of all, especially from an ethnic point of view.

The business sphere's judgements do not appear to be guided so much by ethnic or political considerations but are rather firmly based on economic performance criteria. This sphere is more critical than the other spheres of the Rajoelina, Zafy and Ratsiraka I (1975–90) periods, which were the most disastrous for growth. This interpretation is borne out by the majority positive judgement of the colonial period (the business sphere is alone in this), despite the fact that business elites are generally more often *Merina* and of *Andriana* origin. It is also supported by the economic elites' about-face in judgement between the first and second terms of M. Ravalomanana's presidency, in a swing that plunges over 40 percentage points. Although the businessman-president's profile may have been good news for the business

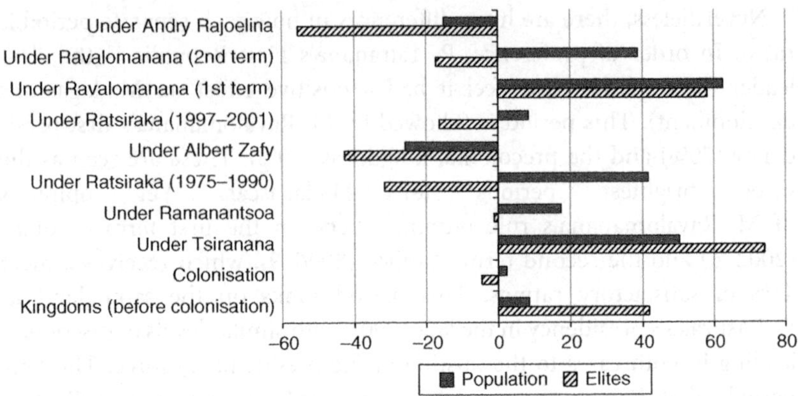

Figure 5.3 Comparative judgements of the different periods by elites and the rest of the population.
Sources: ELIMAD 2012–14 and CITMAD 2013 surveys, COEF Ressources and IRD-DIAL; authors' calculations.

world during his first term of office, the about-turn in this sphere's opinion marks their deep disappointment and their vilification of the presidential family's stranglehold on all the markets to expand its empire. The 'economic operators' were probably the hardest hit by this unfair practice.

The senior public administration profile looks the most like the political sphere, marking the porosity between the two spheres' borders. Last but not least, the 'civil society and others' sphere is found at the end of a spectrum of opinions for most of the periods, reflecting a form of contention already raised between civil society and the political class. This face-off reaches its height over the assessment of the recent transitional period. Just 14% of the elites who belong to neither the political nor the economic sphere and have no responsibilities in public institutions consider this period to be positive (and not one judges it very positively). This proportion is over twice as high (30%) among the political elites. The fact that some of them have held positions in government probably makes them more indulgent.

To conclude, there are striking differences between the elites' judgements and the general public's opinion, as outlined by the balance of opinion chart.[15]

M. Ravalomanana's first term of office meets with unanimous approval, with a positive balance of nearly 60 percentage points (Figure 5.3). The First Republic is also viewed largely in a positive light, albeit more by the elites than

[15] The balance of opinion is the difference between the percentage of positive opinions and the percentage of negative opinions. It is therefore expressed in percentage points with either a positive or negative value.

by the rest of the population (the balances of opinion are respectively +74 and +50 points). However, there is much less agreement over the royal period: 70% of the elites believe it played a positive role as opposed to just 31% of the general public. The positive balance of opinion (9 points) that appears on the chart is due essentially to the fact that four in ten members of the general public did not answer this question. From this point of view, the principle of respect for political leaders and the relative esteem for a '*raiamandreny* state' established in Chapter 4 are no sign of the population's wistfulness for the precolonial system of political organisation.

Conversely, two periods are unanimously seen as dark chapters: the Zafy period, disparaged by 70% of the elites and 54% of the population, and the transitional period, rebuffed by 77% of the elites and 55% of the population. There are also periods over which opinion is divided, such as M. Ravalomanana's second term of office. Whereas the elites are averse, as mentioned above, the population continues to give it some credit albeit with a massive backslide (-24 points). Yet the most divergent judgement probably concerns D. Ratsiraka. Irrespective of the periods and their economic and political turnarounds, the balance of opinion is positive for the population and negative for the elites. This divide, particularly diametrical for the first period (1975–90), underpins the ex-president's oft-heard grievance of being the man the country's elites love to hate (Lavrard-Meyer, 2015). Lastly, the colonial period is for the elites and the population a point of both convergence (with a balance close to zero) and divergence (slightly negative for the elites and positive for the population). From this point of view, the balance of opinion is resonant with the 'ambiguous colonisation' idea put forward by historians P. Brocheux and D. Hémery (2011) in their book on French Indochina.

5.5 Conclusion

The role of the elites in Madagascar's trajectory, especially in the formation and widening of inequalities as a known source of chronic socio-political instability, calls for closer study of the elite group. This chapter establishes a sociography of the elites based on statistical surveys, including a new survey focusing on the Red Island's elites. It provides insights into their strategies to attain and remain in power, but also their opinions on the running of society and especially their views of the obstacles to and drivers of the country's long-term development.

A certain number of key findings are of note. First, the majority of elites are from the old aristocracy. Alongside this poor social fluidity is the elites' straddling of the different spheres of power. For example, the vast majority simultaneously hold positions in different spheres of influence such as government, the National Assembly and the Senate, the army, business, public institutions and civil society. Social capital made up of a rich network in terms of its size, diversity and the intensity of the connections established within the elite circle is used as a strategy to access the highest hierarchical positions.

So without necessarily forming a truly united group, the elites have made use of networks and a specific process of reproduction to more or less directly control and keep control of power over the years. The review in Chapter 2 of the country's long history moreover shows that the power the Malagasy elites inherited from the past (before, during and in the wake of colonisation) and that they managed to use to secure their hold in different spheres (political, economic and bureaucratic) has given them the status of key players in public life and, in a way, has enabled them to claim a certain legitimacy to influence decisions.

Last but not least, this dominant class displays rather mixed attitudes to democratic principles. Although they join the population in criticising the poor successive leaderships, they look as if they are trying to extricate themselves somewhat from their share of responsibility, generally claiming other underlying reasons for Malagasy society's maldevelopment and deadlock: exogenous factors – colonial heritage and donor diktats – and the population's culture and reactionary mentality. Yet the main point of disagreement between elites and the rest of the population concerns the order of priorities on the political agenda. Although maintaining order counts most for the elites, the rest of the population prioritises improved living conditions for the poor. This discrepancy between the elite class's position and the wishes of the vast majority of the people is indicative of the divisions between these two groups. The situation is to the people's disadvantage in that the elites have the privilege of power and more easily influence which political options are taken up. So by maintaining the social order's status quo, the elites have basically protected their status since the colonial period, if not the kingdoms, irrespective of the interests of the vast majority of the population.

General Conclusion

This book has taken an innovative approach to considering how Madagascar functions in order to understand the country's trajectory since independence. The approach has been first to reinterpret Madagascar's history through a political economy lens, presenting the different diagnoses drawn from the data and studies accumulated over time. Empirical analyses of original data, produced mainly with the authors' participation, have then been conducted to identify obstacles and potential levers to set the country on a sustainably positive path.

Madagascar's long-running economic underperformance is not due to the usual suspects found by economic science. Neither is it due to factors associated with history or geography (remoteness, climate, conflicts, resources, etc.), social fragmentation (measured by indicators such as ethnic diversity), inequalities as measured by household surveys (which do not capture the elite) or the quality of the country's institutions (measured by the different international databases). Nor can economic policy choices explain Madagascar's trajectory. The country has explored a succession of different options in keeping with donor-recommended policies in comparable countries. Political economy, particularly the NWW framework, offers an interesting alternative approach to explaining how developing societies function. This framework highlights the role of the elites who manipulate others to their own advantage, capture rents and are non-developmental. We have shown that this model corresponds in part to the case of Madagascar. Nevertheless, our analysis finds a certain number of Malagasy particularities that, when combined, set the country outside the proposed generic framework.

First, Madagascar has often proved its capacity for change. From an institutional point of view, the country has distinguished itself by setting up open access order (OAO)-type formal organisations on the three economic, bureaucratic and political fronts. These achievements belie the notion of the 'structural' inability of developing countries to make such institutions work without misusing them. Second, despite recurring political crises, Madagascar has made little use of political violence as its society harbours a deep-rooted disapproval of any form of violence, regarded as taboo. Last but not least, our analyses stress the fact that the people, and not just the elites, do matter. Although the people are absent from the North, Wallis and Weingast (NWW) approach, which ascribes an exclusive role to struggles and arrangements between elite fractions (reminiscent of 'the 200 families' in France, or conspiracy theory in other cases, and 'the club of 48 families' in the Malagasy case), our findings show that the people, even the poor, play a role in events and in the country's trajectory. They have a form of autonomy and are not mere 'pawns'. Popular discontent has been one of the underlying drivers of the movements in all the crises: whether the people are manipulated or the movements are spontaneous, popular discontent is always found somehow setting the stage. Economic issues can crystallise this discontent, especially inequalities perceived through the magnifying glass of cases of astronomical enrichment by those close to the ruling power, and affairs of grand corruption and poor governance in the public arena or more directly on the political scene (electoral fraud). The combination of an unfair distribution of the wealth produced and serious governance problems is a major element of every crisis. Despite the people's attachment to social stability, they express their demands and seek ways to make their voice heard as much in terms of improving their welfare as democracy. Hence the people, and especially their aspirations, play a role even in the most fragile natural states, a role singularly overlooked by most of the analytic frameworks in political economy.

However, there is evidence of a number of structural obstacles to the country's development. The fundamentally hereditary and hierarchical social structure firmly established since the time of the monarchies is exacerbated by many social divides (distinctions within same-status groups and marked interpersonal distrust) and many geographical divides (town/country split, imbalanced regional development, isolation of certain regions, and a monocephalic capital). Madagascar has all the characteristics of an atrophy of the three main potential channels that usually connect the elites with the population in developing countries: the state, mainly through its redistributive functions (formal links); patronage and clientelism, be they through ethnic groups, castes, regional affiliations or other elements (informal links); and intermediary bodies of different kinds such as political parties, trade unions and associations, churches, local authorities, and traditional leaders (formal and informal links). None of these social elements cements society from top to bottom. Atomisation of the population and weak intermediary bodies prevent the people's needs from being voiced and mean that the authorities are not compelled to respond to them. So, as in modern-day Europe, riots appear to be the only possible form of collective mobilisation (Hobsbawm, 1966). In reality, however, the violence taboo makes riots a rare phenomenon. Although the people lay claim to democratic principles, they are torn between civic aspirations for democracy and meritocracy – part imported, part drawn from the Malagasy cultural wellspring – and the ever-potent traditional values that demand respect for the real and symbolic hierarchies inherited from the past.

The main 'social order' perpetuated over time is therefore the divide/split between the elite and the vast majority of the population. The survey findings bear out that the elites have made use of networks and a specific process of reproduction to more or less directly control and keep control of the power over the years. However, this does not necessarily mean that they have total control over access to power considering that the popular uprisings have taken the elites by surprise, at least in the first three crises. The system is not a totally closed shop, as seen from the dual economic (arrival of a class of new entrepreneurs) and political transition (real uptake of the democratic system by the people) that took place in the 1990s, even though this transition was not consolidated. Similarly, the successive arrivals of M. Ravalomanana, A. Rajoelina (in controversial circumstances) and H. Rajaonarimampianina following the 2013 elections have demonstrated the possibility for political competition from outside the fold. This relatively open political scene is positive, even though it is not really structured and has been appropriated mainly by high-profile figures ('free agents' to start with) who have seized on an opportunity for their own interests.

The elites hence emerge as highly individualistic and incapable of establishing strong organisations and lasting coalitions. This situation enables power to be highly concentrated in the hands of a small number of individuals who are neither compelled nor encouraged to adopt a medium- or long-term vision or to take the interests of the vast majority into consideration. Constantly changing, fragile alliances at the top – confined as they are to those in the president's orbit – exclude and frustrate potentially influential elite groups with the power to destabilise the situation. Given the endemic weakness of the institutions and organisations (formal and informal) and the fact that no one faction has any real ability to rally violence on a large scale, it is easy to topple the government in office with precious few financial and human resources. What is significant, then, is the absence of any long-term vision and, more especially, any strategy to ensure the longevity of the ruling power. This is evidenced for one by the 'quick getaway' attitude[1] found in the corridors of power: those who accumulate wealth do not invest in the country but place their capital elsewhere in full knowledge and anticipation of a short-lived term of office. There may well be a patron–client system in operation, but the rent distribution system tends to remain restricted to the highly exclusive club directly associated with the regime in power. In addition, and unlike other developing countries, those who take office in Madagascar have never sought to develop or particularly support their home regions. So in the case of Madagascar, it is not clear whether the leaders' prime objective is really to maintain order, as posited by North *et al.* (2009, 2012a) because, on balance, order usually tends to be well kept by the culture of consensus and the widespread culture of *fiaraha-monina* ("living in harmony"). The objective once in power tends to be enrichment, but apparently without the concern of building a lasting system (or at least without the ability to do so).

At the end of our analyses, we believe we have shown the extent of the unique, hybrid nature of contemporary Malagasy society and the way it functions. This demonstration of uniqueness was a logical imperative to be able to claim to explain the Malagasy mystery, itself unique. Yet the uniqueness of the Malagasy case also has a universal dimension. The divide between elites and the people, the attitude towards power and the questioning of democracy at the core of the current Malagasy knot are also part of a planetary groundswell that is a cause of concern for developing countries and developed countries alike.

The hybrid aspect, however, is the product of both internal influences, themselves diverse, and external influences. Despite our conclusion that endogenous dynamics are leading the dance, the Malagasy configuration is a melting pot of imported and local elements in constant interaction. Therein lies the rub. For Fremigacci (2014b), the meld of mutually perversive traditional homegrown concepts and Western ideas has given birth to a 'chimera', a monstrous creation that is leading Madagascar to its doom. Although the Malagasy system is so dysfunctional that it might befit the chimera idea, we believe the equation is far more complicated than a head-

[1] This expression was used by a Malagasy politician, Herizo Razafimahaleo, to denounce the fact that all the members of the Malagasy elite make sure they are ready to leave the country at a moment's notice, either because of reprehensible actions in the exercise of their duties or merely to avoid 'going down with the country'.

on collision between imported modernity and traditional local values. Madagascar is clearly torn between contradictory systems of values. The list is endless: between the duty of deference to the *raiamandreny* and democratic civic duty; between the upside of physical violence controlled as being taboo and its downside of an established order maintained by the yoke of strong symbolic violence; between the advantages of an open system and the instability it implies; between the historical strength of the institutions and their state of decay; between the legitimacy bestowed on elected public office and political authorities and their total disrepute; between the churches acting as mediator and pillar of the established order in the same breath; between elites supposed to contribute to development and their role as its main obstacle; between the attachment to legal and bureaucratic procedures and the use of states of exception (Razafindrabe, 2018); and so on ad infinitum.

However, this manifest acute bipolarity is not only (nor even mainly) the product of poorly assimilated or warped imported standards. 'Malagasy tradition' is itself contradictory. We have pointed up the 'antidemocratic' aspect of Madagascar's heritage: a hierarchical, dynastic, ancestral society with its principles of *hasina*, *raiamandreny* and *olomanga*. Yet Malagasy tradition also bears endogenous elements that can be related to the universal conception of democracy, as shown by Raison-Jourde and Roy (2010). The *fanjakana* of royal descent stands opposite the *Fanjakan'ny madinika* (society of equals).[2] For all the Malagasy terms standing for status order, just as many can be found underlying democratic principles: *fokonolona*, *fiaraha-monina*, *firaisan-kina*, *fihavanana*, *soa iombonana*, etc. More subtly, the same word can have all sorts of different meanings and connotations depending on the period of time and the social groups using it.

So a chimera it may be, but not one formed by a head-on collision between Malagasy and foreign influences. It is the product of a dysfunctional entanglement of horizontal and vertical principles from home and away. We consider just three examples of this fateful combination. The fiscal minimum tax (former capitation tax) was scrapped in 1972 with the launch of the *fokonolona* reform. This tax had placed a huge burden on the rural world. Equated with labour duty and its own share of

[2] In the same vein, Graeber (2018) discusses the hierarchy and absolute nature of sovereign power in his study of monarchs in Merina society in the nineteenth century. His analyses show that the conception of royal power meant that monarchs could be controlled as they were considered to be babies: they were highly dependent on their subjects who could reprimand them in a reversal of hierarchical position.

violence, the tax was seen as especially iniquitous in that it had been introduced by the colonial power (Gallieni's famous 'moralising tax'). This act of liberation therefore came as a huge relief to the people. Yet the tax had another symbolic meaning: it stood for the state (the *fanjakana*), the mark of the sacred nature (*hasina*) of subjection to power. So once the initial wave of astonished relief had subsided, its phasing out was also interpreted as the end of the state, of the reign of law. The axing of the tax was immediately followed by a surge of previously prohibited behaviour, such as bush fires, with terrible consequences (Raison-Jourde & Roy, 2010). More generally, this point marked the start of the state's gradual abandonment of the Malagasy countryside, or the end of peasant 'capture' to coin Hyden (1980), from which there has been no return since.

Turning to the second example, a taboo on violence throughout an entire human society is undoubtedly a rare quality. Yet in the case of Madagascar today, this taboo is also partly to blame for the political instability as the cost (in violence) of insurgency bids is particularly low, whether because the legal authority does not have credible deterrents or because the people allow themselves to be easily intimidated by what would be perceived as low-level threats were it not for this taboo. The third example concerns the elites and their at least implicit, if not explicit, strategies. Why do these strategies (or at least why does the upshot of the power struggle between heterogeneous elite groups with potentially divergent interests) ultimately make for the choice of a larger slice of a smaller cake (preference for inequality over growth), rather than a smaller slice of a larger cake (product of stronger inclusive growth)? This choice in all probability makes for a lower value of elite rent. Only the contemporary expression of a hierarchical, infinitely tiered Malagasy society underpinned by the perpetuation of the aforementioned political theology can possibly hold up an edifice that is so counterproductive for all, particularly the vast majority of the population. If the downward spiral underway for at least half a century is to be turned around, there needs to be a change in the combination of elements at work in the social dynamic.

The social order is not set in stone. A number of elements already at work will probably change the game sooner or later. Three elements are worth mentioning here: the emergence of new rents, the decline of political theology and, to a lesser extent, ecological developments. First of all, 'economic' rents have historically been small and not particularly concentrated. However, the discovery of rare new resources (combined with the boom in commodity prices) heralds a new game that counts as both lucky for the country (given the scale of the resources concerned) and risky (given the possible tensions generated by attempts to corner these resources and the associated pressure on the land and ecological risks) (Raharinirina et al., 2018). From 2007 to 2009, a huge influx of foreign investment was attracted by the discovery of mineral sands containing titanic iron ore and zircon near Fort Dauphin, and nickel and cobalt at Ambatovy (DG Trésor, 2011).[3] These mines have gradually ramped up production to make what is already a major contribution in foreign currency (albeit dependent on world price trends), in tax resources and in employment. These mineral rents could be further increased in the future by bauxite mining (the Manantenina deposit could be one of the largest in the Indian Ocean) and, in the longer run, by onshore and offshore oil and gas production (Madagascar was ranked the number two African destination for this type of investment by the Africa Oil & Power initiative in 2016). Madagascar is also one of the target countries for what are known as rare earth elements (earths containing strategic minerals for the high-tech industries), especially tantalum (Ampasindava peninsula). Moves have been underway in recent years to scale up production of the older rents of gold and rosewood to meet an increase in world demand (particularly Chinese). Last but not least, Madagascar's land itself forms a resource for agrarian projects. Raharinirina *et al.* (2018) report that contracts covering 3 million hectares were signed with foreign investors in 2013. From this point of view, Madagascar, hitherto relatively free from the curse of natural resources, could suffer the ills that have hit the most resource-rich countries, especially in sub-Saharan Africa (the first signs of criminalisation of business activities, ecological degradation and conflicts over land tenure are starting to appear).

Malagasy society's long-term social stability is underpinned by a political theology that makes the use of violence taboo and respect for leaders and the hierarchical order a fundamental precept. Yet this political theology is showing signs of waning over time. The crisis back in 2009 already saw new manifestations of interpersonal violence, pillage (such as the *dahalo* rustlers in the rural areas in the south of the country; Pellerin, 2014; Tarabey, 2014) and challenges to the social hierarchy (Galibert, 2009; Vivier, 2010). The social climate has taken a turn for the worse with a growing sense of insecurity, the spread of mob justice often ending in

[3] Investment has slowed down because due to the political instability, the world slowdown in commodity prices and the transition from the commissioning phase to the production phase by QIT Madagascar Minerals (QMM) and Ambatovy (French Directorate General of the Treasury, 2015; World Bank, 2016).

clashes with the police, an increase in land disputes and other socio-political signs of simmering social discontent. In addition to this rising common law violence, there is the risk of a pathogenic spread of state violence. Disturbing cracks are starting to appear in the historically side-lined and relatively law-abiding army, as seen from the admittedly small-scale, but fast-growing mutinies. In an environment of persistent insecurity, there is no ruling out the possibility of a junta taking power (Fremigacci, 2014b).

Lastly, the combination of these elements coupled with the natural shocks to which Madagascar is particularly exposed (UNISDR, 2009) could tip the country into a vicious cycle of institutional decay, economic decline and growing popular poverty. Madagascar's economic deterioration, rising insecurity and development of illegal activities in a climate of political instability have already dragged the country into the group of 'fragile states' (IMF, 2014). A state of chaos is one of the possible scenarios for Madagascar. It is clear at the end of this book that the new period ushered in by the 2013 electoral cycle and extended by the new 2018 presidential change-over has done nothing to change the structural order of the Malagasy equation.

The rhetoric of the providential man emerging from limbo and resurfacing at each election is hollow: not only because no candidate donned such a mantle this time round, as shown by the return of previous presidents to the first three places in the first round of November, but also because even if he did miraculously exist, the institutional arrangements without the above-mentioned safeguards would soon make him devoid of all reality. It is not the least of the paradoxes of the latest elections that the Malagasy voted in a presidential candidate who had already governed with catastrophic results following a coup d'état (2009–13), and whose term of office was considered by both the people and the elites as the worst the country had seen since independence. It is all the more paradoxical because the unknown origin of the funds lavished on the campaign and the rash promises should have made voters more circumspect. However, this was probably more of a Hobson's choice than anything else, as evidenced by the record rate of abstention.

A new crisis could erupt at any moment on the same bases as the previous crises, but on increasingly fragile ground each time. In many areas, economic and democratic governance alike, a body of evidence suggests that there could be a chink in the huge resilience that Madagascar has shown in response to previous crises. In the face of such a disastrous turn of events, the prospect of a military tyranny envisaged by J. Fremigacci (2014a) as an alternative to chaos is hardly cheering.

Yet these real, serious threats are not necessarily harbingers of the country's inevitable fate, given the capacity for reaction and institutionalisation that Malagasy society has shown in the past. Other prospects could shape up for Madagascar. The country ranks among the fragile limited access orders (LAOs), as defined by the framework proposed by NWW (2009, 2012a). Yet we have seen that it also has some of the characteristics of mature LAOs, if not OAOs, in economic, bureaucratic and political areas alike. The two new democratic changes of power (2013 and 2018), two decades after the first two democratic change-overs (1993 and 1996), constitute the most recent demonstration of the capacity for institutional regulation.

Two other less dramatically downhill paths then open up. The first is the road of positive societal changes outlined by the implicitly evolutionary framework developed by NWW (2009, 2012a), with Madagascar becoming a basic LAO mainly due to restored stability (Diagram 6.1). In this scenario, the elites would organise themselves into factions to establish their power with grounded grassroots support based mainly on a more organised top-down patron–client system. They would set up sound, lasting institutions guaranteeing access to rents and the enduring stability of the political system, while providing partial forms of redistribution. The elite factions' monopoly on and threat of violence would round out the system, preventing any protest movement. This scenario would establish a stable social order, but would mean the abandonment of the democratic process. It appears to sit well with the elites' priority of keeping order before any other concern with improving living conditions or the political participation of the people. Such an option could also find favour with the donors, forced to compromise with the members of the elite and seeking to meet the imperative of fast results.

This path is nonetheless not an easy one to set up and recent political developments are not indicative of such a scenario taking shape. Despite repeated talk of 'national reconciliation' (meaning reconciliation among elites) and the passing in December 2016 of an act supposed to finally guarantee the country's stability, everything points to today's alliances being pacts of pure convenience, as in the past (the aforementioned 2016 act can be seen as a way of putting the two previous presidents of the Republic out of the running for the 2018 presidential election). Bear in mind that the conflicts between elites during the mandate of H. Rajaonarimampianina have led to many sticking points (problems appointing a prime minister, changes of political affiliation within parliament, and votes of no confidence in the president and the government) and

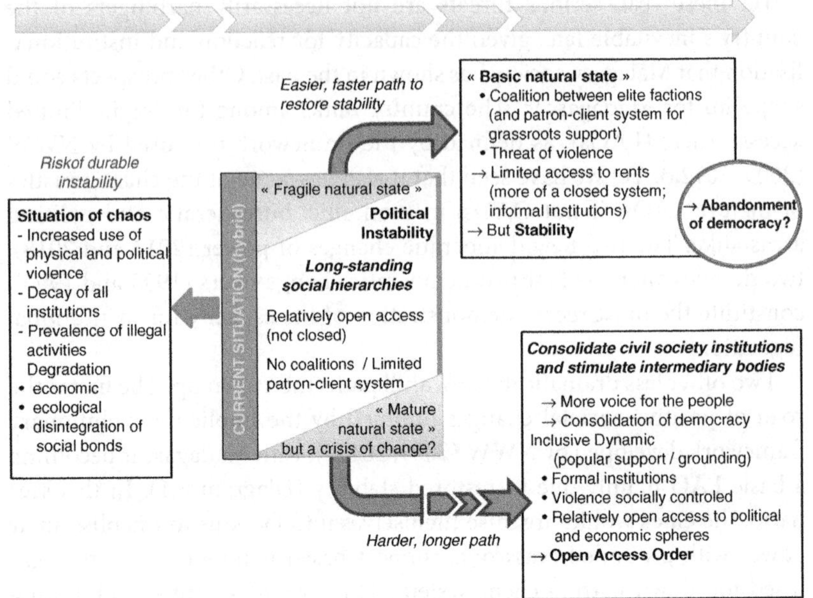

Figure C.1 Future prospects: Three possible institutional configurations for Madagascar.
Note: See Box 1.1 for a presentation of natural states and open access orders.
Source: Authors.

changes of political affiliation. The attempts at institutionalisation moreover seem fragile and prone to challenge as social developments advance (as seen from the conflicts over the introduction of a new mining code in 2015 and a new communications code in 2016).

The second path could organise and galvanise civil society, taking advantage of the absence of strong elite organisations that might close off access to economic and political power. This would consolidate countervailing institutions and develop intermediary bodies, giving more voice to the people. They would therefore bring to the public arena what is still today often more like silent protest (Biaussat & Tabet, 2016). Democratic consolidation would then be achieved by means of an inclusive social, political and economic dynamic. Democratic aspirations continue to run high in Madagascar, even though perversion of the democratic process has caused doubts as to its effectiveness and a downturn in political participation.[4] These aspirations

[4] Voter turnout at the Antananarivo local election in July 2015 was 29% even though the candidacy of L. Ravalomanana, wife of the former president prevented from standing,

can be seen, for example, from the size and length of the 2016 popular protest in Soamahamanina against the granting of a gold mining permit to a Chinese company. The role taken in the public debate by certain civil society associations such as SeFaFi and Justice et Paix in recent years, civic action by diaspora associations such as the Collective for the Defence of Malagasy Land (*Tany*), and the more recent emergence of the peaceful protest movement *Wake Up* also suggest that such a path is not improbable. The same applies to the expression of critical views on social media and in the press. The survey of the elites also shows that those involved in civil society have a particular profile and values. Internationally, there is the tentative emergence of an organised Malagasy diaspora from its French base where it is massively concentrated. Slow to pick up speed, its hitherto marginal role could act as a catalyst, not only because the diaspora is the largest of all the sub-Saharan communities, but also because it is the most integrated and skilled in France (Razafindrakoto et al., 2017).

From a dynamic, non-static angle, it could be said that Madagascar is engaged in a long-term democratisation process, with all its steps forward and back. The country's political instability is ultimately due to there being no coalition among elites owing to the fact that the system is not closed, a factor or element that should be viewed in a positive light. Despite this book's largely negative picture of the situation, especially in the current period, the country's political instability may not be the mark of a decisive divide, but rather a transition crisis, a learning curve crisis in a non-linear process of consolidation marked by the throes of the old order. Madagascar's leaders after all nearly always take power on a democratic footing, seeking democratic legitimacy in an electoral process. Leaders since independence have also been keen to secure the people's support directly, as shown by the particularly high number of referendums in Madagascar's history (eight since independence). There is no official challenge on record to democratic principles. Save for a handful of intellectuals, no group or party has openly taken an anti-democratic stance in any way like the extreme right wing in Europe and fundamentalists in the Muslim world. On a final note, given that democracy building is a long-term process, the fifty-odd years since independence could be deemed a short period in the history of the Malagasy nation. Bearing this in mind, Madagascar could well make the transition from fragile natural state to 'mature' natural state (without passing through the 'basic' phase), and then

should have made it a symbolic platform. She was consequently elected by just 16% of the registered voters.

to an open access order inclusive of all society's stakeholders playing their role to the full in the development process.

This second path is possible and preferable. Yet it is also harder to steer and, most importantly, it would take time. This preference, this choice, is obviously just one point of view, one opinion. Yet may we be so bold in concluding this book as to take off the scientific, analytic hat we have worn up to this point and briefly don our engaged citizen cap to add a personal touch and perchance take sides; the side of a little optimism? The idea here is not to develop a detailed plan of action, a catalogue of policies and measures to be taken to turn the ship around and out of the vortex that is dragging Madagascar down with every passing day. This is a task essentially for the Malagasy people themselves, at all levels of the social ladder. We believe that the analyses developed here provide insights into the Malagasy 'mystery', reveal its drivers and consequently point to courses of action. We hope that this opportunity will be seized. We feel that among the many possible ways forward, there is one that is key and yet overlooked; that is to redefine the relationship between power and the people, between elites and the public at large based on a new social contract and a shared future. On the research front, we will devote the last opus of our *Quartet*[5] to this issue, expanding on Chapter 5 of this book.

On the policy front, and at our modest level of individual 'engaged researchers', we are picking up the proposal we outlined at the last Francophone Summit in Antananarivo in November 2016 (Razafindrakoto *et al.*, 2016), officially supported by the National Organising Committee, to create an institutionalised forum for public discussion and debate focusing exclusively on narrowing the growing divide between the elites and the rest of the population in all its manifold dimensions. The purpose of this forum would be to hatch decision-making assistance proposals informed by the findings of scientific research. It would be opened by a long-established institution[6] and its action would be evaluated and judged.

We recommend that the forum launch a first, particularly rich workstream as a priority to re-explore a certain number of notions and principles seen by all as specifically Malagasy. There is a common consensus today that

[5] In reference to *The Red Island Quartet,* our four-part editorial project on Madagascar mentioned in the introduction with this book as its keystone.

[6] Although a programme of this sort may well warrant the creation of its own organisation, it would more realistically be hosted on a long-term basis by an existing or planned institution, such as the Economic and Social Council (CES) or the High Council for the Defence of Democracy and the Rule of Law (HCDDED), whose creation has already been confirmed.

the terms *fihavanana*, *fiaraha-monina*, *firaisan-kina*, *fokonolona*, *soa iombonana*, *raiamandreny*, *fanjakana*, *hasina* and *olomanga* all exhibit this essential quality. However, as we have shown throughout this book, their sometimes-twisted meaning is not shared by all. In practice, they are often used as an instrument of domination and oppression by the minority over the majority, and their combination has spawned this ominous chimera that we have evidenced. Yet the meaning contained in all these terms is by no means immutable. They are labile, polysemous and constantly evolving over time as witnessed by the articles presented on this point in Kneitz (2014), in the case of *fihavanana*, and those in Raison-Jourde and Roy (2010) for the *fokonolona*. So we need to choose a battery of 'word-concepts' and challenge them for their meaning to evolve, to reconfigure them into a system of Malagasy values conducive to shared, equitable development firmly rooted in history. Perhaps the first consideration should concern the meaning and use of the word *Fanjakana* to refer to the state. It is a vehicle of domination and servitude, as implied by the etymological sense of *manjaka* (to reign). This is precisely how many Malagasy people, especially in rural areas, perceive the state and its Malagasy manifestation. First, however, instead of ruling as an absolute divine ruler, the state needs to take on board democratic aspirations and be accountable for its actions. This would, among other things, address one of the pillars of political theology that we have identified as being one of the main obstacles responsible for Malagasy society's impasse. Second, a fundamental state function needs to be regenerated: the state embodies the vertical link between the population and its rulers and thereby guarantees social cohesion or Malagasy *fiaraha-monina* (living in harmony). Without being naïvely culturalist, we believe this reappropriation process has the potential to be largely embraced and serve as a basis for a process of reconstruction, of rebirth to escape this fate of a country slowly, silently falling, watching as it sinks amidst total indifference. It would put an end to decades of humiliation caused by the gulf between the country's tragic economic and social trajectory since independence and the unanimous conviction that Madagascar is a great nation, beyond compare.

Timeline

Year	Event	Reign	Period
1807	British Parliament decrees slave trade illegal.		Precolonial period
1808	Great Britain takes possession of Mauritius.		
1817	Radama I marches on Tamatave. Treaty with Great Britain: ban on the export of slaves.	Radama I	
1820	London Missionary Society (LMS).		
1828	Radama I dies. Ranavalona I accedes to the throne.	Ranavalona I	
1836	LMS missionaries expelled from Antananarivo.		
1861	Ranavalona I dies. Radama II accedes to the throne. Trade liberalisation. Missionaries authorised to purchase land.		
1863	Radama II assassinated. Rasoherina becomes queen.		
1868	Ranavalona II accedes to the throne. Rainilaiarivony made Prime Minister. Royal code of 101 articles enacted. French-Malagasy treaty (freedom of worship, freedom of trade, right of establishment, French protection, and recognition of the queen's authority throughout Madagascar).	Ranavalona II	
1869	Ranavalona and Rainilaiarivony convert to Christianity, adopted as state religion.		
1876	Schooling compulsory for eight-year-old boys and girls in the highlands region (compulsory royal service). Five-year military service compulsory.		
1877	'Mozambicans', imported slaves, are freed. Government of Antananarivo internationally recognised as the capital of the sovereign state of Madagascar.		
1881	Royal code of 305 articles. Ban on selling land to foreigners.		
1883	Ranavalona III crowned. Start of French military expeditions.	Ranavalona III	
1885	Treaty ending the war against the French. Madagascar becomes a French protectorate.		
1890	Anglo-French agreements. The two powers mutually recognise the other's free hand in Madagascar and Zanzibar.		
1896	France annexes Madagascar. Ban on slavery. Gallieni appointed Governor of Madagascar. Start of the Menalamba uprising.		Colonial period
1897	Abolition of the privileges of the Tompomenakely, feudal lords of Imerina, and end to the Vodivona (fiefdoms) Establishment of Le Myre de Vilers school.		
1900	French Parliament passes legislation requiring the governments of the French colonies to fund their needs from their own resources. Start of the Tananarive–East Coast railway line.		
1904	Institution of the French Code of Indigenous Status in Madagascar.		
1909	Decree of accession to French citizenship for all French-speaking Malagasy with a sound education.		
1913	Creation of VVS: secret political society.		
1916	VVS trial. Creation of the Bank of Madagascar.		
1926	Start of work on the Fianarantsoa–Manakara railway line. Introduction of SMOTIG (Manpower Service for Public Works).		
1927	Creation of six administrative regions.		
1929	Protest in Tananarive for mass naturalisation.		
1930	Decree establishing a press offence.		
1937	SMOTIG scrapped. Press offence repealed. Introduction of first union legislation: trade union rights for literate Malagasy.		
1938	The ashes of Ranavalona III, deceased in exile in Algiers in 1917, return to Madagascar. Extension of Malagasy accession to French citizenship rights.		
1940	Britain imposes economic blockade on the island.		
1942	Britain takes control of the island.		
1944	Brazzaville conference. Reinstatement of the French colonial government.		
1946	France: new constitution establishing the French empire and recognition of French citizenship for all subjects of the colonies. Establishment of the Investment Fund for Economic and Social Development (FIDES). The Democratic Movement for Malagasy Renewal (MDRM) founded in Paris. Parti des Déshérités de Madagascar (PADESM – Party of the Disinherited of Madagascar) founded. Ravoahangy and Raseta submit a bill to constituent assembly to establish Madagascar as a free state within the French Union.		
1947	March: Bloodily repressed uprising against the colonial authority. Dissolution of the MDRM and PANAMA (National Malagasy Party).		
1950	Creation of Crédit de Madagascar. Creation of the rural indigenous authorities (CAR).		
1951	Education reform: end of segregation between indigenous and European schools. Creation of SIM (Madagascar Property Investment Company).		
1952	Creation of SEM (Madagascar Electricity Board). Election of a leader in the 105 Malagasy communes.		

Year	Event	Leader	Republic
1956	French Overseas Reform Act: introducing elections by universal suffrage and a single electoral college (end of colonised/coloniser distinction) alongside an executive council. Administrative decentralisation under the control of elected assemblies. PADESM splits into two parties: Tsiranana's Social Democratic Party (PSD). Tsiranana elected MP for Madagascar to the French Union on a French Section of the Workers' International (SFIO) ticket.		
1958	Referendum: Madagascar becomes an autonomous republic within the French Community. Monja Jaona's Madagascar for the Malagasy (MONIMA). Creation of the Antokon'ny Kongresin'ny Fahaleovantenan'i Madagasikara (AKFM – Congress Party for the Independence of Madagascar) in Toamasina by pastor Richard Andriamanjato calling for immediate independence.	**Tsiranana**	**First Republic**
1959	Philibert Tsiranana elected President of the Republic by the Constituent Assembly. Tsiranana wins victory over opposition in local elections. AKFM wins Antananarivo and Antsiranana; Alexis Bezaka (former AKFM) wins Toamasina; Monima wins Toliara.		
1960	Independence proclaimed on 26 June. Tsiranana is the first President of the Republic. Cooperation agreements with France: defence; foreign policy; monetary, financial and economic policy; and higher education. Creation of an army.		
1961	Creation of the University of Antananarivo. Madagascar admitted as a member of the United Nations.		
1963	Membership of the International Monetary Fund.		
1965	Tsiranana re-elected President of the First Republic by direct universal suffrage. Opening of the Antsirabe Military Academy (ACMIL).		
1971	April: Farmer revolt led by Monja Jaona. Violently suppressed by Gendarmerie Commanding Officer Richard Ratsimandrava. Interior Minister André Resampa arrested for an attempted coup d'état and exiled to Sainte-Marie Island.		
1972	Tsiranana (only candidate in presidential election) re-elected by 99% of voter turnout. April-May: student strikes and general strike bloodily repressed by the Republican Security Forces (FRS) (40 dead). 18 May: Tsiranana hands over power to G. Ramanantsoa. October: Referendum to endorse interim government. A National Popular Council for Development replaces the National Assembly and the Senate. *Fokonolona*-based policy. Abolition of capitation tax and cattle tax. The Republican Security Forces are reorganised into the Mobile Police Group (GPM). Creation of the USM (Malagasy Socialist Union openly declaring itself to be acting in the interests of the *côtier* people). December: Anti-*Merina* riots in Toamasina and Antsiranana.	**Ramanantsoa**	
1973	Madagascar leaves franc zone. Creation of SINPA (National Farm Produce Marketing Board). Withdrawal of provincial budget.		
1975	Failed coup attempt. Conflict between government and the GPM. Ramanantsoa dissolves his government and hands over power to Colonel Richard Ratsimandrava. February: Ratsimandrava assassinated. March-June: Trial of the Century. June: Didier Ratsiraka appointed head of state by military directorate. December: Referendum. New constitution adopted by referendum. Charter of the Malagasy Socialist Revolution. Creation of the Vanguard of the Malagasy Revolution (AREMA).	**Ratsiraka**	
1976	Establishment of a National Front for the Defence of the Revolution: AREMA, Vonjy Iray Tsy Mivaky (VITM – Popular Movement for the Unity of Madagascar, PSD offshoot), AKFM, Union of Christian Democrats (UDECMA). June-August: First wave of 'Malagasisation': nationalisation of banks, insurance firms and the Compagnie Marseillaise de Madagascar, and oil and import–export companies. Nationalisation. Establishment of OMNIS (National Military Agency for Strategic Industries).		**Second Republic**
1977	*Charter of Socialist Enterprises*. Nationalisation of SOSUMAV sugar company, Denis Frères and COROI trading company. MFM joins the National Front for the Defence of the Revolution (FNDR). First use of SDRs (special drawing rights from the IMF).		
1978	Public investment in industrial and agricultural sectors. Establishment of the Malagasy Council of Christian Churches (FFKM).		
1981	First Structural Adjustment Programme. 10% devaluation in the Malagasy franc (MGF).		
1982	D. Ratsiraka elected president by universal suffrage. Inauguration of Andekaleka Hydro-Electric Dam (58 megawatts) financed by the World Bank, Kuwaiti funds and the Arab Bank for Economic Development in Africa (BADEA).		
1983	Partial liberalisation of the rice trade (with the exception of rice in the Alaotra and Marovoay regions). D. Ratsiraka proclaims himself Admiral, becoming the highest-ranking officer in the history of Madagascar.		
1984	Clashes between Kung-Fu fighters and the Tanora Tonga Saina (TTS – 'Aware Youth').		
1985	Total liberalisation of rice prices at the request of the international financial institutions (IFIs). 20% devaluation in the MGF. AKFM loses local elections in Antananarivo. First privatisation: state-owned company TAMALU (Toamasina Aluminium Company) sold to a private firm.		

Year	Events	Period	Republic
1986	First wave of privatisation of public enterprises. Censorship lifted.		
1987	Total liberalisation of exports with the exception of coffee, vanilla and cloves under CASPIC (Industrial and Trade Policy Structural Adjustment Credit). Rescission of pepper export tax and closure of pepper marketing board. 55% devaluation in the MGF.		
1988	Closure of coffee and clove marketing board → significant cut in export taxes. Liberalisation of domestic and foreign trade with the exception of vanilla. End of state monopoly on exports. Public enterprise reform programme with CASEP (Public Enterprise Structural Adjustment Credit). Extraordinary repayment of Madagascar's debt by the Paris Club.		
1989	D. Ratsiraka re-elected. Privatisation of nationalised businesses. Slide in the MGF's parity. Winding up of the FNDR.		
1990	Freedom of establishment of political parties.		
1991	April: Council of Forces Vives. June: Establishment of interim government by the Council of Forces Vives. June–October: Series of demonstrations demanding revision of the constitution and departure of Didier Ratsiraka. General strike. Army opens fire on demonstrators marching on Iavoloha Palace, killing twelve people. July: Parallel rule of the Council of Forces Vives (Hery Velona). 14–15 September: First national conference of federated states. 31 October: Panorama Convention. November: Albert Zafy proclaimed President of High State Authority while D. Ratsiraka remains President of the Republic.	Transition	
1992	August: Referendum on a new constitution. Political leaders referred to by the term of *raiamandreny*.		
1993	February: Zafy wins presidential election against D. Ratsiraka.	Zafy	
1994	Floating exchange rate for the MGF.		Third Republic
1995	Vanilla price liberalisation at the request of the IFIs. Membership of the World Trade Organization. September: Referendum to give President of the Republic the power to appoint the prime minister.		
1996	Second wave of privatisation. September: Parliamentary impeachment and resignation by Zafy. Norbert Ratsirahonana appointed acting president. December: D. Ratsiraka wins presidential election against Zafy.		
1998	Reform of the constitution by President Ratsiraka (referendum). Creation of autonomous provinces.	Ratsiraka	
1999	December: Marc Ravalomanana elected mayor of Antananarivo.		
2001	Birth of SeFaFi. December: First round of presidential election. The results are disputed.		
2002	January: Demonstrations and general strike in Antananarivo, Mahajanga and Fianarantsoa. February: First blockades set up by D. Ratsiraka on road from Antananarivo to Toamasina. April: High Constitutional Court proclaims M. Ravalomanana victor of the election. May: Inauguration of Ravalomanana. July: D. Ratsiraka leaves Madagascar. End of military operations. December: Tiako i Madagasikara (TIM – 'I Love Madagascar) wins general election.	Ravalomanana	
2003	July: Madagascar readmitted to the African Union (AU). December: D. Ratsiraka sentenced to five years' imprisonment.		
2004	The World Bank and International Monetary Fund announce cancellation of approximately half of Madagascar's debt.		
2005	First state to receive development assistance from United States under the Millennium Challenge Account programme. The ariary replaces the MGF.		
2006	Ravalomanana re-elected President of the Third Republic in first round. Launch of Madagascar Action Plan. Creation of integrated growth poles. Creation of one-stop shop for foreign investors (Economic Development Board of Madagascar [EDBM]) under the auspices of the World Bank.		
2007	July: Ravalomanana dissolves parliament September: TIM wins general election, boycotted by part of opposition; constitutional reform. End of the autonomous regions. December: Rajoelina elected mayor of Antananarivo.		
2008	November: Daewoo and Boeing affairs. December: Andry Rajoelina closes Viva TV station following broadcast of an interview with D. Ratsiraka.		

Year	Events	President	Republic
2009	January: Demonstrations calling for a new government. 26 January: Tiko warehouses and national television and MBS TV channels looted. A. Rajoelina forms the High Transitional Authority (HTA). February: On 7 February, security forces open fire on an opposition demonstration; at least 30 dead. Roindefo appointed prime minister of HTA. March: Army Corps of Personnel and Administrative and Technical Services (CAPSAT) soldiers mutiny. Ravalomanana resigns. Military directorate transfers power to Rajoelina. The UA and Southern African Development Community (SADC) suspends Madagascar's membership. June: Ravalomanana sentenced in absentia to four years in prison. August: Talks in Maputo to reach a power-sharing agreement. December: Rajoelina announces withdrawal from power-sharing talks.	Rajoelina	
2010	February: Rajoelina postpones parliamentary elections until May. March: The AU imposes targeted sanctions on Rajoelina and his administration. November: New constitution adopted by referendum establishing a semi-parliamentary system. June: The EU suspends development assistance to Madagascar in the absence of democratic progress.		Fourth Republic
2011	September. The different political protagonists sign a roadmap to appoint a new government representative of the different political sides and the different regions. October: New government, with J.-O. Beriziky as prime minister.		
2013	January: Two opposition journalists sentenced to three years in prison. December. First round of presidential election.		
2014	January: Presidential election. H. Rajaonarimampianina wins the run-off (53.5% of the votes cast). Abstention rate: 38.4% in the first round, 49.3% in the second. April: R. Kolo appointed prime minister. June: Foundation of HVM (Hery Vaovao ho an'i Madagasikara; Nouvelle Puissance Pour Madagascar; New Forces for Madagascar) presidential party. 3,000 tons of rosewood from Madagascar seized in Singapore. October: Return of M. Ravalomanana. Placed under house arrest. November: Outbreak of plague in the capital. December: Abolition of capital punishment. Morondava: Looting and clashes with paramilitary police in conflict between factory workers and management at Chinese-run plant.	Rajaonarimampianina	
2015	January: The government resigns. J. Ravelonarivo appointed prime minister. March: riots in Mananjary. Gendarmes shoot at the angry crowd: five dead. May: End of Ravalomanana's house arrest. May: Motion to impeach president passed by MPs, but rejected by High Constitutional Court. June: ARMADA, political alliance of presidential election losers. July: Vote of no confidence in the government rejected by a margin of just seven votes. Only 17 MPs vote against it. July: Local elections. Lalao Ravalomanana elected Mayor of Antananarivo (56% of the vote by a turnout of 29%). December: National reconciliation act passed. Act to combat rosewood trafficking.		
2016	April: Cabinet reshuffle. O. Mahafaly appointed prime minister. May: Bishops sound alarm over the violence, poverty and misappropriation of natural resources. May-June: National Assembly passes a motion to impeach the president for high treason. The motion is rejected by the HCC (Haute Cour Constitutionnelle; High Constitutional Court). May-October: Protest in Soamahamanina against a Chinese company's gold mine permit. November: Antananarivo City Hall surrounded by armed soldiers for several hours. December: Donors and investors conference in Paris (UNESCO). Resumption of financial support from the international donor community.		
2017	June: Claudine Razaimamonjy, special adviser to Rajaonarimampianina and founding member of the HVM, is imprisoned for embezzlement of public funds, abuse of office and favouritism in the award of public contracts. August: Establishment of a committee for national reconciliation. Cabinet reshuffle. August–November: Pneumonic plague epidemic leaves 200 dead. December: Attack on Ikongo penitentiary and gendarmerie headquarters by 600 villagers.		
2018	January: AVA cyclone: 29 dead and 83,000 victims. April-May: Demonstrations against the new electoral laws (3 dead on April 21). May 3: The HCC rescinds the electoral laws. May 31: Army threatens to intervene in the political crisis. June: Cabinet reshuffle: Christian Ntsay appointed prime minister. November-December: Presidential election. Record abstention rate (46% in the first round and 52% in the second). A. Rajoelina elected with 55.6% vs. 44.4% for M. Ravalomanana. First round scores: A. Rajoelina = 32.9%, M. Ravalomanana = 35.4%, H. Rajaonarimampianina = 8.8%.		
2019	January 8: A. Rajoelina officially elected. January 19: A. Rajoelina sworn in as Madagascar's president.	Rajoelina	

Glossary of Malagasy Terms

Andevo: Descendants of ancient *Merina* society slaves. This slave descent still carries a very low status in Malagasy society today.

Andriana: Nobility status group (or caste) in ancient Merina society. Although this system was abolished, the *Merina* continue to discriminate based on their caste extraction.

Avo razana: High born (*razana* means ancestors and *avo* means high).

Dahalo: Cattle rustlers. The phenomenon of zebu cattle raiding, initially borrowing from the Bara tradition, has grown considerably in the last more than twenty years.

Dina: By-laws enacted by members of a *fokonolona* to govern harmonious community social and economic affairs.

Fady: Taboos passed on by deified ancestors called *Razana*. They remain prevalent in Malagasy society in all sorts of areas such as work, sexual practices and diet.

Fanjakana: The state, the political power.

Fanompoana: Labour duty. Under the *Merina* monarchy, peasants had to provide their sovereign with all manner of services, including work on collective agricultural projects such as dykes and water supply systems, in return for the sovereign's protection.

Fialonana: Jealousy.

Fiaraha-monina: One aspect of *fihavanana*. Living in harmony.

Fihavanana: An essential value of Malagasy society inscribed in the preamble to the Constitution of the Third Republic since 1992. This reputedly untranslatable term is often described as a traditional way of life governing interpersonal relations based on fraternity, mutual respect, consensus-seeking and cordiality.

Firaisan-kina: Solidarity.

Fivondronana: Malagasy administrative subdivision under the Second Republic.

Fokonolona: Local community. Form of local, community-based (originally village-based) organisation of community life calling for close cooperation among members. The *fokonolona* choose their representatives tasked, in addition to tax collection, with overseeing activities to develop and protect the *fokontany*. The *fokonolona* are also entitled to enact their own by-laws or *dina* to govern domestic security.

Fokontany: Village or district. The *fokontany* is the smallest Malagasy administrative unit.

Fomba: Customs.

Fotsy: White. See *Mainty* 2.

Hasina: Invisible essence of power, which the king can bestow on his descendants.

Hova: A pre-twentieth-century *Merina* society status group loosely corresponding to commoners.

Kabary: Great assemblies summoned by Malagasy sovereigns, providing the opportunity to deliver a formal speech, to gain popular consensus for political decisions. Nowadays, kabary refers to a traditional form of public speech.

Karana: Name given to Indo-Pakistanis who arrived in Madagascar in the late seventeenth century.

Lamba: Toga. Traditional peasant attire.

Mainty: 1. Name of the group of slaves emancipated for services rendered. Starting under the reign of Andrianampoinimerina, the *Mainty* were assigned essentially to royal services (royal guard and elite troops). In the late eighteenth century, *Mainty* and *Andevo* linguistically fused. 2. Black. This term is used to make a very general distinction between whites (descendants of the higher status groups) and blacks (descendants of slaves). However, this partly symbolic colour distinction (separating the pure from the impure) is also used to indicate a physical difference: the *Mainty* often have 'African' features while the *Fotsy* are more 'Asian'.

Manjaka: Reign.

Marofotsy: Deserters from the army and forced labour or escaped slaves who lived in the farthest reaches of the areas controlled by the *Merina* kingdom.

Menalamba: Name given to the insurgents who destabilised the French colonial state's establishment in Imerina from 1895 to 1898. From *mena* for 'red' and *lamba* for 'shawl' (the insurgents daubed their clothes red).

Merina: Ethnic groups from the Central Highlands of Madagascar.

Mosavy: Witchcraft.

Mpanjaka (or Ampanjaka): Sovereign (king or queen); traditional leaders.

Mpiavy: Inhabitants of a territory where their ancestors are not buried. Seen as newcomers, they are considered less legitimate than the *tompontany*.

Olobe: Type of traditional leader.

Olomanga: Remarkable, famous, worthy person.

Raiamandreny: Etymologically speaking, father and mother. Name often bestowed on leaders, referring to their legitimacy by right of their status of elder and the wisdom and leadership supposedly associated with this status.

Sampy: Talismans associated with the king's power under the *Merina* monarchy.

Sinoa: Name given to the Chinese who settled in Madagascar.

Soa iombonana: Common good.

Tangalamena: Traditional provincial authority.

Tany: Land.

Tsiny: Wrath of the ancestors for breaking traditional taboos.

TTS: *Tanora Tonga Saina*. Literally, young people with self-awareness. A group of unemployed youths coordinated by the government to propagate violence to support the regime in place.

Vatoeka: A *fokonolona*'s economic committee.

Vonodina: Damages, pecuniary or in kind, owing to the victim and the *fokonolona*.

Zanatany: Descendants of French settlers in Madagascar for generations.

ZOAM: See *ZWAM*.

Zoky: The oldest, but also a person deemed superior or more important.

ZWAM: *Zatovo Western Andevo Malagasy* (Malagasy Western Slave Youth) – *Zatovo* (youth), *Western* (due to their identification with cowboys), *Andevo* (slave), *Malagasy*. An organisation that appeared in 1972 to support the student protests against the laws of President P. Tsirinana. The group then changed its acronym to *ZOAM*, *Zatovo Orin'Asa Malagasy* (Unemployed Malagasy Youth).

References

Acemoglu D., Johnson S. & Robinson J. A. (2001). The Colonial Origin of Comparative Development: An Empirical Investigation. *American Economic Review*, 91, 1369–1401.

Acemoglu D. & Robinson J. (2005). *Economic Origins of Dictatorship and Democracy*. Cambridge: Cambridge University Press.

Acemoglu D. & Robinson, J. A. (2012). *Why Nations Fail: The Origins of Power, Prosperity and Poverty*. London: Profile Books.

AfDB, OECD & UNDP (African Development Bank, Organisation for Economic Co-operation and Development and United Nations Development Programme) (2016). *African Economic Outlook 2016*. Paris: Organisation for Economic Co-operation and Development.

AFP (Agence France-Presse). (2002). L'indépendance des provinces à Madagascar: Une menace symbolique. Dépêche, 2 May.

Afrobarometer. (2008). 2008 Round 4 Afrobarometer Survey in Madagascar: Summary of Results. Available at: www.afrobarometer.org/files/documents

Alexandre C. (2007). *Violences malgaches*. Antananarivo: Éditions Foi et Justice.

Althabe G. (1978). Strikes, Urban Mass Action and Political Change: Tananarive 1972. In P. C. W. Gutkind, R. Cohen & J. Copans (eds.), *African Labor History*, 205–43. London: SAGE.

Althabe G. (1980). Les luttes sociales à Tananarive en 1972. *Cahiers d'études africaines*, 80, 407–47.

Amprou J. & Chauvet L. (2004). Efficacité et allocation de l'aide, revue des débats. AFD, Notes et Documents, 6 November. Paris: French Agency for Development.

Amsden A. H., DiCaprio A. & Robinson J. A., eds. (2012). *The Role of Elites in Economic Development*. UNU-WIDE Studies in Development Economics. Oxford: Oxford University Press.

Anderson K., ed. (2009). *Distortions to Agricultural Incentives: A Global Perspective: 1955 to 2007*. London and Washington, DC: Palgrave Macmillan and World Bank.

Anderson K. & Nelgen S. (2013). Updated National and Global Estimates of Distortions to Agricultural Incentives, 1955 to 2011. Washington, DC, June. Database available at: https://www.worldbank.org/en/research/brief/distortions-to-agricultural-incentives

Anderson K. & Valenzuela E. (2008). Estimates of Global Distortions to Agricultural Incentives, 1955 to 2007. Washington, DC: World Bank, October 2008.

Andriamihaja N. V., ed. (2012). *Madagascar: Crises cycliques, culture et développement: Les conditions de la relance*. Antananarivo: Sevenco. Nota Bene: *The Malagasy Development Journal*.

Andriamirado S. (1977). Heurs et malheurs du Fokonolona. *Autogestion et socialisme*, 39, special issue on Afrique Noire: Des communautés de base au socialisme autogestionnaire, 51–64.

Andrianarison F. (1996). La politique industrielle à Madagascar: Les traits marquants de 1960 à nos jours. Working Paper No. 9606/E. Antananarivo: Madagascar - Dial - Instat - Orstom (MADIO).

Andrianarivo-Razafimanjato V. (2000). Akamasoa ou la réinsertion sociale des sans-abris d'Antananarivo. *Kabaro, revue internationale des sciences de l'homme et des sociétés*, 1(1–2), 185–93.

Andrianjafy-Andriamanindrisoa E. (2004). *Economie populaire, territoires et développement à Madagascar*. Social sciences doctoral thesis, Catholic University of Louvain.

Andrimihaja N. A., Cinyabuguma M. & Devarajan S. (2011). Avoiding the Fragility Trap in Africa. Policy Research Working Paper 5488. Washington, DC: World Bank.

Antoine P., Bocquier P., Razafindratsima N. & Roubaud F. (2000). *Biographies de trois générations dans l'agglomération d'Antananarivo*. Documents et manuels, No. 11. Paris: Ceped.

Araujo Bonjean C. & Azam J.-P. (1996). La libéralisation du riz à Madagascar ou l'ajustement sans croissance. *Région et Développement*, 4, 1–22.

Archer R. (1976). *Madagascar depuis 1972: La marche d'une révolution*. Paris: l'Harmattan.

Arndt C. & Oman C. (2006). *Uses and Abuses of Governance Indicators*. Paris: OECD Development Centre.

Bach D. & Sindjoun L. (1997). Ordre et désordre en Afrique. *Polis*, 4(2), 3–17.

Badie B. (1992). *L'état importé: Essai sur l'occidentalisation de l'ordre politique*. Paris: Fayard.

Badouin R. (1967). Où en est la réforme de l'économie de traite en Afrique noire? *Tiers-Monde*, 32, 1209–1216.

Banerjee A., Deaton A., Lustig N. & Rogoff K. (2006). *An Evaluation of World Bank Research, 1998–2005*. Washington, DC: World Bank.

Bardhan P. (2006). The Economist's Approach to the Problem of Corruption. *World Development*, 34(2), 341–8.

Barro R. J. & Sala-i-Martin X. (2004) [1995]. *Economic Growth*. Cambridge, MA: MIT Press.

Bat J.-P. (2016). Et pour quelques zébus de plus . . . trafics et insécurités à Madagascar. *Libération*. Blog LibeAfrica4, 16 October 2016.

Bayart J.-F. (1993). *The State in Africa: The Politics of the Belly*. London: Longman.

Bayart J.-F., Mbembe A. & Toulabor C. (1992). *Le politique par le bas en Afrique noire: Contribution à une problématique de la démocratie*. Paris: Karthala.

Beaujard Ph. (1991). *Mythe et société à Madagascar*. Paris: L'Harmattan.

Berthélémy J.-C. & Tichit A. (2004). Bilateral Donors' Aid Allocation Decisions: A Three-Dimensional Panel Analysis. *International Review of Economics and Finance*, 13(3), 253–74.

Biaussat A. & Tabet M. (2016). *Zana-Bahoaka. Le néo rebelle malgasy*, Film, 26 minutes. Available at: http://collateralcreations.com/Perceptions-populaires-de-l

Blanc-Pamard C. (1985). Du paddy pour les porcs. Dérives d'une société rurale: L'exemple des Hautes Terres centrales de Madagascar. *Etudes rurales*, 99–100, 327–45.

Bloch M. (1983). La séparation du pouvoir et du rang comme processus d'évolution: Une esquisse du développement des royautés dans le centre de Madagascar. In F. Raison-Jourde (ed.), *Les souverains de Madagascar: L'histoire coloniale et ses résurgences contemporaines*, 265–97. Paris: Karthala.

Bloch M. (1990). *New Foreword*. In O. Mannoni, *Prospero and Caliban: The Psychology of Colonization* [1948], v–xx. Ann Arbor: University of Michigan Press.

Bluhm R. & Szirmai A. (2012). Institutions and Long-Run Growth Performance: An Analytic Literature Review of the Institutional Determinants of Economic Growth. UNU-MERIT, Working Paper Series, No. 2012-033, January.

Blum F. (2011). Madagascar 1972: L'autre indépendance. Une révolution contre les accords de cooperation. *Le Mouvement Social*, 236, 61–87.

Blundo, G. & Olivier de Sardan J.-P., eds. (2001), *La corruption au quotidien: Politique africaine*. Special issue, 83, 5–114.

Boetsch G. & Savarese E. (2000). Photographies anthropologiques et politique des races. *Journal des Anthropologues*, 80–1, 247–58.

Bornschein J. (2008). La politique de M. Ravalomanana à Madagascar. Grin Seminar Paper No. V114813.

Bossuroy T. & Cogneau D. (2013). Social Mobility in Five African Countries. *Review of Income and Wealth*, 59, 84–110.

Bost F. (2010). *L'atlas mondial des zones franches*. Paris: La Documentation Française.

Bourguignon F. (2015). *The Globalization of Inequality*. Princeton, NJ: Princeton University Press.

Bratton M. & van de Walle N. (1997). *Democratic Experiments in Africa. Regime Transition in Comparative Perspective*. Cambridge: Cambridge University Press.

Braudel F. (1967). *Civilisation matérielle, économie, capitalisme (XVe- XVIIIe siècle)*, tome 1. Paris: Armand Colin.

Brocheux P. & Hémery D. (2011). *Indochina: An Ambiguous Colonization, 1858–1954*. Berkeley: University of California Press.

Brown M. (1997). *A History of Madagascar*. New York: Markus Wiener Publishers.

Burnside C. & Dollar D. (2000). Aid, Policies and Growth. *American Economic Review*, 90(4), 847–68.

Burnside C. & Dollar D. (2004). Aid, Policies and Growth: Revisiting the Evidence. Policy Research Working Paper No. 3251. Washington, DC: World Bank.

Butler R. A. (2014). Singapore Intercepts Massive Illegal Shipment of Madagascar Rosewood, Mongabay. Available at: https://news.mongabay.com/2014/06

Butler R. A. (2015). Singapore Court: Illicit Timber Trafficking through Our Ports Not Our Problem, Mongabay. Available at: https://news.mongabay.com/2015/11

Cadoux C. (1993). La constitution de la troisième république malgache. *Politique africaine*, 52, 58–66.

Campbell G. (1991). The Menalamba Revolt and Brigandry in Imperial Madagascar 1820–1897. *International Journal of African Historical Studies*, 24(2), 259–91.

Campbell G. (2005). An Economic History of Imperial Madagascar, 1750–1895: The Rise and Fall of an Island Empire. New-York: Cambridge University Press.

Carayol R. (2010). "TGV, la voie royale?" *Jeune Afrique*. Available at: www.jeuneafrique.com/193330/politique/tgv-la-voie-royale/

Chabal, P. & Daloz, J.-P. (1999). *Africa Works! Disorder as Political Instrument*. Oxford: James Currey.

Chadefaux C. (2012). La France m'a tuer. In M. A. Andriamihaja (ed.), *Madagascar. Crises cycliques, culture et développement: Les conditions de la relance*, 33–8. Antananarivo: Sevenco. Nota bene.

Châtaigner J.-M. (2014). Madagascar: Le développement contrarié. *Afrique contemporaine*, 251, 107–24.

Chazan-Gillig S. (1991). *La société sakalave: Le Menabe dans la construction nationale malgache*. Paris: Karthala.

Cling J.-P., Razafindrakoto M. & Roubaud F. (2005). Export Processing Zones in Madagascar: A Success Story under Threat? *World Development*, 33(5), 785–803.

Cling J.-P., Razafindrakoto M. & Roubaud F. (2009). Export Processing Zones in Madagascar: The Impact of Dismantling of Clothing Quotas on Employment and Labor Standards. In R. Robertson, D. Brown, G. Pierre & M.L. Sanchez-Puerta (eds.), *Globalization, Wages, and the Quality of Jobs*, 237–64. Washington, DC: World Bank.

Cling J.-P., Razafindrakoto M. & Roubaud F. (2013). Is the World Bank Compatible with the "*Socialist-Oriented Market Economy*"? A Political Economy Approach Applied to the Case of Vietnam. In P. Alary & E. Lafaye de Micheaux (eds.), *Political Economy of Contemporary Asia, Revue de la régulation. Capitalisme, institutions, pouvoirs* [online journal] special issue, 13 |six monthly/spring.

Cogneau D. (2015). Après Swiss Leaks, il faut aussi lutter contre la fuite de capitaux dans les pays pauvres. *Le Monde*, 23 February. Available at: www.lemonde.fr/evasion-fiscale/article/2015/02/23/apres-swiss-leaks-il-faut-aussi-lutter-contre-la-fuite-de-capitaux-dans-les-pays-pauvres_4581859_4862750.html

Cogneau D., Dupraz Y. & Mesplé-Somps S. (2017). Public Finance and Investment in the French Colonial Empire 1870–1960. Paris: School of Economics, DIAL.

Cole J. (2001). *Forget Colonialism? Sacrifice and the Art of Memory in Madagascar*. Berkeley: University of California Press.

Collier P. & Hoefler A. (2004). Greed and Grievance in Civil War. *Oxford Economic Paper*, 56(4), 563–95.

Condominas G. (1991). *Fokon'olona et collectivités rurales en Imerina (1961)*. Paris: Editions Orstom.

Crombrugghe de D., Farla K., Meisel N., de Neubourg C., Ould Aoudia J. & Szirmai A. (2010). Institutional Profiles Database III. Presentation of the Institutional Profiles Database 2009. AFD Working Paper No. 89. Paris: French Agency for Development.

Darbon D. & Toulabor. C. (2011). Quelle(s) classe(s) moyenne(s) en Afrique? Une revue de literature. AFD Working Paper No. 118, Paris: French Agency for Developement.

Déléris F. (1986). *Ratsiraka: Socialisme et misère à Madagascar*. Paris: L'Harmattan.

Delval R. (1994). Le fédéralisme, forme nouvelle de l'ethnicité. In F. Deleris (coord.), *Madagascar. 1991–1994. Dans l'œil du cyclone*, 41–66. Paris: l'Harmattan.

D'Ersu L. (2009). Changement d'homme providentiel à Madagascar. *Études*, 4115, 451–61.

Deschamps H. (1960). *Histoire de Madagascar*. Paris: Berger-Levrault.

Devarajan S. (2013). Africa's statistical tragedy. *Review of Income and Wealth*, 59, DOI:10.1111/roiw.12013.

Dez J. (1981). L'illusion de la non-violence dans la société traditionnelle malgache. *Droit et Cultures*, 2, 21–44.

Dezalay Y. & Garth B. G. (2002). *The Internationalization of Palace Wars: Lawyers, Economists, and the Contest to Transform Latin American States*. Chicago Series in Law and Society.

DG Trésor (Directorate General of the Treasury). (2011). Les investissements directs étrangers à Madagascar en 2010. *Publications des services économiques*. Antananarivo: French Embassy to Madagascar.

DG Trésor (Directorate General of the Treasury). (2015). Note sur l'investissement direct étranger à Madagascar en 2013. *Note du service économique*. Antananarivo: French Embassy to Madagascar.

D'Hoore A. (2018). Crises et économie à Madagascar, 1960–2010: 50 ans de pas et faux pas macroéconomiques de la Grande Île. In M. Razafindrakoto, F. Roubaud & J.-M. Wachsberger (eds.), *Madagascar, d'une crise l'autre: ruptures et continuité*, 43–74. Paris & Marseille: Karthala-IRD.

DiCaprio A. (2012). Introduction: The Role of Elites in Economic Development. In A. H. Amsden, A. DiCaprio & J. A. Robinson (eds.), *The Role of Elites in Economic Development*, 1–18. Oxford: Oxford University Press.

Di Tella R. & Schardgrodsky E. (2003). The Role of Wages and Auditing during a Crackdown on Corruption in the City of Buenos Aires. *The Journal of Law and Economics*, 46(1), 269–92.

Dollar D. & Levine V. (2004). The Increasing Selectivity of Foreign Aid, 1984–2002. Policy Research Working Paper No. 3299, May. Washington, DC: World Bank.

Dorosh P., Haggblade S., Lungren C., Razafimanantena T. & Randriamiarana Z. (2003). *Moteurs économiques pour la réduction de la pauvreté à Madagascar: Analyse économique améliorée pour la prise de décision à Madagascar*. Antananarivo: Cornell University, US Agency for International Development.

Droy I. (1996). La multiplication des ONG à Madagascar: Une réponse au désengagement de l'Etat? Working Paper No. 9653/E. Antananarivo: Madagascar – Dial – Instat – Orstom (MADIO).

Dufernez A.-S., Meisel N. & Ould Aoudia J. (2010). Who Ever Saw a Social Order. Presentation to French Agency for Development (AFD), Paris, 7 July.

Easterly W. & Levine R. (1997). Africa's Growth Tragedy: Policies, and Ethnic Divisions. *Quarterly Journal of Economics*, 111(4), 1203–50.

Elias N. (1975). *La dynamique de l'Occident*. Paris: Pocket.

Ellis S. (1998). *L'insurrection des menalamba, une révolte à Madagascar (1895–1898)*. Paris: Karthala.

Expansion Madagascar. (2011). 50 ans d'industrialisation. Un bilan mitigé. *Le Magazine du Syndicat des Industries de Madagascar (SIM)*, No. 7.

Fanomezantsoa A. (1993). Le régicide ambigu ou le mouvement de 1991 vu de Tamatave. *Politique africaine*, 52, 40–9.

Fauroux E. (1999). Une transition démocratique et libérale difficile dans une région périphérique de l'Ouest malgache. *Autrepart*, 10, 41–57.

Fearon J. D. (2003). Ethnic and Cultural Diversity by Country. *Journal of Economic Growth*, 8(2), 195–222.

Fenochietto R. & Pessino C. (2013). Understanding Countries' Tax Effort. Working Paper 13/244. Washington, DC: International Monetary Fund.

Forim (2016). *Étude du profil de la diaspora malagasy en France*. Geneva: Ministère des Affaires étrangère de Madagascar, Ambassade de France à Madagascar, OIM.

Fremigacci J. (1999). Bilan provisoire de l'insurrection de 1947. Nécessité de nouvelles recherches. In F. Arzalier & J. Suret-Canale (eds.), *Madagascar 1947: La tragédie oubliée*, 177–89. Paris: Le temps des Cerises.

Fremigacci J. (2007a). Madagascar 1982: Une économie en crise. Des facteurs traditionnels à la conjoncture récente. *Tsingy*, 6, 55–68.

Fremigacci J. (2007b). La vérité sur la grande révolte de Madagascar. *L'Histoire*, 318, 36–43.

Fremigacci J. (2014a). *État, économie et société coloniale à Madagascar (fin XIXe siècle-1940)*. Paris: Karthala.

Fremigacci J. (2014b). Madagascar ou l'éternel retour de la crise. *Afrique contemporaine*, 251, 123–41.

Fukuyama F. (1995). *Trust: The Social Virtues and the Creation of Prosperity*. New York, The Free Press.

Galibert D. (2004). État et citoyenneté à Madagascar depuis l'indépendance. Conference of 17 February 2004 at the Centre Culturel Alpha à Saint-Pierre de La Réunion, unpublished.

Galibert D. (2009). Mobilisation populaire et répression à Madagascar. *Politique africaine*, 113, 139–51.

Galibert D. (2011a). *Les gens de pouvoir à Madagascar*. Paris: Karthala.

Galibert D. (2011b). Rigidités et globalisation un regard anthropologique sur la crise malgache, 2009–2011. *Les Cahiers d'Outre-Mer*, 255, 413–26.

Galy M. (2009). *Lova, héritage ambigu. Généalogie de la violence politique à Madagascar*. Available at: http://www.madamag.com

Gastineau B., Gubert F., Robilliard A.-S. & Roubaud F. (2010). Conclusion. In B. Gastineau, F. Gubert, A.-S. Robilliard & F. Roubaud (eds.), *Madagascar face au défi des Objectifs du millénaire pour le développement*, 319–27. Marseille: IRD Éditions.

Gendarme R. (1960). *L'économie de Madagascar Diagnostic et perspectives de développement*. Paris: Cujas.

Genieys W. (2011). *Sociologie politique des élites*. Paris: Armand Colin.

Gingembre M. (2011). Match religieux en terrain politique: Compétition entre églises chrétiennes et chute du régime Ravalomanana à Madagascar. *Politique africaine*, 123, 51–72.

Gingembre M. (2012). Les Églises malgaches dans la crise de 2009. In S. Randrianja (ed.), *Madagascar, le coup d'État de mars 2009*. 97–121. Paris: Karthala.

Goguel A.-M. (2006). *Aux origines du mai malgache: Désir d'école et compétition sociale (1951–1972)*. Paris: Karthala et AUF.

Gollwitzer S., Franke C. & Quintyn M. (2014). Doorsteps Toward Political and Economic Openness: Testing the North-Wallis-Weingast Transition Framework. *Emerging Markets Finance and Trade*, 50(4), 212–36.

Goody J. (2010). *Le vol de l'histoire: Comment l'Europe a imposé le récit de son passé au reste du monde*. Paris: Gallimard.

Graeber D. (2018). Le peuple, nurse du roi: Notes sur les monarques enfants dans le centre de Madagascar. In M. Razafindrakoto, F. Roubaud & J.-M. Wachsberger (eds.), *Madagascar, d'une crise l'autre: Ruptures et continuité.* 171–98. Paris: Karthala-IRD.

Gros J.-B., Letilly G. & Martinet S. (2001). *Performances commerciales, compétitivité et diversification des économies subsahariennes.* Paris: Ministère des Affaires étrangères, Direction Générale de la Coopération internationale et du Développement (DGCID), Rapport d'étude.

Gubert F. & Robilliard A.-S. (2010). Croissance et pauvreté à Madagascar: Un aperçu de la dernière décennie (1997–2007). In B. Gastineau, F. Gubert, A.-S. Robilliard & F. Roubaud (eds.), *Madagascar face au défi des Objectifs du millénaire pour le développement*, 25–52. Marseille: IRD Éditions.

Guénard C. & Mesplé-Somps S. (2007). Mesurer les inégalités: Que captent réellement les enquêtes? Discussion et illustration à partir de deux enquêtes ivoirienne et malgache. *Statéco*, 101, 29–51.

Guilloux C. (2010). *Le biais anti-urbain de l'aide au développement.* Paris I- Sorbonne: Mémoire de Master 2. Available at: www.ville-developpement.org/docman-liste/autres/145-110111-memoire-c-guilloux-le-biais-antiurbain-oct2010/file

Gurr T. (1970). *Why Men Rebel.* Princeton, NJ: Princeton University Press.

Gurr T. (2011). Why Men Rebel Redux: How Valid Are Its Arguments 40 Years On? *E-International Relations.* Available at: www.e-ir.info/2011/11/17/why-men-rebel-redux-how-valid-are-its-arguments-40-years-on

Helluin J.-J. (2010). Penser, gérer, aider la ville à Madagascar: Une triple faillite. Communication pour la journée mondiale de l'Habitat, Antananarivo, 4 October. Available at: www.ville-developpement.org/docman-liste/autres/122-101029-la-triple-faillite/file

Herrera J., Razafindrakoto M. & Roubaud F. (2007). The Determinants of Subjective Poverty: A Comparative Analysis in Madagascar and Peru. In S. Klasen & F. Nowak-Lehmann (eds.), *Poverty, Inequality and Migration in Latin America*, 181–220. Frankfurt am Main: Peter Lang.

Hobsbawm E. (1966 [1959]). *Les primitifs de la révolte dans l'Europe moderne.* Paris: Éditions Fayard.

Hübsch B., ed. (1993). *Madagascar et le Christianisme.* Paris: Karthala.

Hugon P. (1974). Conjoncture et politiques économiques depuis l'indépendance. In *Centre d'étude et de recherches sur les sociétés de l'océan Indien: Annuaire des pays de l'océan Indien*, I, 325–44. Aix-en-Provence: Presses universitaires d'Aix-Marseille.

Hugon P. (1976). *Économie et enseignement à Madagascar.* Institut international de Planification de l'Éducation, UNESCO.

Hugon P. (1986). La crise économique à Madagascar et l'intervention du Fonds monétaire international. *Canadian Journal of African Studies*, 20(2), 186–218.

Hugon P. (1989). Incidences sociales des politiques d'ajustement. *Tiers-Monde*, 30 (117), 59–84.

Huntington S. (1991). *The Third Wave: Democratization in the Late Twentieth Century.* Norman: University of Oklahoma Press.

Hyden G. (1980). *Beyond Ujamaa in Tanzania: Underdevelopment and an uncaptured peasantry.* London: Heinemann.

IEP (Institut d'études politiques), World Bank. (2014). *Les crises malgaches: Un diagnostic pluridisciplinaire.* Antananarivo: Institut d'études politiques de Madagascar.

IFPRI (International Food Policy Research Institute). (1998). La structure et le comportement des marchés des intrants et des produits agricoles et la réponse des ménages agricoles face aux réformes des politiques agricoles à Madagascar. Research Findings Interim report. Washington, DC: International Food Policy Research Institute.

IMF (International Monetary Fund). (2014). *Sub-Saharan Africa: Staying the Course.* Washington, DC: Regional Economic Outlook, October.

IMF (International Monetary Fund). (2015a). *Republic of Madagascar: Article IV Consultation.* Washington, DC: International Monetary Fund.

IMF (International Monetary Fund). (2015b). *Republic of Madagascar: Selected Issues.* Document No. 15/25, January. Washington, DC: International Monetary Fund.

Inglehart R. (1997). *Modernization and Postmodernization: Cultural, Economic and Political Change in 43 Societies.* Princeton, NJ: Princeton University Press.

INSTAT (Madagascar National Statistics Office). (2012). *Madagascar en chiffres: Données macroéconomiques.* Antananarivo: Institut national de la statistique. Available at: http://instat.mg/madagascar-en-chiffres/

INSTAT (Madagascar National Statistics Office). (2013). *Enquête nationale sur l'emploi et le secteur informel. ENEMPSI 2012.* Antananarivo: Institut national de la statistique, 1. Available at: http://instat.mg/statistiques/enempsi-2012/

INSTAT (Madagascar National Statistics Office). (2015). *Enquête nationale sur le suivi des Objectif du millénaire pour le développement à Madagascar 2012–2013.* Antananarivo: United Nations, Governance and Institutional Development Program (PGDI), BAD, Common Market for Eastern and Southern Africa (COMESA), World Bank.

Institut d'étude politique de Madagascar & la Banque Mondiale (2014). *Les crises malgaches: Un diagnostic pluridisciplinaire. Mettre fin à la fragilité: 'Construire le présent à partir du futur'.* Antananarivo: Actes de colloque, 16–18 June 2014.

Institute for Economics and Peace. (2016). *Global Peace Index 2016. Ten Years of Measuring Peace.* Sydney: IEP (Institut for Economics & Peace).

ISS (International Institute of Social Studies) (2013). *The Indices of Social Development (ISD).* The Hague: Erasmus University of Rotterdam, June. Available at: http://www.indsocdev.org/

Jacob G. & Koerner F. (1972). Économie de traite et bluff colonial: La Compagnie occidentale de Madagascar (1895–1934). *Revue historique*, 248(2), 333–66.

Jacquemot P. (2013). Les classes moyennes changent-elles la donne en Afrique? Réalités, enjeux et perspectives. *Afrique contemporaine*, dossier spécial *Les classes moyennes*, 244, 17–31.

Jacquier Dubourdieu L. (2002). De la guérison des corps à la guérison de la nation. Réveil et mouvements évangéliques à l'assaut de l'espace public. *Politique africaine*, 86, 70–85.

Jerven M. (2010a). The relativity of poverty and income: How reliable are African economic statistics? *African Affairs*, 109(434), 77–96.

Jerven M. (2010b). Random growth in Africa? Lessons from an evaluation of the growth evidence on Botswana, Kenya, Tanzania and Zambia, 1965–1995. *Journal of Development Studies*, 46(2), 274–94.

Jerven M. (2011). Counting the bottom billion: Measuring the wealth and progress of African economies. *World Economics*, 12(4), 35–52.

Jerven M. (2013). Comparability of GDP estimates in sub Saharan Africa: The effect of revisions in sources and methods since structural adjustment. *Review of Income and Wealth*, 59, 16–36.

Jerven M. (2015). *Africa: Why Economists Get It Wrong*. London: Zed Books.

Jütersonke O. & Kartas M. (2010). *Peace and Conflict Impact Assessment (PCIA): Madagascar*. Geneva: Graduate Institute of International and Development Studies.

Kanbur R. (2005). Réformer la formule: Une modeste proposition pour inclure des critères de résultats dans les procédures d'allocation de l'aide de l'IDA, *Revue d'économie du développement*, 2–3, Sept., 79–108.

Kantorowicz E. (1981). *The King's Two Bodies [1957]*. Princeton, NJ: Princeton University Press.

Kaufmann D. & Kraay A. (2008). Governance indicators: Where are we, where should we be going? *The World Bank Research Observer*, 23 (spring), 1–30.

Khan M. (2010). Political settlements and the governance of growth-enhancing institutions. Working Paper. London: University of London, SOAS Online Library.

Kneitz P. (2014). La paix du Fihavanana. In P. Kneitz (ed.), *Fihavanana-La vision d'une société paisible à Madagascar*, 15–72. Halle and der saale, Universitätsverlag Halle-Wittenberg.

Koerner F. (1994). *Madagascar, colonisation française et nationalisme malgache, XXe siècle*. Paris: L'Harmattan.

Koussoubé E., Loada A., Nébié G. & Raffinot M. (2015). *Économie politique de la croissance au Burkina Faso: Institutions, gouvernance et développement*. DIAL Working Paper 2015/10. Available at: https://dial.ird.fr/publications/documents-de-travail-working-papers#chapitre_4

Lagrange H. (1984). Perception de la violence et sentiment d'insécurité. *Déviance et société*, 8(4), 321–44.

Lahiniriko D.-A. (2012). *Les structures politiques nationalistes tananariviennes de la Seconde Guerre mondiale à la Première République. Union, unanimisme et division partisane dans la culture politique nationaliste (1945–1958)*. Doctoral thesis, Université d'Antananarivo-Université de Paris I, Paris.

Lahiniriko D.-A. (2018). Passé politique ancien et résurgences contemporaines: Le cas de l'insurrection de 1947–1948 à Madagascar. In M. Razafindrakoto, F. Roubaud & J.-M. Wachsberger (eds.), *Madagascar, d'une crise l'autre: Ruptures et continuité*, 305–28. Paris: Karthala-IRD.

Lavallée E., Razafindrakoto M. & Roubaud F. (2010). Les mécanismes à l'origine de la corruption: Une analyse sur microdonnées africaines. *Revue d'Économie du Développement*, 3(2010), 5–47.

Lavrad-Meyer C. (2015). *Didier Ratsiraka: Transition démocratique et pauvreté à Madagascar*. Paris: Karthala.

Leymarie P. (1989a). Le président Ratsiraka, champion de l'entreprise privée. *Le Monde diplomatique*, January, 10–11.

Leymarie P. (1989b). Opération 'sécurité intégrée' contre les voleurs de zébus. *Le Monde diplomatique*, January, 10–11.

Leymarie P. (1995). Espace géopolitique éclaté, états riverains en crise: Longue patience à Madagascar. *Le Monde diplomatique*, Oct., 19.

Lienert I. & Modi J. (1997). A decade of civil service reform in sub-Saharan Africa. Working Paper/97/79. Washington, DC.: International Monetary Fund.

Lindauer D. & Nunberg B., eds. (1994). *Rehabilitating Government. Pay and Employment Reform in Africa*. Washington, DC: World Bank.

Lombard J. (1988). *Le royaume sakalava du Menabe, 17e-20e siècle: Essai d'analyse d'un système politique à Madagascar*. Paris: IRD Éditions.

Maddison A. (2011). *Historical Statistics of the World Economy: 1-2008 AD*. Groningen, University of Groningen. Available at: www.ggdc.net/maddison/oriindex.htm

Mannoni O. (1950). *Psychologie de la colonisation*. Paris: Seuil.

Mannoni O. (1990). *Prospero and Caliban: The Psychology of Colonization [1948]*. Ann Arbor: University of Michigan Press.

Marie A. (1997a). Du sujet communautaire au sujet individuel, une lecture anthropologique de la réalité africaine contemporaine. In A. Marie (ed.), *L'Afrique des individus*, 54–110. Paris: Karthala.

Marie A. (1997b). Avatars de la dette communautaire. In A. Marie (ed.), *L'Afrique des individus*, 249–328. Paris: Karthala.

Marx K. (2005). *The Eighteenth Brumaire of Louis Bonaparte [1851]*. New York: Mondial.

Marx K. & Engels F. (1973 [1850–1861]). *La Chine*. Paris: Éditions 10/18, UGE.

Marx K. & Engels F. (2010 [1853]). *Trois lettres à propos du mode de production asiatique*. Strasbourg: La Phocide.

Médard J.-F. (1992). Le '*big man* ' en Afrique: Esquisse d'analyse du politicien entrepreneur. *L'année sociologique*, 42, 167–92.

Merlin J. (2002). L'assistance médicale indigène à Madagascar (1896–1950): Un exemple d'interactions entre services de santé, appareils administratifs et objectifs politiques. *Clio*, 8. Aix en Provence: Centre d'étude des mondes africains (Cemaf), autumn/winter. Available at: www.cemaf.cnrs.fr/IMG/pdf/8-clio.pdf

Molet L. (1957). Nomenclature des groupes ethniques à Madagascar. *Bulletin de Madagascar*, 129, 163.

Morisset J. (2009). Pour que la terre tourne . . . aussi à Madagascar: Vers un agenda de relance économique. Blog, Africa can end poverty. Washington, DC: World Bank.

Morisset J. (2010). Au cœur des ténèbres: Le renouveau des institutions et de la gouvernance. In *Madagascar: vers un agenda de relance économique*, 23–40. Antananarivo: World Bank.

Naudé W., Santos-Paulino A. U. & McGillivray M. (2012). *Fragile States: Causes, Costs and Responses*. Oxford: Oxford University Press.

Naudet D. & Rua L. (2018). Madagascar: Lfa spirale de l'échec public. In M. Razafindrakoto, F. Roubaud & J.-M. Wachsberger (eds.), *Madagascar, d'une crise l'autre: ruptures et continuité*, 75–100. Paris: Karthala-IRD.

North D. (1990). *Institutions, Institutional Change and Economic Performance*. New York: Cambridge University Press.

North D, Wallis J., Webb S. & Weingast B. (2012a). Lessons: In the shadow of violence. In D. North, J. Wallis, S. Webb & B. Weingast (eds.), *In the Shadow of Violence. Politics, Economics, and the Problem of Development*, 328–50. Cambridge: Cambridge University Press.

North D, Wallis J., Webb S. & Weingast B., eds. (2012b). *In the Shadow of Violence. Politics, Economics, and the Problem of Development.* Cambridge: Cambridge University Press.

North D., Wallis J. & Weingast B. (2009). *Violence and Social Orders: A Conceptual Framework for Interpreting Recorded Human History.* Cambridge: Cambridge University Press.

OECD (Organisation for Economic Co-operation and Development). (2013). Identification and Monitoring of Potentially Under-Aided Countries. Paris: OECD.

OECD (Organisation for Economic Co-operation and Development), AFD (French Agency for Development). (2015). Connecting with Emigrants. A Global Profile of Diaspora 2015. Paris: OECD.

OHCHR (Office of the United Nations High Commissioner for Human Rights). (2018) Rapport sur les droits de l'homme et la pratique de la justice populaire à Madagascar. Geneva, Switzerland: OHCHR.

Olivier de Sardan J.-P. (1999). A Moral Economy of Corruption in Africa? *The Journal of Modern African Studies,* 37(1), 25–52.

Ottino P. (1996). Agir dans les campagnes merina des années soixante. In A. Carénini, & J.-P. Jardel (eds.), *De la tradition à la postmodernité: Hommage à Jean Poirier,* 445–61. Paris: PUF.

Ottino P. (1998). *Les champs de l'ancestralité à Madagascar: Parenté, alliance et patrimoine.* Paris: Orstom/Karthala.

Ould Aoudia J. (2011). Violence et ordres sociaux. North, Wallis, Weingast 2009. Paris: Communication orale à la maison des sciences économiques, 11 January 2011.

Paternostro S., Razafindravonona J. & Stifel D. (2001). Changes in Poverty in Madagascar: 1993–1999. Washington, DC: World Bank, Africa Region Working Paper Series, 19.

Pellerin M. (2009). Madagascar: Un conflit d'entrepreneurs? Figures de la réussite économique et compétitions politiques. *Politique africaine,* 113, 152–65.

Pellerin M. (2011). Le nouvel essor des relations entre la Chine et Madagascar. IFRI paper, March.

Pellerin M. (2014). Madagascar: Gérer l'héritage de la transition. Institut française des relations internationals, Nov.

Pellerin M. (2017). Madagascar face à la criminalité multiforme. Institut française des relations internationals, March.

Pesle N. (2006). *Résurgence d'une nation: Madagascar 2002: 30 semaines de crise.* Antananarivo: Éditions Foi et Justice.

Pierre Bernard A., Ramarosaona F., Razafindrakoto M. & Roubaud F. (1998). *Partis et classes politiques: Les intermédiaires démocratiques jouent-ils leur rôle?* Working Paper 9736/E. Antananarivo: Madagascar –Dial – Instat – Orstom (MADIO).

Pigeaud F. (2006). Madagascar: Entre le marché et le goupillon. *Le Monde Diplomatique,* March, 15–16.

Pigeaud F. (2017). À Madagascar, les paysans 'trouble-fête du bal de la mondialisation'. *Médiapart,* 12 February. Available at: www.mediapart.fr/journal/international/120217/madagascar-les-paysans-trouble-fete-du-bal-de-la-mondialisation?onglet=full

Piketty T. (2014). *Capital in the Twenty-First Century.* Cambridge, MA: Harvard University Press.

Piketty T. & Saez E. (2006). The evolution of top incomes: A historical and international perspective. *American Economic Review*, 96(2), 200–5.

Pryor F. L. (1990). *Malawi and Madagascar, the Political Economy of Poverty, Equity and Growth: A World Bank Comparative Study*. Washington, DC: World Bank, Oxford University Press.

Rabearimanana L. (1980). Un grand journal d'opinion malgache: *Ny Fandrosoam-Baovao*. Deuxième partie: Un nationalisme modéré. *Omaly sy Anio*, 11, 7–48.

Rabearimanana L. (2001). Protestantisme et nationalisme à Madagascar. *Revue historique des Mascareignes*, 3, Chrétientés australes du 18e siècle à nos jours, 177–89.

Rabemananoro E. (2014). Le drame des investissements irréversibles. *Afrique Contemporaine*, 251, 51–68.

Rabenirainy J. (2002). Les forces armées et les crises politiques (1972–2002). *Politique africaine*, 86, 86–102.

Rabetafika R. (1990). *Réforme fiscale et révolution socialiste à Madagascar*. Paris: L'Harmattan.

Radert S. (2008). Économie politique de la décentralisation. Actes du colloque *Économie politique de la décentralisation*. Available at: http://siteresources.worldbank.org/INTMADAGASCARINFRENCH/Resources/ecopol_dec.pdf, 8–20.

Raffinot M. & Roubaud F., eds. (2001). Les fonctionnaires du Sud: Sacrifiés ou protégés? *Autrepart*, 20, special issue, 5–175.

Rafitoson K. (2014). Les crises malgaches vues par la conférence épiscopale de Madagascar: Étude des communiqués publiés de 1889 à 2014. *Afrique contemporaine*, 3/2014(251), 69–92.

Raharinirina V. (2013). Madagascar: Conflits 'glocaux' autour des projets extractifs et agraires. *Alternatives Sud*, 20, 57–65.

Raharinirina V., Douguet J.-M. & Martinez-Alier J. (2018). Néocolonialisme vert, conflits de redistribution écologique et crises malgaches. In M. Razafindrakoto, F. Roubaud & J.-M. Wachsberger (eds.), *Madagascar, d'une crise l'autre: Ruptures et continuité*. 147–67. Paris: Karthala-IRD.

Raison F. (2007). L'Afrique de Didier Ratsiraka, lieu de passage vers la cour des grands. In D. Nativel & F. Rajaonah (eds.), *Madagascar et l'Afrique:Entre identité insulaire et appartenances historiques*, 345–62. Paris: Karthala.

Raison J.-P. (1972). Utilisation du sol et organisation de l'espace en Imerina ancienne. *Tany Malagasy*, 13, 97–121.

Raison J.-P. (1991). Dynamismes ruraux et contrastes fonciers dans Madagascar en crise. *Tiers-Monde*, 32(128), 901–15.

Raison J.-P. (2000). Madagascar, vers une nouvelle géographie régionale. *L'information géographique*, 1, 1–19.

Raison J.-P. (2002). Économie politique et géopolitique des barrages routiers. *Politique africaine*, 86, 120–37.

Raison-Jourde F. (1972). Les ZWAM: Qui sont-ils, que veulent-ils? *Réalités malgaches*, 22, 26–8.

Raison-Jourde F. (1991). *Bible et pouvoir à Madagascar au XIXe siècle: Invention d'une identité chrétienne et construction de l'État (1780–1880)*. Paris: Karthala.

Raison-Jourde F. (1993). Une transition achevée ou amorcée? *Politique africaine*, 52, 6–18.

Raison-Jourde F. (1995). The Madagascan churches in the political arena and their contribution to the change of regime, 1990–1993. In P. Clifford (ed.), *The Christian churches and the democratisation of Africa*, 292–301. Leiden: E. J. Brill.

Raison-Jourde F. (1996). Un deuxième 1947 en 1957? Les prolongements du soulèvement dans la mémoire et dans le contact avec les administrés. *Omaly Sy Anio*, 41–44, 227–44.

Raison-Jourde F. (2002). Les Kung-Fu. *Politique africaine*, 86, 68–69.

Raison-Jourde F. (2014). Avant-propos. In P. Kneitz (ed.), *Fihavanana. La vision d'une société paisible à Madagascar*, 7–14. Halle and der saale: Universitätsverlag Halle-Wittenberg.

Raison-Jourde F., ed. (1983). *Les souverains de Madagascar: L'histoire royale et ses résurgences contemporaines*. Paris: Karthala.

Raison-Jourde F. & Raison J.-P. (2002). Ravalomanana et la troisième indépendance? *Politique africaine*, 86, 5–17.

Raison-Jourde F. & Randrianja S., eds. (2002). *La nation malgache au défi de l'ethnicité*. Paris: Karthala.

Raison-Jourde F. & Roy G. (2010). *Paysans, intellectuels et populisme à Madagascar: De Monja Jaona à Ratsimandrava, 1960–1975*. Paris: Karthala.

Rajaonah F. (1996). *Élites et notables malgaches à Antananarivo dans la première moitié du XXe siècle*. Thèse d'État, Université Lyon II.

Rajaonah F. (2014). Indépendances et identité: Le Fihavanana comme ressource pour les Malgaches au XXe siècle, d'après Paul Ramasindraibe. In P. Kenitz (ed.), *Fihavanana-La vision d'une société paisible à Madagascar*, 74–100. Halle and der saale: Universitätsverlag Halle-Wittenberg.

Rajaonesy G. (2008). Économie politique de la décentralisation. Actes du colloque *Économie politique de la décentralisation*. Available at: http://siteresources.worldbank.org/INTMADAGASCARINFRENCH/Resources/ecopol_dec.pdf, 21–33.

Rakotoarisoa J.-E. (2002). 1991–2002: Le difficile apprentissage de la démocratie. *Afrique contemporaine*, 202–3, 15–25.

Rakotomalala P. (2014). Madagascar: La crise de 2009 ou les aléas de la diplomatie française. *Afrique Contemporaine*, 251, special issue, 2014/3, 93–106.

Rakotomanana F., Rakotondradany I., Calvo T., Razafindrakoto M., Razakamanana N. & Roubaud F. (2016). *L'état de la gouvernance, de la paix et de la sécurité à Madagascar en 2015–2016. Rapport d'analyse du Module GPS-SHaSA*. Antananarivo, INSTAT & DIAL.

Rakotomanana F., Razafindrakoto M., Roubaud F. & Wachsberger J.-M. (2010). L'impact économique de la crise politique sur les ménages urbains à Madagascar. Le marché du travail dans l'agglomération d'Antananarivo en 2010: Une mise en perspective décennale. Antananarivo/Paris INSTAT-DIAL, Policy Brief, July.

Rakotomanga M. (1998). *Forces armées malgaches: Entre devoir et pouvoir*. Paris: L'Harmattan.

Rakotondrabe D. T. (1993). Essai sur les non-dits du discours fédéraliste. *Politique africaine*, 52, 50–7.

Ralaimihoatra E. (1965). *Histoire de Madagascar: Des origines à la fin du XIXe siècle*. Tananarive: Société malgache d'édition.

Ralaimihoatra E. (1966). *Histoire de Madagascar: Le XXe siècle*. Antananarivo: Société malgache d'édition.

Ralibera R. (2008). *Souvenirs et témoignages malgaches, de la colonisation à la troisième République*. Antananarivo: Éditions Foi et justice.

Ralison N. (2011). *Les organismes patronaux à Madagascar de 1946 à nos jours: Forces, développement et faiblesses*: Available at: http://www.cresoi.fr

Ramamonjisoa J. (1984). *Blancs et Noirs: Les dimensions de l'inégalité sociale. Documents socio-linguistiques*. Cahiers des Sciences Sociales, 1, 39–45. Université de Madagascar.

Ramamonjisoa J. (2002). Les relations entre 'ethnies' à Madagascar: Une problématique souvent mal posée. *Afrique contemporaine*, 202–3, Apr.–Sept., 55–71.

Ramasy J. F. (2010). Madagascar: Les forces armées garantes de la stabilité politique et démocratique? *Identity, Culture and Politics*, 11(2), 1–42.

Ramasy J.-F. (2012). Militaires et système politique. In S. Randrianja (ed.), *Madagascar, le coup d'État de mars 2009*, 67–96. Paris: Karthala.

Randriamalala H. & Liu Z. (2010). Bois de rose de Madagascar: Entre démocratie et protection de la nature. *Revue Madagascar Conservation & Development*, 5(1), 11–22.

Randriamaro J.-R. (1997). *Padesm et luttes politiques à Madagascar: De la fin de la Deuxième Guerre mondiale à la naissance du PSD*. Paris: Karthala.

Randriamaro J.-R. (2009). Aux origines des Zwam: Les jeunes des bas quartiers de Tananarive de l'entre-deux-guerres jusqu'à 1972. In D. Nativel & F. Rajaonah (eds.), *Madagascar revisitée*, 463–78. Paris: Karthala.

Randriamarotsimba V. (2005). La malgachisation de l'enseignement. État des lieux et perspectives. In L. F. Prudent, F. Tupin & S. Wharton (eds.), *Du plurilinguisme à l'école: Vers une gestion coordonnée des langues en contextes éducatifs sensibles*, 197–218. Berne: Peter Lang.

Randriamihaingo L. H. (2004). *Les partis gouvernementaux et l'espace malgache de 1960 à 2001*. Antananarivo: Université d'Antananarivo, DEA.

Randrianja S. (2001). *Société et luttes coloniales à Madagascar de 1896 à 1946*. Paris: Karthala.

Randrianja S. (2005). Ravalomanana, 2002–2005. Des produits laitiers aux affaires nationales. Bern: Working Paper Swisspeace, March.

Randrianja S. (2012a). Le coup d'État de mars 2009, chronologie et causes. In S. Randrianja (ed.), *Madagascar, le coup d'État de mars 2009*, 13–41. Paris: Karthala.

Randrianja S. (2012b). Les années Ravalomanana (2002–2009). In S. Randrianja (ed.), *Madagascar, le coup d'État de mars 2009*, 239–77. Paris: Karthala.

Randrianja S., ed. (2012c). *Madagascar, le coup d'État de mars 2009*. Paris: Karthala.

Randrianja S. & Ellis S. (2009). *Madagascar: A Short History*. Chicago: University of Chicago Press.

Ratrimoarivony-Rakotoanosy M. (1986). *Historique et nature de l'enseignement à Madagascar de 1896 à 1960*. Thèse de 3e cycle, Université Paris IV, Centre international d'études francophones.

Ravaloson J. (2000). *Transition démocratique à Madagascar*. Paris: L'Harmattan.

Ravaloson J. (2008). L'affaire Savonnerie tropicale devant le Comesa: Un point de vue internationaliste. *Revue juridique et fiscale de MCI*, 44.

Ravelosoa R. & Roubaud F. (1998). Dynamique de la consommation des ménages de l'agglomération d'Antananarivo sur longue période: 1960–1995. *Autrepart*, 7, 63–87.

Razafimbelo C. (2004). Histoire de Madagascar. L'indépendance. *Didaktika, revue de didactique*, 2, 2e semestre, 63–73.

Razafindrabe T. (2018). État d'exception et péripéties de l'État de droit. La dynamique des crises politiques constitutionnelles à Madagascar. In M. Razafindrakoto, F. Roubaud & J.-M. Wachsberger (eds.), *Madagascar, d'une crise l'autre: Ruptures et continuité*, 283–304. Paris: Karthala-IRD.

Razafindrakoto M. (1994). *État des statistiques économiques sur le secteur industriel moderne: Diagnostic et propositions*. Working Paper 9403/DT. Antananarivo: Madagascar – Dial – Instat – Orstom (MADIO).

Razafindrakoto M. (1996). *Dynamique du secteur industriel moderne sur longue période: 1966–1994 ou comment se perdre en une décennie*. Working Paper 9613/E. Antananarivo: Madagascar – Dial – Instat – Orstom (MADIO).

Razafindrakoto M., Razafindratsima N., Razakamanana N., Roubaud F. & Wachsberger J.-M. (2017). *La diaspora* malagasy *en France et dans le monde: Une communauté oubliée ?* Paris: DIAL DT2017-18.

Razafindrakoto M., Razafindrazaka D. & Roubaud F. (2009a). *La gouvernance à Madagascar: portée et limites de la lutte contre la corruption et du processus de décentralisation*. Afrobarometer Briefing Paper 63. Available at: http://afrobarometer.org/fr/publications/la-gouvernance-%C3%A0-madagascar-port%C3%A9e-et-limites-de-la-lutte-contre-la-corruption-et-du

Razafindrakoto M., Razafindrazaka D. & Wachsberger J. M. (2009b). *Les Malgaches et la démocratie: Principes, fonctionnement, participation*. Afrobarometer Briefing Paper 64. Available at: http://afrobarometer.org/fr/publications/les-malgaches-et-la-d%C3%A9mocratie-principes-fonctionnement-participation

Razafindrakoto M. & Roubaud F. (1996). Ce qu'attendent les Tananariviens de la réforme de l'État et de l'économie. *Politique africaine*, 61, 54–72.

Razafindrakoto M. & Roubaud F. (1997). Les entreprises franches à Madagascar: Économie d'enclave ou promesse d'une nouvelle prospérité? *Revue Économie de Madagascar*, 2, 217–48.

Razafindrakoto M. & Roubaud F. (1999). La dynamique du marché du travail dans l'agglomération d'Antananarivo entre 1995 et 1999: La croissance économique profite-t-elle aux ménages? *Revue Économie de Madagascar*, 4, 103–37.

Razafindrakoto M. & Roubaud F. (2001a). *Pensent-ils différemment? La 'voix des pauvres' à travers les enquêtes statistiques*. DIAL Working Paper DT/2001/13.

Razafindrakoto M. & Roubaud F. (2001b). Vingt ans de réforme de la fonction publique à Madagascar. *Autrepart*, 20, 43–60.

Razafindrakoto M. & Roubaud F. (2002a). Madagascar à la croisée des chemins: La croissance durable est-elle possible? *Afrique Contemporaine*, 202–3, Apr.–Sept., 75–92.

Razafindrakoto M. & Roubaud F. (2002b). Le scrutin présidentiel du 16 décembre 2001: Les enjeux d'une élection contestée. *Politique africaine*, 86, Madagascar, les urnes et la rue, 18–45.

Razafindrakoto M. & Roubaud F. (2003a). Do they really think differently? The voice of the poor through quantitative surveys. In J.-P. Cling, M. Razafindrakoto & Roubaud F. (eds.), *New International Poverty Reduction Strategies*, 126–47. London: Routledge.

Razafindrakoto M. & Roubaud F. (2003b). Wage and corruption: The case of Madagascar. *Global Corruption Report 2003*, Transparency International, 292–4.

Razafindrakoto M. & Roubaud F. (2003c). The existing systems for monitoring poverty: Weaknesses of the usual household surveys. In J.P. Cling, M. Razafindrakoto & F. Roubaud (eds.), *New International Poverty Reduction Strategies*, 2nd ed., 265–94. Paris: Economica/IRD.

Razafindrakoto M. & Roubaud F. (2005). Les pauvres, la démocratie et le marché à Madagascar: Une analyse à partir de trois séries d'enquêtes auprès de la population malgache. *Revue d'économie du développement*, 1(2005), 56–89.

Razafindrakoto M. & Roubaud F. (2010a). Are international databases on corruption reliable? A comparison of expert opinion surveys and household surveys in Sub-Saharan Africa. *World Development*, 38(8), 1057–69.

Razafindrakoto M. & Roubaud F. (2010b). La pauvreté urbaine à Madagascar: Dynamique, déterminants et politiques. In B. Gastineau, F. Gubert, A.-S Robilliard & F. Roubaud (eds.), *Madagascar face au défi des Objectifs du millénaire pour le développement*, 87–118. Marseille: IRD Éditions.

Razafindrakoto M., Roubaud F. & Wachsberger J.-M. (2012). L'enquête auprès des élites à Madagascar: quelles solutions aux enjeux méthodologiques? *7e colloque francophone sur les sondages*, SFdS & ENSAI, 5–7 November, Rennes. Antananarivo: Madagascar – Dial – Instat – Orstom (MADIO). Available at: http://sondages2012.ensai.fr/wp-content/uploads/2011/01/S12P1_RoubaudEtAl.pdf

Razafindrakoto M., Roubaud F. & Wachsberger J.-M. (2014a). Élites, pouvoir et régulation à Madagascar: Une lecture de l'histoire à l'aune de l'économie politique. *Afrique Contemporaine*, 251, special issue 2014/3, 25–50.

Razafindrakoto M., Roubaud F. & Wachsberger J.-M. (2014b). Madagascar, d'une crise l'autre. Introduction thématique. *Afrique Contemporaine*, 251, special issue, 2014/3, 13–22.

Razafindrakoto M., Roubaud F. & Wachsberger J.-M., eds. (2014c). Madagascar: Anatomie d'un état de crise. *Afrique Contemporaine*, 251, special issue, 2014/3.

Razafindrakoto M., Roubaud F. & Wachsberger J.-M. (2015). L'île mystérieuse: Une approche d'économie politique de la trajectoire longue de Madagascar. *Canadian Journal of Development Studies/Revue canadienne d'études du développement*, 36(3), 397–415.

Razafindrakoto M., Roubaud F. & Wachsberger J.-M. (2016). *Restaurer le dialogue entre élites et citoyens à Madagascar: Un impératif de développement*. Antananarivo, oral presentation for 'Élites, démocratie et croissance', Francophone Summit, National Steering Committee (CNO), Malagasy Ministry for Higher Education and Scientific Research (MESUPRES), IRD, 21 November.

Razafindrakoto M., Roubaud F. & Wachsberger J.-M. (2017). *L'énigme et le paradoxe: Économie politique de Madagascar*. Paris: IRD/AFD Editions.

Razafindrakoto M., Roubaud F. & Wachsberger J.-M. (2018a). *Madagascar, d'une crise l'autre: Ruptures et continuité*. Paris: Karthala-IRD.

Razafindrakoto M., Roubaud F. & Wachsberger J. M. (2018b). Violence et ordre politique à Madagascar: Grille de lecture d'un double paradoxe. In M. Razafindrakoto, F. Roubaud & J.-M. Wachsberger (eds.), *Madagascar, d'une crise l'autre: Ruptures et continuité*, 329–60. Paris: Karthala-IRD.

Razafindralambo L. N. (2005a). Construction d'identité et relations de dépendance: Descendants d'anciens maîtres et descendants d'anciens 'esclaves' en Imerina. *Taloha*, 14–15. Available at: www.taloha.info/document.php?id=131.

Razafindralambo L. N. (2005b). Inégalités, exclusion, représentations sur les hautes terres centrales de Madagascar. *Cahiers d'études africaines*, XLV(3–4), 879–903.

Razafindratandra Y. (1993). Le régime malgache de zone franche. *Politique africaine*, 52, 19–21.

Razafindrazaka D., Razafindrakoto M., Roubaud F. & Wachsberger J.-M. (2008). Madagascans and Democracy: Principles, Practice and Participation. Afrobarometer Briefing Paper 64. Available at: www.afrobarometer.org/abbriefing.html

Roubaud F. (1997a). *Les élections présidentielles à Madagascar 1992–1996: Un essai de géographie électorale.* Working Paper 9707/E. Antananarivo: Madagascar – Dial – Instat – Orstom (MADIO). Available at: https://www.instat.mg/

Roubaud F. (1997b). La question rizicole à Madagascar: Les résultats d'une décennie de libéralisation. *Économie de Madagascar*, 2, 37–61.

Roubaud F. (1999). Religion, identité sociale et transition démocratique à Tananarive: De fidèles en citoyens. In R. Otayek (ed.), *Afrique: les identités contre la démocratie? Autrepart*, 10, 135–49.

Roubaud F. (2000). *Identités et transition démocratique: L'exception malgache?* Antananarivo, Paris: Tsipika, L'Harmattan.

Roubaud F. (2001). Démocratie électorale et inertie institutionnelle à Madagascar. In P. Quantin & C. Toulabor (eds.), *L'Afrique Politique 2001: Réformes des États africains*, 85–98. Paris: Karthala.

Roubaud F., ed. (2002). Madagascar après la tourmente: Regards sur dix ans de transitions politique et économique. *Afrique Contemporaine*, dossier spécial, 202–3, Apr.–Sept.

Sarraut A. (1923). *La mise en valeur des colonies françaises.* Paris: Payot.

Saura A. (2006). *Philibert Tsiranana premier président de la République de Madagascar*, t. 1: *À l'ombre de Gaulle*, t. 2: *Le crépuscule du pouvoir*, Paris: L'Harmattan.

SeFaFi (2003). *Militarisation et démocratisation politique.* Communiqué du SeFaFi, Antananarivo, 14 March.

Sen A. (2005). *La démocratie des autres. (Democracy as a Universal Value and Democracy and Its Global Roots).* Paris: Payot.

Singly F. (de) & Thélot C. (1988). *Gens du privé, gens du public: La grande différence.* Paris: Dunod.

Spacensky A. (1967). Regard sur l'évolution politique malgache 1945–1966. *Revue française de science politique*, 2, 263–85.

Spacensky A. (1970). *Madagascar: Cinquante ans de vie politique, de Ralaimongo à Tsiranana.* Paris: Nouvelles éditions latines.

Swamy A., Knack S., Lee Y. & Azfar O. (2001). Gender and corruption. *Journal of Development Economics*, 64(1), 25–55.

Tarabey B. (2014). *Madagascar dahalo: Enquête sur les bandits du Grand Sud.* Paris: L'Harmattan.

The Indian Ocean Newsletter. (2002). *Madagascar. Who's Who.* Paris: Indigo Publications.

Tilly C. (1976). *From Mobilization to Revolution.* Reading, MA: Addison-Wesley.

Treisman D. (2000). The causes of corruption: A cross-national study. *Journal of Public Economics*, 76, 399–457.

Tronchon J. (1974). *L'insurrection malgache de 1947: Essai d'interprétation historique.* Paris: Maspero.

Tronchon J. (1995). Madagascar: Église et non-violence. *Autres Temps. Cahiers d'éthique sociale et politique*, 46, 52–77.

United Nations, Department of Economic and Social Affairs. (2015). *Trends in International Migrant Stock: Migrants by Destination and Origin.* United Nations database, POP/DB/MIG/Stock/Rev.

UNISDR (United Nations Office for Disaster Risk Reduction). (2009). *Global Assessment Report on Disaster Risk Reduction.* New York: United Nations.

Urfer S. (1993). Quand les Églises entrent en politique ... *Politique africaine*, 52, 31–39.

Urfer S. (2012a). *Madagascar: Une culture en péril?* Antananarivo: No comment éditions.

Urfer S. (2012b). Madagascar: Une société en mutation, pour quel développement? *Nota Bene: The Malagasy Development Journal*, 1, 21–6.

Vahabi M. (2011). Compte rendu de la publication de Douglass C. North, John Joseph Wallis et Barry R. Weingast (2010). In *Violence et ordres sociaux.* Paris, Gallimard, *Revue de la régulation, 9, 1er* semester. Available at: http://regulation.revues.org/9088

Vanf. ed. (2012). Madagascar. Crises cycliques, culture et développement: Les conditions de la relance. *Nota Bene, The Malagasy Development Journal*, 1.

Van Rijckeghem C. & Weder B. (2001). Bureaucratic Corruption and the Rate of Temptation: Do Wages in the Civil Service Affect Corruption, and by How Much? *Journal of Development Economics*, 65(2), 307–31.

Verdier I. (1995, 2000, 2002). *Madagascar: Les hommes de pouvoir. Biographies exclusives.* Paris: Indigo Publications.

Vérin P. (1990). *Madagascar.* Paris: Karthala.

Véron J.-B. (2010). L'Afrique post-indépendance: 50 ans de crises? *Afrique contemporaine*, 235/3, 115–26.

Vivier J.-L. (2007). *Madagascar sous Ravalomanana: La vie politique malgache depuis 2001.* Paris: L'Harmattan.

Vivier J.-L. (2010). *Madagascar, une île à la dérive: Les années 2007–2010, de Ravalomanana à Rajoelina.* Paris: L'Harmattan.

Wachsberger J. M. (2007). Les Malgaches et la politique: Quelques enseignements tirés des enquêtes Afrobaromètre de 2005. Afrobarometer Briefing Paper 47.

Wachsberger J. M. (2009). *L'intégration sociale hiérarchisée: Le cas d'une métropole en développement, Antananarivo.* Lille: ANRT.

Wachsberger J.-M., Razafindrakoto M. & Roubaud F. (2016). *Étude sur les perceptions et attentes citoyennes concernant l'exercice du pouvoir à Madagascar.* Paris: Collateral Creations et Katsaka.

Wantchekon L., Lahiniriko D. L. & Garcia-Ponce O. (2011). Echoes of the Malagasy uprising: Estimating long-term effects of political repression on political attitudes in Madagascar. Paper presented at the APSA Annual Meeting in Seattle, 1–4 Sept.

Wapenhans W. (1992). *Effective Implementation, Key to Development Impact.* Washington, DC: The World Bank, Report of the Portfolio Management Task Force.

Weber M. (2003 [1921]). *Économie et société.* Paris: Agora Pocket.

Willame J.-C. (1994). *Gouvernance et pouvoir: Essai sur trois trajectoires africaines: Madagascar, Somalie, Zaïre.* Paris: L'Harmattan.

Williamson J. (1990). What Washington Means by Policy Reform. In J. Williamson (ed.), *Latin American Adjustment: How Much Has Happened?*, 7–20.Washington, DC: Institute for International Economics.

Wisner B., Blaikie P., Cannon T. & Davies I. (2014). *At Risk: Natural Hazards, People's Vulnerability and Disasters.* London: Routledge.

World Bank. (1995). *Madagascar, New Horizons. Building a Strategy for Private-Sector, Export-Led Growth. A Private Sector Assessment.* Report No. 14385-MAG.

World Bank. (2000). *Reforming Public Institutions and Strengthening Governance: A World Bank Strategy.* Washington, DC: World Bank, Public Sector Group.

World Bank. (2008). *World Development Report 2008: Agriculture for Development.* Washington, DC: World Bank.

World Bank. (2009). *Pour que la terre tourne . . . .aussi à Madagascar: Vers un agenda de relance économique.* Available at: http://blogs.worldbank.org/files/africacan/Madagascar_Update_in_French.pdf

World Bank. (2010). *Madagascar governance and development effectiveness review. A political economy analysis of governance in Madagascar,* Report No. 54277-MAG.

World Bank. (2012). *CPIA, Africa: Assessing Africa's policies and institutions.* Washington, DC: World Bank, June.

World Bank. (2014). *Opportunites et defis pour une croissance inclusive et resiliente: Recueil de notes de politique pour Madagascar* [Opportunities and Challenges for Inclusive and Resilient Growth: Compendium of Policy Notes for Madagascar]. Antananarivo: World Bank.

World Bank. (2015). *Madagascar: Systematic Country Diagnostic.* Washington, DC: World Bank.

World Bank.(2016). *Madagascar Economic Update.* Available at: https://openknowledge.worldbank.org/bitstream/handle/10986/25745/110674-WP-MadagascarEconomicUpdate-PUBLIC-ENGLISH.pdf?sequence=1&isAllowed=y

World Bank. (2017). *World Development Report 2017: Governance and the Law.* Washington, DC: World Bank.

World Bank. (2018a). *World Development Report 2019: The Changing Nature of Work.* Washington, DC: World Bank.

World Bank. (2018b). *Madagascar. Évolutions économiques récentes. Favoriser l'inclusion financière,* June. Available at: http://documents.banquemondiale.org/curated/fr/592831532449183076/pdf/128782-WP-PUBLIC-FRENCH-REVISED-Digital-MEU-Favoriser-LInclusion-Financiere.pdf

You J.-S. (2012). Transition from a Limited Access Order to an Open Access Order: The Case of South Korea. In D. North, J. Wallis, S. Webb & B. Weingast (eds.), *In the Shadow of Violence. Politics, Economics, and the Problem of Development*, 293–327. Cambridge: Cambridge University Press.

Zafimahova S. (1998). *Jeu de fanorona autour de la privatisation. Le désengagement de l'État des entreprises publiques: Frein ou arme de développement? (Le cas de Madagascar).* Antananarivo: Éditions Orsa Plus.

Index